American
Neo-Noir
the movie never ends

American
Neo-Noir
the movie never ends

Alain Silver &
James Ursini

Foreword by Walter Hill

This book is dedicated
to the memories of our colleagues
Robert Porfirio
and
Lee Sanders

Published in 2015 by

Applause Theatre and Film Books
An Imprint of Hal Leonard Corporation
7777 West Bluemound Road
Milwaukee, WI 53213

Trade Book Division Editorial Offices
33 Plymouth Street, Montclair, NJ 07042

Photo permissions can be found in the Acknowledgments on page 7.

Book and cover design by Alain Silver

Printed in the United States of America

Library of Congress Cataloging-in-Publication Data is available upon request.

ISBN 978-1-4803-8626-6

www.applausebooks.com

Front Cover: *Body Heat*

Frontispiece: *The Driver*

Contents page: Jack Nicholson in *Chinatown*

Back Cover insets, clockwise from top left: Jodie Foster in *Silence of the Lambs*; Izabella Miko in *Dark Streets*; Samuel L. Jackson in *Pulp Fiction;* Javier Bardem in *No Country for Old Men.* Background: Golden Gate from the San Francisco Mission Inn, photo by Linda Brookover.

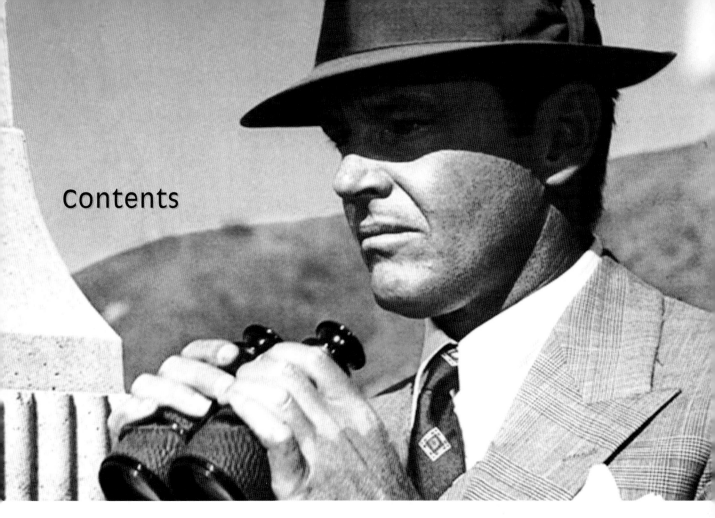

Contents

Acknowledgments

Thanks, first of all, to our frequent collaborators the late Robert Porfirio, Elizabeth Ward, and Linda Brookover for their suggestions about this volume and whose own writing underlies many of our comments. Another colleague, Paolo Durazzo, assisted on the Filmography. Todd Erickson coined the term *neo-noir* and provided quotes from David Mamet and others. Obviously, a special thanks to Walter Hill for graciously adding his auteurist perspective (and for the production still from *The Driver*).

Besides our present publisher John Cerullo and editor Carol Flannery at Applause, we would like to acknowledge the long-term support we received from their predecessor, the late Mel Zerman, on the entire Film Noir Reader series. The groundwork for this volume was laid in an essay written for the second and expanded in the third edition of *Film Noir the Encyclopedia*. It was revised and expanded again in 2011 when we were asked by Roberto Cueto to contribute an article to the program notes for a neo-noir retrospective at the San Sebastián Film Festival.

Many of the illustrations in this volume are from our personal collection, but for others we are grateful to the late Lee Sanders, Timothy Otto, and visual archivists, too numerous to cite individually, who share their material online.

Stills are courtesy of Avco-Embassy, Buena Vista, Castle Hill, Castle Rock, Columbia, Dimension, De Laurentiis, Fineline, Fox Searchlight, Island, Kings Road, Lions Gate, MGM/UA, Millennium, Miramax, New Horizons, New Line, Orion, Paramount, Polygram, Promark, Sony, Touchstone, Trimark, TriStar, 20th Century-Fox, Universal, Vestron, Warner Bros., Zanuck, Zoetrope, and many other production companies and distributors.

Walter Hill (in cap above) on the set of *The Driver*.

Foreword

Noir.
As someone said,
'More than a style,
Less than a genre...'
But we know it when we see it.
At least we think so.
And now:
Neo Noir.

***

I grew up watching film noir.
Of course, we didn't call it that back then.

The plots were usually about crime, always about human misbehavior featuring killers, thieves, rogue cops, edgy private eyes... There were dream sequences and flashbacks, amnesia or men hung up on beautiful women they couldn't have, until they could. Sometimes they were about grifters or ex-cons or some hapless guy who didn't do it but had to go on the run anyway. Maybe they cleared their names, maybe they evened the score, or maybe they ended up dead. When we heard the ominous minor chords of the title music, that told us we were going to watch people fighting for their lives in a story of desperation and anxiety. In short: We knew what it was before we knew it was film noir.

***

I agree with the two gentlemen who wrote this excellent book that the "classic period" started before I was born and ended around 1960. I agree, too, that era is over and done with, and you can't go back. But when I had the good fortune to write and then direct my own films, I wanted to try to recapture some of that feeling I had watching these stories as a child and a teenager. The first film I wrote was premised on the idea that people like Hickey and Boggs still had dramatic life even though they may have outlived their time, played out their string. When I became a director, I continued to believe truly noir characters could have dramatic focus, as in *The Driver*, where the players didn't even need names for an audience to grasp who they were, what they were about; as in *Johnny Handsome*, where the protagonist's criminal code becomes his destiny; as in *Undisputed*, where meaningful victory is compromised by the inability to alter one's fate.

I hope to have a chance, or two, to tell that kind of story again.

W.H.

Lee Marvin as Walker in
Point Blank.

Part One

Classic Becomes Neo

A Definition

After many years, decades actually, of critical debate about what constitutes a film noir, the issue is still not entirely resolved. For us, film noir was never a genre but an American film movement that was defined by style as much as content, which began around the same time as World War II and ended just twenty years later.

That time frame, at least, is now almost universally accepted. The classic period of film noir spans the years in which American filmmakers created and sustained the cycle over the course of more than four hundred feature films. It began just after 1940 with *The Maltese Falcon* and wound down around 1960 or shortly after *Touch of Evil* (1958). Certainly there were prototypes and precursors of the movement going back to the acme of the gangster genre in the early 1930s. And there were many stragglers, late entries by Sam Fuller and other independent directors, but before the mid-1960s film noir's classic period had run its course.

There is no precise moment or movie that marks the beginning of neo-noir. For us, neo-noir is more genre than movement, a mimicking of the style and content of the classic period, the best early example of which is John Boorman's 1967 *Point Blank*, an adaptation of *The Hunter*, part of a postwar, hard-boiled series of "Parker" novels about the criminal underworld by Donald Westlake writing as Richard Stark. Like its antecedent and from the first, neo-noir would also be tied closely to a literary movement, riffs on the work of Hammett, Chandler, and McCoy, starting with the gritty exploration of sociopathy by Jim Thompson, the smug mysogyny of Spillane's Mike Hammer and then a next generation that included Westlake, Ross Macdonald, and Elmore Leonard.

While such novelists pushed their violent protagonists even further down Chandler's mean streets dark with something more than night, the neo-noir genre was defined by screenwriters and directors who had grown up watching movies during the classic period. Some of the early neo-noir were "retro-noir," narratives set in the not-to-distant past, whose characters wore period costumes and drove vintage cars, such as the private detectives Jake Gittes in *Chinatown* (1974), the classic-period icon Robert Mitchum as an older and more

fatigued Philip Marlowe in *Farewell, My Lovely* (1975), or Det. Tom Spellacy investigating a fictionalized "Black Dahlia" in *True Confessions* (1981). The multinational creative personnel of a movie like *Chinatown* written by American Robert Towne and directed by Polish émigré Roman Polanski, reenacted such classic-period relationships as Raymond Chandler and Billy Wilder crafting *Double Indemnity* or Herman Mankiewicz and Robert Siodmak on *Christmas Holiday* (both 1944).

The most self-conscious of the early neo-noirs came from writer/directors. Walter Hill—who had previously scripted the 1972 paean *Hickey & Boggs* where old-school PIs discover that "there's nothing left of this profession...it's all over, it's not about anything"—infused 1978's *The Driver* with a noir style that echoed Kubrick's *The Killing* (1957) and De Toth's *Crime Wave* (1954). Hill's characters are so pointedly archetypal that they do not even have names:

Above, Jack Nicholson (right) as 1930s P.I. Jake Gittes with corrupt financier Noah Cross (John Huston) in the "retro-noir" *Chinatown*.

Opposite, Sterling Hayden as hard-bitten Det. Lt. Sims (left) and Gene Nelson as small-time crook Steve Lacey in *Crime Wave*.

they are simply the Driver, the Detective, and the Player. Three years later *Body Heat* (1981), Lawrence Kasdan's homage to *Double Indemnity*, set a new standard for femme fatales. By 1987 the double-crosses and twisted psychology in David Mamet's *House of Games* (1987) fully evoked its creator's intent: "I am very familiar with noir...and I love it. I tried to be true."

At the height of the classic period individual noir films transcended personal and generic outlook and reflected the cultural preoccupations of America no matter where the filmmakers were born. From the late 1970s to present, in a "neo-noir" period, many of the productions that again create the noir mood, whether in remakes or new narratives, have been undertaken by filmmakers cognizant of a heritage and intent on placing their own interpretation on it. As the various interviews conducted by scholar Todd Erickson and reproduced in his thesis where the term *neo-noir* was coined affirm, most of the filmmakers approach neo-noir with a conscious, expressive intent.

If neo-noir is to some extent, as in the classic period, America's stylized vision of itself, one might expect a cynicism made even harsher by decades of cold war, nuclear peril, fiscal uncertainty, the threat of terrorism, millennial dystopia, and cultural upheaval. While the emphasis may have shifted among these social realities, the outpouring of films has continued. The actual results

ove, Ryan O'Neal as the title character in *The Driver.*
posite, more 1970s retro-noir: Robert Mitchum (left) as Marlowe with Moose

remain mixed. One aspect of film noir that many filmmakers have chosen to underscore is its forlorn romanticism, the need to find love and honor in a new society that venerates only sex and money. Many others have followed alternative narrative paths blazed in the classic period, and as a result any overview such as this needs a new "family tree" to trace through the titles. Of course, as with critic Raymond Durgnat's original essay, many of the categories overlap and intersect, and many titles crossover several branches.

Creating the Genre

The core conundrum of *Point Blank* sets the tone for much of the neo-noir genre: is the entire narrative imagined by a dying protagonist in the manner of Ambrose Bierce's story "An Occurence at Owl Creek Bridge"? Is it like that story's alternate title "A Dead Man's Dream"? In the end, whatever the reality and as with many of the classic period's convoluted plots, it is the monomaniacal obsession of *Point Blank*'s Walker that most powerfully evokes the ethos of the just-ended movement. Like the doomed Frank Bigelow of *D.O.A.* (1950), Walker simply wants to root out and bring to justice all those involved in the plan to murder him. Unlike Bigelow, Walker never considers simply reporting them to the police.

Because it is situated physically in the normal world and emotionally in the shadows of the same noir universe that enveloped so many classic-period protagonists, *Point Blank* is less a stylistic than a thematic paean to core noir. The same could be said of *Warning Shot* (also 1967), a mirroring narrative in which a straight cop struggles against appearances that paint him as a rogue. The respective stars of *Point Blank* and *Warning Shot*, Lee Marvin and David

Above, Lee Marvin (right) as one of the titled "cool" killers with sidekick Clu Gulager in Don Siegel's remake of the key classic-period movie. Below, a somewhat less cool Charley Varrick (Walter Matthau) in disguise to rob what turns out to a mob bank.

Janssen, typify the new school of noir protagonists. The gray-haired Marvin progresses from the cheap hoods of *The Big Heat* (1953) and *Violent Saturday* (1955) to a seriously deadly criminal focused on his self-serving quests in both *The Killers* (1964) and *Point Blank.* Janssen established his survivor's credentials over several seasons of TV's *The Fugitive* before returning to features in *Warning Shot* as a framed cop who is older, wearier, but just as dogged as any classic-period character in refusing to accept fate.

Don Siegel was one of the few directors with significant credits in both the classic period and early neo-noir. It could be argued that his remake of *The Killers*, like Fuller's *The Naked Kiss* released the same year, was one of the last vestiges of classic-period sensibility. Certainly it follows the same narrative line as the 1946 adaptation, which used Hemingway's short story as a springboard to a complex flashback of obsessive love and betrayal after caper. A key distinction is the perspective, which switches from that of an insurance investigator to the titled killers themselves. More remarkably, despite its title and violent narrative, Siegel's adaptation was originally intended to be broadcast on NBC to be, before rival network ABC coined the term, the first movie of the week. That its unwholesome content precipitated a change of plan by Universal and a theatrical release, is indicative of where neo-noir was headed, into a world where the violence, illicit sex, and other "bad" behavior would be more literal than stylized and metaphorical.

Siegel's next classic-noir remake *The Hanged Man* transposed the events of *Ride the Pink Horse* (1946) from New Mexico to New Orleans. It was also a made-for-television and, having lost much of the undertone of Robert Montgomery's original, did debut on the airwaves in late 1964. Siegel lost the distinction of being director of first MOW to *See How they Run*, an very early neo variation on "kid noir" about three children stalked by a criminal cartel. From these first examples right after the classic period ended, television had a significant role in neo-noir. As many examples later in this survey will demonstrate, when premium cable channels began producing their own feature-length originals without the content restrictions on broadcasters, the bad behavior of neo-noir characters became a salacious-content sellling point for the subscribers.

One of the motifs in neo-noir is blurring the lines in traditional roles. Cops who may not be outright criminals, but rogues in terms of methods that push the boundaries, a prototype defined by the title character in Siegel's *Dirty Harry* (1971) and refined from those in the earlier *Madigan* and *Coogan's Bluff* (both 1968). Conversely there are criminals who follow a code and assume the narrative position of sympathetic protagonist as in Siegel's *Charley Varrick* (1973), released the same year as the similarly themed and much more brutal *The Outfit.* Siegel's title crook suffers a typically noir mischance when he inadvertently knocks over a syndicate bank. As portrayed by Walter Matthau, Varrick is homespun and self-effacing while also being what the tag line calls "the last of the independents." In contrast, Madigan and Coogan are aggressive cops who, unlike the compulsive and disturbed figure in the classic-period *The Detective Story* (1951), use violence as an investigative tool.

Neither, of course, compares to the "go ahead, make my day," magnum-wielding Inspector "Dirty Harry" Callahan, a character so intense, so casually cruel but compelling (and also profitable), that he spawned a spate of sequels—four over fifteen years from *Magnum Force* in 1973 through *The Drowning Pool* in 1988. On several levels, Callahan continues to define the neo-noir detective. Although he never crosses the line into fully felonious behavior, like the detectives in Siegel's *Private Hell 36* (1954), Callahan is not conflicted about his behavior. He may patrol the streets of San Francisco that are photographed in color but he sees them through the black-and-white prism of such classic-period detectives as Sims in *Crime Wave* or Wilson in *On Dangerous Ground* (1951).

From its opening shots of the deserted New York City streets at daybreak. *Madigan* evokes the ambience of two decades earlier and the Hellinger/Dassin *Naked City*. From his classic-period work, Siegel was certainly familiar with the approach of Mark Hellinger, the producer who had considered him to direct for the original version of *The Killers*. Siegel manages the complex narrative and constricted time frame through intercutting between the efforts of Detectives Madigan (Richard Widmark) and Bonaro (Harry Guardino) to recapture an escaped murder suspect and the political "damage control" of Commissioner Russell (Henry Fonda). While Russell's moralizing over police integrity may seem simplistic, the dark and duplicitous undertones echo those of co-screenwriter Abraham Polonsky's classic noir *Force of Evil* (1948).

Below, Clint Eastwood as the comsumately cool and quick-on-the-draw inspector in Siegel's *Dirty Harry*. Opposite, *Madigan*, a rumpled but dogged Richard Widmark (center) has gotten careless in middle age.

Although Russell may regard him as the epitome of a bad cop, Madigan is not untroubled by that. His own alienation in the classic noir tradition from *Scene of the Crime* (1948) to *The Big Combo* (1955) is more purely existential. Although he is neither a rogue cop, nor an embezzler as in *Private Hell 36,* Madigan does appreciate the meager perks of the job. Being stripped of his gun by a felon, like the hapless Det. Cates in Walter Hill's later *48 Hrs.* (1982), has embarrassing connotations for Madigan; the most disturbing aspect is the threat to his life style. Madigan's off-handed violence, whether overturning a secretary's desk or blackmailing part-time pimp, is much closer to Hammer in *Kiss Me Deadly* (1955) than to Cates. Madigan perishes then not in expiation for being unscrupulous or immoral but by the same quirk of fate that destroyed so many of his classic-period prototypes.

The Conscious Auteurs

One of the most stylized examples of conscious and relatively early neo-noir is *The Driver*. Like its characters, the narrative is laconic and spare, alternating balletic interludes of high-speed chases down dark, wet streets or in claustrophobic parking structures with terse, expository scenes. The Detective is so obsessed with catching the Driver that he blackmails another criminal into setting him up. The woman known as the Player is so obsessed with gambling that she is unable to give the Driver any emotional support. While *their* motivations are reasonably clear, the Driver's never is. Being the "best wheel man in town" leaves him in the grip of some quasi-existential anguish. Like many classic noir

Hickey & Boggs: above, a pair of neo-noir's first old-school the P.I.s of the title, Robert Culp (left) as Frank Boggs and Bill Cosby as Al Hickey. Below, even with larger-caliber wheel gun, Boggs and Hickey are sorely pressed by attackers in a helicopter with high-powered auto-matic weapons and must take cover behind some pricey vehicles on a beach in Malibu.

figures, wandering through dark rooms, silhouetted or in sidelight, the Driver lives on the edge of an ill-defined underworld. Like the title figure in Melville's *Le Samourai* (1967) he lives by an unwritten code, but it seems mostly to burden him as relentlessly as Sisyphus' stone. When he finally violates its basic tenet ("Never carry a gun") in what could be either a liberating act or a hollow triumph, it merely completes the Driver's transformation into a cipher.

The viewer can accept a noir protagonist without a name but not one without an identity. Both as a film and as a character, *The Driver* takes the concept of action as being, creates dramatic conflict, then leaves it unresolved. Hill's later *48 Hrs*. comes closer to a genuine noir ambience. Having two seemingly antithetical characters—a rumpled, alienated detective and a glib well-dressed convict—thrown together by circumstancescreates a stronger central irony than in *The Driver*. As in *Hickey & Boggs*, "It's not about anything anymore," for Detective Jack Cates in *48 Hrs*. who has to wrestle with his lost idealism. Literally and figuratively emasculated by the loss of the gun, Cates is inevitably partnered with the smooth Reggie Hammond, an impromptu partnership that mirrors the ethnic mélange of *Hickey & Boggs*. The idea of a right way and wrong way for any enterprise, a unwritten book of rules for cop and criminal alike to follow, is rooted in Hill's screenplays for that picture and *The Getaway* (1972), as well as his first writer/director project *Hard Times* (1975). From street fight promoters in Depression-era New Orleans to the syndicate solders in Los Angeles or the forlorn criminal couple Doc and Carol McCoy, characters are driven and controlled by established codes.

That the titled private detectives of Hickey and Boggs even have personal demons plays against the types established for Bill Cosby and Robert Culp (who also directed) in the *I Spy* television series. The darkest scenes, emotionally and physically, are coupled to their romantic obsessions. Their compulsive behavior night after night vis-à-vis their ex-wives mirrors their professional lives, careening around the Los Angeles underworld during the day. While they may share the independent spirit of their earlier counterparts in classic noir, they differ in the extent to which they can control their situation. Roughly a decade after the end of the classic period, the neo-noir protagonist has lost the ability to effect change in a modern world, and this increasing powerlessness is a correlative of diminishing social morality. This powerlessness is encapsulated in Frank Boggs remark after a shoot-out: "I gotta get a bigger gun. I can't hit anything." His revolvers, small and large, are trademarks of his profession, icons that recall the "gats" and "roscoes" of a more colorful era. As symbols of both his personal power and genre identity, they are nothing compared to the modern arsenal of weapons possessed by the gangsters and the political guerrillas, who annihilate one another with carbines and high-caliber automatic rifles at the film's climax on a beach in sun-drenched Malibu.

Unlike their classic-period counterparts, at home in Chandler's mean streets, Hickey and Boggs are too washed up to control anything. Boggs, the dissolute believer in a bygone heroism, seemed to understand their existential dependence on this profession and insists it is important to "try and even it up, make it right." This sequence recalls a similarly extravagant ending as the unstable "great whatsit" explodes to conclude *Kiss Me Deadly*. In this sardonic variant the detectives walk off into the sunset, together but not side by side.

Hickey asserts, "Nobody came, nobody cares. It's still not about anything." Boggs wearily replies, "Yeah, you told me." Hickey and Boggs have survived only because they are unimportant.

Hill's *Johnny Handsome* (1989) posits a small-time crook, betrayed by his associates, whose grotesque facial features are ameliorated by a prison doctor before his parole. The concept of an identity change harks back to *Dark Passage* (1947) and *The Hollow Triumph* (1948), but the theme here is revenge. In the jewelry store robbery sequence, Hill immediately includes the violent action opening, which typifies his work from *The Warriors* (1979) and *Streets of Fire* (1984) to *Extreme Prejudice* (1987) and *Red Heat* (1988); but the other thrust is toward the mood of noir. Of Hill's action movies, in particular because it recalls the uneasy collaboration between the hard-nosed cop Sims and grifter Steve Lacey in *Crime Wave*, the protagonists of *48 Hrs.* are noir figures, especially Det. Jack Gates (Nick Nolte). His quest to retrieve both his lost gun—his relationship to the weapon recalls that of a samurai to his sword—and his lost honor probes the mind-set of a contemporary cop caught in a deeper existential bind than a classic-period semi-rogues like Sims.

The seamier quartiers of New Orleans (a setting Hill revisited in *Johnny Handsome*) in the period piece *Hard Times* provide the dark, wet streets that are the stereotypical noir locus. But unlike *Hard Times* or *The Warriors*, where Hill successfully merged genre expectations and a dark visual style to create set pieces more reminiscent of the samurai film than noir, *Johnny Handsome* struggles to find its core narrative line. Bronson's character in *Hard Times* is more effectively a noir-cum-samurai protagonist. The same could be said regarding

Charles Bronson as the aging street fighter grapples with an opponent in *Hard Times*.

Last Man Standing (1996), the retro-style remake of *Yojimbo* that overlays a noir look onto another samurai/gangster genre hybrid. Similarly the dilemma of the imprisoned boxer in *The Undisputed* (2002) channels the ethos of Robert Aldrich's *The Longest Yard* more than that of *The Set-Up* (1949) or *The Harder They Fall* (1956), noir films set in the prizefight milieu.

If there is a contemporary actor who could typify a youthful neo-noir *angst*, Mickey Rourke or Sean Penn seem the likeliest candidates; yet the portrayal here alternates between undercurrents of sensitivity and psychoses that are more baffling than ambiguous. As revenge ends in self-destruction, the potentially powerful irony is slightly undercut by the commentary of Lt. Drones, the detective who has dogged Johnny's trail. From *Hickey & Boggs* on, in his action films Hill has been as or more conscious of the workings of genre expectations and the noir tradition than any other writer or director. He has often called *Johnny Handsome* a film noir, and it is certainly neo-noir; but perhaps what this film demonstrates is that mere consciousness does not always align precisely with the sensation of classic film noir.

More than three decades after its release, *Body Heat* is the earliest and perhaps best example of neo-noir films that directly confront the love/sex, honor/money dichotomies. A less-than-average lawyer gets involved with Mattie, a rich man's wife. Despite clear warnings from both law-enforcement and criminal associates, he then devises a scheme to murder her husband. Lawrence Kasdan's screenplay boasts as many twists and turns as the most

Tacky femme fatale Ellen Barkin with Mickey Rourke as *Johnny Handsome*.

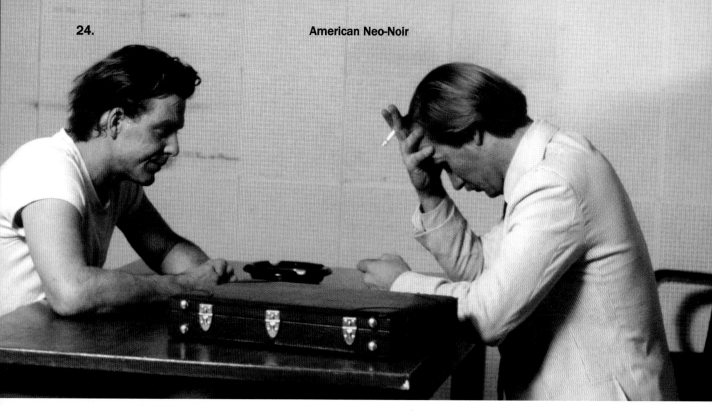

complicated classic period narrative. As many commentators have noted, *Body Heat* is *Double Indemnity* for the post-Code era, a conspicuous reworking of the Cain novel as adapted by Chandler and Wilder without being an official remake or even acknowledging its source. *Body Heat* also offers the neo-noir viewer what an audience in 1944 could only imagine. When Walter Neff dug his fingers

into Phyllis Dietrichson's sweater and said, "I'm crazy about you, baby," the scene ended. *Body Heat* opens with a naked, sexually sated Racine staring out a window at a distant fire, wondering if a client of his is responsible. Of course, while Walter Neff is a top agent with Pacific All Risk, attorney Ned Racine is a low-rent mouthpiece who, as a judge remarks, is sorely in need of a better class of client.

In one of the many bits of dialogue that mirror the slightly more oblique double entendres in *Double Indemnity*, Matty remarks that her "engine runs a little hotter than normal." As with Neff and Dietrichson, this reckless passion for each other makes it difficult for them to stay apart after the murder of her husband. Ultimately Racine is emotionally closer to Steve Thompson in 1949's *Criss Cross* than Walter Neff in *Double Indemnity.* Unlike Neff who, after the crime is committed, compels Phyllis to meet him guardedly in a local market and despite the fact that Edmund's niece is staying in the house, Ned rushes over to Matty in the throes of uncontainable desire, as if to demonstrate the truth of her early remarks: "You're not too smart, are you? I like that in a man." The complications that ensue continue to mirror *Double Indemnity, a*lthough like Neff, Racine does suspect that Matty may be setting him up. Still as the investigators become more suspicious of the accidental nature of the death, they naturally focus on the wife, he never manages to give the lie to her assessment of his intelligence. That leaves him vulnerable to the ultimate double cross by

Body Heat: opposite, Ned Racine (William Hurt) with his pyromaniacal client (Mickey Rourke, top left) and après sex with Matty (Kathleen Turner). Below, an insouciant Matty dines with cuckolded husband (Richard Crenna).

Violence in the movies: Robert De Niro as Travis Bickle in *Taxi Driver*.

a 1980s femme fatale more cunning than most of her antecedents.

The final mirror between the adulterous killers is their last fateful and fatal meeting. By the boat house, Matty again confesses her love for Racine, even though she no longer thinks he believes her. Despite luring Neff into her darkened parlor, the inability of Phyllis to shoot again and finish him off unexpectedly confirms her emotional attachment to him. Matty is a blacker widow. While Neff can look back, accept that he killed for money and a woman, and ruefully conclude, "I didn't get the money, and I didn't get the woman. Pretty isn't it?" the imprisoned Racine continues to delude himself that his purposes were somehow purer than Matty's, that she was and is a woman "who could do what was necessary, whatever was necessary."

In typical classic noir, a female criminal, no matter how appealing or wronged, like Debby March in *The Big Heat,* had to suffer and die for her mistakes. In neo-noir the murdering couple does not ride the streetcar to the end of the line together and the femme fatale gets away with it by finding a corpse to stand in for her. Kasdan uses unexpected detail, such as the wind-chimes in the early conversation on the porch or the dancing prosecutor, to distract both viewer and protagonist from the sordidness of the underlying reality. Because the viewer co-experiences his betrayal, *Body Heat* evokes the noir sensibility much more powerfully than do many of the films that followed it.

While more involved with the resurrection of the gangster genre than neo-noir, few directors could bring as broad a knowledge of the period titles to 1976's *Taxi Driver* as Martin Scorsese. Although scripted by Paul Schrader, the foundation was as much Dostoievskian as noir. As iconic as Robert De Niro's personification of loner Travis Bickle may have become, it began as a straightforward, sociopathic loner. While Bickle never rationalizes his erratic and deadly behavior in a Raskolnikovian way, his core belief does participate in the dialectic of ordinary and extraordinary and empowers him to eradicate what he perceives to be evil. Certainly Scorsese's vision of New York at night, the wet and steamy streets that Bickle traverses in his cab from midnight to dawn, echoes a "Naked City" going back beyond Hellinger and Dassin to Arthur "Weegee" Fellig, but one of Bernard Herrmann's final scores, full of plaintive jazz riffs, creates the firmest sense of alienation.

With his adaptation of *The Manchurian Candidate* (1962), John Frankenheimer pushed beyond the limits of the waning classic period and turned fever-dreams into fierce social satire. While his 1975 *French Connection* sequel ihas aspects of neo-noir, the investigator who discovers an indigenous conspiracy by white supremacists in *Dead Bang* (1989) resembles diverse and dogged predecessors in the murky depths of the classic-period underworld.

Three other examples of highly reflexive neo-noir are *Tough Guys Don't Dance* (1987), *Shattered* (1991), and *Final Analysis* (1992). Norman Mailer's adaptation of his own novel, itself a pastiche of Hammett and Spillane, could be considered a neo-noir attempt to cross over from journalism and prose fiction to screenwriting and direction in the manner of Samuel Fuller. Unlike Fuller,

Below, *Tough Guys Don't Dance*: Not looking as smooth as in *The Driver*, Ryan O'Neal behind another wheel, facing another guy with a gun.

Mailer brought a heavy burden of post-realistic pretension to this feature and, despite script-doctoring by Robert Towne, the movie had none of the spontaneous angst epitomized by the impromptu brawl with co-actor Rip Torn in the earlier *Maidstone* (1970).

It would be hard to imagine a greater pastiche of noir elements than *Shattered*: a nearly fatal car crash, a femme fatale (perhaps two), amnesia, an identity changed through plastic surgery, a quasi-amateur private detective (he also owns a pet shop), flashback truths and flashback lies, corrupt deals for public works, the list goes on. It would also be hard to imagine a poorer result. As part of a small neo-contingent of German and Hungarian émigrés in Hollywood, director Wolfgang Peterson and cinematographer Laszlo Kovacs must have more than a casual awareness of the tradition of Siodmak, Lang, de Toth, and Curtiz. Nonetheless the visualization full of dark corners and sinister landscapes is also full of slow-motion and opticals that make for a curious mixture. Given the narrative convolutions of *Shattered*, which are certainly not without antecedents in the classic period, what was needed was a compelling protagonist to create a through-line. On an expressive level Don Merrick is a lot more like Bigelow in *D.O.A.*, trying to piece together a picture puzzle whose subject is unknown, than the amnesiac in *Somewhere in the Night* (1946) or Bogart in *Dark Passage*. Of course, while it may not be a surprise to many in the audience, Merrick does not even know plastic surgery has changed his identity until near the conclusion. Giving out bits and pieces of this information in flashcuts creates more confusion than suspense, for the protagonist and for the audience. Likewise a surfeit of red herrings creates too little tension and too much of a fishy smell.

Compared to *Shattered*, the self-consciousness of *Final Analysis* seems almost restrained. Neither director Phil Joanou nor director of photography Jordan Cronenweth are émigrés; and Cronenweth was certainly one of the most remarkable of contemporary American cameramen whose style stresses source light and naturalistic effects. While it has distinctive plot twists of its own, *Final Analysis* is not a narrative pastiche, but more of a reverse of the earlier neo-noir *Jagged Edge* (1985). Given the noir sensibility of Joanou and Cronenweth's earlier collaboration on *State of Grace* (1991), the unsubtle echoes in *Final Analysis*, in particular the insistent allusions to *Vertigo* (1958), that reduce it to cartoonish parody are somewhat unexpected. Despite the self-awareness of the psychiatrist protagonist who actually says, "I want to be surprised," and remarks on "existential angst," the story line is simple: two sisters trap him into unwittingly assisting in murder. But *Final Analysis* is not *Vertigo*, and no amount of suffused sidelight coming off wood-paneled rooms, depth of field holding full face and silhouette in close two-shots, or tracking back into empty space from figures at the edge of a great height can underscore character emotion that is never developed. After watching Richard Gere hang precariously over an abyss, seeing Kim Basinger plunge to her matte-shot death, followed by an epilogue in which Uma Thurman seems to assume her dead sister's identity, one realizes not only that it would have been no better with James Stewart, Kim Novak, and Barbara Bel Geddes but also how thin the line between masterful and turgid can be.

Above, amnesiac (Tom Berenger) with the P.I. (Bob Hoskins) hired to help find his identity in *Shattered*. Below, dueling femme fatales (Uma Thurman, left, and Kim Basinger) with psychiatrist Isaac Barr (Richard Gere) in *Final Analysis*.

The Hard-boiled School and Remakes

The thinness of that line is also exemplified in the 1983 television remake of *Double Indemnity*. Very little is changed from the original script, one of the noir movement's finest, and the lead actors are arguably just as talented. The result is nonetheless mediocre.

  Against All Odds (1984) and *No Way Out* (1987), the remakes of *Out of the Past* (1947) and *The Big Clock* (1948)respectively, may have their plots dressed up with sports car chases or computers, but dramatically they are somewhat retrograde. Where the protagonists perished in *Out of the Past, Against All O*dds merely condemns them to a narrative limbo, apart but alive. And the cold-war plot revelation that concludes *No Way Out* is less novel than anticlimactic. Other remakes such as *The Big Sleep* (1978) and *The Postman Always Rings Twice* (1981) are even further off the mark. In the former, Robert Mitchum reprises Philip Marlowe; but the battered idealism that sustained *Farewell, My Lovely* has become mere indifference as the filmmakers inexplicably relocate Raymond Chandler's quintessential Angeleno from L.A. to London. In the latter, Nicholson and Lange in the Garfield/Turner roles recapture the impulsive sexuality but little of the determinism of Cain's original or the 1947 adaptation. *Sharky's Machine* (1981) takes the central premise of *Laura* (1944) and little else. The detective's obsession with a high-priced call girl he thinks is

dead is a small noir twist in a very tangled scenario.

Kiss Me A Killer (1991) is a Latino remake (without crediting Cain) of *The Postman Always Rings Twice*. In fact, the narrative borrows liberally from other types of films, from Siegel's *Crime in the Streets* (1956) to Hitchcock's *I Confess* (1953) ; but the narrative centers on the Mexican-American wife of a white bar owner and a guitar-playing drifter named Tony who helps transform the place into a salsa hot spot. Like Visconti's 1943 *Ossessione*, this unsanctioned adaptation of Cain's novel emphasizes the loutish qualities of the husband and builds audience sympathy with the killers. There are several interesting narrative inventions: the dream sequence in which Teresa imagines her spouse mounted like a game fish on the wall of the bar and the ending in which Tony is killed by a former friend who resents being "set up" in the first attempt on the husband.

The better-known remake of *Postman* is from 1981, a studio project with a screenplay adapted from Cain by David Mamet and Jack Nicholson and Jessica Lang as the doomed couple. As in the first adaptation, the novel's café somewhere "near Glendale" again becomes a highway truck stop. It is now a retro noir, and the passions of the protagonist, which are more explicitly depicted are

Classic versus neo, doomed couples (No. 1) in Mexico: opposite, Robert Mitchum as Jeff Bailey and Jane Greer as in *Out of the Past*. Below, Jeff Bridges and Rachel Ward in *Against All Odds*.

perhaps meant to be even more shocking in a period context. Mamet's spare script should have been be underplayed, but the lustful Nicholson (although his performance is subdued compared to others in his career) as Frank and pouting, pointedly sultry Lange as Cora are somewhat off that mark particularly compared to Garfield and Turner in the original. Ultimately neither version can supersede the classic-period version that MGM had to wait ten years until censorship relaxed after World War II or for that matter Luchino Visconti's stylish neo-realist bootleg *Ossessione*.

   If Cain, Chandler, and other authors published in the French *Série Noire* have not led to inspired filmmaking in the last decades, their narrative preoccupations have been borrowed quite liberally by writers of original scripts. Cain's motifs of doubt and trust underscore the plots of such diverse original scripts as *Jagged Edge*, *Still of the Night* (1982), and *The Morning After* (1986). Yet none is truly effective as film noir, none discovers the unstable undercurrent at the core of such similarly plotted films as *Beyond a Reasonable Doubt* (1956)*, In A Lonely Place* (1950)*,* and *Blue Gardenia* (1953). An auteurist explanation of this phenomenon might cite the passing of Fritz Lang and Nicholas Ray, each of whom directed a half-dozen or more noir films. But the stylistic touches of Lang and Ray, the slow, ensnaring dolly moves or the disorienting cuts during panning shots, are used just as often by contemporary filmmakers. The most derivative direction, such as Brian De Palma's unabashed recapitulations of Hitchcock in *Dressed to Kill* (1980)*, Blow Out* (1981)*,* and

Body Double (1984), may slightly enrich or impoverish the basic material but cannot overwhelm it. De Palma's *Obsession* (1976) may be his most egregious pastiche, an incongruous mélange of *Vertigo* and *Marnie* (1964) underscored, literally and figuratively, by composer Bernard Herrmann. Although set in 1959, the undercurrent is not retro, despite its convoluted plot, which includes a double for a dead wife, who turns out to be a daughter.

One writer whose novels have been adapted several times in neo-noir is Jim Thompson, whose only work in the classic period was dialogue credit for Stanley Kubrick on *The Killing*. In the past decades Thompson's "rediscovery" has led to adaptations of many of his books. The best known, thanks to Anjelica Huston's award-winning performance, is *The Grifters* (1990). While clearly meant to be faithful to Thompson's unrelentingly bleak vision, *The Grifters* presents its cast of "losers" straightforwardly but fails to capture fully the novelist's undercurrent of forlorn perseverance that mutates into classic existential despair.

The 1976 film *The Killer Inside Me* lacked the chilling tone of Thompson's saga of a small-town psychopath who happens to be a cop, a novel that typified his leitmotif that "You can't hurt people who are already dead." Not even the combined efforts of Sam Peckinpah, Walter Hill, and Steve McQueen in *The Getaway* translated this aspect of Thompson to the screen. In the adaptors' hands, the novelist's usual assumptions about the sordidness of crime and its corrupting influence on the criminal's will, became instead a story of betrayal

Classic versus neo, doomed couples (No. 2): opposite, John Garfield and Lana Turner as Frank and Cora in *The Postman Always Rings Twice*. Below, Jessica Lange and Jack Nicholson reprise the roles with some more explicit carnality.

and redemption, of self-righteous violence and paranoiac romance. In these terms and as a fugitive-couple narrative, the 1972 version of *The Getaway* provides an expressive link to the films of the classic period of film noir. The opening focuses on "Doc" in prison. Carol is first seen in the form of two snapshots taped to the wall of his cell. Moreover Peckinpah unabashedly puts forth his typical naturalistic metaphors. The first shot is of a kneeling doe, followed by a stag. From this, there is a pan up to reveal a prison watchtower. Finally a long shot of sheep zooms back to reveal rows of cell blocks. Noise from the prison textile mill fades in. The isolated male and female animals prefigure Doc's overwhelming sense of sexual repression. The machine noise; Doc's upsetting chess pieces and his opponent's remark, "Oh, man, it's just a game"; the destruction of the matchstick bridge—all this overt symbolism establishes a deterministic undertow; and even though the machine noise stops with marked abruptness when Doc is released, this undertow will grip Peckinpah's fugitive couple unrelentingly.

Throughout the film, other elements from Lucien Ballard's flat lighting scheme to the clipped dialogue adapted by scenarist Hill from novelist Thompson, reinforce the realism. In the escape from the bank robbery, a crossing guard stops Doc and Carol's car. The red, hand-held Stop sign which she holds up for them to see is a typical expression of noir fatalism always threatening to capsize a scheme that goes back to the grind of the starter motor in *Double Indemnity*. For Wilder and Chandler adapting Cain, the engine finally starts. For Peckinpah and Hill interpreting Thompson, the delay creates a moment of chaos and violence, which the characters must stoically endure. The supporting players are nasty, garrulous, and otherwise unattractive in line with Peckinpah's naturalist bent and, of course, given to offhanded and extreme violence. His car chases are full of odd angles and cut points. The sound effects complement the lighting: they are muted and hollow.

For Peckinpah, violent action is a transcendent activity. The slow motion and other stylistic manipulations create a distorted perspective for the viewer that is meant to be roughly equivalent to the temporal and sensory distortions that real violence imposes on its participants. For Thompson, the ultimate irony of *The Getaway* is the very title. Just as Lou Ford does in *The Killer Inside Me,* his Doc and Carol learn in Mexico that "I'll never be free as long as I live..." This is not to disparage the Peckinpah/Hill version of *The Getaway*; but its alterations of the novel move it farther from rather than closer to films of the classic period like *Criss Cross* or *The Killing*. After two French adaptations of the early 1980s, *Série Noire* (1979 from Thompson's *A Hell of a Woman*) and particularly Bertrand Tavenier's *Coup de Torchon* (1981, from *Population 1280*), American filmmakers discovered Thompson again in the 1990s.

In contrast director-writer Maggie Greenwald's low-budget 1989 adaptation of Thompson's 1957 novel *The Kill-Off* manages to capture more of the author's brutality and naturalism. The film opens on shots of the economically depressed, semi-deserted factory town (enhanced by the muted colors and low-key photography) and its corrupt inhabitants, which include drug dealers, prostitutes, vicious gossips, child molesters, and alcoholics. Luane operates as the poisonous center of this corrupt town. As she lies in her invalid's bed, surrounded by cheap jewelry and tattered clothes, spreading gossip about the town's denizens, like some small-town Hedda Hopper, the camera pans across the phone lines. On the soundtrack her words are electronically accelerated as they spread her invidious message. We see the first result of her words as a brother and sister accused of incest commit double suicide.

This noir doom that awaits the other characters in the film is further reinforced by the musical "fate motif": the minimalist repetitive chords reminiscent of composer Philip Glass, which act as the soundtrack for the film. Probably the most poignant character in the film is Myra (portrayed by Jorja Fox—best known from the influential TV noir show *CSI*). With her stooped posture, her face cov-

Fugitive couples à la Jim Thompson: opposite, *The Getaway*, Doc (Steve McQueen) and Carol (Ali McGraw) on the run in a blue sedan. Below, *After Dark, My Sweet*, Collie (Jason Patric) and Fay (Rachel Ward) similarly on the run.

ered by her long hair, she is the ultimate victim. Raped by her father Pete, the bar owner, beaten repeatedly by her drug dealer boyfriend Bobbie, she finds her only release in the heroin her boyfriend supplies her. It is, however, Myra who ultimately survives the "kill-off" of the final scenes of the movie. Pete first murders Luane, who knows his secret of what he did to his own daughter. Then he kills Bobbie before he can get away with Pete's money and Myra; but before he can harm her again, Myra uses Bobbie's gun to kill her father. Finally seizing control of her own life, Myra's action is equal parts vindictive desperation and bitter empowerment.

The Kill-Off was actually the first released of the 1990 Thompson adaptations and the most deliberate attempt to retain the multiplicity of viewpoints used in many of the novels, cutting between narrators who are each trapped in what Thompson saw as personal hells. At times The Kill-Off does suffer from its lack of budget, particularly in the uneven performances of its quasi-professional actors. As it happens, The Grifters, with its still modest but substantially larger budget, has much the same problem. The characters in The Grifters are people whose business is deception, whose emotions are concealed to all but a few. John Cusack's laconic rendering of Roy does not catch the glib turns of the con man, especially if compared to a performance like Joe Mantegna's in Mamet's House of Games or Anjelica Huston's as Roy's mother. It is precisely because Thompson's personages are so often trapped in these personal hells, that the business of deception applies to others and to themselves.

Others are the victims of physical or emotional turmoil, such as "Collie" in After Dark, My Sweet. For Thompson and many of the filmmakers who have adapted his work, point of view is crucial. A remarkable performance by Jason Patric's portrayal of "Collie" anchors the 1990 adaptation of After Dark, My Sweet. The credit sequence is an expressionistic rendering of the prizefight in which Collie kills his opponent. Midway through the titles, a sound-buffered jump cut takes the viewer to a tight close-up of him as he now is. After Dark, My Sweet is a first-person film on several levels from the voiceover narration to the optical and sound effects, which intermittently externalize his troubled mental state. Employing these stylistic elements typical of the classic period permits all the narrative tensions to be laid out effectively within the first few minutes. A cut back from the close-up reveals the protagonist in a desert landscape coming out of an escarpment of large stones. As he shuffles across the highway, the narration rambles over shot: "I wonder where I'll be tomorrow..." The key phrase is "I couldn't walk away." As he enters the town, the sound of a train is heard and a sudden, sidewise camera move swings past him but holds the figure in a 180-degree arc, fixes his body in the sun-bleached highway. It prevents him from walking out of the shot, figuratively holding him as firmly as his troubled memories grip his mind.

Like all Thompson's characters, Collie is slowly dying in this personal hell. When Fay (Rachel Ward), a femme fatale in sandals and a straw hat, picks him up, she treats him like a stray puppy, patting the car seat and saying, "Come on, now, there's a good boy," to entice him in. Her directness—she wants to call him "Collie" because he reminds her of a shaggy dog—is what makes her ambiguous, what sets her apart in a Thompson-esque milieu of con men and petty crooks. The desert itself with its clean, brightly lit vistas is in constant contrast to the emotional darkness within. But it is through Patric's performance, full of tics, stumbling, and false starts, that *After Dark, My Sweet* evokes the hopelessness of both Thompson and neo-noir more forcefully than *The Grifters* and more pointedly than *The Kill-Off.*

Whether from a position of ignorance or knowledge, the interaction of protagonist and viewer seems much more seldom to reveal the instability, the dark undercurrent that served as a thematic constant of the noir cycle. That "Fate or some mysterious force" that destroyed or endangered scores of characters like Frank Bigelow and Al Roberts in *Detour* (1945) is less often a factor in neo-noir. If the remake *D.O.A.* (1988) illustrates anything, it is that the arbitrariness of death in an era of yuppie values and AIDS can still matter. The remake is stylistically too self-conscious, not just in the black-and-white sequences that bracket the flashbacks of college professor Dexter Cornell (the new Frank Bigelow) flashback story of how he was killed, but in the diffused, desaturated color scenes as well. The key story point—that Cornell (Dennis Quaid) has been poisoned because he might recognize a novel, the student-author of whom has been killed by an another professor who wants to publish it as his own—is even more suggestive of ethical values gone totally awry.

Martin Scorsese's *Cape Fear* (1991) epitomizes the synthesis of a conscious auteur and the remaking of a picture from the classic period. Even more than the 1962 original, the new *Cape Fear* transforms Al Roberts' lament into a relentless litany. As the sense of helplessness grows in the family tormented by a vindicative ex-convict, the sense of menace is as palpable as in the original or *The Killer is Loose* (1956). In another remake, *Desperate Hours* (1990), the posturing of the criminals never seems as threatening to the family as its own inner turmoil. Scorsese unabashedly creates a preternatural figure with Robert De Niro's portrayal of Max Cady, a tattooed, vindictive, self-righteous brute, whose monomania becomes, for his victims, the pointed finger of the mysterious force.

Scorsese puts De Niro back in a theater seat as the crazed Max Cady in *Cape Fear*.

Victims of Circumstance—Love with an Improper Stranger

Even when Roberts' "mysterious force" does appear to be in play, the result can be quite different. The failure of a film like *Out of Bounds* (1986) to be anything more than a "kid noir" parody is the failure to exploit viewer expectations. The motivating plot element, picking up the wrong bag, is accomplished with a lot more verisimilitude than in *Too Late for Tears* (1949); but little else is. Hunted by both a murderous pusher and the police, helped only by a Hollywood pun-kette, the fresh-from-the-farm protagonist perseveres where many a noir hero would have despaired, or at least faltered. This combination of violence and teen-grit falls a bit short of the noir sensibility.

On the other hand, the popular success of a picture like *Fatal Attraction* (1987) is more dependent on the noir formula. Certainly its very title is in the same "boldface" used by so many classic-period films and more on the money than the earlier neo *Play Misty for Me* (1971, discussed below in "Auteurist Riffs"). Despite that, it manipulates viewer expectations. More significantly, it manipulates them by drawing the viewer into the protagonist's point-of-view. The audience fails to discern the latent psychoses of Alex Forrest, fails to read any real menace in her slight lack of focus or an occasional nervous gesture, because Dan Gallagher does not see it. Alex Forrest is no femme fatale, luring the unwary hero down a deadly path of criminal activity or other degradation. Like the woman in *The Locket* (1946), the veneer of normality is enhanced by her sexual vulnerability. From the protagonist's, and audience's, frame of reference, her behavior is more disturbing for its unexpectedness. Like many noir figures before him, Gallagher's inability to anticipate or respond is the real source of peril. Like Sam Bowden in *Cape Fear*, he finds that the very social

order which he thought would protect him, only makes him and his family easier to assail.

Neo-noir has fatal men as well as women, although the cultural prejudices that helped create the femme fatale are still in play. Tim Whelan, the protagonist of *Masquerade* (1988), is a gigolo intent on seducing an heiress. Like Nick Blake in *Nobody Lives Forever* (1946), the victim's naivete gives Whelan pause; but in the typical schematic of neo-noir, nothing can prevent his destruction. Despite its literally explosive conclusion which annihilates the protagonist, *Masquerade* is a flaccid reflection of the classic period. Equally ineffective is the similarly plotted second adaptation of the Ira Levin novel *A Kiss Before Dying* (1991). The low-budget *Blue Desert* (1991) centers on a woman who works as a comic book artist and whose experiences in New York drive her from the city to a what she expects will be a safe community in the desert. Her involvement there with a drifter and a local policeman lead her to discover that deception and menace are not uniquely urban problems.

In *Fatal Attraction*, *Masquerade*, and *A Kiss Before Dying*, in films as diverse as *Sea of Love, Mortal Passions, Paint It Black* (all 1989), *Blue Desert,* or *The Hot Spot* (1990), what makes many of the figures in neo-noir into victims of circumstance is their proclivity for love with an improper stranger.

The Hot Spot is a reciprocal of *The Strange Love of Martha Ivers* (1946) or what might have happened if Martha Ivers had accomplished her aims. The film's fatal woman, Dolly Harshaw, does manage to kill her husband and trap the protagonist in her black widow's web. Of course, Harry Madox, *The Hot Spot*'s protagonist, is a con man, bank robber, and killer, who in the film's final

Opposite and below, *Fatal Attraction*, before and after: when a neo-noir femme fatale lets herself go then opts for a kitchen knife instead of a styling brush.

words accepts his fate: "I found my level, and I'm living it." *The Hot Spot* is fully as self-conscious of the noir tradition as *Shattered* and *The Final Analysis*. If it succeeds where they fail, part of the reason is a directness that verges on parody. From the opening titles, revealing its "hero" among sand dunes under a blistering sky as a hawk screeches on the soundtrack, director Dennis Hopper uses the shorthand of iconic indicators like a wry commentary. The robbery, the extortions, the seductions are secondary elements in a plot hinging an allegorical triangle that seems descended from those of noir novelist David Goodis. On the one hand is the lascivious, animalistic Dolly, repeatedly posed with her legs parted on a car seat or covered with shaving cream, linked in fatalistic side moves of the camera with a rearing polar bear, or, in the penultimate sequence, crawling on the floor and counter-posed with a stuffed cougar. On the other hand is Gloria, demure, virginal, blackmailed by Frank Sutton who has photographs of her in an apparently lesbian interlude. "That little gal's got you all stoked up," Sutton correctly observes to Harry; and what Don Johnson's performance suggests has Harry stoked up is the hint of sordidness in Gloria. It is the sights and sounds of the milieu where the buzz of a fly on Sutton's hand is like the stench of corruption, where Madox's black-finned Studebaker swoops down on Sutton's place like a bird of prey, which truly situate *The Hot Spot* and enclosed Harry Madox in a personal hell as fiery as any of Jim Thomspon's.

Variants of obsessive love are as commonplace in neo-noir as they were in the classic period. The difference between *Revenge* (1990) and *Cat Chaser* (1989) is one of tone. The latter has script work by Elmore Leonard from his own novel and, in Peter Weller, an actor who could blend the resignation of Sterling Hayden and the edginess of John Ireland while delivering lines such as

Opposite and below, *The Hot Spot*: Harry Madox (Don Johnson) wth Gloria (Jennifer Connelly) and (Dolly) Virginia Madsen. Can one tell who is working harder on her femme fatale credentials?

Jane Fonda as call girl Bree Daniel in *Klute*.

"Sometimes you see somebody and you see yourself going down a road you could have gone." Ultimately while it may be the least violent of director Abel Ferrara's neo-noir credits, *Cat Chaser* is too caught up in the conditional mode and its impact diffracted through a supporting cast of losers and thugs. It is the aspects of irresistible compulsion and betrayal that make a less complex film like *Revenge* at least superficially truer to the noir tradition.

These subthemes of betrayal and mistrust that were at play in *Out of the Past* and *Criss Cross* also find diverse new examples in *Klute* (1971), *The Last Embrace* (1976), *Sea of Love*, *Kill Me Again* (1990), and *Deceived* (1991). The last of these is a pallid echo of *Suspicion*, using stray cats for shock cuts but less suspenseful than another Hitchcock-inspired (by 1935's *The 39 Steps*) Goldie Hawn vehicle, *Bird on a Wire* (1990), which is essentially comic. Jonathan Demme's early *The Last Embrace* (1979) is an even greater conflation, with its plotted maladies ranging from a simple nervous breakdown to psychopathic schizophrenia tied into arcane Judaica and a trip down Niagara Falls without a barrel. The earliest of these, *Klute*, sets a pattern for plot and character development, aspects of which are echo throughout neo-noir. Bree Daniel

is the target of a killer and also a prostitute. As with Bigelow, circumstances not her line of work, have put her in jeopardy. The scenes which track Bree plying her trade, at auditions, at her therapist's are part of a parallel schematic with John Klute, the small-town cop investigating his friend's death, and Peter Cable, the killer trying to cover his tracks. The discussions about love and trust are direct reflections on themes from the classic period. From the costumes and characterizations down to sound effects and underscore, the style is expressive of the interplay of the noir underworld and "normal" society.

Also of interest in terms of narrative structure are *Sea of Love* and *Kill Me Again*. Both were sold to audiences as erotic thrillers but the key to each is not whether the female lead is a femme fatale as much as how the male detective (police and private respectively) perceives her. When the protagonist in *Sea of Love* finds himself fixated on a woman whom he suspects is a "lonely hearts" killer, there are two possible narrative resolutions: either she is or she is not. The conflict becomes an inner one fixed on his inability to trust his feelings. This is not uncommon and is often situated outside of a noir environment. With *Kill Me Again* as in *Criss Cross*, the question is not whether the object of the detective's attraction is capable of lying to him, for he knows she has done that

repeatedly, but whether she will continue to do so. In the end, *Kill Me Again*'s Jack Andrews is neither Walter Neff nor Steve Thompson; but like other noir and neo-noir P.I.s, from Sam Spade on, he is capable of hedging his bets.

Cops—Good, Bad, and All Dead Inside

Early neo-noir saw both retro P.I.s and retro cops, although the no-nonsense and cynical detective in *True Confessions* and the titled character in Warren Beatty's stylish if insubstantial *Dick Tracy* (1990) are worlds apart. The former movie imagines how Los Angeles cronyism continued to generate shady real estate schemes and cover-ups a decade after the events of *Chinatown.* The latter one visualizes a squared-jawed detective picking his way through an irreal landscape filled not only with literally comic-strip villains but also sleek cars and sleeker women. Conversely, *Robocop* (1987) minimalized the sci-fi and maximized the brutal violence in the grim streets of future Detroit. While there were overt existential implications in transformation of Murphy the cop into Murphy the machine, in the end his mantra of "Dead or alive, you are coming with me" made him closer to a Lone Ranger in a tin suit.

The concept that "anyone can be killed" is central to John Flynn's *Best Seller* (1987). A hired killer named Cleve wants Dennis Meechum, a detective/novelist, to write his biography and expose his former employer, a noted philanthropist, who, like the syndicate figures in Flynn's earlier *The Outfit* (1972) that "act like they own the world," needs his comeuppance. Cleve also asserts that he and the cop are a lot alike, a notion which the detective must

Opposite, top, *Sea of Love*: a NY detective (Al Pacino) and his lonely-hearts femme fatale (Ellen Barkin); bottom, some fatal women even pick up gats, Joanne Whalley-Kilmer in *Kill Me Again*. Below, cop/novelist Dennis Meechum (Brian Dennehy) and his hit man/literary adviser/snitch Cleve (James Woods) in *Best Seller.*

Above, metrosexual FBI profiler Will Graham (William Petersen) pays the first neo-noir visit to serial killer Hannibal Lecter (Brian Cox, opposite) inside the remarkably clean psycho ward in Michael Mann's *Manhunter.* Below, Petersen as an edgier street cop in *To Live and Die in L.A.*

resist. The same contention is made by a mass murderer to the detective in *Manhunter* (1986). For the latter protagonist, in particular, getting inside the criminal mind has had psychically damaging implications. For both men, the most alienating aspect of their job is the latent fear that they are indeed becoming like the criminals they track. Director Michael Mann, who brought a noir viewpoint to the small screen with *Miami Vice*, has his camera constantly gliding behind the title character in *Manhunter,* picking up disturbing resonances of fear and death. Graham is actually more disturbed by his visits to the imprisoned Dr. Lecter than by his attempts at mind-melding with the "tooth fairy." In the scene where he tells Lecter how he managed to capture him ("You had certain disadvantages." "What disadvantages?" "You're insane."), Graham fidgets nervously in the chair. When he feels the fabric of the victim's clothing in the evidence room and asks the absent killer out loud, "What is it you're

becoming?" Graham seems totally in control. From that scene, Mann cuts to the killer's home and a close-up of William Blake's watercolor of "The Red Dragon," the being with which the psychopath identifies. For Meechum and Graham, being touched by the pollution and sordidness of the noir underworld is part of the job description. Unable to behave like the brutal cops in *The Detective Story* or *Where the Sidewalk Ends* (1950), these more modern policeman suffer from a job-related, mental dysfunction that makes them feel more like the ex-con Galt in *The Dark Corner* (1946), "all dead inside."

By its very title, *Murphy's Law* (1986) epitomizes the narrative counter-influences on neo-noir. When the viewer expects things to go wrong for the pro-tagonist, they invariably do; but when the protagonist expects things to go wrong, the delicate balance of the noir universe is upset. What keeps many of the Charles Bronson pictures after *Death Wish* (1974) and the Clint Eastwood vehicles after *Dirty Harry* from evoking the noir sensibility is the grim miens of their stars, the lines in their faces that suggest they are beyond wondering about the vagaries of life. The antithesis of these portrayals would be Bruce Dern as the Detective in *The Driver*.

The distinction between police conscience and police corruption can be finely drawn in neo-noir. Eastwood's slightly kinky detective in *Tightrope* (1984) cannot help but see a little of himself in the sexually frustrated killer he is stalk-ing. Even as the implacable "Dirty Harry" in *Sudden Impact* (1983), he becomes so involved with a woman tracking a gang of murderous rapists that he lets her go at the film's conclusion. By 1990, in *The Rookie* Eastwood is a necessarily older, somewhat less-reckless detective, mentoring the title character but still getting caught up in violent encounters.

The federal agents in *To Live and Die in L.A.* (1986) get so caught up in the underworld they are combing for a master criminal that they cross the line, as do the street cops in *King of New York* (1990). Even *Stakeout* (1987), which is seriocomic in depicting a detective's unforeseen affair with a woman he has under surveillance, is just slightly removed from the darker implications of the classic period's *Pushover* (1954). Like *Someone to Watch Over Me* (1987), which reduces the concept to soap opera, *Stakeout* does confront the issue of conflict of interest as a human failing with possibly fatal results.

Obviously none of these characters is a "bad cop" in the classic sense, accepting bribes like the title figure in *Rogue Cop* or killing for money as in *Shield for Murder* (both 1954). The police figure in *The Big Easy* (1987) is on the take and happily so. The bounty hunter in the semi-comic *Blue Iguana* (1988) also skirts the rules, which makes him susceptible to being blackmailed and co-opted. As with the cliquish detectives in *Prince of the City* (1981), it's easier to be part of the game than to buck the system. Even after being caught, the character's remorse is more over the possibility of losing a job he's good at and a love interest who is a district attorney than from any sense of wrongdoing. Ironically, the character's easy virtue makes him all the more guilty when he discovers the extent of the corruption in his department.

Besides "Dirty" Harry, perhaps the best known of cops that push the boundaries is Jimmy "Popeye" Doyle. Certainly as portrayed by Gene Hackman in *French Connection* (1971) and *French Connection II* (1975), Doyle is a hardscrabble, unkempt roughneck in a felt porkpie, the uncool, New York variant of Eastwood's smoothly coiffed Inspector Callahan. Doyle's red-faced frustration during the celebrated car chase under the el train, is also in stark contract to Callahan's control.

The string of corrupt cops featured in early neo-noir is long and varies from *The Border* (1982) to *Black Rain*, *Q & A*, *Last of the Finest*, and *Internal Affairs* (all 1990) not to mention where such characters are less prominent, as in *Witness* (1985) or *Narrow Margin* (1990), but still central to the plot. Given the cross-cultural thrusts of *The Border*, *Black Rain*, and even *Q & A*, only *Internal Affairs* is as focused on bad cops as *The Big Easy*. Like many who stretch the rules, the squad of narcotics investigators in *Last of the Finest* are disgusted by a system that often protects the guilty, so they devise a vigilante financed operation by robbing dealers.

Below, *Black Rain*: bad and good cops in an alien environment, Dets. Nick Conklin (Michael Douglas, right) and Charlie Vincent (Andy Garcia) in Tokyo. Opposite, Douglas as the addicted but well-coiffed Det. Nick Curran with murder suspect, novelist and party girl Catherine Trammell (Sharon Stone) in *Basic Instinct*.

What separates and sometimes redeems the rogue cops of neo-noir is their motivation. Of those involved in crime, the supporting characters in *The Border* or *Witness* are merely venal and either perish or are caught. The characters in *Q & A* and *Black Rain* are a bit more complicated. But neither the former who administers his own justice nor the latter who rehabilitates some of his honor in Japan seems troubled by the fact of his imperfect behavior as by its consequences. Ultimately the protagonists in *The Border* and *Internal Affairs* are closer to the classic tradition. The former who accepts the corruption around him and almost falls prey to it because he needs money cannot accept the devaluation of human life that his working environment fosters. Unlike the title character in the earlier *Serpico* (1973), whose outrage at larcenous cops is met by institutionalized disregard, the investigator in *Internal Affairs* is charged to uncover bad cops. Consequently, *Internal Affairs* is even more overt in its treatment of corruption as latent in everyone; but the dark possibilities of transference of guilt that it raises are left underexplored at its end. Conversely, a picture such as *The Onion Field* (1979) initially makes transference a keynote; however, the guilt which one cop feels after his partner's murder is quickly subsumed to the study of the criminal mentalities of the two killers, which is ultimately closer to the "true story" connotations of *In Cold Blood* (1967) than to neo-noir.

The cops of the classic period from 1941's *I Wake Up Screaming* to *Pushover* or even *Laura* who were compromised because of sexual obsessions are less common in neo-noir. Certainly *Sea of Love* might have taken that narrative direction but did not. There are sexual overtones in *Internal Affairs* and even *The Border*, but they are secondary considerations. Essentially the protagonists of both those films act out of idealism, compromised idealism, perhaps, but sufficiently intact to compel their outrage when they discover inhuman and murderous behavior.

By 1992 idealism is in short supply. The protagonist of *Basic Instinct* (1992) is a cop whose cocaine addiction may have driven his wife to suicide, who has had an affair with his psychotherapist and is seduced by a murder suspect. Beneath the surface flashes of violence and sex, the potential alienation

of *Basic Instinct's* wayward cop is lost in a miasma of plot convolutions and quirky nostalgia, as in the casting of Dorothy Malone, a classic-period icon, as an older psychopath. The similar themes of such modestly budgeted efforts as *To Kill For* or *Criminal Intent* (both 1992) provide telling comparisons with *Basic Instinct*. The San Francisco detective in *To Kill For* is similarly seduced by a female suspect and the brutal cop in *Criminal Intent* is being investigated by internal affairs. While neither film succeeds where *Basic Instinct* fails in truly evoking a noir ambience, these failures are, at least from the viewpoint of time and money involved, much more modest. Even a true idealist, such as the deputy sheriff in *White Sands* (1992), who becomes enmeshed in an labyrinthine plot involving corrupt operatives from several federal agencies simply because he is diligently investigating a murder, is extricated from the potential miasma of neo-noir alienation by some convenient plot twists.

Dennis Hopper as Harry Niles, a "pissed-off white cop who's been suspended," does embody some of that alienation in John Flynn's *Nails* (1992). His portrayal, despite snippets of personal philosophy, such as "Cautious men die; the reckless survive," is ultimately more style than substance. Where Harry Niles is a self-professed relic, the character of John Hull in *Deep Cover* (1992) puts a new spin on the noir hero. Opening with an incident from the protagonist's childhood twenty years in the past (he sees his father gunned down while robbing a liquor store) and using voiceover narration throughout, *Deep Cover*

incorporates many traditional noir elements with such newer optical devices as step printing, staggered zoom shots, and interlaced montages. This staccato imagery combined with a pulsing underscore and the main character's monotone narration create a kind of "rap noir," an emblem of 1990s alienation entirely appropriate to an example of neo-noir focused on drugs, racism, and mixed loyalties. Even as tilted angles externalize Hull's sense of disequilibrium, the surface irony remains that the street cop protagonist is more at home undercover than in uniform, that he is full of anti-authoritarian tendencies that lead the federal agent who recruits him to observe that "undercover all your faults will become virtues. You'll be star there, John." Compounding this is the perspective of first-person recollection, a commentary that reveals a deterministic overview: "I felt that it would be the biggest mistake of my life, and I was right." Through a series of violent and chaotic set pieces, that determinism drives the narrative toward a climactic moment when the protagonist must make a choice typical of the noir underworld, not just between good and evil, but between past and present, rich and poor, old allegiances and new. Clearly the undercover agent's criminal partner, though white and middle class, is a mirror of his own "dark" side. Because it focuses more on the cop than the criminal than such films as *New Jack City* (1990) or *King of New York*, the viewer expects from the first what that choice will be. If there is a false note in the conclusion of *Deep Cover*, it is not the protagonist's survival as much as the reversal of his position with a system that has manipulated him from childhood.

Essentially the neo-noir cop begins with three Frank Sinatra pictures of the late 1960s: *The Detective* (1968), the centerpiece book-ended by the P.I. pictures *Tony Rome* (1967) and *Lady in Cement* (1968), in an informal series with the same director, producer, cinemagrapher and so on. The iconic playing with type and exploiting both the professional and private personas of the actor-singer could not sustain those pictures nor the later *The First Deadly Sin* (1980). But they are significant in helping define a type, a world-weary investigator whether carrying a gold shield or a private investigator's license, more effectively portrayed in *Madigan* or *Hickey & Boggs.* In *The Detective*, while he investigates the grisly murder of a gay scion of a notable New York family, Sgt. Joe Malone is surrounded by old-school cops who want to beat up "fags," while his captain covers up racism and wants him to kowtow to politicians. Stylistically, despite occasional foreground clutter, some layered flashbacks, and a jazzy score from Jerry Goldsmith, just a few years from the classic period, the staging by director Gordon Douglas and cinematographer Joe Biroc is more doc that noir. When his sociology professor wife (Lee Remick) mirrors his ethical concerns and suggests that he could quit, his existential reply is "What else am I good at?" The same question could have been asked by Sinatra the year before as the title character in *Tony Rome*, which features irrational ingénues, missing diamonds, and competing clients. By *Lady in Cement*, Rome may be dodging both cops and criminals in the best Marlowe-esque manner, but noir undertone is most absent.

As in his own classic-period noirs, director Robert Aldrich keys the mise-

Opposite, criminal mouthpiece and dealer David Jason (Jeff Goldblum) with undercover operative Russell Stevens aka John Hull (Laurence Fishburne, right) in *Deep Cover.*

Above, Phil Gaines (Burt Reynolds) and Nicole (Catherine Deneuve) in *Hustle*. Opposite, Det. Murtaugh (Danny Glover, right) is close to retirement and unhappy with his unstable new partner Riggs (Mel Gibson) in *Lethal Weapon*.

en-scène of *Hustle* (1975) to the protagonist's alienated point of view. An opening sequence of LAPD Detective Phil Gaines in the home of his hooker girlfriend is remarkably diffracted from its aerial shots to close-ups. The color and details of the setting are attenuated by the high contrast and hard edge in the lighting. "Dirty Harry" Callahan may take to the streets in search of confrontation and catharsis, but Gaines retreats from oppressive realities into himself. He is openly nostalgic: "I like the thirties, Cole Porter, Dizzy Dean," which suggests the same fallen romanticism of another Callahan, Aldrich's character in *World for Ransom* (1954). Although portrayed by Burt Reynolds, Gaines has no false bravado and is not inured to the violence of the world, not even when he administers a coup de grace to a homicidal mental patient, so that the man will never be allowed to go free again. Gaines adopts metaphors for this violence, his favorite being the movie version of *Moby Dick*. If Gaines does see himself as Ahab, driven mad by his own moral outrage, he must also see his reflection in the felons and psychopaths who wage their own war against society and the system. For a street cop in the context of neo-noir, there may be an emotional equation between self and other; each action against the social outcasts may reflectively become an action against the underpinnings of his own persona. By the time Nicole comes home to find him watching *Moby Dick* on television and crouched in the shadows like Charlie Castle in Aldrich's *The Big Knife* (1955), the myths have lost their therapeutic value for Gaines with fatal consequences. Reynolds reprised more job-weary, burnt-out cases, plodding on because the alternative to enduring is expiring in such pictures as *Malone* (1988) and *Rent-a-Cop* (1988), iconography without substance.

　　　　Perhaps the most estranged for the least apparent reason is the suicidal vice cop in *Lethal Weapon* (1987). He is, as it happens, a Vietnam veteran who has lost a loved one. Like his G.I. counterparts back from World War II, he neither thinks nor acts normally: he is as likely to push a jumper off a roof as pull him back. Like Gagin in *Ride the Pink Horse*, the unforeseen association with his new partner's family brings him back from the brink. Unlike Gagin's experience, or that of any classic noir protagonist, his catharsis is a torrent of violent action culminating in hand-to-hand combat on his partner's lawn. Given the restorative impact of *Lethal Weapon*'s narrative on the alienated protagonist, it is not surprising that *Lethal Weapon II* (1989), *III* (1992), and *IV* (1998) lack the nervous energy of the first picture.

More variations are *Cop* (1988), *Dead-Bang*, *State of Grace*, *Homicide* (1991), *Thunderheart* (1992), and, of course, *Deep Cover*. The first two are versions of the burnt-out case, investigators estranged from their families and bending the rules as they doggedly pursue leads and try to convince others of the connection in a string of crimes. *Cop*, in particular, dwells on the brutality that is both suffered and inflicted by its protagonist. In the conclusion of *Lethal Weapon* Riggs gave the taunting killer a duelist's chance; but in this picture Hopkins has a different response to the jibes of the captured murderer. Having seen the victims' bodies and imagining a trial where pleas will be entered and facts distorted, Hopkins realizes that, while "I'm a cop and I've got to take you in," he is suspended from duty. He says as much to the suspect and then blows him away.

The latter two films, in particular, unflinchingly question many values in the standard cops and robbers or good guys versus bad approach of many law enforcers. The undercover cop in *State of Grace*, who is sent back to his old neighborhood to bring down the friends of his childhood, has a very different experience than the detective in *Cry of the City* (1948). As the distinction between good and evil is increasingly blurred, the warring factions do not mere-

ly murder in the cold-blooded tradition of the 1930s gangster film but rational-
ize it as well. As the hospital-endowing drug lord of *King of New York* remarks
on his rapacious victims, "Those guys are dead because I didn't want to make
money that way. I never killed anybody that didn't deserve it." As in *Deep
Cover*, ethnic prejudice is also a key issue in both *State of Grace* and *Homicide*.
Although guilt-ridden undercover officer Noonan in *State of Grace* may try to
achieve catharsis by confronting his antagonists and opening fire, there is no
simple method to expiate the convoluted betrayals in *Homicide*. The frustration
and confusion that plague Noonan are not only disquieting but they short-cir-
cuit the kind of Hawksian professionalism through which he thought he had
found an identity. The film's ending, in which he is blackmailed by those he
thought were his new brothers and loses his partner as a consequence of his
personal failure, are not so much anti- as pre-Hawksian, the descent into self-
loathing from which redemption may or may not be possible. A similar theme,
with a slightly more upbeat conclusion, is explored in *Thunderheart*. While the
Native American FBI agent is not directly betrayed by the inhabitants of the
reservation where he goes to investigate a murder, he does discover that many
of them are not above selling out. In that sense, even as mysticism mixes with
identity crisis, the concept of betrayal is still in play. It remains to be seen
whether *Thunderheart* and *The Dark Wind* (1990), based on a series of novels
by Tony Hillerman featuring a reservation policeman, fully constitute a sub-cat-
egory of Native American noir.

    For all the police characters in neo-noir films, violence betokens both
solution and problem, dispelling a physical threat but compounding a moral
dilemma. Some protagonists, as in *Best Seller,* manage to resist the temptation of the quick fix; others, as in *To Live and Die in L.A.*, are consumed by it.

Serial Murder and Psychopaths—The Killer Inside Me

Perhaps the explicit threat of transference, of mentally trading places with the criminals they pursue, experienced by the detectives in *Best Seller* and *Manhunter*, is epitomized by the female investigator in *Black Widow* (1987). Like her male counterparts, she is warned about her "obsession," about her abnormal relationship with the woman she is pursuing. Other noir protagonists have established relationships with suspects—Fallon in *White Heat* (1949) and the undercover cops in *Street with No Name* (1948) and *House of Bamboo* (1955)—but they never forgot they were playing a role. In *Black Widow*, the protagonist's involvement, first with the suspected murderess and then with her fiancé, violates all the usual rules. The scene in which she gives her adversary a black widow brooch clarifies the nature of the deadly duel in which the two women are consciously locked: a conflict not just of crime and law, of chaos and order, but, like Det. Diamond and Mr. Brown in *The Big Combo*, a conflict of sheer will as well.

Transference is also a factor in such diverse productions as *Mike's Murder* (1984), *52 Pick-up* (1986), and *At Close Range* (1986). In *52 Pick-up*, twenty-five years after *The Manchurian Candidate*, John Frankenheimer's adaptation of Elmore Leonard explores the intrusion the underworld of sex and drugs into the clean, well-lit lives of a small businessman and his politically active wife. At first, the protagonist seems unable to deal with the coldblooded, anonymous extortionist who suddenly turns his world upside down; but as he first tracks down his antagonist and then confronts him, the victim becomes the aggressor. *At Close Range* is quite memorable for director of photography Juan Ruiz

Sean Penn in early neo-noir: below, gangster-in-training Brad Whitewood Jr. with patriarch Christopher Walken in *At Close Range. Opposite* as undercover cop Terry Noonan with sketchy muscle Jackie Flannery (Gary Oldham) in *State of Grace.*

Anchía's hard-lit images. The plot, a criminal father's seduction of his sons into the life he and his own brothers live, never develops beyond its "based on a true story" pathos. Eventually, even the austere side-lit close-ups and dark frames cut by white light, visualizations in the noir tradition that subtly suggest the violence smoldering just below the surface, lose their impact, drowned by listless staging and an overused underscore.

The Bedroom Window (1987) is little more than a pastiche of Woolrich and Hitchcock. Not until the last third of its narrative, when the original victim returns to help clear the innocent protagonist does the production do more than simply borrow plot from a film like Phantom Lady (1944), too late to create anything more than a superficial noir ambience. Mike's Murder is a bit more ambitious. Unlike the male figure in 52 Pick-up, the woman's odyssey into the same subculture of sex and drugs in Mike's Murder is a voluntary one. After a series of bizarre encounters, like those of Van Stratten in Mr. Arkadin (1955), what she discovers about herself as well as about her murdered friend is that the noir underworld is indeed still just beneath the surface, menacing those who probe too deeply. Moreover, in this film and Black Widow, Debra Winger takes on roles that are traditionally male and gives them a new perspective. While her characters have a situational resemblance to the Ella Raines' portrayal of a woman trying to clear the boss she secretly loves of murder in Phantom Lady, Winger's sexuality is more of a tool than a motivation. In Betrayed (1988) Winger plays an FBI agent enamored of the white supremacist whose group she has infiltrated. The ending in which the undercover agent

Debra Winger (below left) was a sincere and dogged female investigator in both Mike's Murder and Black Widow. Right, Theresa Russell incarnates the titled serial killer in the latter movie.

must accept that she has been intimate with a killer, and shoots him, is effectively a reversal of *Phantom Lady*.

Given its narrative pretexts and its source material, the sequel to *Manhunter*, *Silence of the Lambs* (1991) is remarkably asexual. In expanding the character of Hannibal Lecter, both novelist and filmmakers create a cipher for all the psychopaths at large in the neo-noir underworld. What fascinates Lecter is the grim skull beneath the skin, the chaos beneath the surface order. As disquieting as he may appear strapped to a stretcher in a straightjacket and mask, his bare face is even more disturbing. His leering offer to the young female FBI trainee, "I'll help you catch him, Clarice," is more carnivorous that lubricious. "Hannibal the Cannibal," "The Tooth Fairy," "Buffalo Bill," all the epithets suggest a search for food, not sex. Lecter and his ilk also represent the most fundamental assault on the ostensibly normal, ordered world of the protagonists. "Don't tell him anything personal,"Clarice is advised, "You don't want Hannibal Lecter inside your head." Since Lecter's price for information is being permitted inside her head, the final face-to-face meeting is both terrible and cathartic for Clarice. The visual style alternates tight, low-lit close-ups of Lecter with slow zooms into her face, externalizing the process of his mind penetrating hers.

For the FBI agent in a picture such as *Shoot to Kill* (1988), the psychopath, the victims, the alternate lifestyle of his back-country guide are all secondary considerations, in a stereotypical and one-dimensional portrait of a law enforcer. For Clarice Starling, as it was for *Manhunter*'s Will Graham, whose name and history are directly invoked in *Silence of the Lambs*, Lecter is frightening in and of himself and also as a symbol of the terrifying underworld that was integral to the classic noir narrative. Unlike Graham, Clarice is not an empath whom Lecter brings face to face with his own dark side. Lecter's prob-

Clarice Starling (Jodie Foster) visits the downscale asylum cell of Hannibal Lecter (Anthony Hopkins) in *Silence of the Lambs*.

ing of her past and her values never menaces her life and ultimately reinforces her own sanity.

During and just after the classic period, encounters between cops and serial murderers were less frequent and more predictable: Dirty Harry shot him, tortured him, and shot him again at the end. Neo-noir has many variants that blur the distinction from the simplistic, blue-lit, low-budget *The Rain Killer* (1990), in which the FBI man is the psychopath, to *Relentless* (1989), in which the killer's father was a policeman, to *Miami Blues* (1990), in which the criminal impersonates a cop. In a production like *The Rain Killer*, where the poor technical choices and poorer acting discredit the entire effort, the viewer is not encouraged to consider the elements of transference in the plot. *Miami Blues* actually focuses on that concept in opposing a killer who wants to try a normal domestic life in which murder and robbery are his nine-to-five job with a cop who might be happier on skid row.

One of the most unsettling example of the domestic serial killer is *White of the Eye* (1988). In confronting the question of the killer inside, director Donald Cammell drags along often inappropriate effects from *Performance* (1970) and stages the killings as repellent ballets of death. A shot of a victim reflected in an extreme close-up of an eye may be a less than subtle statement of intent about re-creating the killer's point of view; but without benefit of the killer's identity, the crimes are anonymously grotesque. For most of the narrative the viewer is encouraged to believe that the killer is actually an innocent victim, whose only "crime" is cheating on his wife. It is, in fact, the wife's point-of-view that is most severely manipulated; yet the ironic flashbacks and the encounter with her old boyfriend who has mysteriously returned to Arizona after a prison sentence create an aura less of vague apprehension or even dislocation than of ennui. The final sequences where "all is revealed" have some chilling moments as the psychopath puts on his ritual costume and terrorizes his own wife and child, but nothing of that comes close to the effect of a single low-lit view of Lecter in his glass cage.

Victims of Circumstance II—Welcome to My Nightmare

Just as there were in the classic period, there are other types of victims of circumstance in neo-noir. Certainly Frank Bigelow and Al Roberts are paradigm of the extreme twists of fate, where the victim perishes. In neo-noir, the parallels are more often to pictures like *Nightfall* (1957) or *The Hitch-Hiker* (1953), where the protagonists manage to overcome the forces that menace them. Edmond O'Brien played Bigelow, Ray Collins in *The Hitch-Hiker*, and Mal Granger in *711 Ocean Drive* (1950). While all three characters share an iconic and narrative typing and react similarly to the perilous events that suddenly threaten them, the latter figure is lured into criminal activity by the prospect of being well paid for his technical skills. Like the couple in *Too Late for Tears*, he is typical of those who are wholly or partly responsible for their dilemmas. Analogs in neo-noir of those trying to seize an opportunity of easy money are the protagonists of *Atlantic City* (1981) or *Who'll Stop the Rain* (1978).

From *Hardcore* (1979) or *Eyewitness* (1981) to the self-conscious, almost "new age" tone of *Union City* (1980) or *Slam Dance* (1987), the linking principle is, exactly as it was with *The Hitch-Hiker*, the lack of security and stability in everyday living, no matter how commonplace. Some of these figures, like the janitor in *Eyewitness* who pretends to know a killer's identity to prolong his association with a female reporter, do contribute to their problems. The cartoonist hero of *Slam Dance* is initially short-circuited by his own disbelief, which seems an occupational hazard. Even the self-righteous father in *Hardcore* must ultimately accept that his own stern behavior toward his daughter makes him partly responsible for her disappearance. Perhaps the noir credo is that no one, not even the women in *Narrow Margin* (1990) or *Someone to Watch Over Me*, is entirely blameless on some moral or ethical level when fate points the finger. That is certainly the underlying concept that inspired the first script of *The Bodyguard* (1992), which mixed the disturbed psychology of repressed siblings with ecology, feminism, professionalism, et al. Because the title character's self-awareness never transcends the tenuous allusions to *Yojimbo* or *Star Wars* to become a "dark past," an atmosphere of alienation or obsession never materializes. As in *Someone to Watch Over Me*, the concept of not being able to do one's job and be emotionally involved with a "client" cannot generate or sustain a noir tone alone. The motiveless killer in *The Hitcher* (1986) recalls the fugitive in the classic period Lupino movie, but the preternatural, murderous gasoline truck in Spielberg's television movie *Duel* (1971) is not neo-noir.

Before *The Hot Spot*, Virginia Madsen was the seductress Yolanda Caldwell who caused cartoonist C. C Drood (Tom Hulce, left) to stray in *Slam Dance.*

Along those lines, *Paint It Black* is also typical. After an opening scene in which police investigate an art theft, the protagonist is introduced: a sculptor who believes that he is being misled by his agent/mistress. He has two unusual encounters: a woman swerves to avoid a pedestrian and hits his car; he finds an injured man in alley and helps him home. He begins an affair with the woman; and when the young man comes by to thank him, he confides in him about his problems. Shortly after he breaks into his agent's office to verify that he has been cheating him, she is killed by someone else. It turns out that the new girlfriend is the daughter of a well-known art agent and that the killer is the young man, who is sexually fixated on the sculptor and wants to represent his work. Fearful of being incriminated and under threat from the young man, he can tell no one.

Such a story line might work if the actors and filmmakers were less conscious of its unwieldy convolutions; but in a post-De Palma era, it takes more than visual and musical homages to Hitchcock to bring off such a movie. *Paint It Black* is only one low-budget variant of the miscues of *Shattered* or *Final Analysis*. *Call Me* (1988) has a female protagonist who mistakes an obscene caller for her boyfriend, which leads her to a seamy bar where she witnesses the murder of a pusher in drag in the ladies' room. Such a plot needs more than elements from *Sorry, Wrong Number* (1948) or *Experiment in Terror* (1962) for success. *An Innocent Man* (1989) starts with bad cops who break into the wrong house and brazenly frame its occupant then refocuses on the victim of that circumstance. When its innocent protagonist lands in prison, it becomes a narrative of survival and then of revenge. In *Ricochet* (1991) a vindictive killer escapes from prison, fakes his own death, then discredits and frames the cop-now-district-attorney who wounded and arrested him years earlier. The plot may recall aspects of *Cape Fear* or, in the frenzied portrayal of the antagonist, *White Heat*'s Cody Jarrett, but the through-line is derailed and muddled by an oblique indictment of the media.

P.I. Private Investigations (1987) attains a measure of impact by holding down the sheer volume of unfavorable circumstances, for, as in the classic period, one mischance can prove more than perilous enough. *Red Rock West* (1992), written (as was *P.I. Private Investigations*) and directed (as was *Kill Me Again*) by John Dahl, uses the same technique. A drifter from Texas arrives in a small Wyoming town and is mistaken by a bar owner for another man from Texas hired sight unseen to kill his wife. The drifter not only takes the money and goes to warn the wife, but calmly accepts another sum from her to kill the husband instead. Just when the mischance is about to turn into an unforeseen profit, his car breaks down just outside of town.

Bad Influence (1990) is a new twist on the darkly humorous *The Devil Thumbs a Ride* (1947). Using Rob Lowe as the manipulator turned killer and extortionist exploits the same iconic values as *Masquerade* but allows for a different type of ironic realization. Here the seductive elements are connected to power rather than sex, and the misled hero finds himself ensnared by his previously unrealized desire to control his own life. *Mortal Thoughts* (1991) has a similar theme involving two women. In this instance, also, one character is so much a participant in the other's perspective that their experience becomes a sort of shared nightmare, so convoluted but palpably real that memories may become distorted and flashback recollections may lie. The living nightmares of *Bad Influence* and *Mortal Thoughts* recall the oneiric mode of classic film noir. Both end with their respective male and female protagonists waiting to tell the police what really happened.

If there is an archetypal situation for victims of circumstance in neo-noir, it might be as the target of an obsessive, possibly deadly stalker in the manner of either version of *Cape Fear*. *Lady Beware* (1987), *Fear City* (1984), *Out of the Dark* (1988), *Scissors*, *Intimate Stranger*, *Sleeping with the Enemy* (all 1991)—in all of these films, as in *Klute,* the victims are women. The particulars do vary. One is already a fearful neurotic set up by her psychiatrist (*Scissors*). Another is fleeing her abusive husband (*Sleeping with the Enemy*). Several work in telephone sex (*Intimate Stranger, Out of the Dark)* and, like *Klute*'s Bree Daniel, might be likelier to encounter deadly sexual deviates. Another works as a window dresser (*Lady Beware*) but is similarly plagued. Some of these women try to flee; most, to confront their tormentors. Some perish, but most survive. The results are mixed, but most, concentrating on the idea of suspense rather than the sense of disruption, fail to evoke a noir sensibility.

Criminal Law (1988) incorporates diverse elements without having recourse to extensive narrative complication. The premise is direct: an aggressive attorney successfully defends a client who is accused of a brutal rape and murder. After the not-guilty verdict, the attorney learns that the client actually committed the crime. The character motivations are also direct. Not only must the attorney blame himself for leaving a dangerous psychopath at large, but he

At right, early neo-noir hook-up with the improper stranger finds Julia Roberts as the fearful and disheveled young wife menaced by her controlling hubby Patrick Bergin in *Sleeping with the Enemy.*

Below, wifey has finally had enough.

Above, *Criminal Law*: high-priced attorney Ben Chase (Gary Oldman, center left) meets the press with his exornerated but guilty client Martin Thiel (the slyly smiling Kevin Bacon). Opposite bottom, Axel Freed (James Caan) confers with his bookie Hips (Paul Sorvino) in *The Gambler*.

would still be ethically compromised if he used information acquired within the context of attorney/client privilege against him. A version of the same dilemma confronts the assistant district attorney in *Presumed Innocent* (1990), for as he investigates the murder of a colleague with whom he had an affair, he finds that much of the physical evidence could incriminate him. In this picture and the earlier *Frantic* (1988), Harrison Ford's portrayals capture the edge between panic when confronting circumstances beyond one's control and resilience while fighting to regain it.

What separates the moral problem of these attorneys, initially at least, from those in *True Believer* (1988) or *Suspect* (1987), from courtroom drama, is the profundity of their error. The defense attorneys in *True Believer* and *Suspect* are idealists at heart, whose discovery of corruption within the system does imperil them, but whose faith in that same system is ultimately redemptive, particularly in *True Believer*. The protagonist of *Criminal Law* is closer to Frank Bigelow in his determined resolve to put things right. When his client threatens another woman with whom the attorney is emotionally involved, the web of circumstances closes and creates a quandary as dark as Vanning's in *Nightfall*. Like other neo-noir victims caught in such a web, thrashing about is futile. Only those able to find assistance manage to escape.

Liebestraum (1991) or "love dream" takes its name from a Liszt piano piece and its dreamlike style is as insistently imposed as the droning underscore. As in *At Close Range* cinematographer Juan Ruiz Anchía's hard light knifes though the images, both real and dreamed, to create a tangible fatality. The plot, which brings a celebrated young architect to a small town to meet his birth mother who is dying of cancer, turns on a deadly lover's tryst in a 1950s-style department store. That scene is staged or remembered—the first of many narrative uncertainties—in the movie's opening sequence. Because the point of view may be either omniscient or subjective, whether the events of the scenes are actual or imagined is always in question. It is in the protagonist's flashbacks, where shafts of light seem to pierce passing hopper cars, that the style and sensation of the first sequence most impinge on the present; but its tone hangs over the entire film and welcomes the viewer to his nightmare.

When the architect begins an affair with the photographer wife of a college friend who is dismantling the department store building, the line between dream and reality, past and present is further blurred. The audience can fully empathize with the chance remark of the cab driver who takes the architect to the college friend's party: "You mind if I ask you a question? I feel like I know you. You on TV or what?" As he squirms inexplicably in the back seat, patches of white and red light cut in and out of the frame, the architect's reply can only be an ambiguous "What." Because the entire film is suffused with an hallucinatory languor, seeming at times to move in slow motion, it not only tests the limits of photographic reality but of what the viewer will tolerate. By the time, the end credits arrive and a young girl plays "liebestraum" on the piano in an unlikely homage to *Guest in the House* (1944), some points have been clarified, but most have not. This leaves *Liebestraum* as much a neo-Jungian, plastic-fantastic voyage as neo-noir.

Despite his Dostoievskian roots the gambler protagonist is not that common in the classic period. Certainly a lot of characters are depicted playing cards or standing at a roulette wheel; but the crew planning a caper in *The Killers* are just passing the time and the bookie haunts and illegal clubs from *The Big Sleep* to *Force of Evil* are just background settings for shysters and P.I.s. Johnny Farrell in *Gilda* (1946) is a gambler and a cheat; but most noir protagonists who turn to crime to pay of debts owe money for reasons other than gambling. *The Gambler* (1974) is certainly amd self-consciously both Dostoiekskian and neo-noir, even more so than the later *Taxi Driver*. Its protagonist Axel Freed (James Caan) is no Travis Bickle, no alienated loner, but a university professor addicted to betting and unable to pay back his patient but

menacing bookie Hips (Paul Sorvino). In the manner of classic-period boxing pictures from *City for Conquest* (1940) through *The Set-Up*, the plot turns on Freed's rigging a sporting contest by having one of his students shave points in a basketball game. Although his scheme succeeds, Freed's final action is as a dark as Bickle's when he provokes a fight and viciously beats a pimp, is slashed by a hooker, but regards his wound with a twisted pride in primordial triumph.

Gangsters, Pushers, Pimps, and Con Men

As in the classic period, neo-noir does occasionally feature protagonists who are professional criminals. While the pitilessness of such characters remains constant, the other aspects—their greed, their thirst for power, their code of behavior—have taken new turns. As a genre, gangster films can stand alone, imbued with their own expectations and iconic values; but crossovers and connections with film noir remain.

While Coppola's Godfathe*r* series has often been cited by other commentators on neo-noir, those pictures exemplify the evolution of the gangster genre. Although they share an evocation of period with other films, like *The Untouchables*, their focus on the inner workings of criminal syndicates is unwavering. On the other hand, unlike "pure" gangster pictures from *The Brotherhood* (1968) to *Scarface* (1983), part of the Godfather saga's appeal, particularly in the first and final parts, is the sense that war hero Michael

Tom Reagan (Gabriel Byrne, left) calmly preparesto lights coffin nail while all hell breaks loose in *Miller's Crossing*.

Corleone's criminal career was to some extent forced on him by outside events.

Even though the *Godfather* films never fully cross over into the noir mode, other period films like *Miller's Crossing* (1990) may. If anything, *Miller's Crossing* stresses the question of ethics to the point of exaggeration. The musings of Johnny Caspar—"You double-cross once, where does it all end?"—are a bit incongruous from one who teaches his killers to put "one bullet in the brain." The real enigma of *Miller's Crossing* is Tom Reagan, a gangster without a gun. His odd traits from attachment to his hat to fixation on his boss' "twist" could easily relocate him into a Western or a noir milieu. The narrative asserts only that he has no heart. There are stylistic elements of *Miller's Crossing* that recall the classic period. Dark rooms where harsh sidelight bisects the actors' faces create a mood. Sequences from the tableaux of a boy and a dog finding a body in an alley or the tommy-gun battle accompanied by the strains of "Danny Boy" to the tilted angles and demented screams when Caspar bludgeons his own lieutenant to death all reinforce the sense of chaos. In the end, for all the dramatic impact of its set pieces or the stylistic evocation of the noir underworld, *Miller's Crossing* leaves the viewer, like its protagonist, leaning against a tree in the middle of nowhere.

There are fewer capers in neo-noir. One of the earliest examples is *The Split*, released the year after *Point Blank* and like it adapted from a Parker novel and centered on suspicion and betrayal among thieves and a crooked cop. The careful plan gone awry by mischance in *The Asphalt Jungle* (1950) or *The Killing* becomes a disintegration in psychoses and recrimination in *Dog Day Afternoon* (1974). The bank robbery planned by disaffected Vietnam vets in *Special Delivery* (1976) is so logistically complicated that it falls apart from sheer inertia. Only the early 1990s *Reservoir Dogs* uses a caper in a classic way; but even that is merely as a hub for other explorations.

The Outfit is also loosely adapted a "Parker" novel. Again the central figure is a freelance robber who finds himself suddenly under attack from organized crime and decides that his best chance of survival lies in active retaliation. The adaptors of *The Outfit* confront a central narrative that suggests an existential set piece in which a loner salves his alienation through murderous violence. It is also a mock epic in which the "little man" defeats the dehumanized, organizational machine. The closing shot of *The Outfit*—a freeze-frame of defiant "independents" smiling in exhilaration at their victory—would seem to fall into the latter category, particularly in contrast to the ambiguities of *Point Blank*. This ending does not controvert the fundamentally noir vision of the film, which situates itself wholly in a dark, parallel world, where the uncertainty of surface appearances undermines the very concepts of victory or defeat.

Macklin's response to his situation, accentuated by the laconic performance of Robert Duvall, that is reminiscent of Robert Montgomery's in *Ride the Pink Horse* and that of many other noir figures, all mindful of their own possible destruction but compelled to even the score. He has the ruthlessness of Hammer in *Kiss Me Deadly* without his egocentricity, the inside knowledge of Kelvaney in *Rogue Cop* without his indecision, and the sheer killing ability of Callahan in *Dirty Harry* without any pretense of abiding by the law. Macklin can with equal dispassion release a man sent to kill him with the offhand remark, "Die someplace else."

Above, Robert Duvall (right) as Macklin robs a card game in which the unhappy mob enforcer Jake Menner (Timothy Carey) happens to be holding a hand in *The Outfit.*

Opposite, the neo-noir Mr. Brown, ruthless analog of the smug mob in *The Big Combo*: Wesley Snipes as Nino in *New Jack City.*

If Macklin appears to move through the array of noir cons arrayed against him—from Robert Ryan and the maniacal Timothy Carey as the syndicate man to such bit players as Elisha Cook Jr., Marie Windsor, and Emile Meyer—it may be because they evoke, like the old car parked outside Macklin's first heist, an antique vision of the noir underworld. Unlike Dancer in *The Line-Up* (1958), infuriated by his exasperating inability to reconcile the syndicate boss to his honest mistake, Macklin understands from the start that he will never be able to do that, that the unwritten rules, which are the only element of stability in the noir underworld, have condemned him.

The figures in Abel Ferrara's *King of New York*, and Mario Van Peebles' *New Jack City*, and Carl Franklin's *One False Move* (1992) are more representative of the neo-noir criminal. Both of the 1990 films also feature portraits of policemen, whose antagonisms are much more forthright than in *Cry of the City* or even *The Big Combo*. *New Jack City* has its own Mr. Brown, who like Frank White in *King of New York* imagines that he is a servant of his oppressed community. As he explains to the vice cop who infiltrates his gang, killing is part of business not personal, a sentiment that echoes Sollozzo's excuse in *The Godfather* even before it becomes the motto in *Diary of a Hitman* (1992).

Both these characters, who seem to be named by their skin color, have a point of view, however twisted. That "philosophy" becomes a mocking reply to the cops who try to rebuke them. For those cops facing this scorn, the temptation to cross the line is intensified. The fact that the police in *King of New York* take the law into their own hands and that those in *New Jack City* almost do but stop short is less significant that the blurring of distinctions between cop and crook, the reaffirmation of Cleve's point in *Best Seller*. As Frank White sardonically confesses, "My feelings are dead. I got no remorse." For Frank White and Nino Brown, the universe is born of injustice and sustained by fury.

Stylistically, both films recruit cultural indicators such as hip-hop, whether creating an insistent, chaotic buzz on the soundtrack in *New Jack City* or the occasional litany of death as in Jimmy Jump's rap in *King of New York.* Abel Ferrara's staging in the latter film not only creates killing scenes that are at once graphic and surreal but constructs sequences that manifest an awareness of abstract terror. In a sequence at a theater where White's envoy meets with a Chinese gang and discuss their antagonisms and demands in a private theater, the Asian gangsters watch Murnau's *Nosferatu*, either not noticing or not caring about how much they resemble the grotesque images projected on the wall. Throughout the film, Ferrara's relentless use of close-ups holding the figures in tight hard-lit frames creates a sense of deterministic constriction.

There are also some old-school gangster types in early neo-noir in films such as *The Friends of Eddie Coyle* (1973), *The Nickel Ride* (1975), and *Straight Time* (1978). As in *Farewell, My Lovely,* Robert Mitchum again provides a link to the 1940s noir, but this title character is a long way from Marlowe. Eddie Coyle is a small-timer facing a life term as a chronic offender and trying to exchange information for a reduced sentence. In any underworld, just plain noir or neo, that is a losing formula.

Above, *The Nickel Ride*: Turner (Bo Hopkins) is too cool to be deferential to old-school small-timer Cooper (Jason Miller).

The Nickel Ride's criminal protagonist, Cooper, is another throwback, a warehouse manager/bagman for the mob's loot, whose sense of self-worth depends on the respect he commands from his cronies. Coop's growing paranoia about his position follows a direct line from a classic-period personality like Shubunka in *The Gangster* (1947). Cinematographer Jordan Cronenweth's scheme for the urban scenes is grainy and drained of color, which aptly types Cooper's neighborhood as a small and inconsequential part of a large city.

Straight Time is even grimmer as its protagonist Max Dembo spirals down from harassed parolee, to betrayed and recidivist robber, to cop killer, and then part of a fugitive couple. While lacking the doggedness of any of the movie incarnations of Parker, Dembo does have a quirky code, so that after he extracts revenge on a craven accomplice, he refuses to take along the woman who loves him on what is likely a final and fatal flight.

The pimps and pushers in films as diverse as *The Killing of a Chinese Bookie* (1976), *Year of the Dragon* (1985), and *Eight Million Ways to Die* (1986) are characters that could only be implied in the classic period, when production codes made drug addiction and prostitution unfit subjects. In the ten years between John Cassavetes' *The Killing of Chinese Bookie* and Hal Ashby's *Eight Million Ways to Die*, the sense of honor among thieves eroded completely. By using brutish character actors like Morgan Woodward and Timothy Carey to portray the cheap hoodlums who hound nightclub owner Cosmo Vitelli to kill the bookie in lieu of paying a gambling debt, Cassavetes suggests that life is cheap because killers are inept and grotesque. In *Eight Million Ways to Die* the slick, evil pimp and pusher portrayed by Andy Garcia kills and tortures because he likes to. Dennis Hopper's performance as drug lord in *Midnight Heat* (1992) is a smarmy stereotype but the only anchor in a muddled narrative.

Presenting "working girls" and "candy men" for what they are in neo-noir changes the impact and the tone. As the violence and the sordidness in the milieu froth on the surface rather than simmer below it, perhaps the outrage of the authority figures from *Cop* to *New Jack City* becomes understandable if not acceptable. Outside of the Thompson adaptations discussed earlier and a few other titles, there are not many pictures that assume the criminal's point of view. *Tequila Sunrise* (1988) attempts it through the guise of a love triangle and old friends on opposite sides of the law, a common motif in the gangster genre. Portraying the racketeer as sincere and the detective as manipulating may seem novel on paper, but the film is merely perplexing, especially its romantic ending. *Pacific Heights* (1990) features a con man and gigolo who exploits his landlords through a complicated narrative that seems designed to create menacing situations no matter how contrived.

Thief (1981) is director Michael Mann's antecedent to *Manhunter*. Like *Miller's Crossing* or the Godfather films, its perspective is wholly within the criminal underworld. Like Hill's Driver, Mann's Thief, is a nonviolent specialist, a safecracker. Unlike the Driver, he has a name, Frank, but only a first one. In the neo-noir underworld such nonviolence and no last name are not protection. As Frank's mentor nostalgically observes when he visits him in prison, there is no sense of honor anymore in the big house or outside. On a narrative level, *Thief* is about betrayal: Frank's betrayal by the cops who beat him, by the mob types who exploit and extort him, by a thieves' code that he trusted. In that sense,

James Caan as the title figure in *Thief*.

the destruction and death that he effectuates at the conclusion are an outraged response. Mann's stylized treatment of the events, as Frank systematically demolishes his links with underworld, also suggests a redemptive ritual in the classic noir tradition.

For the grifters and con artists in *House of Games*, *The Horseplayer* (1991), or *Night and the City* (1992), redemption is not an issue. In the earlier film, the con itself is the ritual. As the female psychiatrist who believes she has stumbled into their world discovers, they are like the scorpion in Mr. Arkadin's parable: they cannot help but con, it's their nature. The lack of perception by a psychiatrist who has studied and written about compulsive behavior may lack verisimilitude; but in the enclosed world of marks and cheats that writer/director David Mamet creates, misperception is the key to making a buck. Caught up in that illicit milieu and its freedom from responsibility is a giddy experience for the protagonist. Her outrage at betrayal is both the fury of a woman scorned and of a child deprived of her secret playground, motives quite different from if not opposite of Frank's in *Thief*. In that sense, her real crime at the film's conclusion also becomes ritual reversal. It is a full and final initiation into the noir underworld that fascinates her and makes the premise and the title of her new book, *Forgive Yourself*, disturbingly ironic.

"Viewed from the proper angle, all our lives are a little bit sordid." *The Horseplayer* puts a new twist on *Scarlet Street*. An artist has his girlfriend pose as his sister and seduce subjects for his surrealistic paintings. The latest victim is a "horseplayer" and a creature of habit in a very insular world: he works in a "box," a liquor store freezer compartment, restocking the shelves. Filled as it is with oppressive close-ups, *The Horseplayer*'s tortured relationships are full of

Below, Mike the con man (Joe Mantegna) and his intense pupil/lover psychiatrist Margaret Ford (Lindsey Crouse) in *House of Games*.

Opposite, Forest Whitaker plying his trade as Dekker in *Diary of a Hitman.*

overtly symbolic behavior, as when the artist draws a scar on the girl's face with a china marker, while telling her "You're like a mirror to me. I can see myself reflected so clearly."

Superficially *Night and the City* is a straightforward remake moved from postwar London to contemporary New York. Its protagonist, Harry Fabian, is still a cheap hustler, still trying to muscle in on the fight game and conning money from Helen Nasseros with a forged liquor license. The changes—the missing characters, the rougher language—are relatively minor; but the tone is different. Richard Widmark's Harry Fabian never was more than a hustler, an American in a strange country trying to turn a buck. Robert De Niro's Fabian is an attorney who admits to chasing ambulances in his own neighborhood: "I never been out of New York practically. One time I was gonna move to L.A. I wanted to be a talent scout, but..." Where Widmark's character seemed trapped by circumstances of time and place and driven by a need to score big, De Niro's seems to be where he is by his own choice looking for an easy buck because it's easy. Both Fabians make the same play and meet the same fate; but in the remake, the ironies, like the scams, are mostly off the mark.

Two modestly budgeted pictures confront the issue of criminal "professionalism" most directly: *Diary of a Hitman* and *Reservoir Dogs* (1992). Although he is killer for hire, the title figure of *Diary of a Hitman* more closely resembles John Hull in *Deep Cover* than he does the dozens of analogs in other neo-noir films. Unlike *Deep Cover,* the real irony of *Diary of a Hitman* may be unconscious in casting an African-American actor in a part not necessarily written for one. Also unlike Laurence Fishburne in *Deep Cover*, Forest Whitaker does not bring an iconic signature to *Hitman*, does not suggest (there's no other way to put it) a "black" noir persona. His character, Dekker, is a throwback and the film's narrative style follows suit. The story unfolds as a flashback, a message that Dekker is leaving on his "booking agent's" answering machine, and his voiceover narration is used heavily throughout. Early on, Dekker confesses

Reservoir Dogs: Messrs. Blonde (Michael Madsen), White (Harvey Keitel), and Pink (Steve Buscemi) peer into a car trunk.

to being troubled by his work and maintaining the illusion that "it's not personal." He even consults a psychiatrist, to whom he confesses the killings as "bad dreams." Because *Hitman* ultimately becomes a performance piece for Whitaker and Sherilyn Fenn as his last victim, Jain, most of these echoes of classic noir are left unexplored.

Dekker's key comment is "I was a pro. A pro is a pro, right?" The answer from Mr. Pink in *Reservoir Dogs* is "A psychopath ain't a professional." From the perspective of the classic noir style and narrative, *Reservoir Dogs* is pointedly aware of a relationship to that tradition. As was noted, the plot of *Reservoir Dogs* derives from the caper film. An organizer brings a group of otherwise unrelated criminals together for one job and keeps their true identities from one another with "colorful" names. The botched robbery itself is never seen, only its aftermath as the survivors come to the rendezvous point and argue over what happened and what to do now. Flashbacks within flashbacks create narrative layers that are both "traditionally" noir and endistance the modern view from identification with the criminal protagonists. Equally endistancing are slow-motion optical effects and moments of grisly, self-conscious humor. The psychopathic Mr. Blonde might well be alluding to *Point Blank* when he confesses to being "a big Lee Marvin fan"; but his character grimly transcends the violence of that type of picture when he cuts off the ear of a police hostage and talks to it. In the end, *Reservoir Dogs* is also about self-immolation, but not just because the characters shoot one another in an absurd, quasi-parody of a Mexican standoff. There is an also existential justice in the fact that what may be Mr. White's one redemptive quality—his sense of loyalty to the severely wounded Mr. Orange—is also his undoing. That personal connection to a cohort who is actually an undercover cop is both human and, in the noir scheme of things, appropriately deadly.

The Neo P.I.— Retro, New-Age, and De-Tech Noir

The prototype of retro noir, a neo-noir production set in the years of the classic period is *Chinatown.* While protagonist J.J. Gittes is an ex-cop now private detective specializing in divorce work—something Raymond Chandler's investigators would never do—the evocation is both noir and hard-boiled. Client Evelyn Mulwray wants to know if her husband has been unfaithful and Gittes must follow a twisted path to find an answer. For screenwriter Robert Towne as with Chandler and the creators of early noir, the mean streets prewar Los Angeles hold the same dark secrets as they did in the classic period. While Gittes may traverse them with a "what's in it for me?" attitude that is more aligned with Mike Hammer in the 1955 adaptation of Mickey Spillane's *Kiss Me Deadly* than an incarnation of Philip Marlowe, his growing involvement with the glamorous Mulwray leaves him vulnerable to the same emotional wounds.

By incorporating historical events in which a thirsty Los Angeles schemed to acquire water from elsewhere, Towne finds the same vestiges of corruption that underlie surface society as did Chandler and even Spillane. When Mulwray is widowed, she becomes neither a black one nor a traditional femme fatale. If anything, like Hammer in the Aldrich/Bezzerides *Kiss Me Deadly*, Gittes is a fatal man, one who ignores the warnings of both colleagues and antagonists with deadly consequences.

Marlowe himself was also rediscovered and reinvented by neo-noir filmmakers, initially becoming the title character in the 1969 *Marlowe*, an adaptation of Chandler's Hollywood novel, *The Little Sister*. Like the ill-conceived remake of the *The Big Sleep*, *Marlowe* is not retro although it posits that the detective's late 1960s office is in the vintage Bradbury Building, a frequent classic-period location. *Farewell, My Lovely* is full-on retro. Noir icon of the 1940s Robert Mitchum is the only actor to have portrayed Marlowe twice. Ironically he

Below, after his being injured and told to back off, shady private eye Jake Gittes (Jack Nicholson) meets again with his wealthy client Evelyn Mulwray (Faye Dunaway) in *Chinatown.*

Despite the intimidating destruction of his office by Winslow Wong (Jackie Chan), James Garner as a dogged contemporary (1969) version of Chandler's urban knight is also disinclined to desist from his investigations in *Marlowe.* Opposite, Harrison Ford as Deskard in the future world neo-noir *Blade Runner.*

did so when his physical age far exceeded Chandler's perennially 39-year-old character. At 58 (and past 60 in *The Big Sleep*), Mitchum was a decade older than Bogart and his drooping face and fatigued stride across the period streets suggest that more than a little tarnish has accumulated on the armor of Chandler's urban knight.

If the 1970s were a transitional period for the attitudes of police protagonists, a resolution was always available through their criminal nemeses. The world-weary attitudes of the private investigators in *Hickey & Boggs* were somewhat mirrored in the Marlowe portrayed by Elliott Gould in the Robert Altman/Leigh Brackett 1973 adaptation of *The Long Goodbye*. Although set twenty years after the novel, and shot in everyday Hollywood and hip Malibu, Gould's rumpled personification is retro, as he is verbally and physically abused by both cops and mobsters. Only when he takes justice into his own hands at end of the narrative does *The Long Goodbye* embrace a neo sensibility.

Actors like Steve McQueen or Clint Eastwood, playing skip tracers in *The Hunter* (1980) and *Pink Cadillac* (1989) respectively, rely on genre expectations of rugged individualism closer to the Western than to film noir. The comic aspects of De Niro in *Midnight Run* (1988) outweigh the noir sensibility, but that film's use of technological props are part of a new tradition that goes back to Coppola's *The Conversation* (1974).

Harper and *The Drowning Pool* (1975) where Paul Newman impersonates Ross MacDonald's "Lew Archer," whose name comes from Sam Spade's partner in Hammett's iconic *Maltese Falcon* and whose attitude from Chandler, represent just about the last vestiges of the classic gumshoe, working with just his wits and luck through plots as tangled as that of *The Big Sleep* or *Lady in the Lake*. By the time of the 1982 remake of 1953's *I, the Jury*, the consummate cynicism of Mike Hammer is drowned in a sea of car chases, automatic weapons, and naked woman that have very little to do with either Spillane's original or film noir.

Warren Oates in *Chandler* (1971) says, "I'm a relic"; and the picture is littered with shoeshine stands, bars with pool tables in them, and incongruous old cars that seem left over from *The Big Sleep*. Chandler's attitude toward women—his last words are "You'll do"—is especially regressive. Despite the train rides and cameo appearances by Gloria Grahame and Charles McGraw, Chandler's clipped dialogue and conscious nostalgia ("That's Chandler, as in Raymond") are also part of the crossover of old-time private eyes into a new age. In that same year, another title character, John Klute, took a remarkably different slant from his technical methods to his attitude regarding the woman he was following. The process is a continuing one and could ultimately lead to "contemporary" versions of *Blade Runner* (1982) or *Total Recall* where Philip K. Dick's visions of a noir future become reality.

Although it does includes a noirish opening, *Total Recall* (1990) is mostly off-world. *Blade Runner*'s dystopian vision, however, is rooted in Los Angeles of 2019, a city of polluted rain and perennial dusk, far removed the "land of

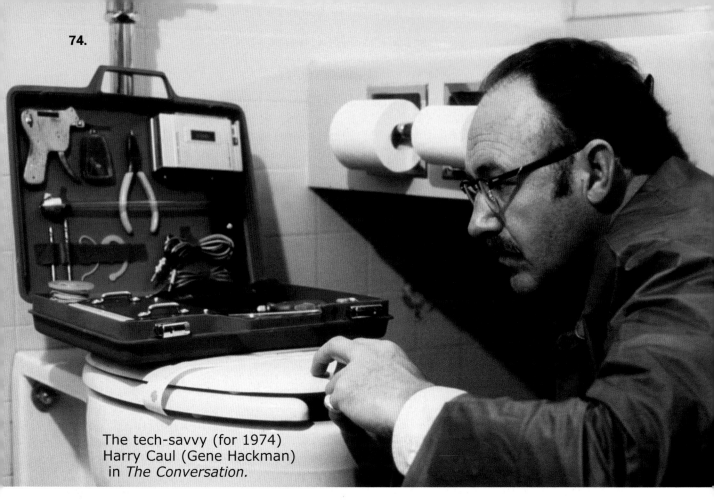

The tech-savvy (for 1974)
Harry Caul (Gene Hackman)
in *The Conversation*.

sunshine and flowers." The streets are crowded with a listless population over-whelmed by the darkness and corruption, all looking for a way "to score" or to leave the planet. Most of the upper class has already deserted earth for colonies in space where "replicants," artificial humans, serve as slaves. While this may seem the antithesis of retro, *Blade Runner* makes extensive use of locations from the classic period: from the deco Union Station to a Lloyd Wright house in the Hollywood Hills to Chinatown, which is now a neon-lit swamp of water, steam, and human excess, and a final confrontation in the Bradbury Building. Equally and self-consciously retro are narration through which Deckard fills in backstory with a sardonic tone and the look of the femme, or rather replicante, fatale Rachael whose with makeup and hairdo recall the looks of Stanwyck in *Double Indemnity* or Crawford in *Mildred Pierce* (1945). Roy Batty, the ostensible antagonist to Deckard's sci-fi P.I., in many ways becomes the noir figure of the movie's second half. His existential anguish mirrors that of doomed accountant Frank Bigelow in *D.O.A.* that plays out in the same marble and iron-grated confines of the Bradbury Building interior.

Klute's techniques include wiretaps, recordings, and slides of typewriter fonts. Harry Caul (Gene Hackman) in *The Conversation* is a technical legend and a loner who guards his privacy with a paranoiac fervor. Caul takes satis-faction in being the best but is troubled by the current job eavesdropping on a couple as they walk in a crowded square. As he mixes a version of their con-versation together, Caul cannot help but think that they may somehow be in danger. When a rival tells a story at a party of how Caul once bugged a crooked union official, who assumed his accountant had betrayed him and had his family murdered, Caul realizes that he "can't let it happen again." After his master tapes are stolen, Caul decides to try to warn the couple.

Coppola's visualization is keyed to the technology. The spaces of the loft that house Caul's operation are compartmentalized by grilled enclosures, so that even at the party characters are constantly framed against electronic equipment and metal. Caul's bus ride back from his girlfriend's apartment, which he leaves abruptly because she asks too many personal questions, is a long side-angle close-up with his silhouette framed against the studded white-painted wall and dark window of the bus, his face isolated against stark manufactured forms. It is only in his traditionally furnished apartment, playing his saxophone, that Caul lets down his guard and reveals his humanity. Unlike *Chandler* where the riffling piano underscore contributed another layer of heavy nostalgia, David Shire's clean, jazzy measures are a contrast, an element of irregular, non-mechanized expression. It is in the final sequence, when Caul discovers that things were the opposite of what they seemed, that his insular world collapses. The final pan as he sits playing the sax after tearing up the wall and floors of his apartment, searching for a bug, reveal a disturbing metaphor. For in divulging the industrial underpinnings behind the walls and under the floors, Caul himself has created an apparition of technical ruin that undermines his belief system, an imagistic analog to Lector in or out of his straightjacket.

As he did with Popeye Doyle and Harry Caul, Gene Hackman injects an undercurrent of compulsion into Harry Moseby the private detective in *Night Moves* (1975) On the surface, Moseby is a traditional investigator, somewhat insightful, somewhat cynical, and sometimes wondering like Hickey and Boggs whether the job is about anything. Where Moseby ends up, wounded on a rudderless boat, suggests that the answer is no.

Like the name of the disco in *The Terminator* (1984), *Blade Runner's* vision of Los Angeles, where aerocars navigate through smog zones that are reserved for the lowest castes of a new society could be dubbed "tech noir." In that case, *Dead Again* (1991) is "karmic noir." As in *Liebestraum*, *Dead Again's* characters are more than casually affected by a past crime. The elaborate "past life" recollections, shot in black-and-white, are at once a plot device and a stylistic commentary on the classic noir style. If the flashbacks, trances, and other hocus-pocus are a bit forced, they continue, via stylistic dissertation, to function as a form deconstructing itself as relentlessly as Harry Caul's prying up floorboards with a crowbar. In this sense, *Dead Again*, like such earlier period films as *The Two Jakes* (1990) and *Hammett* (1983), is both a throwback and a look back, a film that can re-create but never reenter a period. It is not coincidental, that while they may not be as forthrightly comic as the parody *Dead Men Don't Wear Plaid* (1982), the two retro noirs—a long-planned and often derailed sequel to *Chinatown* and a "real life" imagining of hard-boiled writer's actual expoints as a P.I.—contain more than a few moments of tongue-in-cheek humor. Where *Hammett* plods through with an enforced nostalgia as poorly fit to the plot as the padded shoulders on its wardrobe, the self-indulgence in *The Two Jakes* is more humorous, as when the double-breasted, fedoraed form of Jack Nicholson is catapulted across the frame in slow motion, a truer relic of classic noir than all of the old cars in *Chandler*.

Neo-noir has produced other "throwbacks," but almost always with a twist. An early example is *Shaft* (1971), which features a tough-talking, New York City-based private detective reminiscent of Mike Hammer, who is black. Shaft is hired to rescue the daughter of a black mobster from Italian kidnappers in a straightforward narrative. A few years later, *Black Eye* (1974) sends its rogue detective, suspended for killing a drug pusher, down a crooked trail of Jesus freaks and sexual deviants while investigating the murder of a silent movie star. While early neo *The Split* starred Jim Brown as its "Parker," most full-on "blaxploitation" titles of the early 1970s turned on a revenge motif in such films as *Slaughter*, *Black Gunn* (both 1972), and *Coffy* (1973).

More recently, the main character who pieces together the puzzling clues in a string of killings in *The Rosary Murders* (1987) is a skilled amateur and also a priest in the mode of G.K. Chesterton's iconic Father Brown. The title figure in *V.I. Warshawski* (1991) is a wisecracking, two-fisted, gun-toting private dick, who happens to be a woman. *The Last Boy Scout* (1991) features a down-on-his-luck, former Secret Service agent, who's a sucker for home and family. For all his cynical veneer, when the private detective in that film asks the de facto partner of his last adventure to formalize their relationship, one might imagine that was how the title figures in *Hickey & Boggs* got together; and the cycle begins again.

Kid Noir

As progenitors of "kid noir," one could cite *The Window* (1949) or *Talk About a Stranger* (1952), films with youthful protagonists whom the adults won't believe. That same concept is the core of *Night Visitor* (1989). Within films like *Out of Bounds*, adolescents are featured, but the problems they face are those of adults. In 1983 two adaptations of S. E. Hinton's young-adult novels, *The*

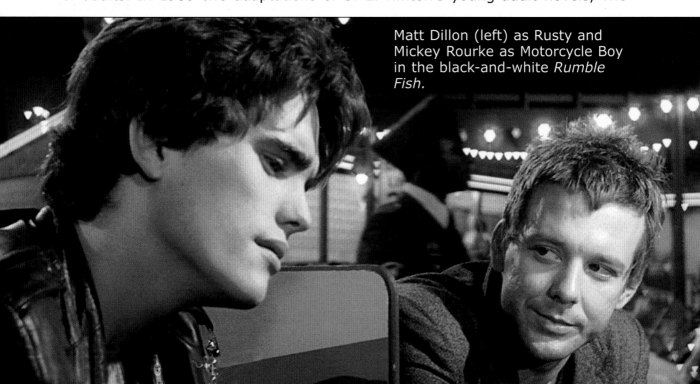

Matt Dillon (left) as Rusty and Mickey Rourke as Motorcycle Boy in the black-and-white *Rumble Fish.*

Outsiders and *Rumble Fish*, both directed by Francis Ford Coppola, were released. The gangs in both films are teenagers facing actual adolescent dilemmas, growing up in different social strata but equally prone to violence to settle childish grievances with deadly consequences, a much truer sort of kid noir.

Bad Boys (also 1983) is as much a gangster film as kid noir, with rival factions and racial antagonisms in the manner of *Miller's Crossing* or *State of Grace*. *Run* (1991) posits a victim of circumstance with a *39 Steps* plot, who just happens to be a college student. What separates them in terms of noir sensibility are the emotions of the characters. Sean Penn's performance in *Bad Boys* is as much about the painful transition to adulthood as it is about the codes of behavior imposed by gangs and prisons. His anger and catharsis are more proximate temporally and emotionally to James Caan's in *Thief* than Bobby Driscoll's in *The Window*. Patrick Dempsey's portrayal of a victim of circumstance in *Run*, on the other hand, has little progression. His character is not so much matured by the experience as he is delivered from it.

Blue City, *Dangerously Close* (both 1986), *Gleaming the Cube* (1988), *Prime Suspect* (1989), *Night Visitor* and *Out of the Rain* (both 1990) are several films having a story line where a young man, often still in high school, investigates the death of a friend or loved one. Adapted and produced by Walter Hill, the protagonists of *Blue City* were made younger and cast with two Brat-Packers from the previous year's *The Breakfast Club*. The loved one in this movie is the murdered mayor of a small Florida town, but only his prodigal son and two of his friends care about who killed him.

Dangerously Close and *Gleaming the Cube* are a bit like "Bill and Ted's Excellent Mystery"; but they do use the fact of an adolescent hero as plot keys. Ultimately *Dangerously Close* drowns in its own incoherencies that have nothing to do with kid noir. *Gleaming the Cube,* in which a ne'er-do-well skateboarder refuses to believe that his Vietnamese-born, adopted brother committed suicide, introduces many other issues, from racial tensions to the judgment of teenagers based on their appearance. All of these are brushed aside in the rush to a climactic action sequence of boys on skateboards chasing crooks in cars on the freeway.

The narrative structures of *Out of the Rain* and *Prime Suspect* are more traditional but equally listless. As in *Gleaming the Cube*, *Out of the Rain*'s protagonist refuses to believe his brother's suicide. In an ending that involves a merry-go-round rather than skateboards, the psychopathic killer is revealed. That it is the girl whom both brothers loved should be a poignant disclosure rather than merely predictable; but the protagonists of kid noir may seem as empty of feeling as the most hardened adults. *Prime Suspect* begins on a chilling note with a precredit sequence of a little girl's witnessing her mother's murder. But the music box motif that carries through on the soundtrack over the credits is the end of that point of view. Plot entanglements follow: the girl is killed as a teenager and her boyfriend, who witnesses the murder from the center of a small lake, is so traumatized that he loses his voice. He is put in an asylum, where a woman psychiatrist is pressured by a supervisor (who, of course, turns out to be the killer) to certify him fit for trial. The woman's boyfriend is the local sheriff, so when the young man whom she believes innocent overpowers a sadistic, bisexual orderly and escapes, her loyalties are divided. After another murder and false leads involving a violent, sociopathic cook, who is another of the woman's patients, and the PCP-ingesting restaurant manager who single-handedly decimates the sheriff's department before the boy intervenes, the real killer is finally revealed, stabbed with his own knife, and, when he gets up for more, pushed out a window. This is the short version of a convoluted story line that might have worked for Woolrich, but not here.

From *Union City* to *Final Analysis* neo-noir has outrageous or derivative plots in abundance; and those may be part of its wry outlook. What neo-noir does not have is the permeating influence of being part of the classic tradition rather than merely alluding to or recalling it. From the perspective of the 1990s, a film like *Night Visitor*, which is most notable for such outlandish scenes as Elliott Gould and Michael J. Pollard dueling with shotgun and chainsaw in a basement, seems likelier to evoke the gothic excesses of *Whatever Happened to Baby Jane* than *Talk About a Stranger*.

Whether a film such as *Drugstore Cowboy* (1989) is kid noir or neo-noir is debatable. The pathetic crime spree of its drugged-out protagonists seems to owe more to Maxim Gorki than James M. Cain. The death by overdose and the impact of that event on its main character is the stuff of television movies. The ending suggests that the tentacles of the noir underworld are a factor; and the film as a whole uses the youth of its characters to enhance rather than obviate dramatic irony. Kid noir is not yet a rich tradition, but in certain aspects of these films and others, such as *Guncrazy* (1992), which is discussed later, it holds promise for the future.

Still Out for Revenge

The original *Death Wish* may not be that far removed from *The Big Heat* or *Underworld U.S.A.* (1961). Unlike the figures in those classic-period features, Paul Kersey, the protagonist of *Death Wish*, never found the actual street punks who killed his wife and raped his daughter and ultimately no longer cared. *Death Wish* brought the audience as forcefully into the revenge seeker's point of view as had any film of the classic period and then, in its own self-aware use of prop newspaper headlines and magazine covers, mocked its own viewers for empathizing with that point-of-view. Long before 1994's *Death Wish V,* when keeping track of the body count was literally impossible, a different kind of mockery was in question.

In their *Panorama du Film Noir Américain*, Raymond Borde and Etienne Chaumeton perceived certain aspects of the classic noir figure in James Bond. If Bond's sardonic, world-weary, and increasingly mechanistic actions are spun off from the alienation of the noir hero, the newest incarnations are the seemingly invulnerable and usually vindictive martial arts protagonists. The pictures starring Chuck Norris and more recently Steven Seagal and Jean-Claude Van Damme often hinge on a character's seeking revenge for the murder or maiming of a close relative or friend. It would be hard to equate Van Damme's smirk or Seagal's perpetual scowl in films with such interchangeable titles as *Marked for Death* or *Hard to Kill* with a mask of alienation, even if there were some doubt about their ultimate triumph over scores of leering antagonists. In the best Seagal vehicle, *Out for Justice* (1991), the search for his partner's killer leaves a trail of battered and dead men and women that is not easily tallied. More significantly, although has the same director as *Best Seller* and *Rolling Thunder* (1977) and *Lock Up* (1989), John Flynn, *Out for Justice* is a Seagal picture before all else and unambiguous about his inevitable conquest.

In certain films, Chuck Norris comes closer to an evocation of a noir persona, as in *The Hero and the Terror*, which uses flashbacks to flirt with the sometimes psychic relationship between detective and serial killer probed more deeply in *Manhunter*. Perhaps the inevitable expression of the vengeful and alienated superhero is the Australian-made *The Punisher*, based on a comic-book character and appropriately cartoonish. The same principle of invincibility creates an "anti-noir" iconic typing is at work in mainstream films and prevents characters portrayed by Sylvester Stallone in *Cobra* (1986) or *Lock Up* or Arnold Schwarzenegger in *Raw Deal* from becoming neo-noir.

Rolling Thunder involves a returning veteran, more specifically a Vietnam war POW. As in scenarist's Paul Schrader's *Taxi Driver*, the expressions of the protagonist's maladjustment alternate between rage and despair, most memorably when he shoves his arm into a garbage disposal. Major Ranes' experiences as a prisoner of war and the brutal assault he suffers on his return would seem to give him more cause for alienation than Travis Bickle; but in numbing himself to torture, Ranes has detached himself from feeling. Unlike Bickle's experience, the brutal hunt for his assailants is more an expression of personal than social or existential outrage.

The low-budget pictures, *The Killing Time* (1987) and *Jezebel's Kiss* (1990), both feature youthful revenge seekers and might alternately be con-

Below, ready to even the score: Wiliam Devane and Steven Seagal (inset) level their weapons in *Rolling Thunder* and *Out for Justice,* both directed by John Flynn.

sidered as kid noir. The key to both stories is revealed in flashback: they have returned to obtain reprisal for the death of a parent that they witnessed as children. Both films are situated in small California coastal communities, and the deaths are tied to land swindles. *The Killing Time*'s protagonist murders and takes the place of the small town's new deputy sheriff and features a performance by Kiefer Sutherland that evokes Jim Thompson's Deputy Lou Ford. *Jezebel's Kiss* features another Thompson-esque creature, a ruthless ingenue (Katherine Barrese), who arrives on the scene on a motorcycle and uses her sexuality as well as a weapon to even the score.

Ms. 45 (1981), *Positive I.D.* (1987), *Alligator Eyes* (1991), and *The Hand That Rocks the Cradle* (1992) all feature women seeking revenge. Like *Jezebel's Kiss* these productions are mostly low-budget. As it happens the costliest of these, *The Hand That Rocks the Cradle*, is the least interesting. There is a decidedly disturbing tone in a narrative which features a deadly nanny trying to steal the family of a woman who accused her doctor-husband of improper sexual advances that led to his suicide and her miscarriage. This victim of circumstance-cum-psychopath who could be pathetic is merely vindictive; and overhead shots of her thrashing around in a bathroom stall make her look silly, not angst-ridden. At the other extreme is *Alligator Eyes*, which features a blind woman who also witnessed a parent's murder as a child, which is also recalled in flashback. Her interaction with the trio of vacationers that pick her up hitchhiking is more eccentric than noir in mood.

Ms. 45 (featuring a haunting performance by Zoe Tamerlis in the role of the protagonist Thana) also features a disabled victim, a mute who is raped twice in the same afternoon and kills her second attacker with an iron. Afraid that her actions will be misunderstood, she decides to dismember the body and discard the parts throughout the city, a procedure which makes her understandably apprehensive, so she takes the gun with her. Her wordless descent into psychosis leads her to gun down a string of real and imagined rapists before being killed herself. Like *Alligator Eyes* and *Ms. 45, Positive I.D.* is shot in a gritty, quasi-documentary style atypical of neo-noir. What sustains a noir ambience is the heroine's monomaniacal plan to murder the man who brutally raped her, creating a bar-girl alter ego but abandoning both new identity and family after exacting retribution.

Opposite, Jamie Lee Curtis as Policewoman and stalker victim Megan Turner in *Blue Steel.* Below, the many faces of Thana (Zoe Tamerlis)—short for "Thanatos" or death?—in *Ms. 45.*

If women are freer in the context of neo-noir to join men in seeking revenge, they are still portrayed as more prone to psychological imbalance after being victimized. Thana's reaction is no more violent than that of Major Ranes or Paul Kersey, no more demented than Travis Bickle's. The real difference is her fate.

Women in Film Noir

Recent neo-noir examples of women fighting prejudice in assuming traditional male roles are *Blue Steel* (1989), *Impulse* (1990), and *Love Crimes* (1992). Not coincidentally, all three films are directed by women, Katherine Bigelow, Sondra Locke, and Lizzie Borden respectively. Women directors are also responsible for *Lady Beware*, *Stripped to Kill* (both 1987), The *Kill-Off, Body Chemistry*, *Rush* (all 1990), *Past Midnight* (1992), and *Guncrazy*. Although it might surprise die-hard male chauvinists, it is not coincidental either that most of these titles deal with women in law enforcement.

The earliest, Katt Shea's *Stripped to Kill*, is probably also the lowest in budget. On a narrative level it employs elements of the stalker film in the relationship between the male and female detectives; but its main thrust is a common a motif in later pictures: the undercover cop who gets caught up in the cover identity. When compared to *Impulse* or *Rush*, getting too involved in the role of exotic dancer may seem trivial next to becoming prostitute or drug user; and stripping to earn a living may be seamy but is certainly not criminal. In fact, the very seaminess, triviality, and the momentary desire, which grips the female protagonist to be as good or better than the other dancers, enhance the dramatic irony; and when her partner tells her to come to her senses, it also reveals the depth of his own prejudice.

In *Blue Steel* the question of role ambiguity is introduced in the title sequence as an androgynous form puts on a police uniform. In its early stages, *Blue Steel* develops the issue of prejudice against women in male roles merely

ENTRANCE

Color TV
PHONE
AIR COND.
HEATER

VACANCY
DRIVE-IN

LAS PALMAS AVE.
← 1400 N.

as ironic undercurrent, as the main character (Jamie Lee Curtis) faces the prejudice not only of her colleagues but of her own family. Eventually the woman protagonist's struggle with an obsessive killer becomes the narrative focus, and the film becomes a conventional, quasi-noir *policier*. That its heroine uses violence to overcome her nemesis is less liberating than constricting, a validation of the usual male technique. There is much more of a noir undertone in Bigelow's *Point Break*, where through what is almost a parody of male-bonding an undercover FBI agent begins to identify with the zen-surfer philosophy of the bank robbers he is trying to convict and irreparably compromises himself from an ethical standpoint.

Impulse also features a female cop (Theresa Russell). Here harassment is more overt in that she must deal with the sexual advances of a superior officer, but the core premise is that the central character, who works undercover as a prostitute, gets caught up in the lifestyle. When a man who picks her up in an upscale bar is murdered, she conceals the fact that she was present. The film could be viewed as a gender-switching variant on pictures where male cops stray from ethical behavior, from *Where the Sidewalk Ends* to *Point Break*; but, as with *Blue Steel*, the plot twists draw the film back to a traditional line. Less traditional is Lily Fini Zanuck's *Rush* (1991), ostensibly focused on the male protagonist, who has been undercover and using drugs for much longer. Much of his ethical deterioration is seen from the point of view of his newly recruited female partner. Clearly her entry into the twilight lifestyle is full of ironic transference, admiration for her more experienced and "dedicated" partner that becomes love, sympathy for the petty criminals she helps entrap which frustrate attempts to help save them, sexual and maternal instincts twisted and turned awry often by a sense of professional obligations. *Rush* is not about good and bad cops, categories into which the detectives' supervisor and the chief of police fall respectively, nor even about good/bad cops, as much as about a young woman almost destroyed by a rash of sometimes macho, sometimes pathetic, seldom heroic male values. Stylistically long takes and a rock-derived driving underscore may occasionally suggest a sense of entrapment or compulsion but may also give a techno-pop patina that can trivialize the subject.

Right, director Sondra Locke replicates the ironic scene from *Blue Steel*: a female cop, a large wheel gun, a grocery aisle.

Opposite, undercover policewoman Lottie Mason walks the streets of Hollywood.

Patrick Bergin as "David Hanover" menaces another woman: Sean Young as D.A. Dana Greenway in *Love Crimes*.

Love Crimes (1992) and *Past Midnight* are two more in this category. The latter resembles movies from *Deceived* back to *Suspicion* in its main plot: a social worker's relocating a parolee who committed a particularly brutal murder and becoming intrigued by inconsistencies in the case file. Of course, the inevitable liaison develops, and the equally inevitable questions about whether the man did commit the crime and will or will not murder her. Despite the performances of Natasha Richardson and Rutger Hauer, *Past Midnight*'s now all-too-familiar "suspense" style undercuts much of the would-be noir mood.

The troubled production history of *Love Crimes*, with scenes re-shot and performances altered in post-production, make for an aesthetic result that is uneven at best; but *Love Crimes* is probably the most iconoclastic statement from a woman filmmaker using elements of neo-noir. In pop-critical jargon, Lizzie Borden takes a cinematic ax and gives her audience forty whacks. From the first scene, which frames the narrative and in which Johnson, a black, female police lieutenant, makes a statement about a woman prosecutor, the point is things would have gone differently "if she wasn't a woman." The androgyny of the prosecutor, Dana Greenway (Sean Young), from her name to her hairstyle, is both subtler and more significant than in *Blue Steel*. As in *Impulse*, the protagonist's first scene involves an undercover officer posing as a prostitute; but in this case, Greenway is using her friend Johnson to trap fellow officers preying on hookers.

Ultimately, the narrative is encumbered with numerous complications, most notably from the flashback-within-flashbacks to Greenway's apparent abuse by a father who kills her mother. On one level the focus of *Love Crimes* is the transference relationship between Greenway and the man she is personally pursuing, a charlatan who poses as a photographer to seduce and abandon women. The revelations in flashcuts that he resembles her abusive father who also locked her in a closet as a child are timed to create visual irony but blur the issue of women's fighting male stereotypes. It is that stereotyping which, on another level, the two female protagonists are actually confronting and which in the end they can only overcome by acting unethically and destroying evidence. The narrative ironies are multiform. When Greenway changes her hair and her clothes and abandons her masculine style to "go undercover" posing as a schoolteacher on vacation, she is falling back on those stereotypes, perhaps more consciously than do the protagonists of *Blue Steel* or *Impulse* but entrapped by them nonetheless. When "David Hanover" (whose real name is never revealed) holds her hostage, his mind game is to convince Greenway that he can set her free of her inhibitions. When circumstances impugn her behavior, even Johnson assumes that she may have succumbed to the strange allure of her antagonist. The gender of the sexual dynamics may differ but the issues become much the same as in *Manhunter* or *Point Break*: agents of law enforcement encounter the surprisingly complex criminal mind and are misled by the charm of the sociopath.

The final irony is that it is Greenway's unexpected resistance to that charm of his that traps "Hanover," makes him unable to go back to seducing others until he has settled his score with her. In the climactic scene, the flashes of his camera strobe violate her more profoundly than any physical assault, triggering more flashbacks and pulsing through the frame as if to externalize her psychic spasms. It is that strobe, which keeps going even after he is struck down and drops the camera, which is isolated in a final close-up, and which triggers a white optical that blots out the frame, that is the mechanistic metaphor for the social strictures that hinder Greenway, Johnson, and all the other women "victims." In that context, Greenway's burning the Polaroids that "Hanover" had taken while he held her hostage becomes less an act of destruction than one of liberation from her dark pasts, both distant and immediate.

The New Fugitive Couple

Sexuality in the noir cycle figured most prominently in the narratives of fugitive couples, the *amour fou* of *Gun Crazy* or the entrapment of *Where Danger Lives* (both 1950). Along with *The Honeymoon Killers* (1969 and discussed later), *Pretty Poison* (1968) was one of the earliest neo-noirs to feature a crime spree by a fugitive couple; and with its darkly comic undertones and teenage femme fatale is an obvious antecedent to *Badlands* (1974). Based not just on the exaggerations of once institutionalized Dennis Pitt (Anthony Perkins) but also the pouty, manipulations of the Lolita-like Sue Ann Stepanek (Tuesday Weld), *Pretty Poison* follows a clear line from *Gun Crazy* than looks forward to *Badlands* and beyond. In fact, as the more ruthless of the couple, Sue Ann is arguably neo-noir's closest double for *Gun Crazy*'s Annie Laurie Starr.

It is surprising that more neo-noir films of the 1980s and 1990s did not follow this line. *Blood Simple* (1986) and *Wisdom* (1987) both engage the concept. The former may attempt to be more than another cross of Woolrich and Hitchcock, but it is still less than full-on noir. There is a deterministic aura that hangs over films like *Liebestraum* and *Blood Simple*, much of it created by the low-key photography and austere production design. In *Blood Simple*, the characters' halfhearted flight is just one component in an conscious attempt to substitute style for substance. *Wisdom* sets itself up as a conscious parable of modern youth; but the conclusion, revealing that the entire narrative is daydream, is more parody than parable. Unlike *Pretty Poison* or Terrence Malick's quixotic *Badlands* it never completes the bridge between black comedy and noir film.

Part homage to the 1950s, part naive noir, the first-person narrative of *Badlands* is straight out of movie magazines that youthful fugitive Holly Sargis reads as she travels the back roads of the Dakotas with her personal James

Below and opposite, *Badlands*: the bizarre romance of Kit (Martin Sheen) and Holly (Sissy Spacek) begins in town and ends with him in handcuffs.

Dean, garbageman turned killer Kit Caruthers. The landscape of this film, framed by her teen-diary-like narrative, is spectacular; but at the same time Holly's detached commentary is as if she were recalling another lifetime. *Badlands* skirts the dark corners of classic noir. Its horizontal aspect created by the meeting of land and sky is closest to the few examples of open landscapes of the classic period such as *Nightfall* or *Ace in the Hole* (1950). The fateful quality of the first meeting of the soon-to-be fugitive couple is both reinforced and mocked by Holly's voiceover as she explains that it was "better to spend a week with one who loved me for what I was than years of loneliness." Her rural accent with its meticulous inflection create an unrelenting and almost mocking tension in her voiceover. While that tradition is deeply imbedded in noir, classic-period femme fatales rarely addressed the viewer directly. Mallick's script infuses both voiceover and dialogue with a banality that contrasts chillingly with the violence.

For Kit, being part of a fugitive couple is the existential self-expression of one who unhappily collected the discards of others. Holly is less love object than decoration: he would "love" her or anyone else that had been in her place. Their dance to Mickey and Silvia's "Love is Strange" is one the most savagely comic moments of neo-noir. As the couple sways languidly, eyes closed, Holly barefoot, Kit in his cowboy boots, the music and their aspect in wooded hideaway are a long way from the young love of Bowie and Keechie in *They Live by Night* (1948). Still almost twenty years before the excesses of *Natural Born Killers* (1994), the mix of ingenuous angst and sudden death in *Badlands* make Kit and Holly ring truer than Oliver Stone's twisted fugitives in a postmodernist context.

This is not to say that homage cannot evoke the noir ambience, as is the case with François Truffaut's couple in his adaptation of Woolrich novel *Waltz into Darkness*, *Mississippi Mermaid* (1970), or even when the fugitive couple goes to the land of Oz in *Wild at Heart* (1990). In a film like *No Mercy* (1986), the fugitives are thrown together by circumstance, not passion. The noir mood in *No Mercy* derives as much from the cop-protagonist's desire to avenge his

Above, *No Mercy*: Det. Eddie Jilette (Richard Gere) goes from vindictive cop to part of a couple fleeing through the bayou with the enslaved Michel (Kim Basinger).   Opposite, Howard (James Le Gros) and Anita (Drew Barrymore in *Gun Crazy.*

murdered partner, as from the love interest that develops later. The narrative actually begins in the tradition of *The Big Heat* or *Dirty Harry,* only to shift focus in midstream to that of the fugitive couple. *Breathless* (1983) is an indirect homage, by way of Jean-Luc Godard's original, that works as *amour fou* if not necessarily as film noir. The level of self-consciousness in *Breathless* is even higher than in *Mississippi Mermaid.* Truffaut is content to re-create the suspenseful long take from the rear seat of the car, an angle first used in *Gun Crazy,* but *Breathless* has its lovers embracing behind the flickering screen of a movie theater that is actually showing *Gun Crazy.* Richard Gere's kinetic portrayal is in some ways closer to Cagney's Cody Jarrett in *White Heat* than either Belmondo in *Breathless* or John Dall in *Gun Crazy.* Although *Breathless* actually reverses the male/female roles of *Gun Crazy,* it reaffirms that even in 1990s certain men and women still combine explosively "like guns and ammunition."

Another twist on the fugitive couple was 1991's *Thelma and Louise,* two women on the run. The narrative setup, in which Louise shoots a drunken rapist who attacks Thelma, is straightforward enough; but the rest of the picture moves from set piece to set piece without developing a point of view. Certainly there are overtones of liberation in the women's behavior, whether it is Louise's coming to terms with the troubled relationships of her past, Thelma's discovering orgasm, or both of them blowing up the tankers of a leering trucker. Ultimately guns are not empowerment, and the women's decision to never be taken alive is at once an extravagant homage to an inappropriate desperado tradition and at the same time pointlessly romanticizes their fate. In the noir tradition, fugitives die because they must, because fate, mischoice, or the burden of their crimes compels it. Occasionally there is a redemptive context to death; in *Thelma and Louise,* there is a freeze frame emblematic of futility.

Guncrazy is not a remake, but a mélange of the fugitive couple and kid noir concepts. The script posits a high-school girl, living in a trailer with her

Above, *One False Move*: fugitive trio Pluto (Michael Beach, left), Fantasia (Cynda Williams) and Ray (Billy Bob Thorton) plan their next move.

mother's abusive boyfriend while Mom turns tricks in Fresno, who becomes pen pals and eventually marries a young ex-con with a fascination for handguns. The film echoes classic-period titles in both visual imagery reminiscent of the original *Gun Crazy* in scenes of the couple locked in a parody of embrace while they shoot at cans and bottles and also in its use of ingenuous dialogue in the manner of Nicholas Ray's *They Live by Night*. Because the characters themselves, Howard and Anita, are much more like Ray's Bowie and Keechie than those in Robert Altman's aimless, direct remake, *Thieves Like Us* (1974), they naively romanticize their sordid dilemma, epitomized when they break into a house and dress up for a candlelit dinner. Their inadvertent, grisly killing spree often becomes darkly comic. In a sense, perhaps the strongest allusion and the blackest joke is in the implicit parallel to *Tomorrow Is Another Day* (1951), as the mocking Freudianism of the Howard's high-caliber impotence and idealization of Anita despite her numerous sexual experiences are the 1990s equivalent of Steve Cochran's character in *Tomorrow* having gone through puberty in prison and fixating on a taxi dancer. When Anita fulfills her promise to Howard, who purposely walks into a hail of police gunfire, and glances up from his body to flatly intone, "He made me do it," the emotional transaction is much closer to *They Live by Night* than is the quirky neo-realism of Altman's pastiche. There is, in fact, a different kind of transference at work, more akin to the love of kidnapper and victim in Robert Aldrich's bleak period picture *The Grissom Gang* (1971) based on the celebrated novel *No Orchids for Miss Blandish*. In a sequence such as when Howard and Anita bury their first victims, the high school boys who have tormented her, shot in one take with the camera looking up from inside a shallow grave at their silhouettes against the sky and ending as the last shovelful of dirt covers the lens, both the narrative and the grimly humorous style most closely echo those of *Badlands*.

Like so many classic-period antecedents the relatively low-budget *One False Move* parallels the narrative of fugitives, in this instance a couple and another man and the pursuers. From an opening killing spree tied to money and drugs, after which the trio hits the road to turn the pilfered cocaine into more cash, the early scenes with the fugitives are mostly at night in the urban sprawl of Los Angeles and on the highways out of town. When LAPD detectives follow their leads to a small town in Arkansas, they gradually discover that the local sheriff was intimately involved with one of the purported killers. At the core of the narrative is racial. Although they work in tandem, the male criminals are a glib, good old boy Ray (Billy Bob Thornton) from the deep South and the nerdish yet menacing Pluto (Michael Beach) from the projects. The woman along for the ride has two names, Lily Walker and Fantasia (Cynda Williams), which reflect her dual status: exploited Black teenager in Arkansas who became an exotic starlet in Hollywood. As she rides from one locus to the other, Fantasia morphs from femme fatale back to Lila, a protective mother who steals from her partners to help her child.

As with *Blue Velvet* (1986), David Lynch's saga of a fugitive couple from Cape Fear, *Wild at Heart* is full of comic and surreal twists and marginally noir. Lynch's Sailor and Lula become a happy at the end, and in their own warped way so do the full-blown psychopaths in Oliver Stone's *Natural Born Killers*. Ultimately Stone's insistence on pushing the narrative envelope, as if to anticipate and out-do Tarantino, makes his unnatural couple as marginal as Lynch's.

Ironically, perhaps the most traditional of fugitive couples is early neo-noir are in sci-fi noir *The Terminator*. Thrown together by circumstance, tracked simultaneously by a relentless killer and the police, this couple only become lovers after fleeing, and the male ultimately lays down his life to save his companion.

Neo-B

Guncrazy is also a low-budget picture, as were *Ms. 45, Positive I.D.*, and many other features already discussed. In the classic period, film noir may have been disproportionately involved with productions done on limited means. The original *Gun Crazy* as well as *Kiss Me Deadly, D.O.A., Detour*, and score of others were all made on limited budgets and shooting schedules, which seemed to mesh well with the spare, ill-lit locales that typified the noir underworld. In many ways, the resurgence of interest in the noir style by low-budget film-makers represents a return to the roots of the cycle. The "B-film" or "pro-grammer," the less costly productions of the 1940s and 1950s from the major studios such as *Thieves' Highway* (1949, Fox), *Scene of the Crime* (MGM), or *Black Angel* (1946, Universal), whose second-tier actors, writers, and directors were featured on the bottom half of double bills, transformed itself into the limited release and made-for-video efforts of the 1980s and 1990s. While other than theatrical productions are only tangentially considered in this study, the low-budget feature, made pre-digitally at a cost ranging from less than $500,000 to $3 or 4 million, is. Such project could not be financed based on US theatrical prospects alone but must follow the dictates of the foreign, DVD, and cable markets. Not only do those markets still prize the "action" picture or "thriller," whose spare narratives translate more easily for non-English-speaking audiences, but the violence and compulsive sexual behavior that has always been part of film noir are more "saleable" than ever. Since many productions of the classic period were criticized at the time for their violence and unsavory themes, this is just another aspect of neo-noir's return to its roots. At the lowest of budgets the results can admittedly be marginal. *Blue Vengeance* (1989) uses cross-bows, strobe lights, and lots of stage blood in a failed attempt to mask its limited means. The plot of the *Dark Side* (1987) finds a taxi driver embroiled with a porn-star fare who fears she may be cast in a snuff film.

Most of the films already discussed, from *Guncrazy* to *After Dark, My Sweet*, have worked within the range of limited budget and successfully evoked the noir tradition. In fact, in the worst of neo-noir, the failing is seldom because of monetary restrictions. *Hit List* and *Relentless* (both 1989) are two interesting productions directed by William Lustig, which both feature obsessive cops and victims of circumstance. The setup in *Hit List* is prototypical: a dying cop wants to put away a racketeer and has a protected witness to use against him. A hit man sent to eliminate him literally goes to the wrong address and wreaks havoc on the inhabitants of the house across the street. The twist has the inno-

Delusion: Hit man Chevy (Kyle Secor) plays cat and mouse with his target Larry (Jerry Orbach) while girlfriend Patti (Jennifer Rubin) chats with hapless Jim Metzler (George O'Brien), handcuffed to the trailer awning in the background.

cent victim recruiting the witness to help retrieve his kidnapped son. What imbalances the picture are the performances, with Rip Torn, Lance Henriksen, and Leo Rossi performing at one level and Jan-Michael Vincent and Charles Napier at another.

If *Hit List* turns on the concept of the wrong address then the modus operandi in *Relentless*, where the killer chooses his victims by opening a page at random from the telephone directory, is even more arbitrary. Although Judd Nelson's portrayal of the psychopath brought the picture much opprobrium, his manic interpretation works within the context much as did Richard Basehart's in *He Walked by Night*. The ironies of the displaced cop (Leo Rossi) trying to prove himself and the old veteran (Robert Loggia) dying because of his carelessness are reinforced by the iconographic context of prior work, particularly Loggia's in *Jagged Edge*. In this sense, *Relentless* maximizes the impact of its limited means. While the flashbacks to the killer's abused childhood at the hands of his police officer/father may seem an "antique" device, they economically fulfills a necessary narrative function.

Not only is such economy the key in "neo-B," it helps generate a higher percentage of films that are rooted in the noir tradition without overwhelming it like such high-budget efforts as *Shattered* or *Final Analysis*. In copying *Fatal Attraction*, *Body Chemistry* must circumvent the obstacles of short schedule, less celebrated actors, and certainly had no budget to re-shoot endings after test screenings. Despite that, the result is both stark and affecting. Without the clutter of freight elevators or operatic arias, *Body Chemistry* focuses relentlessly on the central premise; and when the "hero" is gunned down it arrives literally and figuratively at a very different conclusion. *Mortal Passions* takes types from the James L. Cain mold. Its plot, which turns fraternal loyalty into betrayal and has a would-be femme fatale fall in love, recalls more than anything in its final sequence Cain's ending to *Double Indemnity,* the novella.

Such titles as *Genuine Risk* (1990), *Delusion* (1991), even *Femme Fatale* (1990) are remarkably unambiguous. Equally remarkable is how well these pictures succeed as neo-noir. *Femme Fatale* is the most complicated, recalling elements of *The Locket* and *Chicago Deadline* (1949), in which a man marries a woman who turn outs to be someone else or more accurately, someone suffering from a multiple personality disorder. Like the reporter in *Chicago Deadline*, her husband pieces her other lives together through a succession of leads, while dodging some street hoodlums whom another of her personalities swindled.

Delusion is more derivative of Al Robert's "mysterious force" in *Detour* or *The Hitch-Hiker*. Embittered over his long-time employer's sale of the company, George O'Brien has embezzled a million dollars and is driving to Las Vegas with the cash in his trunk. He stops to help a young couple, Patti and Chevy, in a car that has swerved of the road, and they abduct him. O'Brien does not realize that the young tough has not been planning to kill him and does not know about the money, until Chevy kills someone else. Now O'Brien is a witness; and they dump him in the desert. He survives; but by the time he tracks them down, Patti has found the money and is preparing to go off on her own.

Stylistically both of these films benefit from the isolated or seedy locales, which permit a spare and stark visualization in the manner of *Border Incident*

(1949) or *On Dangerous Ground.* As in *After Dark, My Sweet* or *Kill Me Again*, the desert locations in *Delusion* permit an arrangement of figures in a landscape that create a sense of otherworldliness or mirage (the film's original title), of acting out a bad dream without having recourse to optical effects or mood lighting. At the victim's trailer site or in a rundown motel at the aptly named Death Valley Junction, the isolated environment underscores the narrative tension in the classic noir manner. The last shot literally drives away from O'Brien as he stands looking off from the wounded Chevy lying in the dusty driveway and continues down the road for the entirety of the end credits. When that shot cedes to Patti, back to working as a showgirl and singing "These Boots Are Made for Walking," the final note is both sardonic and deterministic.

Genuine Risk has the deadliest of the femme fatales and is the most traditional in approach. It is also the most self-conscious, as locations, lighting style, and art direction constantly underscore the sordidness of the milieu. Even more overt is the script which features lines like, "A racetrack is like a woman...A man weathers so much banality in pursuit of the occasional orgasmic moment." What distinguishes *Genuine Risk* is the offhandedness of its violence, where people are beaten or die painfully, abruptly and without reason in stagings that capture the disturbing tone of videotapes of real events from surveillance cameras. It also has some wryness and novelty in its plot and casting, most notably Terence Stamp as a 1960s British pop star turned petty mobster. Although deceived by this mobster's wife, the "hero," a hapless petty criminal and compulsive gambler named Henry, survives while just about everyone else perishes and goes back to the track for another play.

The plots of these pictures, all budgeted at under a million dollars, take only what they can afford from the classic tradition; but that is a considerable amount. All have enough money for a femme fatale, a hired killer or two, a confused and entrapped hero, an employer ripped off, a shakedown. Two have

Fatal Instinct.

flashbacks, two have gang bosses, one a psychiatrist. The locations vary from Los Angeles to Las Vegas, from Death Valley to Big Bear Lake, but two have mansions, two, cheap motels, two, isolated rural locales where killers take their proposed victims. Like its antecedent, neo-noir—and neo-B in particular—makes few if any extravagant demands in terms of production value.

Fringe Areas

From television to comic books, film noir has exerted and continues to exert its narrative and stylistic influence. Concurrent with the classic period were not just the docu-noir series *Dragnet* but also *M Squad*, *Man with a Camera*, and *Johnny Staccato*. A generation of neo-noir series began with *The Fugitive, Run for Your Life*, and *Harry-O* as network television series and then cable programming continuously explored the noir terrain, frequently in retro mode. Concurrent with *Miami Vice*, Michael Mann created the period cop show *Crime Story*. Chandler's main character first headlined a series in contemporary private eye in 1959, returned in retro mode via a cable mini-series in 1983 and currently prowls the streets of 1950s Tokyo on the Japanese television adaptation of *The Long Goodbye.* From the first, television also parodied noir, and after *Fish Police* could it be long before an angst-ridden Bart Simpson skateboarded down his own mean streets?

Neo-noir titles again tell the tale: the words "kill" or "dead" or "black" appear in a score of them. Characters are deceived, shattered, and sleeping with the enemy, presumably with one eye open. The impersonal aspect of urban sprawl is the visual motif in the main title sequences of *New Jack City*, *V.I. Warshawski*, and *Run*, which feature helicopter shots sweeping over New York, Chicago, and Boston respectively. Echoes of the classic period from its undercurrent of despair to its the dark visual style continue to manifest themselves in other types of films, in political thrillers from *The Parallax View* (1974) and *Winter Kills* (1979) to *JFK* (1991), in the surreal *Blue Velvet*, the docu-drama *Henry, Portrait of a Serial Killer* (1990), the dark corridors of the spaceship Nostromo in *Alien* (1979) where an inhuman serial killer prowled, or the big-budget, adaptations based on the comic book *Batman*, which after were taken over by Christopher Nolan would became unrestrained visual homages to classic noir style with a "dark knight" patrolling a menacing urban landscape.

One of the surest indicators on a neo consciousness of that style were the parodies and not the just the retro *Dead Men Don't Wear Plaid* with its clips from classic-period features fully integrated into the narrative. A decade later in *Fatal Instinct* (1993), *Dead Men* director Carl Reiner pointedly mocked purely visual moments in noir, such as femme fatales enveloping their prey in cigarette smoke. *Get Shorty* (1995) cast neo-actors from the large and small screen, such as Gene Hackman and Dennis Farina, to parody themselves.

Well before the end of the 20th century and less than seven decades from the inception of the original movement, American neo-noir was firmly established a a vibrant genre and ready to branch out through a new generation of filmmakers, auteurs conscious of both the original and its spin-off, of both *Double Indemnity* and *Body Heat.*

L.A. Confidential: 1950s LAPD
Detectives White (Russell
Crowe, left) and Exley (Guy
Pearce).

Part Two

The Evolution of Neo

Introduction–High and Low, Side by Side

It should be clear from Part One that the early 1990s were a turning point for neo-noir. In fact, interest in neo-noir waxed and waned from the end of the classic period until that powerful resurgence from 1990 to 1992. From that point on it was not just the narrative preoccupations rooted in the 1940s that were replicated. As more and more of the generation born after the classic period ended became filmmakers, the reflection on the movement became less nostalgic and more stylistic.

The visual impact infused into so many noir films by cinematographers such as John Alton, John F. Seitz, or Nick Musuraca reappeared across genres. Although far from homogenous, a neo-noir style was applied to the retro and to the futuristic and identified itself from crime films to sci-fi. Straightforward tales of sirens and scammers shared the noir platform with space travelers and satirical riffs. Strictly in terms of budget, neo-B noir continues to reach new lows. From shot-on-film features that cost one or two hundred thousand dollars twenty years ago, digital moviemakers have created features on aglet budgets. While it may not be possible to determine who made a movie for the smallest tip of a shoestring, Daniel Casey's *The Death of Michael Smith* (2006) at $541 may be the winner.

Where the genre has gone in the past two decades, the evolution of neo-noir in a post-postmodern era, has been along two distinct paths, both of which are keyed to the development of 21st-century technology. The first, as just noted, moved with the professional and prosumer equipment for recording images and sound that burst on the market at the latest turn of the century. From 1990 to 2010, the typical method of recording movies went from film to videotape to the same medium on which this sentence is being recorded, a digital drive, from analog images encoded on celluloid or magnetic oxide to a binary series of 0s and 1s. Of course, even when a camera loaded with film is still used to shoot a movie, in all but a few cases that negative is essentially discarded, transferred to the digital intermediates used to edit, score, and create the final images and sounds of almost all motion pictures. Inevitably even the most die-hard of "filmmakers" will be making their movies without the film.

Once "normal" high definition equipment, such as the heavy CineAlta cameras with 1080 lines of resolution recorded in 24p ("progressive" frames) on large videotapes and famously used in 2000 for the production of *Star Wars*

Above, parking-garage pursuit in *Beyond A Reasonable Doubt.* Opposite, the sci-fi fugitive couple Ricks (Elias Koteas) and Cash (Agjelina Jolie) in *Cyborg 2.*

II: Attack of the Clones (2002), have been obsolete for years. Those first-generation HDcams with their 1K resolution cost over a quarter of million dollars to buy. While 1080p may still be the standard for consumer televisions, the lightweight Red cameras record at more than 4 times the acuity but are priced at less than one-tenth as much. Among the most popular cameras for the past few years, the Canon Ds, cost even less. While meant for still photography, they are capable of shooting rings around the CineAltas of a decade and a half ago, at 1/100th the cost. Among the studio-budgeted neo-noirs discussed in this part of the book, *Beyond a Reasonable Doubt* (2009), was made with a Red; *Sin City* (2005) on the latest, lightweight CineAlta; *Deception* (2008) with the Panavision Genesis; and *Zodiac* (2007) used the Thompson Viper. The studio publicity for *Zodiac* trumpeted the fact that, until some film release prints were struck, none of the movie existed on either celluloid or videotape.

To illustrate the effect of technological evolution from personal experience, the kid noir titles produced by Alain Silver in the late 1980s, *Prime Suspect* and *Night Visitor*, had budgets of $400,000 and $850,000 respectively, They were shot on film, transferred to reference-tape dailies, and cut experimentally using the ECS90 video system. In 1992, *Cyborg 2* was also shot on film with Panavision anamorphic lenses for a wide-screen aspect ratio on a $6-million budget. It was cut on an Avid editing system that had been invented 3 years earlier. Before the millennium, high-definition had come into existence, so that when a negative cutter ruined large portions of *Palmer's Pick-up* (1999), the production company's only recourse was to what might well have been the first "digital intermediate" to repair the damage and "blow up" the 16mm neg-

ative to 35mm prints non-photographically. That process alone cost over $100,000 or more than the entire budget of the digital feature made the next year, *Bel Air.* A more recently completed digital movie, *Crashing* (2007) was made six years later with a prosumer miniDV camera and cost just over $6,700 to shoot. Of course, that's still ten times more than Daniel Casey and his colleagues spent on *The Death of Michael Smith.* For low-budget filmmakers (the term will likely survive even if the medium is destined for extinction) an important parallel is the creation by the industry guilds and unions of side-letters that variously reduce minimum salaries and other working conditions at tiers ranging from $500,000 to $9 million.

The other parallel path, of course, is digital distribution. Less than 20 years ago *Cyborg 2* was released on VHS tape in a pan-and-scan format to fit 4:3 television screens. At that time only a fraction of classic-period titles discussed in the third edition of our *Film Noir: An Encyclopedia Reference to the American Style* were available. Since 2000 low- and ultra-low-budget productions have had a reasonable chance of recouping their miniscule costs first on DVD and now via streaming video-on-demand in 16:9 and other widescreen formats. Aesthetically creators of the neo-Bs discussed below could watch most of the classic-period movies and make whatever style notes they wanted. It also makes easier than ever our repeated encouragement for the reader over numerous studies of noir to go back to the movies themselves.

Perhaps the best illustration of these introductory remarks, is to examine side by side the same subject dramatized by high- and low-budget movies. Although they portray many of the same events, the differences between the $1-million-budgeted *The Zodiac* (2006) and just plain, no-film-used *Zodiac*, the project funded by two major studios officially at $65 million but estimated by

some sources to be over $100 million, are as much about fundamental approaches to neo-noir as about funds available to make the movie. While its script and performances often betray its limited resources, *The Zodiac* more distinctly echoes the classic period. The unrelenting, amped-up character of Detective Parish recalls monomaniacal cops as varied as Culloran in *The Beat Generation* (1959) and Capt. McQuigg in *The Racket* (1951). While the iconic status of Justin Chambers, who portrays the lead detective in *The Zodiac*, is a far cry from Robert Mitchum's in *The Racket* or even Steve Cochran's in *Beat Generation*, the alternate narrative points of view from Parish's wife and son, a wistful young man whose single expression suggests extreme emotional repression, create the same undercurrent of chaos lurking in the shadows that was common in classic period productions. There are repeated visual links between the lurking Zodiac, whose face is never seen, and Johnny Parish, which simultaneously suggest a dark menace and a mirror, as if the Zodiac were watching a flashback to his own dysfunctional childhood. The Zodiac hates his mother, suggests a glib psychiatrist whom the detectives consult. While young Johnny may not hate her, he runs away from his mother when she plans to leave Parish and their home.

Like the main titles and stock footage of the moon landing, some of the exterior daylight scenes in *The Zodiac* are staged in a documentary style. Like the clips from *The Most Dangerous Game* (the 1932, public-domain version), which appear in a screening attended by the killer and in a montage flashback, the use of car beams and flashlights in the night sequences and a low-key and semi-monochrome scheme saturated in yellow and green inside the Parish house play against any sense of documentary reality. During the attacks and other scenes, there are also shots from the Zodiac's point of view. Some are straightforward depictions of the killer's eye-line during the violence. Others, as in a brief encounter with a waitress in a diner, are fractured and overlaid, a severe disruption of realistic perspective that is easily read as the killer's emotional point of view, severely distorted and dissociative. While one actor portrays the killer on screen, another gives voice to the letters. The fact that this

voice is measured and slightly over-modulated, reminiscent of HAL in *2001*, is subtle and disturbing, running against viewer expectations even as it invokes an aural archetype for a dysfunctional machine. The explicit ironies at the end of *The Zodiac* also work at different levels somewhat counter to normal. Parish's demotion permits a tenuous reconciliation with his son and his wife who has repeatedly accused him of ignoring his family and of being a possible threat to them. The voice of the Zodiac has the last words taken from his final letter: "I am waiting for a good movie about me. Who will play me?"

The events from *The Zodiac* make up only the first half of the narrative of the more recent *Zodiac*. Parallel investigative stories involving San Francisco Detective Inspectors Toschi (Mark Ruffalo) and Armstrong (Anthony Edwards)

Opposite, light glints off the glass of the killer in a darkened movie house in *The Zodiac.* Above, amateur sleuth Robert Graysmith (Jake Gyllenhaal) explores a possible suspect's basement. Below, Det. Matt Parish (Justin Chambers) from *The Zodiac* seems to confer with Det. Dave Toschi (Mark Ruffalo) from the larger-budget movie.

and newspapermen Avery (Robert Downey Jr.) and Graysmith (Jake Gyllenhaal), move into high gear after receipt of letters by the *San Francisco Chronicle*. Unlike the ten-month span of *The Zodiac*'s plot line, the narrative of *Zodiac* covers over twenty years and several other killings and contacts that have never been certainly linked to the serial killer. The last portion revolves around Graysmith's disintegrating marriage as he obsessively completes the research for his book, in the process often revealing facts to police officials from various jurisdictions that their counterparts had kept from them. As does the fictional Parish in *The Zodiac*, Graysmith focuses on a possible acquaintance of the second woman killed. He runs down one false lead and then discovers that Arthur Leigh Allen, the likeliest suspect of detectives Toschi and Armstrong, also knew the woman. After a survivor of the second attack identifies Allen, the ending titles disclose that he died of natural causes before he could be arrested.

From the first *Zodiac* implies that it will strictly adhere to the facts. Using graphics that repeatedly set date, time, and location, the first half of *Zodiac* is a more detailed and dispassionate reenactment than *The Zodiac*. One hundred minutes into the movie, there is a narrative fulcrum when handwriting analysis seems to clear the perfect suspect. After Detective Toschi confesses that he can no longer tell whether he is disappointed because he strongly believed the man was guilty or strongly wanted the case to end, his captain suggests that he take some time off. It is nothing like the scathing lecture that

Above, heavy side-light illuminates Dets. Parish and Martinez (Rex Linn) in *The Zodiac*. Right, fuller lighting is used on Toschi and partner Amstrong (Anthony Edwards) in *Zodiac*.

Parish receives in *The Zodiac*, and Toschi is not demoted back to uniformed patrolman. But in terms of dramatic arc, the movie could end here.

Instead the film continues for another hour, as the shared perspective refocuses predominantly on the writer Graysmith. Near the end, after Graysmith's wife has left him and taken his children because she fears his monomania will destroy them all, there is an extended sequence when Graysmith visits retired theater owner Bob Vaughan and learns that his hand-writing, a possible match for the Zodiac's, is on the posters. The forced creepi-ness—Graysmith is compelled to follow Vaughan into his basement and when his fearful departure is stopped by a locked door—creates pointless suspense. The encounter leads nowhere and does little except to underscore Graysmith's social and emotional dyslexia. Certainly that "dyslexia" could be taken as a par-allel for whatever drives the actual killer. But as Jake Gyllenhaal's performance turns on this detachment, the audience no longer has the easy identification it made with Mark Ruffalo and Anthony Edwards as partners Toschi and Armstrong. It doesn't even have a character like Parish who is coming apart melodramatically. Without that *Zodiac* trudges with hollow footsteps to its nec-essarily enigmatic conclusion. In doing so, it demonstrates again that the most effective evocations of the noir sensibility are not about A-budgets and extraor-dinary resources.

Femmes Fatales

The fatal women of the classic period and most of their early neo sisters were sleek and sexy, most often blondes in tight-fitting gowns who sang torch songs in smoky lounges and whose fates were bound up with the men in their lives. Their explicit liberation in neo-noir began with *Body Heat* and broke out in the early 1990s with features such as *Basic Instinct* and *The Last Seduction* (1994). With its liberated heroine who "fought fire with fire" (to paraphrase Naomi Wolf in her book of the same name) and used all weapons at her disposal, including sexual ones, *Basic Instinct* set the bar for third-wave feminist femme fatale movies, post-1990. That San Francisco detective becomes obsessed with Catherine Tramell, a cool, complex, and blond "ice princess," is expected from the genre indicators. So is his attempt to understand/possess/save her to the point that he becomes unhinged physically as well as mentally. Catherine the novelist is in many ways the metaphorical writer of the movie. She scripts the narration and action, and Nick is a man out of his depth, pulled by women who control him in various ways.

Not all the entranced men are cops or criminals. The protagonist of *The Harvest* (1992) is a screenwriter doing research in Mexico. You'd think he would understand the concept, but he never sees a dangerous woman for what she is until he wakes up missing a kidney. In *The Edge* (1997) the femme fatale is mostly absent. Competitors Green (Alec Baldwin) and Morse (Anthony Hopkins) are stranded in the mountains after a plane crash. Instead of expending most of their energy trying to survive, they spend most of their time arguing while planning and executing revenge strategies against each other because Green is having an affair with the Morse's much younger-model wife

Above, *The Last Seduction*: manipulatuve fatal woman Bridget Gregory (Linda Fiorentino) attracts the attention of the eager Mike Swale (Peter Berg).

Opposite, *Body of Evidence:* D.A. Robert Garrett (Joe Mantegna) watches a sex tape of murder suspect Rebecca Carlson (Madonna).

Another new generation femme fatale is Bridget Gregory aka Wendy Kroy, portrayed with cutting sexuality by Linda Fiorentino in *The Last Seduction*. Bridget/Wendy is a manipulative, sexually aggressive, and smart female who makes her own rules and refuses to recognize middle-class mores. She leaves her drug-dealing husband and steals his "take" after he strikes her; she plans his murder as a form of revenge after he stalks her. Like many third-wave feminists she has co-opted negative male language and made it her own: Mike: "I'm trying to figure out whether you are a total fucking bitch or not." Bridget: "I am a total fucking bitch." Like a macho man she peppers obscenities throughout her speech, uses her new lover Mike Swale (Peter Berg) like a "sex object," and disdains "sharing" feelings.

In counterweight to Bridget is the masochistic Mike who is drawn to her the first time she walks into the bar and, after being ignored, yells, "Who do I have to suck off to get a drink around here?" When his friend asks what he sees in her, he replies, "Maybe a new set of balls." Hers, probably. For the power dynamic of this couple rests on a reversal of traditional gender roles. Mike complains about her "zipless fucks" (to use writer Erica Jong's term): "[You] treat me like a 4H experiment" and misses the tenderness and emotional connection: "I'm having more and more trouble with this, Wendy." He is also by implication bisexual as the audience and Bridget find out later when she tracks down his hidden transvestite wife.

Body of Evidence (1993) is among the most interesting examples of new-wave femme fatale film largely because of its main character Rebecca Carlson, played by pop star Madonna, another edgy blonde. Like Catherine in *Basic Instinct*, Rebecca is unashamed and forthright about her "perverse" proclivities. She seeks out men like a predator, potentially submissive men who will form

Above, the original *Poison Ivy*: Drew Barrymore as the troubled teen seductress of the title.

erotic/romantic fixations on her and thereby play by her "rules," her "way." When the film opens Rebecca is standing trial on the unique charge (one that in reality would not hold up in most courts) of using her "body as a lethal weapon." Again, almost psychically, she attracts a lawyer—Frank (Willem Dafoe)—who is not even aware of his masochistic tendencies but finds Rebecca irresistible. For as she hints to him in a crowded restaurant, he has the "same tastes as [she does]…[but] doesn't know it yet."

As much as Frank tries to maintain his ethical detachment from Rebecca (after all, he is her lawyer), he cannot. Slowly he discovers—to use Freud's term in a positive rather than negative manner—the polymorphously perverse side of himself. Rebecca straps him down with his own belt, pours hot wax on him, and forces him down on a bed of broken glass atop a car while he services her orally. In a short amount of time he becomes addicted to her and the world she has opened up to him. Even when Frank begins to doubt her veracity at the trial and loses the trust of his wife in the process, he cannot stay away. Refusing to heed the advice of the district attorney (Joe Mantegna), "Trial's over, Frank. Walk away," he still clings to the role of savior. He wins the case for her and almost saves her life in the final scene when she is attacked by one of her jilted ex-lovers. He fails, however, and can only look in despair as his blond femme fatale falls to her death.

Director-writer Katt Shea's 1992 *Poison Ivy* marks the beginning of a series of post-feminist teen femme fatales drawing heavily from influences like Vladimir Nabokov's pedophiliac novel *Lolita* as well as the landmark psycho female revenge neo-noir *Fatal Attraction*. These nymphets, stretching from Drew Barrymore's Ivy through Alicia Silverstone's Adrienne in *The Crush* (1993) and Denise Richard's Kelly in *Wild Things* (1998) to Erika Christensen's Madison in the 2002 *Swimfan* (to name but a few), are as symbolic of the threat of female power (sexual and otherwise) as their older femme fatale sisters in noir.

The audience first views Ivy swinging on a rope in slow motion. As the protagonist and narrator of the piece, Sylvie (Sara Gilbert), describes this free spirit, the camera lingers on her tattoos, her piercings, her full lips, and blond mane, obviously as fascinated with this contrasting vision of youth and decadence as the intellectual misfit who describes her. Sara strikes up a friendship with the mysterious Ivy and soon the femme fatale has taken up residence in her palatial home in the hills above Los Angeles. Gradually Ivy intertwines her emotional tendrils around the three dysfunctional inhabitants of the house—Sara, her ailing mother Georgie (Cheryl Ladd), and her self-important news commentator father Darryl (Tom Skerritt). Ivy is driven by two impulses: to seek the family she never really had (she gives moral support to all three, particularly the shy Sylvie) while indulging her more transgressive impulses by disrupting that same family.

Besides turning the hypocritical Darryl into her love slave (we see him on his knees, caressing her feet and legs, which symbolizes his complete submission), she wins Georgie over by sharing her anguish over the death of her own drug-addicted mother and by bringing her a little closer to her daughter. Eventually Ivy loses control of her destructive impulses—pushing Georgie to her death over a balcony (incidentally, a death she had always desired)—and driving herself and Sylvie into a tree. When the delirious Sylvie escapes from the hospital to return home, now convinced Ivy is psychotic, she discovers her father and Ivy in bed. She then begins to see a vision of her mother coming close to her and kissing her on the lips. As that hallucination turns into the reality of Ivy embracing her, she struggles with her, causing her to fall to her death.

Sylvie's experience with Ivy has its positive aspects (she absorbs some of Ivy's confidence and strength), so in director Anne Gorsaud's sequel, *Poison Ivy II* (1996), the diffident Lily (Alyssa Milano, with whom the director worked on the erotic vampire movie *Embrace of the Vampire* the year before) becomes liberated by reading Ivy's diary. Gorsaud uses the *Poison Ivy* franchise to flesh out ideas about the process of becoming an artist. We first see Lily as she arrives at the "big city" art school from the "heartland." Her clothes are frumpy and her manner self-deprecating. But inspired by her unsettling sexual experience with the womanizing art instructor Falk (Xander Berkeley) as well as the nude images she finds of Ivy, Lily decides to explore her own "demons," as Falk advises, and free herself for her art. A change in dress and makeup accomplishes the exterior transformation into femme fatale but the interior makeover comes with greater difficulty. She teases and plays with both Falk and her more sincere lover, the sculptor Gredin. As her art blossoms, her personal life spins out of control when Falk forms a full-blown obsession with Lily, painting her compulsively and then stalking her. In a feminist twist, Gorsaud shifts the nexus of punishment and has the male antagonist fall to his death rather than the femme.

The popular (on video, that is) Poison Ivy franchise lasted through several more incarnations. In director Kurt Voss's *Poison Ivy: The New Seduction* (1997), the story and characters become more codified and stereotyped. In this newest incarnation Ivy's sister Violet, played with great irony and erotic power by Jaime Pressly, pulls no punches in her sexually subversive ways. She is a dominatrix on the side, wears leather and latex outfits, and makes her men submit to her with a directness and violence rarer in the earlier versions of the character. Her search for affection and drive towards destruction is far more palpable as she ties the mewling patriarch of the family (and it is suggested her real father, who had an affair with Violet's mother when she was a servant in his house) to his bed and whips him or as she seduces the boyfriend of her childhood friend Joy (Megan Edwards) and then injects him with an overdose of drugs—all in order to keep Joy close to her. As in the first film it is the shy friend who puts the Ivy character to rest, again with a push from a balcony.

China Moon (1994) follows the pattern of classic noirs like *Double Indemnity* and *The Postman Always Rings Twice.* A "chump," in this case a detective—Bodine (Ed Harris), falls for a sexually charged and in this case, somewhat ethereal (symbolized by the "china moon") femme—Rachel (Madeleine Stowe). As with the film's forerunners like *Double Indemnity,* the viewer never really doubts that there is a love connection between the criminal protagonists (they become involved in the murder of her husband). Also like many neo-noir femme fatales, Rachel is the only character left alive in the end to enjoy the fruits of her labors. Joan Chen made her name as a femme fatale in foreign films like *The Last Emperor* and *Temptation of a Monk,* and in David Lynch's surreal television series *Twin Peaks* (1990-91). In all of these movies

Below, in *Posion Ivy: The New Seduction*, Jaime Pressly is sister Violet who adds more overt eroticism.

Opposite, *China Moon*: fatal woman Rachel (Madeliene Stowe) casts a shadow on the mottled face of Det. Bodine (Ed Harris) in their post-coital clinch.

she plays with the Western stereotypes of Asian women: namely, the Madame Butterfly/Dragon Lady dichotomy.

Playwright David Henry Hwang's *Golden Gate* (1994) is a fine example of this deconstruction of stereotypes. Here the dichotomy is between the Asian Goddess of Mercy and the Chinese warrior woman Fa Mulan. The Chen character Marilyn Song narrates the movie that recounts the story of a cocky 1950s FBI agent, David Walker (Matt Dillon), who precipitates the eventual suicide of Marilyn's labor organizer father by persecuting him for his "communistic" activities. Soon Walker finds himself haunted by these actions (he witnesses the suicide of the father from the Golden Gate Bridge) as well as the image of the defiant young daughter who, he imagines (?), gives him comfort in a rainy alley one forlorn night. Time passes and Walker again encounters the daughter (this time a young woman) while surveilling Chinatown for purported subversives. She is crying on a rooftop. Taken by her beauty and her perceived vulnerability, he shifts into White Savior mode (this motif can also be seen in Hwang's *M Butterfly*) and tries to protect her from the investigation.

Walker also starts to date Marilyn, lying to her about his job and his involvement with her father's downfall. She finds out the truth from a friend and then, as she says, transforms herself from the Goddess of Mercy, Guanyin (a figure she had told Walker about), to the warrior Fa Mulan, trashing his apartment and scrawling graffiti in blood on his walls. This does not end Walker's obsession Marilyn. Instead of cleaning his apartment, he leaves the graffiti up and builds a shrine to both Marilyn and Guanyin. Walker again encounters Marilyn and in order to make reparation steals the file on her father so that she may reveal to the press the truth about the FBI's persecution of her father.

Above, Christopher Walken (Left), Anne Heche, and Joan Chen (center) are a triangle in *Wild Side.* Another Chen character enraptures and dooms Matt Dillon (right) in *Golden Gate.* Below, *Dream Lover*: Ray (James Spader) and Lena (Mädchen Amick).

When they meet in an alley, she kisses him, knowing that her kisses, as she tells him, give him life. She is only partially right. For on her wedding day, Walker finds the exact place on the Golden Gate Bridge where her father had died and commits suicide himself, finding his redemption in that act.

In 1995 Chen starred in director Donald Cammell's last movie, *Wild Side* (2005). In it she plays Virginia, the seductive wife of an out-of-control money launderer named Bruno Buckingham (Christopher Walken). The protagonist of the movie, bank accountant/call girl Alex Lee (Anne Heche), falls under Virginia's spell and attempts to help her escape Bruno who is trying to set his wife up for a fall as well as steal some of Bruno's illegal profits.

Mädchen Amick, coming off her success on David Lynch's *Twin Peaks*, took on the role of the neo-noir femme fatale in two films: *Dream Lover* (1994) and *Love, Steal and Cheat* (1996). In the first film Amick portrays Lena, a grifter who sets her sights on an arrogant, recently divorced architect, Ray

(James Spader), and through a game of tease and denial captivates him. Her first encounter with Ray is at an art gallery where she berates him for accidentally spilling wine on her dress and then verbally upbraids him for neglecting his "girlfriend." Intrigued with her attitude and dark beauty, Ray tracks her down and attempts to date her. She alternates between friendliness and cold distance until one night she lets him into her apartment and while sitting wet and naked under a Japanese robe, she unravels her tale of woe and abuse (all of which turns out to be fiction).

Drawn in by her poignant story and addicted to her sexual energy, Ray marries Lena. Their marriage turns sour soon as Ray sinks into paranoia, convinced his wife is cuckolding him with other men (which, like most examples of paranoia in noir, proves to have a basis in fact). Confronting her with evidence he strikes her after she admits the affair and taunts him with the details. As Lena falls to the ground, she tells him that she knew that eventually his violent side would emerge. Calling in the police and her lawyer, Lena has him committed to an institution for psychiatric evaluation. Ray slowly plots his revenge while resisting medication and treatment. In one of Lena's final visits, Ray reveals the depth of his understanding when he calls her a "psychopath" and accuses her of never loving him. Much like Phyllis in *Double Indemnity*, she responds by telling him that even a psychopath can love, thereby exposing the emotions beneath her hard shell. Ray then proceeds to strangle Lena to death in one final obsessive embrace.

Amick in *Love, Steal and Cheat* plays Lauren, the young loving wife of middle-aged bank executive Paul Harrington (John Lithgow) and ex-wife of psychotic bank robber Reno (Eric Roberts). The reappearance of Reno disrupts Lauren's idyllic marriage as she finds herself drawn to his rough trade ways. While posing as her brother in order to stay in the Harrington house and plan a bank heist, Lauren gives into Reno's sexual advances, including an erotic scene where Reno performs oral sex on Lauren while Paul awaits her in the next room. In a series of twists, the audience begins to believe that Lauren has joined forces with Reno to rob Paul's bank. The robbery turns violent and during an exchange of monies, Paul, it seems, takes revenge on Lauren by shooting her repeatedly. But after Reno is taken down by the police, the movie cuts to a relaxed Paul sitting in a garden. He turns and his expression changes from quizzical to contented as the camera reveals Lauren walking toward him. They had staged her murder in order to fool Reno as well as the drug cartel.

In *The Crush*, the teen femme fatale Adrienne (Alicia Silverstone) is a melding of Lolita and Alex Forrest from *Fatal Attraction*. In the first sequence the male protagonist Nick (Carey Elwes) almost runs into this rollerblading nymphet as he is searching for an apartment to rent. The camera lingers on his look of shock and awe as she seemingly appears out of thin air, like a dangerous vision. She is dressed in tight shorts and sporting Lolita-style sunglasses. She displays not an iota of fear on her face as her gaze locks with his, establishing early the dynamics of the couple.

Nick finds what he is looking for in the quaint guest house of a rich couple, whose "headstrong" (her mother's words) daughter turns out, to Nick's surprise, to be Adrienne. The fourteen-year-old Adrienne's seduction of Nick is gradual and effective. She begins by spying on him as he goes about his daily routine (including a scene where she delightedly stares at his naked rear in the bathroom, again reversing the more typical pattern of a male spying on a female who is eventually naked). As she watches him she compulsively records every detail in her diary like a journalist. For as Nick soon learns, this teen is sly beyond her years. At one point she even hacks into his computer and rewrites his "mediocre" article, to the delight of his editor. It is this young woman's keen intelligence and willful nature, however, that results in Nick's undoing and eventually her own. His attraction to her is undeniable. He takes her to a romantic lighthouse and kisses her there. He in turn spies on her sunbathing below his window. He even hides in her closet, while snooping, and watches her undress. Adrienne is, of course, complicit in all three incidents, brought home to the audience when the camera cuts from the lust-filled eyes of Nick through the slats of the closet door to a cut to Adrienne's own eyes as she acknowledges his presence.

But when Adrienne turns violent, after Nick retreats emotionally following warnings from both her father and his new girlfriend, Nick's illicit passion transforms itself into fear mingled with revulsion. In Adrienne's mind, however, violence and passion are one (her favorite novel and film is *Wuthering Heights*). Love for her knows no boundaries, and neither does she. She releases deadly wasps in a darkroom where Nick's girlfriend is working; she crashes a business event and slaps Nick in front of his colleagues. And in the climax she beats Nick senseless with a cane (her own phallic symbol) in hysterical rage at his "infidelities." Nick escapes with his life and Adrienne is institutionalized but it is implied in the final scene that she may find yet another object for her overwhelming passions and live on to upset and terrorize yet another duped male.

Rose (Jane March) in *Color of Night* (1994) is everyone's "fantasy girl."

Below, *The Crush*: Darian (Alicia Silverstone) and older man Nick (Cary Elwes).

Opposite Dr. Capa (Bruce Willis) canoodles with patient Rose (Jane March) in *Color of Night*.

She suffers from a diagnosed "multiple personality disorder" ("a charming chameleon with a scorpion's sting") that allows her to prey upon others' fantasies in order to act out on her own history of abuse from both her father and her brother Dale (Andrew Lowery). To please her brother Dale, she takes on the personality of their dead brother Richie—an alienated, inarticulate abuse victim himself (in this mode she whips herself raw and accepts crucifixion via nail gun at the end of the movie). For the members of her therapy group, she acts out numerous other roles: a dominatrix for the painter Casey (Kevin O'Connor) who paints her in fetish gear on canvas after canvas in his loft; a little girl for the embittered cop (Lance Henriksen) who lost his family; a seductive, jealous lesbian for the sexually promiscuous Sondra (Lesley Ann Warren), and so on.

But Rose's most fascinating and ultimately, for her at least, most therapeutic object is the guilt-ridden (his arrogance caused the suicide of a patient) psychiatrist Bill Capa (Bruce Willis). For him she appears out of nowhere like "quicksilver" (his words), first smashing into the rear of his car and then showing up unexpectedly at the house he is occupying. And each time Rose (her name connoting not only the color red but passion itself) dons a new persona: a seductress in red dress and red car sporting red lipstick (ironically, Capa can no longer see the color red since his patient's death, a color that his psychiatrist friend tells him represents emotions).

As a seductress she manually stimulates him in front a hotel, invades his home, and has numerous sexual encounters with him and then disappears (Capa: "She floats away on her sweet young legs"). Dressed as a schoolgirl fresh from class with backpack and all, she mounts her "daddy." In an apron and nothing else she cooks him dinner, taking on the male fantasy of a sexy housewife. In this fashion, as Capa points out to Rose, she maintains the upper

hand in the relationship, "You have all the power. I just sit around and wait for you." Capa, however, cannot wait forever. It is not in his nature. He is a savior figure, a psychiatrist pledged to transforming "sick" patients into functioning members of society. In investigating a series of murders involving the therapy group he has inherited from his murdered psychiatrist friend, the clues eventually lead him to Rose. He finds her in a loft downtown where her brother Dale has nailed her to a chair. Capa frees her and she in turn saves Capa by killing the nail-gun-toting Dale. Traumatized once again by her act, Rose runs out to the roof. In the pouring rain Capa begs her not to jump: "If you go, I'll go." Before either can fall, Rose embraces him. They hold onto each other for dear life and kiss. And so Capa has been given his second chance and in the process allowed to "save" the chameleonic Rose.

Joe Eszterhas' script for director William Friedkin's *Jade* (1995) tries to exploit some of the more salacious elements of his earlier *Basic Instinct*. Trina (Linda Fiorentino) is a liberated postfeminist who takes pleasure in S&M games as well as sex with multiple partners. She may also be capable of murder. In *Never Talk to Strangers* (1995) Antonio Banderas plays that fairly rare twist on the femme fatale, the homme fatal (Van Heflin in Joan Crawford's *Possessed* (1947) is a model from the classic noir period). His seductive techniques and deviousness pushes his lover and psychologist (Rebecca De Mornay) off the deep end. Director Gus Van Sant's *To Die For* (1995) is a darkly ironic critique of the cult of personality as well as media in general. A narcissistic blonde, played by Nicole Kidman, will do anything to become a television personality, including seducing teenagers and murdering her husband.

Steven Soderbergh's remake of Robert Siodmak's classic-period *Criss Cross*, *The Underneath* (1995), follows the basic plot line of the original film but with some significant changes that mark it as postfeminist film. Soderbergh

Below and opposite, *The Underneath*: a wide-screen remake with moments of monochromatic, imbalanced frames, in which low-key and rim light evoke the noir undercurrennts that swirl around the doomed relationship of Michael (Peter Gallagher) and Rachel (Alison Elliot).

delves into the married life of the noir couple—here named Michael (Peter Gallagher) and Rachel (Alison Elliott)—in an attempt to shift the sympathy away from the male protagonist onto the female protagonist while humanizing the character of the femme fatale. Although Rachel does, like Anna in *Criss Cross*, love money and sex (in one scene we see her happily manipulating both her lover's penis as well as a bag of illicit money with her naked foot), she is also a wronged woman. She attempted to establish a solid relationship with her husband Michael, a scalawag with a gambling addiction, but he refuses to accept responsibility and uses her ticket money for an audition in Los Angeles to buy a car and a large screen television ("You never do what you say you're going to do.") and keeping her at a distance even during their lovemaking (Rachel: "I'd like to be close."). Ultimately he deserts her and his friends and skips town after accumulating too many gambling debts.

Michael only realizes the depth of his love once he has lost Rachel. Returning to town he finds her engaged to a local hood, Tommy Dundee. Now that she is technically unobtainable he pursues her with an overwhelming, masochistic passion: watching her with glazed eyes as she dances to a rock band; seeing her image when he is making love to a one-night stand; even coming up with the heist plan to win her back (Rachel: "You know I like money."). But her bitterness toward him remains palpable as she reproaches him repeatedly for his betrayal of her. Even though they unite to perform the heist, the viewer is never convinced of Rachel's commitment to him. And in the final scene not only does she betray him but also leaves him to take the rap for

the death of Dundee. Like other postfeminist femme fatales before her, Rachel is allowed to escape ("Now I understand the power of just walking away."), although in this case there lingers a suggestion that she may be pursued by the rest of Dundee's heist mob.

   Playing God (1997) allows Angelina Jolie to once again stretch her femme fatale muscles as the girlfriend—Claire—of a egomaniacal criminal (played with great menace by Timothy Hutton) who employs a discredited and drug-addicted doctor named Sands (David Duchovny) to "fix up" his minions when they are wounded. As a doctor who falls hard for Claire, at the risk of his own life, Sands resonates with characters portrayed by James Mason in the classic-period *Caught* (1949) and particularly *One Way Street* (1950). Robert Altman tries his hand at adapting novelist John Grisham in *The Gingerbread Man* (1998). Weak-willed lawyer Magrudger (Kenneth Branagh) falls without much thought for the "white trash" country girl who dresses in fishnets and sports tattoos. He is bamboozled by her from the beginning and pays for it in the end.

   Steve Shainberg (who would go on in 2002 to make the kinky indie hit *Secretary*) adapted Jim Thompson's novel *A Swell-Looking Babe* in 1996 and called it *Hit Me*. Elias Koteas plays with manic energy the alienated bellhop Sonny who rails out quietly at his dead-end job and then returns home to a house in disarray and a mentally retarded brother. Sonny's chance to escape

this stultifying life comes, as it often does in noir, in the form of a femme fatale. Finding a woman lying in a bathtub with slit wrists, he saves her life by bandaging her wounds and forming a bond with her. For Monique (Laure Marsac) also wishes to escape her life and her involvement with criminals now intent on pulling a heist during an illegal high stakes card game.

Sonny hides Monique out in his house where she becomes a surrogate mother to his brother, restores a bit of order to their house, as well as their lives and even saves Sonny's life during a gun battle with the criminal gang. But when the heist goes wrong and Sonny escapes with the money, he is pursued by his violent cohorts, including the cocaine-addicted, philosophical Lenny Ish (played disturbingly by Philip Baker Hall of P. T. Anderson's brilliant neo-noir *Hard Eight*). In the end Sonny loses everything, including the girl, who cannot stay with a man who can only offer her love. And so she walks off into the night, her souvenir of the Eiffel Tower (they planned to run away to Paris) clutched to her breast. Like his *Natural Born Killers*, Oliver Stone's *U Turn* (1997) showcases an hallucinatory style with flashbacks, visions, and mundane reality interwoven in this tale of an arrogant, none-too-bright hustler—Bobby (Sean Penn)—who while escaping criminal creditors (they cut off two of his fingers in a flashback) finds himself stranded in an Arizona desert town. His travails escalate exponentially when he falls under the spell of a local femme fatale—Grace (Jennifer Lopez), who takes out her anger at her rich husband/father—Jake

Opposite, *Playing Code*: Claire (Angelina Jolie) and Dr. Sands (David Duchovny).
Below, *U Turn*: Grace (Jennifer Lopez) and Bobby (Sean Penn) on the run.

(Nick Nolte)—by cuckolding him with various men. Unable to resist her plaintive "little girl" pleas or her voluptuous body (which Stone literally fetishizes in lingering shot after shot), Bobby falls into a morass of complications.

For nothing Bobby does seems to go right. Much like so many victims of circumstance and stupidity in noir (stretching all the way back to the protagonist in *Detour*), Bobby cannot see beyond his own desires and needs. After being caught in flagrante delicto with Grace by Jake (and beaten by him), he agrees to murder her for money. Then when Grace ignites him sexually on a mountainside while appealing to his sympathy by telling how Jake raped her as a child and caused her mother's death, he changes sides and agrees to murder the husband and steal his fortune. But even this "simple" act of murder is botched by Bobby. Discovered breaking and entering into the house while Jake and Grace are having sex (he calls her "daddy's girl" as he penetrates her violently), Bobby in one of his many cowardly moments agrees to kill Grace in order to save his own life. Grace puts an end to this new agreement by beating Bobby and killing Jake. She then forces Bobby to make love to her while Jake bleeds to death next to them ("Let him watch. I want him to know what he's missing.").

During their flight from town, the fugitive couple is stopped by the sheriff who is also one of Grace's lovers. He is outraged at her infidelity to him. Grace then dispatches him, pushing him over a cliff, the same cliff from which they will throw Jake's body. Unable to trust Bobby again, Grace lets him join her other lovers by pushing him over the cliff. When she realizes he has the keys to the car, she crawls down to him. The broken Bobby strangles her. The camera in an overhead shot ironically frames the bodies of Grace and her lovers scattered over the ravine. In a final desperate act Bobby drags himself up the cliff and into the car. Elated over his final success, he starts the car but the radiator hose in his car blows and he is stranded. In an overhead shot, Bobby screams and the film leaves him to his fate.

Palmetto (1998) features two femme fatales: the indomitable Gina Gershon as the domineering girlfriend of the protagonist/chump of the piece, Harry (Woody Harrelson), and Elisabeth Shue as the deceptive Rhea. Both women lead the often dense Harry around by his sexual desire, causing no little distress to the befuddled ex-reporter who finds himself involved in kidnapping. The filmmakers of *Wild Things* fill their work with so many twists as to make it a labyrinth of lies and deception typical of both classic and neo-noir. But the key characters in the movie are the two femme fatales of the title, the "wild things," who manipulate the other characters of the film, including the two male leads. The film opens on the everglades of Florida with its wildlife cavorting in the waters of the swamps, particularly centering on the alligators rising from the depths. Like these predators Kelly (Denise Richards) and Suzie (Neve Campbell) are often associated with water. There are numerous shots of the spoiled, upper-class "mean girl" Kelly dripping wet: from the hose of a car wash, from the shower, and the central soft-core lesbian sex scene in the movie between Kelly and Suzie occurs in a pool.

But what is most surprising about the movie is that the most fatale of the two femmes turns out to be the more distracted, submissive Suzie. After Kelly is murdered by her accomplice, the "dirty" cop in the central scam of the movie,

it is Suzie who plans the cop's murder by her teacher-lover and then peremp-
torily knocks the teacher overboard after he has offed the cop. In the final
scene a triumphant Suzie, who has traded her slutty goth look for a brightly
colored bikini and blond hair, sails away into the warm Caribbean waters. There
were several sequels to the successful original film. The first, *Wild Things 2*
(2004), features Susan Ward and Leila Arcieri as teen "bad girls," who "love,
cheat, and steal," as the trailer says. In *Wild Things: Diamonds in the Rough*
(2005) the bad girls become jewel thieves. In *Wild Things: Foursome* (2010)
the filmmakers up the ante by having, as the title so subtly indicates, a sexual
foursome in the movie rather than the traditional threesome.

In many interviews, actor Asia Argento credits maverick director Abel
Ferrara with giving her the confidence and encouragement to develop her persona and finally to direct her own movies. Argento first worked with Ferrara on
his 1998 film *New Rose Hotel*. Not only was Argento able to hold her own
against such powerful actors as Christopher Walken and Willem Dafoe but
Ferrara, in an attempt to support her creative growth, also allowed her to direct
several scenes in the movie. Based on a story by cyberpunk writer William
Gibson, Argento plays Sandii, a femme fatale with ambiguous motives and
mysterious roots. Fox (Christopher Walken), an eccentric industrialist/hustler,
hires Sandii after watching her sing in a nightclub where she is caressed and
fondled by several young women as she croons in a raspy voice a torch song
(immediately typing her as a femme fatale of the Dietrich variety). Fox, in collusion with his buddy X (Willem Dafoe), pays her to seduce the scientist Hiroshi

Below, *Palmetto*: Harry (Woody Harrelson) in the clutches of the conniving but
pretty-in-a-print-dress Rhea (Elisabeth Shue).

away from his wife and the Maas Corporation and into his service. However, X, who directs the operation, falls in love with Sandii. Trying to fathom this complicated, secretive woman, he falls deeper into an intense sexual relationship with her, pieces of which are seen throughout the movie repeated from various angles, reinforcing the notion that X, and through him the viewer, are now obsessed with unraveling the mystery of Sandii.

Of course, director Ferrara, famous for his love of ambiguity, never allows that. By the end of the movie, the viewer realizes that Sandii in fact controls the narrative by not allowing either the audience or the men in the film to penetrate her emotionally and intellectually. She betrays X and Fox by siding with the Maas Corporation. Fox kills himself and X retreats to a coffin-like cubicle in the New Rose Hotel where he reruns in his head images of Sandii, still trying to possess her by understanding her. The final images of her ambiguous smile after X suggests they give up the mission (in flashback) says it all and yet says nothing at all.

Night Train (2000) is an extremely low-budget movie that does manage to capture the nightmarish atmosphere of the border town of Tijuana. In addition, it features twin femme fatales. In 2001 writer/director Michael Christofer reunited with star Angelina Jolie, with whom he had collaborated on in the award-winning biopic *Gia,* to film noir novelist Cornell Woolrich's *Waltz into Darkness*. *Original Sin* adhered closely to Woolrich's concept of the perversity and sexual power of the femme fatale but also, in a typically postfeminist move, gave her control of the narrative.

The Julia/Bonnie of *Original Sin* is, like her predecessor in the novel, a sexually charged, cigar-chomping seductress who delights in her power over men (enhanced the presence of Jolie who has developed that image off and on screen). To the colonel who is courting her in the second half of the film, she is a dominatrix who makes him beg outside her door and dismisses him with a threatening wave of her cane. To her lover and criminal accomplice Billy, she indulges her sadomasochistic urges, which include blood-drinking, cutting, and rough sex. To her duped husband Luis she is "the death" of him, someone he "can't live without." The film opens on Bonnie's close-up in prison (this framing device and the twist ending are two major changes made to the novel) as she narrates the story: "This is not a love story. This is a story of love and the power it has over life...the power to heal or to destroy." When she arrives in Cuba to marry her coffee magnate, she initially takes on the more demure facade of the real Julia but soon discards that and reveals the sexually insatiable woman beneath.

After her theft of Luis' money, Bonnie returns to her life of a courtesan and card shark. When Luis tracks her down, after losing himself in the flesh of prostitutes who resembled her, she easily turns him back into her lover by placing the barrel of his gun against her partially revealed breasts. Luis collapses emotionally and physically, unable to resist her appeal: "Don't you see I can't live without you?" From that point on Luis demonstrates his willingness to love her unconditionally, although often intermingled with great angst: "If I ever lost

Opposite: nail-biting, black-cigarette-smoking Asia Argento as Sandii in *New Rose Hotel.*

Below, *Original Sin*: an early meeting in the period-accurate adaptation of Woolrich's novel, the soon-to-be fugitive couple Bonnie (Angelina Jolie) and Luis (Antonio Banderas).

you, there would be nothing left for me." He murders (or thinks he does), cheats at cards, evades the law, and even submits to her cuckolding of him with her ex-lover Billy (again an element resurrected by the filmmakers from Woolrich's novel). Like Louis in Truffaut's film he also gladly accepts death at her hands and drinks the poison: "No matter the price you cannot walk away from love."

Again like Truffaut, the filmmakers of *Original Sin* do take mercy on their fugitive couple, as opposed to Woolrich in his original story. Bonnie is sentenced to death for the murder of Billy. She escapes by seducing an innocent monk to whom she tells her story (the framing device of the movie). In the final scene she is radiant again, draped in an expensive gown and sporting pricey jewelry. She walks around a table of gamblers, pouring them drinks as she signals to Luis, using a code to indicate the hands of the other men. In a final close-up she smiles and runs her finger across her throat, signaling on one level a dangerous card hand while at the same time expressing to the audience the danger of her character and the price one must pay to be with such a woman.

Like *The Crush*, *Swimfan* (2002) posits a teenage love terrorist. The "monstrous-feminine" this time is named Madison (Erika Christensen), like "Alex" in *Fatal Attraction* a threateningly androgynous name. Although the filmmakers do try to create a certain amount of sympathy for Alex by showing her as an accomplished musician who escapes from the world through her cello ("I float out of my body...up above my music.") and by revealing the trauma she suffered when she lost her boyfriend to a coma (visualized nicely by a series of jagged jump cuts whenever a lover disappoints her in some way), she still remains at base an almost superhuman, mentally unstable "girlfriend from hell," as the tagline for the movie identifies her.

As is the pattern in these types of movies, Madison's obsession with high school swim champ Ben (Jesse Crawford) escalates rapidly. After some innocent repartee at the locker and while giving her a ride home (she appears out of nowhere in front of his car as did Adrienne in *The Crush)*, Ben takes her back to the school pool, where he demonstrates his swimming skills while she undresses and seduces him in the water. As they have sex, she says, "Tell me you love me. You don't have to mean it." And of course, like any testosterone-driven teenage boy, he agrees. Although sexually attracted to Madison, Ben finds more security and peace in the arms of his supportive and far less "exciting" girlfriend Amy (Shiri Appleby). He tries to break off the relationship, but like any modern virago Madison will have none of it. She appears at his house with flowers on his mother's birthday, makes friends with Amy, and sends nude photos of herself via email under her screen name "Swimfan85."

Ben refuses to respond and tells her in no uncertain terms that he does not love her. When she responds sadly by saying "You told me you loved me," he reminds her that it was in the throes of passion. Madison follows a much stricter code of behavior, believing that when you have sex with someone "your body makes a promise." In order to punish Ben for his perceived faithlessness and win him back, Madison begins a campaign of terror. She appears at his practice sessions and stands over him, displaying her pantyless crotch. She begins dating his best friend (whom she calls "Ben" while "making out"). When none of this works, she taints his urine sample with steroids so he will be disqualified, gets him fired from his hospital job, and attacks his mother and girl-friend—planting evidence linking Ben to the attacks. The climax of the film is extremely mechanical, reflecting the formula of these films. There is a convoluted chase in which the male protagonist confronts the murderous and powerful femme fatale several times, finally defeating her in a violent culmination (in this case she drowns in the school pool), and then returns to the arms of his girlfriend, safe from the mad love of a more threatening female presence.

In *Wicker Park* (2004) Rose Byrne gives an emotional performance as the obsessed actress Alex who admits that love leads you to do "crazy things." In this case she takes on the persona of another in pursuit of her obscure object of desire. *El Cortez* (2006) narrates the story of an ex-mental patient, Manny (Lou Diamond Phillips), who becomes involved in a gold mine heist. One of his main motivations is pleasing the seductive femme Theda (referencing the first movie vamp Theda Bara), played by Tracy Middendorf. In *Last Time Forever* (2007) a sleazy divorce lawyer gets involved with a married woman who ensnares him in her blackmailing scheme.

Many post-*Body Heat* neo-noirs feature a deadly female whose hapless victim someone manages to reverse the process. In *Derailed* (2005) a woman on a train meets and agrees to a tryst with a financially troubled executive Charles Schine. When La Roche, a gunman colluding with hotel security guard, interrupts their liaison, he begins to blackmail the would-be adulterer. Only

Rose Byrne as Alex in *Wicker Park*.

after he has been cleaned out, embezzled funds from his employer, and an ex-con who tried to help him is killed does the victim discover that he was set up. He manages to interrupt an encounter with a new victim in which all the schemers are shot and killed. In the final twist, he is convicted of embezzlement, sentenced to community service, and while conducting a class in prison reencounters his violent blackmailer who survived. The smug criminal imagines he is back in control only to discover he has been set up. In terms of genre expectations, Schine stabbing an astonished La Roche with a prison shank is the kind of reversal that Racine would have wished to visit upon Matty.

The neo-noir action film *Hitman* (2007), based on the video game of the same name, introduced to the world of neo-noir actress Olga Kurylenko as the femme fatale Nika. The unnamed "47" (Timothy Olyphant) is an accomplished assassin, who was trained (we see in opening flashbacks) in a monastery where he learns killing techniques as well as anchorite practices, turning him into a priest-like hit man, seemingly devoid of desires, including sexual ones. In an early scene he is approached by a beautiful woman in a bar. He shyly demures, to the lady's shock, and returns to his hotel room to secure his perimeter and meditate.

Below, assignation interrupted, Charles Schine (Clive Owen) and Lucinda (Jennifer Aniston) in *Derailed*. Opposite, a girl with a dragon tattoo on her face: Olga Kurylenko as Niki in *Hitman*.

Nika is, of course, the uncontrollable female catalyst that upsets this emotionally shut-down antihero's world, in more ways than one. Sent to eliminate her because, supposedly, she witnesses him assassinate the Russian leader Belicoff, 47 cannot complete the assignment once he sees her face tattooed with a small dragon, a reminder of the bar code on his own skull put there by his trainers. Instead, uncharacteristically for him, 47 becomes her protector. Nika is the mistress of Belicoff, abused by him (we see her naked and being whipped). Although she is initially distrustful of 47, she does sense his perverse attraction to her because, as she says, he cannot "kill [her] or fuck [her]." During their flight from the various government forces pursuing them, Nina relishes taunting her "savior." She walks around naked ("It's not polite to stare."), mounts him after dinner, only to be shot with a sedative by the asexual 47, and nags him for his lack of communication skills. However, as their platonic relationship develops, she opens up to him emotionally, even though he remains shut down. In the final scene he leaves her to fight on, but as a gift gives her the vineyard she had talked about owning. As she walks up the street, deed in hand, he stands above her on the roof (having just dispatched a killer sent to assassinate her) like a bald guardian angel in black.

Kurylenko's character in *Max Payne* (2008) is as femme fatalish as the one in *Hitman* but unfortunately she is killed very early in the film. The camera, often in low angle, emphasizing her stature and long legs, presents her as

seductive spider woman who attempts to seduce the vengeful cop Max Payne. She spreads her black-stockinged legs for him but he does not succumb. Instead, she is ripped apart by bullets from her mobster cohorts.

Set in Israel and dealing with human sex trafficking, *The Assassin Next Door* (2009) features Kurylenko as a prostitute/assassin named Galia, who eventually revolts against her bosses in order to get back her daughter and save the woman next door from a life of abuse and sorrow. The film draws heavily for its inspiration from Luc Besson's landmark *La Femme Nikita* (1990) in the character of Galia as well as the neo-noir feminist couple film *Thelma and Louise* in its climax in which the women take off together pursued by the mobsters. In *Deception* (2007) Michelle Williams plays the mysterious, sexually liberated "S." At first she seems simply like a high-powered executive seeking a little sexual release. But by the denouement, the audience finds out that she is an iconic neo-noir femme fatale, willing to commit murder to achieve her ends and walking away at the end, unpunished, unlike so many of the femmes of the classic period.

Dark Streets (2008) is an anomaly in noir, in that it is a musical that features several full-scale numbers in a club, as well as a wall-to-wall blues soundtrack. Set in the 1930s, the narrative is recounted in flashback by an aging EMT (Noel Arthur), who was the lead dancer at the club. With great precision director Rachel Samuels converts the streets of Los Angeles into the dark and narrow back streets of the French Quarter of New Orleans. The chiaroscuro corridors of the Quarter are lit with neon, and the historical buildings open up to reveal antique décor from various periods of its history—an art deco municipal

Below, a hit woman in femme fatale gear: Olga Kurylenko goes over a wall in fishnets as the title fgure in *The Assassin Next Door.*   Opposite, top, Michelle Williams as "S" in *Deception.* Bottom, Crystal (Bijou Phillips) and Chaz (Gabriel Mann) in the retro *Dark Streets.*

building, a bordello-like nightclub—and reflect the grandeur as well as the decadence of the Quarter. The filmmakers further enhance the noir mood by punctuating the film with periodic power blackouts, caused by the *Chinatown*-like "robber barons" of the piece, that plunge the Quarter into darkness.

The protagonist is Chaz (Gabriel Mann), a wealthy playboy and scion of the family that seeks to control the entire power industry of the state. As the film opens Chaz's father has apparently committed suicide (although we later find out he has been murdered by his own power-hungry brother). This event propels the otherwise womanizing, alcoholic Chaz into action, as he searches for the mystery surrounding his father's demise. As a further complication, chanteuse Madelaine (Izabella Miko) enters the club with her protector/servant,

a police lieutenant (Elias Koteas) who resembles Nosferatu with his shaved head, leather corset, and preternatural powers more than he does a typical noir cop. Like Rita Hayworth in the seminal noir *Gilda*, who comes to dominate the film from the first shot of her, flipping her mane of red hair, Madelaine seizes the discourse away from the weak-willed Chaz as well as his singer paramour Crystal (Bijou Phillips) with her own entry, dressed all in white, her blond locks glistening off her shoulders. Sizing up the pusillanimous Chaz immediately, she arrogantly flashes him a few seconds of thigh in order to get his attention and then proceeds to take over the spotlight of the club from the now discarded ex-junkie Crystal and to turn Chaz into her "love slave."

Like Delilah, as the narrator opines, Madelaine is not satisfied with her seduction of Chaz but uses her intelligence and sexual prowess to find the document Chaz's murderous uncle is looking for and thereby obtain control of the club itself. In a final bit of intercutting, Chaz is transported by the lieutenant to the outskirts of the Quarter and there executed, while Madelaine, now all in black and framed by a neon sign proclaiming her ownership of the club, performs a number for the new clientele of her club, including Chaz's uncle, who bows before her, kissing her hand in the final scene. Once again the femme fatale is triumphant and invulnerable in the world of modern neo-noir.

The Perfect Sleep (2010) could be called the postmodern "grandchild" of Raymond Chandler's classic *The Big Sleep* (in both novel and movie form). Although the movie is set in present-day Los Angeles, it utilizes retro locations (most extensively the Bradbury Building) as well as retro outfits and 1940s-style repartee. Chandler's cynical knight errant Marlowe has become in the hands of writer Anton Pardoe (Pardoe also plays the unnamed narrator/protagonist) a masochistic, taciturn bleeding pulp whose sole mission is, as one of the characters says sarcastically, to show his "worship" of his lost love femme Porphyria (played imperiously by Roselyn Sanchez, the sultry FBI agent on Jerry Bruckheimer's neo-noir television series *Without a Trace*) through suffering and endurance. Like a character in a Russian novel (the milieu here is not accidentally that of the Russian mob), the protagonist suffers, miraculously as he admits, assault after assault from his former relatives and friends within the mob as he attempts to save the now-married Porphyria from the patriarch of the clan, Nikolai.

After rescuing Porphyria's daughter from Nikolai, the protagonist returns to his family house to commit suicide like his mother did, pathetically trying to hoist his broken body up with his belt and then cast himself down the stairs. Porphyria enters and chides him for his cowardice. She takes the belt from him and beats him for wanting to desert her and this world. His response is to show her the metal end of the belt so that she might do a better job and fulfill his oft-stated dream—to drift into a "perfect sleep." He, of course, obeys her, encouraging her to return to her waiting husband and child while he returns the windmills in the desert (the first shots of the movie) to dream a little longer.

David Fincher's *Gone Girl* (2014) is based on the best-selling neo-noir novel of the same name by Gillian Flynn (who also penned the script). Critics

The Perfect Sleep, where a pair of retro femme fatales dominate the frames: opposite, Rosalyn Sanchez as Porphyria; below, Scarlett Chorvat as Tatiana.

have categorized Flynn's novels (*Gone Girl, Dark Places, and Sharp Objects*) as "domestic noir," complex studies of violence and twisted psychology set largely within the microcosm of family relations. *Gone Girl* takes its inspiration from the real-life Scott Peterson case, in which the disappearance of his lovely wife and his eventual conviction fed the cable scandal media for years in the early part of the millennium.

Fincher's movie hews to the book fairly closely. As in many modern and postmodern movies and novels, the narrators of the discourse are unreliable. Nick is the first narrator as we see the events following his wife Amy's disappearance from his perspective although not in voiceover. Nick is a laid-off journalist who has uprooted his wife from diverse Manhattan to the "white-bread" suburbs of Missouri. There he uses her money to open an unsuccessful bar. Through the first half of the movie and book Nick comes off as a laid-back, handsome, even likable protagonist. Still there are cracks in that persona. Underneath this calm facade is an anger that the viewer first sees when he picks up his senile father who has wandered away from a rest home. Nick exudes contempt for his father who incomprehensibly mutters about "bitches," a line Nick himself repeats when he complains about the media doyennes who are "picking away" at him on the 24-hour cable networks. The violence he is capable of is finally confirmed toward the end of the movie, after his wife has returned, and she smashes her head against a wall.

Gone Girl: right, much of the narrative is flashback, such as the library "meet cute" between Nick (Ben Affleck) and Amy (Rosamund Pike). Below, obsessed suitor Desi Collings (Neil Patrick Harris) is a search volunteer along with Nick's twin sister (Carrie Coon). Page 132, Nick meets with the investigarors and Amy's parents.

The point of view of the film changes once Amy's diary is found by the police. The events of the diary are narrated by Amy, detailing her husband's seductive courtship and then consequently the friction that develops after he loses his job. Once Nick moves them to Missouri, the division between them becomes deeper. He isolates her in a suburban track home while he goes off with a teen mistress; he also beats and verbally abuses her. And then the diary ends with a line confirming her fear for her life. Eventually Nick is arrested and then turned over the spit of scandal television.

But the brilliance of the film is that within a few cuts the audience learns that much of what the diary purported is pure fiction as we are treated to yet another narration from point of view of "Amazing" Amy" (the name her parents gave a storybook character they created, thus it is implied stealing her childhood from her) point of view. She dispassionately narrates her meticulous plan to frame her husband for her murder. She sees herself as an avenger for all the abused women (reinforced by a shot of her floating under the water in the company of other female victims—she plans to drown herself to cement her frame). Through this narration we also learn that like many women, she had altered her looks and demeanor to become what she thought her husband wanted, a blonde sexually charged beauty. When she finally returns to Nick near the end of the movie, deciding to torture him for his crimes in life rather than in death, she tells him: "I'm the cunt you married. The only time you liked yourself was when you were trying to be someone this cunt might like. I'm not a quitter, I'm that cunt…You think you'd be happy with a nice midwestern girl? No way, baby! I'm it."

Nick accepts her ultimatum as they turn the media on its head and become "reality TV" stars, with a book deal —Amy finally has reclaimed her childhood by publishing her own "Amazing Amy" book—and lucrative TV deals. In the final shot of the movie, which repeats the first shot of the movie, the audience finally understands the mysterious look in Amy's eyes as her husband wonders, "What are you thinking? What are you feeling? What have we done to each other? What will we do?"

Quasi-remakes and Vendettas

While the narrative events of both versions (1972 and 1994) of *The Getaway* are closely aligned—not surprising given that Walter Hill's adaptation of Thompson's book is the starting point for each—the subversive undertone of Peckinpah's version in 1972 is severely restricted in the remake.

Roger Donaldson, the director of the 1994 *The Getaway*, stages and edits the same action sequences in a more standard way. Although the viewer/camera rides along in the careering vehicles with the fugitive couple, the mechanics of the editing scheme have a depersonalizing effect. The screen personas of both Carols, Ali MacGraw in 1972 and Kim Basinger in 1994, "glamorize" the character, but the greatest shift in emphasis between the versions is between the proto-feminist portrayal by MacGraw and the more explicitly liberated posture of Basinger. Doc's reaction when he learns of Carol's infidelity remains understandable in a patriarchal context, but the 1994 Carol challenges this perspective more emphatically when she asks, "You'd do the same for me, wouldn't you, Doc? You'd humiliate yourself for me?" As a "1990s woman," Bassinger's Carol not only wants the biggest gun, she wants to control her own destiny. MacGraw's Carol winces when she shoots people; but she does shoot them. When Bassinger expertly plays the dumb decoy or runs interference for her husband's scam from the driver's seat, it belies her ability to drive, shoot, and even throw a punch like a man. In this sense, she is closer to Annie Laurie Starr of Joseph H. Lewis' *Gun Crazy*. The title sequence of the latter version exemplifies this.

Compared to the introduction of the MacGraw Carol as she visits Doc/McQueen in prison, the Basinger Carol is first seen at target practice. A slow-motion, extreme close-up of a finger pulling a trigger injects a note of genre awareness that verges on parody. The actors' names are superimposed as the frame widens via a zoom back to reveal the muzzle flash and recoil of the shots and a cutaway reveals tin cans jumping as they are hit. Doc and Carol are first seen in a two shot. She wears a sleeveless turtleneck under a black halter top, the lines of which mirror his shoulder holster. The first shot of her

Below, Kim Basinger and Alec Baldwin as Carol and Doc in *The Getaway* remake.

alone is as she fires a smaller-caliber handgun. She wants the .45, but a smiling Doc asserts that "It's mine." Her answer—"But I want it"—effectively summarizes the dynamics of their relationship. The associations of gunplay and sexplay develop naturally from the staging and statements ("We go together...like guns and ammunition...") of more than forty years earlier in *Gun Crazy*.

Why anyone would want to watch a virtual line for line and shot for shot remake of an earlier film is beyond us. But Wade Williams did that exactly in his 1992 remake of Edgar G. Ulmer's 1945 *Detour*. The director even went to the trouble of casting Tom Neal's son in the main part.

Barbet Schroeder's remake in 1995 of director Henry Hathaway's 1947 *Kiss of Death*, like De Niro's *Cape Fear,* revolves around the expressionistic performance of star Nicolas Cage. Playing the muscle-bound, emotionally immature psychotic Little Junior Brown, Cage makes Richard Widmark's snortling Tommy Udo from the original film seem tame in comparison. Bouncing up and down like an overgrown child, bench pressing a stripper, or spouting New Age nostrums, Cage manages to make the otherwise lackluster remake watchable. *Caught* (1996), unrelated to the classic period Ophuls film of the same name, reworks James M. Cain's story for *The Postman Always Rings Twice* and plops it down in the middle of a fish market in New Jersey. Maria Conchita Alonso

Below, neo "Tommy Udo" Junior Brown (Nicolas Cage) attacks neo "Nick-Bianco" Jimmy Kilmartin (David Caruso) in the remake of *Kiss of Death.*

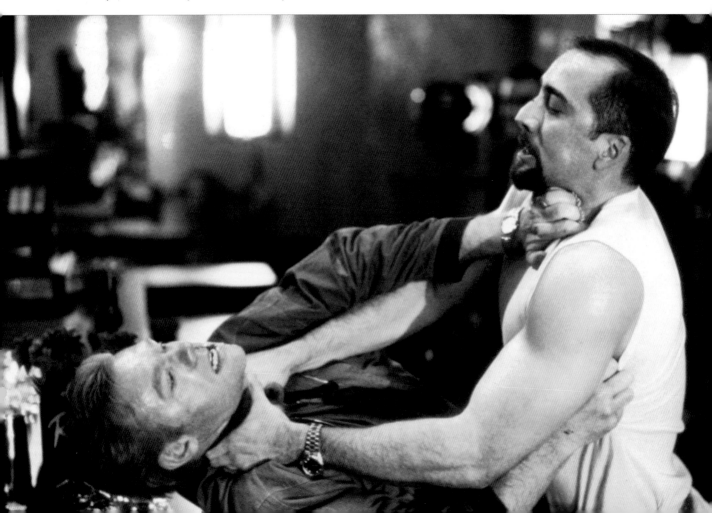

plays a repressed wife who has drifted apart from her older husband, played James Edward Olmos. In walks the drifter who ignites the wife's passion as well as the remaining complications of the story.

Diabolique (1996) is a remake of the Henri-Georges Clouzot French noir *Les Diaboliques* (1955). As the sarcastic, devious blonde, Sharon Stone assumes the role of the mistress of the cruel schoolmaster, while the ethereal Isabelle Adjani is the long-suffering wife. This dark and light pair plot and execute the murder of the schoolmaster; or at least that is what the audience initially surmises, until the surprise twist.

The central concept of Donald Westlake's novel *The Hunter* is the monomaniacal small-mindedness of its protagonist. In its first movie adaptation, *Point Blank*, the "hunter" is called Walker and portrayed by Lee Marvin, whose character unveils dark layers of a criminal underworld lurking beneath the surface of the contemporary world, killers passing for ordinary citizens in clean, well-lit homes by the beach. In the adaptation called *Payback* (1999), de facto executive producer and star Mel Gibson as Porter preserves the small-mindedness and opts as well for a minimalist performance of a well-dressed man moving through a world of back rooms and petty mobsters who mostly wear their occupations on their sleeves. As part of this transformation, the antisocial violence becomes a much grimmer, impersonal type of mayhem in a movie whose central axiom is, as the title suggests, that "payback is a bitch."

With his quest for revenge being as dogged as a samurai's, at times Porter evokes that antique ethos as when a small-time hoodlum he is questioning near a playground asks, "Are you going to kill me?" and Porter answers simply that he would not do that in front of children. While Walker discovered that betrayal was a reflex, in writer/director Helgeland's would-be postmodernist approach, treachery is replaced by honor and code, an almost military adherence to a chain of command but all of it among thieves. Certainly there are "parody" elements, most notably the Asian-American dominatrix Pearl (played by Lucy Liu) who is paid to inflict sexual pain, the ultimate expression of which is her comment when she and her cohorts drive up expecting to kill Porter: "Hubba, hubba."

"Hubba. hubba."

Terence Stamp as the title character in *The Limey*.

The desaturated colors and vaguely period (set in the Nixon era) ambience, in which suits are retro rather than costume and cars are classic rather than antique, create a mood that is at times nightmarish but mostly bring to mind a graphic novel or just-plain comic book. The aspect of *Payback* that most heavily evokes the classic period of noir is its narration. Porter's observations reverberate laconically over the soundtrack from the first scene: lying on a table in some grimy background as an overweight, inebriated "doctor" pulls bullets out of his body and blood streams down his distorted features, Porter notes that in the lawful world medical institutions must report gunshot wounds which they call GSWs as if that would insulate them from the material world of real violence and death.

While *The Limey* (1999) is not a remake, director Steven Soderbergh again takes a fairly common noir plot—a man seeks revenge for the death of a family member, as in *The Big Heat* or *Cry Vengeance* (1954)—and gives it his signature postmodern treatment. The story is fractured much like the mind of the career criminal Wilson (played with a combination of world-weary humor and suppressed grief by Terence Stamp) who is beset by feelings of guilt and rage over what he believes is the murder of his estranged daughter Jenny. Lines of dialogue and significant shots of his daughter are repeated, conveying their emotional weight in his mind. Images from the past constantly wash over him—his daughter, phone in hand, threatening to turn him in if he commits another crime; her smiling face as she frolics at the beach; his relationship with her mother (where Soderbergh cleverly inserts shots from Ken Loach's 1967 film *Poor Cow* which starred a young Terence Stamp). This subjectification of the movie draws the viewer even further into the mind of this man who rarely shows his emotions to the world, playing instead the "limey" street tough.

The casting of 1960s icon Peter Fonda as the venal record producer Terry Valentine also helps create the irony inherent in the film. His shallowness (we see him rhapsodizing incoherently about the "sixties" to his newest nubile girl-friend—the one who replaced the dead Jenny—while flossing his newly capped teeth) and lack of courage (he runs away from his problems as when he accidentally kills Jenny and leaves his "right-hand man" Avery to clean up the mess and fake a car accident) contrast with the gritty combativeness of Wilson. Wilson, ultimately, finds his redemption via Valentine, on a beach not unlike the one his daughter loved. About to kill Valentine, he remembers the image of his daughter's holding the phone and threatening to turn him in if he committed another crime. And so out of love for her, he refrains from eliminating her murderer and walks away, returning to London to find a little peace, or so he says.

Despite the desert locale of its title, *Salton Sea*'s (2002) highly stylized neo-noir tale of vengeance and redemption is mainly set in the seedy meth-infused industrial streets of Los Angeles. Mired in this carefree world of fast-talking yet directionless groups of young people, protagonist Danny Parker leads the viewer through mind-numbing detective work, aided by his amazing photographic memory, while he teeters on a fine line, often falling victim to the foggy world engulfing him. Like Frank Bigelow in *D.O.A.*, Danny is a walking dead man, if only in his heart and soul. He is forced into doing his own detective work because there is no other help in sight. As he plunges deeper into hopelessness, the only grip he has on sanity is to rummage through an old suitcase cradling his trumpet and to connect to his past as a reminder of his true identity and as a reason to stay alive.

Val Kilmer as Danny Parker play his horn by the shore of the actual Salton Sea.

Above, Det. Alex Whitlock (Eva Mendes) and ex-hubby Matt Lee (Denzel Washington), a local sheriff for whom every day if casual Friday in *Out of Time.* Opposite, who's scheming on whom, Rowena Price (Haile Berry) and Harrison Hill (Bruce Willis) in *Perfect Stranger.*

As in Orson Welles' *A Touch of Evil* (1958), the audience is deposited into a world of colorfully dangerous people, all motivated by a desire to maintain their small piece of the power pie. As director D. J. Caruso pushes deeper into Danny's pain-filled past, he creates a fever dream populated by characters from that classic noir underworld full of paranoia and moral ambiguity. At first Danny seems to be using everyone to untangle the true identities of the masked men who murdered his wife. Gradually Danny's true position is revealed as an anti-hero on the edge, uncertain of who he is, what he is doing, or how to carry out his plan. Despite cravenly witnessing his wife's death, Danny becomes a sympathetic character by default.

Red Dragon (2002) is the the second adaptation of the novel by Thomas Harris and a pallid remake of *Manhunter*, inspired mainly by the success of Anthony Hopkins' portrayal of Hannibal Lecter in *Silence of the Lambs*. It pointedly fails to measure up to either of the earlier movies.

In *Out of Time* (2003)—an unofficial third adaptation of Kenneth Fearing's novel *The Big Clock*—Denzel Washington plays Whitlock, a police chief set up while trying to perform an act of charity for an ailing mistress. Whitlock decides to clear his name while making those who tricked pay for their perfidy. *Deepwater* (2005), like so many films before, recycles the plot of Cain's *The Postman Always Rings Twice*. A drifter finds himself working for an older man with a beautiful young wife in an isolated motel. He falls for the wife and they plot their escape from the older man. *Beyond a Reasonable Doubt* (2009) has none of the moral ambiguity and subtlety of Fritz Lang's 1956 original. It is a pale imitation of one of the landmark noir films of the 1950s, a disquisition on fate as well as an attack on the American judicial system.

In *Perfect Stranger* (2007) Halle Berry as Rowena Price plots revenge against the man she believes is the killer of her friend. In order to accomplish that, she goes undercover after she suspects that her childhood friend Grace was murdered by suave executive Harrison Hill (Bruce Willis). What follows conforms to a trend toward narratives that are over-burdened with multiple twists and shocking revelations. Rowena's nerdy friend Miles (Giovanni Ribisi) provides Rowena with evidence that gets Hill prosecuted for the murder; but he knows the truth. As a convenient flashback reveals, Rowena and her mom murdered her incestuous father and buried the body in the backyard. Grace saw this and was extorting money for her silence until Rowena finally killed her, too. Miles would like his silence to be purchased with sexual favors. Rowena prefers giving him a knife blade to the chest.

Based on a purported true story of sex trafficking (the victim was eventually discredited), *Eden* (2012) presents the harrowing tale of a Korean-American teenage girl Hyune Jae (Jamie Chung), who is kidnapped and forced into prostitution by a criminal syndicate, the American branch of which operates in Nevada and is headed by a US marshal Robert Gault (Beau Bridges).

After disturbing cries in the darkness and the sound of hip hop on a car radio in the opening scenes, the film moves into a flashback to the early 1990s. Here it presents a familiar view of an immigrant family's life. Jae as well as her mother and father work diligently at their second-hand store while Hyun studies hard in order to graduate. On the surface Jae seems almost a stereotype: a shy, obedient daughter who casts her eyes downward when speaking to her parents, particularly her "tiger mother" who seems hypercritical and overprotective toward her daughter. Director Megan Girffiths and her fellow filmmakers do hint at a more rebellious spirit within Jae. She sneaks smokes with her friend and convinces her mother to let her stay to do the books of the business while planning to sneak out to a bar, where Jae, who must avoid smiling in order to hide her braces and thereby reveal her age, falls for the uniform and the gentle ways of a young firefighter.

Her would-be tryst ends in her adduction and transportation to a storage facility in the desert from which the traffickers send out girls to clients. After being drugged repeatedly and acculturated to the routine of a sex worker, Jae is given a new name by Gault. The bible-quoting marshal christens her "Eden" after the Hebrew word for "delight"—it also happens to be the name of the trailer park her family lives in. There is a scene early in the movie that captures the smooth-talking Gault killing two men who find the body of a would-be escapee, which establishes his ruthlessness. Despite his threats, Jae does try to escape

Below, Jamie Chung as Hyune Jae in *Eden*.
Opposite, serial killers, paranoia, and confinement a full menu of neo-noir afflictions are served up to Jill (Amanda Seyfried) in *Gone*.

several times. In once incident, while dressed as an Asian schoolgirl to fulfill the "yellow fever" fantasy of an older john, she bites the penis of the client and takes off into the desert, blood dripping from her mouth. All the girls wear tracking anklets, so she is quickly recaptured by Vaughan (Matt O'Leary), the crackhead overseer of the girls who forms a quasi-romantic attachment to Jae. Finally realizing that escape is not an option, Jae decides to survive the best way she can by becoming useful to the psychotic Vaughan (Gault calls him "section 8," referring to his discharge from the military as mentally unfit) while keeping an eye open for another way out. She spends a year as a factotum for Vaughan, answering phones, helping on errands, even participating in the disposal of the bodies of girls who have outlived their usefulness. Given the possibility of being sent en masse to the middle east, Jae must seize the moment. In a brutal conclusion, she laces Vaughn's crack pipe with deadly poison, cuts of her anklet, kills another captor and escapes. From a desert payphone, she calls her mother.

Released the same year as *Eden*, *Gone* immediately takes the viewer into the mind-set of a young woman, Jill (Amanda Seyfried), who is suffering from PTSD after being abducted by a serial killer. Although she escaped, Jill's mental health is severely compromised. She obsessively revisits the area of her kidnapping, a woodland park outside of Portland, Oregon, hoping to find the hole in which she was kept prisoner (the police doubt her story because they could

find no evidence). Her relationship with her recovering alcoholic sister Molly (Emily Wickersham) is strained not only by her kidnapping but by the earlier death of their parents in an accident. When she walks at night, her anxiety level increases whenever she sees a lone male figure in the shadows. In her martial arts class she beats down a male partner who makes the mistake of calling her "sweetie" and brushing her hair from her face. When Jill returns home to find her sister "gone" without warning, she moves into hyperdrive and rushes off to the police to report the "kidnapping." The police listen to what they consider her hysterical rantings (the police had her involuntarily committed to a mental hospital for six months) with expressions of exasperation. When they refuse to act, Jill decides to take matters into her own hands and the film neatly transforms into vigilante mode. Finding out that a "squirrely" neighbor had seen a lock repair company truck outside her house the night of the disappearance, Jill takes off on a crime spree of her own. She threatens the owner's son with a gun for information, lies pathologically in order to obtain leads, escapes the police (who are pursing her after they learn she has a gun) by shooting out a window screen lock in a bathroom, becomes the object of a police pursuit but finally after several change of cars finds the phone number of the man for whom she is searching.

Once contacted the killer leads Jill by phone back to the scene of her crime, the forest and the supposed location of her sister. In a particularly tense night scene Jill drives her car down an isolated forest road where there is no longer cel reception. Finding a tent with the photos of several other women he has killed, Jill approaches the hole fearfully, calling for her sister. The killer (Socratis Otto) appears out of the dark. After a struggle, Jill shoots the killer but promises not to kill him if he tells her where her sister is. Instead she shoots him repeatedly in his limbs. He tells her that his sister has been tied up under their own house all the time. Jill then takes a can of gasoline and pours it into the hole where the killer lies and then throws in his lantern. When he screams that she promised not to kill him, she answers dispassionately in true urban avenger style, "I lied."

Oldboy (2013), Spike Lee's "reimagining" of Chan-wook Park's 2003 film of the same name, outraged many of the fans of the original Korean neo-noir. For some it was a pale imitation; for others it pushed the transgressiveness of the original too far. Remaking a cult film like Park's invites controversy, so in most of his public statements Lee and his writer Mark Protosevich emphasized the point that they went back to the original manga for inspiration rather than be restricted creatively by Park's movie. Whether this is true or not is unimportant, as Lee's *Oldboy* stands on its own: a perverse tale of incest, human cruelty, and possible redemption.

From the first frames of the movie, Josh Brolin's performance as Joe Doucett projects the alienation and damaged psyche of a neo-noir protagonist. He shows up to work drunk and disorderly. He offends a potential client by coming on to the client's wife. He curses out his ex-wife who berates him for not showing up for their young daughter's birthday. He is, in short, a disreputable human being. Consequently when he is, without explanation, kidnapped and imprisoned in a small room, one finds it hard to feel sympathy for him. Only after a decade of imprisonment and drunken self-pity (his captors supply him with liquor) does Joe's character change, thereby allowing a shift in the audience's sympathy. After his captors show him footage of his wife being murdered and his daughter Mia adopted by a "caring" family. Joe finally begins regenerating himself. He stops drinking, he works out while watching martial arts movies and exercise shows on the cable feed supplied in his makeshift prison. He writes heartfelt letters to his daughter, asking her forgiveness. And then one day he finds himself free, deposited in a trunk in an open field, events consistent with the Kafka-esque undertone. And like many of the characters in Kafka's work, Joe finds himself up against forces much more cunning and powerful than he. A do-gooder ex-addict named Marie (Elizabeth Olsen) latches onto him as her personal "redemption project" and assists him in solving the puzzle of why he was imprisoned and who is responsible. They become lovers in a particularly passionate scene. But, of course, the guilty party is ultimately Joe himself. Through a series of bloody encounters (including a macabre, almost humorous one with a Mohawk-sporting Samuel L. Jackson as his jailer) he is led back to the shocking truth, which resonates on so many levels.

The film's resolution is a disturbing net of incest and murder that one-ups Park's movie. In a series of flashbacks in which the characters narrating the

Below, *Oldboy*: Joe Doucett (Josh Brolin) prepares for some serious conversation with the trussed-up Chaney (Samuel L. Jackson).

events enter into the scenes of the past, the audience learns that Joe's tormentor—Adrian (Sharlto Copley)—was involved in an incestuous family triangle involving his father and sister. Ultimately Adrian reveals that the daughter Joe had idealized during all the time imprisoned was not the one seen in videos but is actually, his lover. Anguished by this discovery of his incest, Joe begs for death; but instead Adrian shoots himself, leaving Joe to face the existential horror of his actions. In the end, Joe is locked up again. He can only smile enigmatically as the camera cuts to his daughter/lover Marie, who remains unaware of their familial relationship and drives off into the horizon with a toy duck on her dashboard as a memento of her time with Joe.

Although originally to be directed by Martin Scorsese, the actual remake of *The Gambler* (2014) is marginally neo-noir. While the stakes are literally higher, mostly because of inflation in the real world, the situation for the new "Axel Freed," Jim Bennett (Mark Wahlberg), is much the same. But this is no primordial act after Bennett manages to combine fixing a game and the single spin of a roulette wheel to extricate himself completely. This character, rather, sprints across town to celebrate with his student girlfriend in a manner that suggest his next stop will be a Gambler's Anonymous meeting.

A Newer Kind of Neo-Noir

By 1995, writers and directors of neo-noir had shifted emphasis from remaking or re-creating the twisted narratives and relationships of the classic period to a deeper re-imagining of that original noir ethos with an emphasis on an angst that anticipated the end of a millennium. In many ways, Quentin Tarantino epitomizes the pastiche approach to postmodern filmmaking, noir and otherwise. while his better-known and unrelentingly self-conscious *Pulp Fiction* (1994) suffers dramatically from his pointed deconstruction and endistancing that made it a critical favorite but marginal neo-noir. The hit men, petty thieves, addicts, gangsters, and, yes, an aging boxer who accepts a bribe, then won't take a dive—so many types from the classic period that it's hard to keep track. They became part of a stylized dance through a time-traveling, achronological plot line that Tarantino would choreograph even more extremely in *Kill Bill* parts 1 and 2, where switchblades grow into samurai swords and revenge is first referred to as "best served cold." By then neo-noir and its particularly genre expectation have been left far behind. *Reservoir Dogs* much more effectively embraces the classic noir style and narrative, starting with the casting of classic period B-budget icon Lawrence Tierney as Cabot.

Forest Whitaker is again a hit man in *Ghost Dog: The Way of the Samurai* (1999) for director Jim Jarmusch, who grafts the code of the Japanese samurai onto a modern American urban setting represented by hip-hop anti-hero "Ghost Dog." Whitaker's melancholic cadence again defies viewer expectation. The "Ghost Dog" is a hired killer (or, as he prefers, "retainer") for the mob wise guy Louie who saved his life as a teen. He walks through the streets of the inner city to the beat of his own drummer. With his braided hair, black hoodie, and RZA rap music, he is a self-contained vision of integrity and power, respected by all elements within the ghetto—from violent gangs to Black consciousness advocates. "Ghost Dog" has managed to conform on his existence to the tenets of *bushido* or "the way of the warrior," which he learned from the *Hagakure,* an traditional book of wisdom designed for medieval samurai. Bits of *kōan*-like insight from the book appear periodically on the screen with the protagonist's voice reading them.

On a roof with carrier pigeons—the only medthod by which he communicates with his boss to the comic dismay of the other hoods—"Ghost Dog" meditates in front of his makeshift altar and practices martial arts with both swords and guns. In order to maintain the purity of hiss way, he has isolated himself from others. He does befriend a young girl, Pearline (Camille Winbush), with whom he shares a love of books, and a French-speaking Haitian ice-cream vendor with whom he shares no common verbal language. When a hit goes awry, the semi-comic Italian mob comes after him. Although filled with overweight, aging wise guys who can hardly climb stairs, they do destroy his lair, kill his pigeons, and shoot innocent bystanders whom they think might be him. In order to protect himself as well as his "streets," the hit man eliminates the entire mob, leaving only his boss Louie untouched. In the final scene he gives his money to the illegal alien Haitian and his books to Pearline and goes out, gun unloaded—for a samurai cannot kill his "lord" no matter the reason—to face Louie. His perplexed boss outdraws "Ghost Dog" in a Western-style showdown and, in a final irony, kills the man whose life he once saved.

Forest Whitaker at work as the titled assassin in *Ghost Dog.*

Above, *The Usual Suspects*: Keaton (Garbiel Byrne, right) watches as McManus (Steve Baldwin) lines up a head shot on Kobayashi (Pete Postelthwaite).

Opposite, the deadly couple Violet (Jennifer Tilly) and Corky (Gina Gershon) in *Bound*.

The Usual Suspects (1995), director Bryan Singer's breakout movie, carries over a noir theme that reappears in most of Singer's other movies (*Apt Pupil, X-Men, Valkyrie,* etc.)—the pervasiveness of evil and corruption, even in the most innocuous of settings or within the most ordinary of people. And of course no one could be more innocuous, on the surface at least, than the mass murderer and criminal kingpin Keyser Soze. As played by Kevin Spacey, Soze is bland and unassuming in appearance and affect. That is why it is so easy for him to blend into his surroundings, becoming for the purpose of this story a physically handicapped minor criminal. He epitomizes what the philosopher Hannah Arendt called "the banality of evil."

Consequently, when Soze (aka "Verbal") is rounded up for questioning in an early scene of the flashback, he goes almost unnoticed in a jail cell filled with flamboyant master criminals. He sits quietly against the wall and only appears in the shot after a camera pan reveals him when one of the criminals derides him. But that chameleon quality is Soze's genius. He not only manipulates all the men in that cell, without their or the viewers knowing it, so that they will give their lives in a final caper that eliminates Soze's betrayer, but he also controls the narrative of the movie itself. He tells his tale, as "Verbal," to a federal agent. When it is finally revealed at the end of the movie that Soze and "Verbal" are one and the same, the audience is left to question how much of the narrative was true and how much of it was the creation of his criminal psyche.

Dual-Personality Directing

The Wachowskis, who brought their noir sensibilities to their epic multi-part sci-fi film *The Matrix* three years later, repackage a number of themes, archetypes, and motifs from such classic-noir heist films as *Criss Cross* and *The Asphalt Jungle* in their first neo-noir movie *Bound* (1996). Trust, betrayal, corruption, and *amour fou*, all noir staples, inform this tale of a criminal couple in love who decide to steal mob money and live happily ever after. The significant difference, however, between this heist film and its predecessors is simply that the couple consists of two women in what may be the first mainstream lesbian noir.

Corky, as played with a brooding intensity by a "butch" Gina Gershon, is a traditional noir protagonist—a cynical ex-con who against her better judgment falls for a slinky, goth Violet (Jennifer Tilly in a performance laced with kink and sexuality), the "moll" of mob launderer Caesar (Joe Pantoliano). As in most heist films, the primary theme is trust and its constant companion—betrayal. Corky has been burned before, by a former girlfriend, and so is gun shy when Violet turns on the femme fatale sex appeal to seduce and then involve Corky in her plan to free herself from the bondage (hence the title) imposed by Caesar. Like Violet, Corky, too, has endured her own bondage. Her five years in prison for theft is the same amount of time Violet has spent with Caesar, linking them even further.

In order to further reify this theme of bondage, the filmmakers have Caesar tie up both women toward the end of the film and verbally abuse them by calling them "dykes." In fact, Caesar seems more outraged by the fact that they are lovers than by the reality that they have stolen mob money and made him their patsy. Symbolically, it is crucial that the women free themselves from

the ropes as they free themselves of Caesar's oppression. It is Violet who takes the lead, demonstrating her fidelity to Corky by shooting Caesar to death. In the last sequence, as Tom Jones sings on the soundtrack "She's a lady," Corky and Violet climb into their new truck and join hands as they take off for their "happy ever after"

Since their debut film *Blood Simple* the brother Joel and Ethan Coen have maintained an ongoing if somewhat tortuous relationship with noir. There are traces of it in their gangster pastiche *Miller's Crossing*, faux Hollywood gothic *Barton Fink* (1991), and grisly crime comedies *Raising Arizona* (1987) and the breakthrough *Fargo* (1996). Even *The Big Lebowski* (1998) with its narrative core of mistaken identity throws a dark cloak around its humorously ill-fated protagonist. In terms of conscious nods to the classic period, few neo-noir efforts surpass *The Man Who Wasn't There* (2001), their unwieldy black-and-white mélange of Cain and Woolrich with a hard-boiled kitchen sink thrown in.

While it may not be far in terms of discordant monikers from Nirdlinger—the name lifted directly from Cain's *Double Indemnity* that adorns the department store in *The Man Who Wasn't There*—to the pitiless Anton Chigurh, the characters in *No Country for Old Men* (2007) are physically and figuratively in another world. Certainly it was helpful for admirers of Peckinpah, such as the Coens, to have Cormac McCarthy's novel as a neo-noir template. Reverential in their adaptation, the Coens extracted the Jim Thompson-esque essence from the novel and more than thirty-five years after *The Getaway* used its narrative violence to choreograph deadly encounters in the Peckinpah style. Although there are many parallels between *The Getaway* and *No Country for Old Men*, from their simple satchels of money to deadly encounters in Texas hotels near the Mexican border, while McCarthy's characters are often trying to escape across that border and can be as nasty, garrulous, and otherwise unattractive as any of Thompson's or Peckinpah's, as given to offhand and extreme violence,

Blood Simple.

Javier Bardem as the relentless and socio-pathic hitman Anton Chigurh in *No Country for Old Men*.

Above, *The Man Who Wasn't There*: James Gandolfini as the shadowy store owner Nidlinger, with a name from Cain but a physical presence like Gutman's in *Maltese Falcon*.

the focus of *No Country for Old Men* novel and film is on a more sympathetic if hapless character. Llewellyn Moss is not cut from quite the same cloth as Thompson's Lou Ford in *The Killer inside Me*, even though Chigurh could be taken as the killer inside the contemplative Sheriff Bell. Whereas Thompson's Doc McCoy in *The Getaway* was a postromantic criminal trying to reconcile the fact that his wife's sacrifice for him required her infidelity, Moss is just a man trying to get away to a better life with his faithful wife.

Nor is Moss a typical character for the Coens. While there may be resonances to a figure like McDunnogh in *Raising Arizona*, there is none of the quirkiness that is the sine qua non of their oeuvre. The intricate and ultimately imprudent murder schemes of Joe Wilmot, the small time projectionist in Thompson's novel *Nothing More than Murder*, and Ed Crane, the seemingly mild-manned barber in the Coens' original screenplay for *The Man Who Wasn't There*, are both about cheating wives, anger at the world's indifference, and the killer that can be inside almost anyone. Whereas Thompson's naturalism was a perfect fit for Peckinpah, the Coens' vision of ordinary people confronting twisted killers has tended towards grim irony and little more. *Blood Simple* was just that, while being stylistically akin to the classic period and Hitchcock's cinematic essay on how hard it is to kill in *Torn Curtain* (1966). In a new millennium and in a semi-retro-noir set in 1980 West Texas, just a few years and a few miles removed from the Thompson/Walter Hill/Peckinpah *The Getaway*, the Coens have let Cormac McCarthy's characters override their typical inclinations. In doing so, they have resurrected their neo-noir credentials and created a tableau of darkness deep in the heart of Texas that captures the vision Thompson and McCarthy share.

Like the Coen brothers Scott McGehee and David Siegel, the directing duo behind *Suture* (1993) and *The Deep End* (2001), are hyper-aware of the heritage of noir. The ironies of the black-and-white *Suture*, like the stolen identity movie *The Hollow Triumph* or various amnesia narratives of the classic period, create a layer of quasi-existential angst. Even more striking in this perceptual experiment is the literal blindness, color and otherwise, of its characters who do not share the audience's inescapable perspective, which has an African-American actor being mistaken for his half brother portrayed by a white man. Among many homages are the explicit reference to Keyes' lecture on suicide in *Double Indemnity*, delivered in *Suture* by a police detective: "I've see a lot of suicides: poison, gas, narcotics, leaping suicides, suicides with guns, handguns, rifles, shotguns...but never have I seen a suicide with a self-activated, remote-control car bomb."

Their next movie, *The Deep End*, was is a remake of Max Ophuls' 1949 *The Reckless Moment*. The films use the same story by Elisabeth Sanxay Holding as their source, and both explore a common noir theme: the unpredictable moment in which a reckless act can allow the dark underworld of violence, desire, and corruption into the upper world of middle-class normality as was also pointedly developed in Andre De Toth's *Pitfall* (1948). Siegel and McGehee carefully establish the milieu of Margaret Hall: her spacious lakeside home isolated from the congested city of Reno; her life of carpools, jogging, and errands; her loneliness as she tries to contact her absent husband (he is in the navy). Margaret is in fact a model housewife, juggling her children's schedules, taking out the trash, keeping her home immaculate.

So, it is not such a stretch to believe that when the underworld, represented by her son's hustler boyfriend, invades this domestic security; and when the boyfriend falls to his death, Margaret takes care of the sticky situation with the much efficiency she applies to running her household. She sinks his body in the lake with an anchor, drives his car back into the city, then cleans up blood and fingerprints with hardly missing a beat. Of course, the problem in noir is

Below, a dual-personality study in self-conscious black-and-white: the half brothers (Dennis Haysbert) and (Michael Harris) in *Suture.*

Stylized visualizations of a woman with a problem: above, Tilda Swinton as the anguished Margaret tensed against a field of red in *The Deep End.*

Opposite, Joan Bennett as Lucia Harper, posed in a spotlight adjacent to with an oddly positioned branch in the Max Ophul's original *The Reckless Moment.*

that once you have touched that underworld it is hard to disentangle yourself from it, and the filmmakers use the motif of water to convey the feeling of losing control, of being overwhelmed.

Margaret's relationship with the compassionate blackmailer Al becomes the core of the remainder of the film. In the world of neo-noir brief encounters can easily turn into erotic fixations and even full-blown obsessions. And that is the case here. To Margaret, Al is a man who cares for her. She begins dressing up for their clandestine meetings, where Al listens patiently to her problems, even when she is berating him. Unlike her absent husband, it is the handsome and dangerous Al, who rescues her. He also resembles the man who seduced her son. For Al, Margaret represents an unknown world, and his envy of her situation is conveyed as he wanders through her house, sadly touching photos of her family members and caressing the furniture. His final sacrifice, dying for her on the road while sending her back to her family, has several layers of bittersweet irony. As she tries to save him, their faces briefly touch like lovers'. In the final shot, Margaret lies on her bed weeping as the camera tracks slowly into her face. She opens her eyes wide to reveal her grief and despair. She is now back to her insular home, safe from the underworld. But at what price? Is this even a world she wants anymore, a world of routine, a world bereft of passion and excitement, a "safe" world? In neo-noir it is difficulty to come back to that, after you've gone off the "deep end."

Twins Jonas and Josh Pate, directed *Deceiver* (1997) from their own script. Detectives who have themselves involved been involved with marginal if not outrightly corrupt behavior, investigate the contemporary, Black Dahlia-esque murder of the a prostitute. Ultimately an overlay of visual style (including frequent POVs) fail to stitch the self-conscious red herrings and narrative coincidences together. The Pates wrote the less stylish but still intense caper/falsely accused/revenge story *The Take* (2007), in which an armored-car driver, who is robbed, left for dead and suffers from memory loss, is accused of being complicit and must find the real culprits on his own.

Filmmakers Diane Doniol-Valcroze and Arthur Flam co-wrote and directed the B-budget on a the docu-neo-noir *Kill by Inches* (1999), a descent into madness built around a crazed young killer. They also co-wrote *Hit and Run* (2009), a promising but poorly realized (by someone else) about dual victims of circumstance. In *Random Acts of Violence* (1999, aka *Fast Lane*) the micro-budget co-directors used limited means in an attempt to re-imagine early Tarantino but accomplished little beyond an ultraviolent conclusion that piles up countless bodies. In the dual-personality low-budget *Another Man's Son* (2009), a corrupt official solicits help from a subordinate to cover-up a death, a very low-rent riff on *No Way Out* and *Absolute Power* (1997).

Auteurist Riffs

David Mamet returned to neo-noir with the quirky *The Spanish Prisoner* (1997), which like *House of Games* revolves around a long con. In fact, the title, entirely unrelated to the plot, refers to a scam still in play today in which a wealthy person or warehoused funds a being held in a foreign country. In this instance, the compulsive behavior of the con men that underlaid the neo-noir underworld of *House of Games* is masked and its psychological ironies give way to a plot that hinges on the set-up and the sucker. Prolific and preeminent Western-movie auteur Clint Eastwood entered the genre early with his first feature as director *Play Misty for Me.* Inspired by his collabortions across genres with Don Siegel, Eastwood quickly found his own voice and cast himself as an emotionally shallow and hedonistic disc jockey who underestimates the fury of a scorned female fan whom he discards after a one-night stand. After three decades as a director, Eastwood did not need to appear in *Mystic River* (2003) a neo-riff on mistrust, betrayal, and revenge in the small-time criminal underworld of Boston. This movie's detective is the least violent and most reflective of its principal characters, a far cry from Dirty Harry's speak softly and carry a big gun approach.

Many of the self-conscious movies produced during the evolution of neo-noir were more retrograde than retro, such as the *Snake Eyes* (1998), with more incongrous twists that its titular reptile, and the overheated *Carlito's Way* (1993), both from derivative specialist Brian De Palma. Of course, nothing could be as fevered as a kingpin's rise and fall in De Palma's gangster remake of

Scarface (1983). From its very title to its opening clip from *Double Indemnity*, there is nothing subtle about the source code for De Palma's *Femme Fatale* (2002), in which comic-book characters are put through predictable neo-noir paces. In a final, distorted homage to the marginal plot devices in such classic-period staples as *Woman in the Window* (1944) much of what happens in this movie turns out to be a reverie.

Perhaps the most egregious example of self-consciousness gone awry come from John Frankenheimer in *Reindeer Games* (2000), a pastiche of convoluted caper planning and a doubly deceptive femme fatale, which suffers from disinterested performances and absurd plot twists. The unwitting self-parody is quite far removed the trenchant humor of *The Manchurian Candidate.* In 2003, William Friedkin moved from the quasi-rogue cops of *French Connection* to the rogue operative in *The Hunted*, where a Rambo-like run-amok sustains a killing spree until he is tracked down by his old mentor.

P. T. Anderson's *Hard Eight* (1996) is anchored by the performance of Philip Baker Hall as the "old hood" Sydney. Although not yet known by the viewer, Sydney is searching for redemption—a constant theme in classic noir as well as neo-noir—when he picks up the disheveled and dirty John (John C. Reilly) in a café near the Las Vegas airport. The younger man is the down-and-out son of someone Sydney murdered. Acting like "St. Francis," which is John's initial sarcastic epithet for him, Sydney begins a mentoring process that covers how to act (no profanities except when under stress), dress (suit and tie always), and "game" the casinos (only on a small, safe scale).

Title cards are used to indicate the passage of time, during which John has become a duplicate of Sydney. What Sydney cannot teach John is common sense or strength of will; and when he marries the hooker/waitress Clementine (Gwyneth Paltrow), whom Sydney is also trying to rehabilitate, John's life

Opposite, Joe Ross (Campbell Scott, left) and Jimmy Dell (Steve Martin) in *The Spanish Prisoner.*

Below, the camera focus is on the reflections of Sydney (Philip Hoffman) and John (John C. Reilly) in *Hard Eight.*

Hard Eight:
Gwyneth Paltrow
as Clementine.

begins to disintegrate. After they handcuff and beat a john who tries to stiff Clementine—who has not given up "hooking" even after her marriage—into unconsciousness, a frightened and tearful John calls his surrogate father for help. Sydney cleans up the mess and helps the couple escape. Just as the repercussions from the incident seem to have subsided, the hustler Jimmy (Samuel L. Jackson) tries to blackmail Sydney, who is disdainful of anyone that represents a new breed of profane and careless hoods. Jimmy does know from his connections back east that Sydney killed John's father and threatens to reveal this. Unwilling to let John become estranged like his biological children, Sydney breaks into Jimmy's place and calmly pumps the cheap gangster full of lead.

In both *Lost Highway* (1997) and his later neo-noir *Mulholland Drive* (2001) David Lynch takes the audience into the mind of a psychotic, blending fantasy and reality with overlapping, sometimes ill-defined narratives folds. *Lost Highway* is a homage to Robert Aldrich's *Kiss Me Deadly* (1955), with titles superimposed over a highway at night. Rather than 1955's Nat "King" Cole crooning, "I'd rather have the blues than what I've got," the source music on the car radio is David Bowie singing "I'm Deranged." The movie segues to the moderne Hollywood Hills house of saxophonist Fred Madison (Bill Pullman) and his wife Renee, who is played in arch femme-fatale style by Patricia Arquette, as her auburn wig and 1940s-style clothes create a cross between Rita Hayworth in *Gilda*—Lynch also uses Hayworth as his model for the amnesiac "Rita" character in *Mulholland Drive*—and Barbara Stanwyck in *Double*

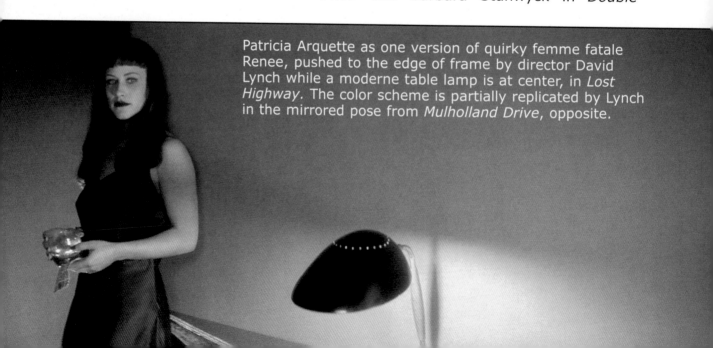

Patricia Arquette as one version of quirky femme fatale Renee, pushed to the edge of frame by director David Lynch while a moderne table lamp is at center, in *Lost Highway*. The color scheme is partially replicated by Lynch in the mirrored pose from *Mulholland Drive*, opposite.

Indemnity. Madison can never quite read his wife, who keeps a cool distance from him and is mysterious about her shady past. As his jealousy grows, so does his psychosis, best objectified by the presence of the demonic "Mystery Man." Played grotesquely with pasty-face makeup and cheaply dyed black hair by Robert Blake, this personnage seems to have privileged access to not only Madison's house but his mind as well.

After Madison is convicted of murdering his wife, his psychosis moves into overdrive. He "reincarnates" himself in the body of the young mechanic Dayton. In this alternate universe, his wife is also "reincarnated," this time in the form of Alice, also played by Arquette with a blond wig à la Stanwyck in *Double Indemnity*, a far more sexually liberated doppelgänger of his wife, who keeps multiple lovers, including himself, and presses him into service in her liberation from her mobster boyfriend. It is clear that Lynch uses twins and mirros as a conscious evocation of the ethos of noir, where multiple identities are a staple. The scene where Dayton and Alice make love in the Mojave Desert, as the red sands swirl around them and the lights of the car overexpose their bodies, is the climactic moment for Madison as he again tries to possess his wife, who tells him in no uncertain terms that he can never really have her. Without her, there is nothing left for Madison, now back in his original body, and so he once again sinks into his mind, visualized in the final scene by his screaming face altered digitally to resemble Munch's painting *The Scream* as he races down the highway, police in pursuit.

Present-day Hollywood in the final stages of decay is the setting for Lynch's *Mulholland Drive*. It is the most caustic attack on the mores of Hollywood since Nathaniel West's bitter narrative *The Day of the Locust*. As in West's novel, director Lynch turns Hollywood into a surreal nightmare of greed, lust, betrayal, jealousy, and hypocrisy, and of course noir dystopia.

Above, a more painterly composition with profiles cubistically arrayed: "Rita" (Laura Harring)and Diane/"Betty" (Naomi Watts) in *Mulholland Drive*.

The film is the story of struggling actress Diane Selwyn (Naomi Watts) who, like the protagonists in other Lynch films such as *Lost Highway*, leads a schizophrenic life: half-real, half-dream. In the early part of the movie the audience sees Diane (in her dream form "Betty") arriving at LAX from the "heartland." She is full of Middle American aspirations and naïveté: "Of course I'd rather be known as a great actress than a movie star. But, you know, sometimes people end up being both. So that is, I guess you'd say, sort of why I came here."

Staying in her aunt's Spanish stucco apartment, "Betty" becomes involved with a classic femme fatale—"Rita," who has been in an accident on Mulholland Drive and wandered in a daze into the courtyard apartment of "Betty's" aunt. "Rita" is clearly the reincarnation of Rita Hayworth in *Gilda*, a poster for which she sees before assuming the name of "Rita" (she suffers from amnesia). Her sultry looks and voluptuous figure, as incarnated by actress Laura Harring, are irresistible to the innocent "Betty," and so they become lovers. In the dream form of this relationship, the love is as tender as in any pulp romantic novel. "Betty" then takes the lead as she assists her amnesiac lover in her search for her true identity.

But when the film relocates from dream life to Diane's real life in the last part of the movie, the audience realizes that "Rita," whose real name is Camilla, is the actually the dominant one. Camilla taunts her ex-lover Diane with her new fiancé, the director Adam Kesher, as well as other female lovers at a party. Diane retreats again into her dream world, which is much more comforting, as the two lovers, like girlfriends in a Nancy Drew mystery, go hunting for the "key," literally and figuratively in this case, to the crime seen at the beginning of the movie, and in the process become inseparable.

There Are Still Victims of Circumstance—Welcome to My Nightmare

If any theme could be said to have proliferated as neo-noir evolved, it would have be the victims of circumstance. Dozens of titles from the mid-1990s to present have explored every imaginable (at least, until now) aspect of fate pointing the finger as it did at Al Roberts in the classic-period *Detour*. Fortunately most of these movies are more inventive than that remake of Ulmer's paean to mischance. There are plenty of falsely accused, a smattering of amnesiacs, a spate of conspiracy theorists, even more kidnap victims, a whistleblower or two, and even some evil stepfathers, so that even the sub-genres number in double figures. Unfortunately the existential promise of a title like *As Good As Dead* (2010), in which a wrong man is abducted by cultists seeking revenge, is not always realized.

In *Blink* (1994) and *Enough* (2002), *Thunderheart*'s director Michael Apted explores the woman-in-peril movie. Although the latter might more properly be classed as a case of love with the improper stranger, both have strong female protagonists determined to overcome a stalker. In that it also has a slightly obsessed detective and a victim uncertain as to whether or not her newly restored sight is playing tricks on her, *Blink* has echoes of *Laura*. Since the stalker in *Enough* is a smug and violent ex-husband, the narrative follows a more predictable and uninspired course. *Copycat* (1995) has two female protagonists, the academic who was previously attacked a serial killer and is now in the sights of a copycat and the police inspector assigned to her case. In a tepid finale that questions the inspector's competence and plays off the victim's trauma-induced agoraphobia, the copycat is revealed to have been coached by the original, who already has a new protégé.

Above, Morgan Freeman, in his first appearance as FBI psychiatrist Alex Cross, ponders a victim display in *Kiss the Girls*.

Kiss the Girls (1997) is one of several adaptations of the "Alex Cross" novels of James Patterson, with another serial predator, another series of female victims, and more collaborating killers—this time across the country—but with a forensic psychiatrist (the title character portrayed by Morgan Freeman) and a victim who escaped teaming to solve the crime. In a predictable turn the East Coast killer turns out to be local cop. Clearly dilemmas such as being stalked by a serial killer or taken hostage are not to be taken lightly. What tinges them with noir is when the unforeseen becomes inescapable peril, as in *P2*, a variant on the *Duel* dynamic, in which a woman trapped in the a level of a parking garage that gives the movie its title, is repeatedly cornered in an everyday location by a deranged assailant.

In a more traditional wrong-place, wrong-time mode are *Freeway* (1995), another cop and civilian/witness teaming, and *Things to Do in Denver When You're Dead* (1995), the first feature of "Alex Cross" director Gary Fleder, in which a group of Tarantino-esque, exotically named, and somewhat inept local hoods botch an assignment from a local kingpin. Although initially spared from retribution by the serio-comic hit man Mr. Shhh (Steve Buscemi), Jimmy Tosnia (Andy Garcia), whose debt put the fateful events in motion, decides to even the score. Like Jimmy, the money-troubled nightclub manager (Lorenzo Lamas) in the low-budget *Undercurrent* (1998) agrees to perform services to retire the debt. Here that plot becomes mostly an excuse for Lamas to remove his shirt.

The tragic ironies of *House of Sand and Fog* (2003) are more solidly in the noir mode. After losing her home due to a bureaucratic error, Kathy Nicolo

Above, Lucinda (Fairuza Balk) and the doomed Jimmy (Andy Garcia) in *Things to Do in Denver When You're Dead*.   Below, the dispossessed Kathy Nicolo (Jennifer Connelly) in *The House of Sand and Fog*.

(Jennifer Connelly) tries to convince the ex-army officer from Iran (Ben Kingsley) to do the right thing. When that fails, rather than sue, she goes femme fatale on the sheriff who evicted her and convinces him to bully the new owner. That, too, fails, but her botched suicide in their driveway does elicit some sympathy. Of course, mischance brings down all involved: the deputy is arrested: the family son is killed which prompts the father and mother to self-immolation. "Lucky" Kathy only loses her house.

As in the classic period, 21st-century noir is also rife with memory troubles and outright amnesiacs. Christopher Nolan's neo-noir breakthrough film *Memento* (2000) tells its non-linear story of a man with short-term amnesia searching for the supposed murderers of his wife. As Leonard (Guy Pearce) cannot be sure of any of his memories, he compulsively writes notes and tattoos his body with messages so he will remember them when he awakes. In this manner Nolan subjectifies this movie as do such classic noirs as *The Lady in the Lake* (1947) and *Dark Passage*. This way, the audience is never allowed out of the point of view of the main character, casting doubt as to how reliable the narrating character is, as the viewer has no outside corroboration against which to measure his facts.

Released the same year *Pilgrim,* (also known as *Inferno*) opens as Jack (Ray Liotta) regains his senses in a southwestern desert but only remembers he had some money, in search of which nasty types soon turn up. Not to be outdone, the protagonist of the ultra-micro-budget *Silent Voyeur* (2005) comes to naked in the middle of the everglades and conflicting *Rashomon*-like flashbacks fail to clarify how he got there. With a budget a thousand times greater, *Unknown* (2011) can incorporate some pricier locations, name actors, and less inventive twists from the same base line of "I forget I was a criminal." There are also noir tinges in *Angel Eyes* (2002) and *The Forgotten* (2004) but the closest to neo alternates to Woolrich's *Black Curtain* novel and film are the British book and movie *Before I Go to Sleep* (2014).

Even more popular as a neo-noir theme is hostage taking. The roadside abduction sub-set is best known from *The Hitcher* (1986, remade 2007) and *Hitcher II: I've Been Waiting* (2003), all of which reiterate the common sense of 1953's *The Hitch-hiker*: give rides to strangers at your peril, as they may be packing more than a duffel. Still the somewhat prototypically named and psychotic "John Ryder" in both *The Hitcher*s is more an incarnation of the nameless and faceless antagonist in the "road horror" imagined by Richard Matheson

in his story and script for *Duel* (1971). Although this "Jack," a villain without a surname in *Hitcher II*, seems more flesh and blood, the credibility of that narrative is most tested by the fact that the doomed Jim Halsey (reprised by C. Thomas Howell) happens to encounter another roadside maniac. While unmistakably micro-budget *The Hitchhiker*, which was meant to ride the 2007 coattails of the much better-funded *Hitcher* remake, is in some ways more noir, like 1947's *The Devil Thumbs a Ride* on acid. Jack Carter (Jeff Denton) is as craven as all the other hitchhikers and abducts a mini-harem of women, some of whom he simply kills; one of them becomes a romantic love object. That Melinda (Sarah Lieving) survives is remarkable; that a wounded Jack recovers, escapes custody, and tracks her down is hard to believe; but that Melinda puts one bullet in his gut then another in his face is actually noir.

Opposite, the protagonist of *Memento* (Guy Pierce) uses Polaroids to help his faulty memory. Above, the original *Hitcher*, Jim Halsey (C. Thomas Howell), momentarily gets the drop on the original antagonist (Rutger Hauer). Below, in the remake Sean Bean menaces Grace (Sophia Bush) who cowers behind bulletproof glass.

Above, professional assassin Vincent (Tom Cruise, left) pursues adbucted cab driver Nax (Jamie Foxx) into the subway in *Collateral*.

Michael Mann's *Collateral* (2004) blends and alters narrative dynamics from *Taxi Driver* and *The Hitchers* in that cabbie Max Durocher (Jamie Foxx) is actively looking for strangers to whom he may offer rides. When a sharply dressed man named Vincent hails his vehicle, Max ignores the rules and accepts an offer of $600 to drive him for the entire night. As with many noir figures, this small transgression is enough to suck Max deeply into the menacing underworld that lurks around every dark corner on the streets of downtown Los Angeles. After the first body falls on his car, Max learns that Vincent is a hit man and that his own ride service is no longer voluntary. As the bodies pile up and Max realizes that Vincent's last target is a female prosecutor who was an earlier fare, his only recourse is to crash and flee. While Max survives the nightmare, the thought of almost having been collateral damage in a criminal rampage leaves an existential scar.

Many of these neo-noir hostages are taken by serial killers and other psychopaths. That is certainly the case in *Kiss the Girls,* and also with *The Vanishing* (1993), director George Sluizer's remake of his 1988 Dutch original. In *Funny Games* (2007), director Michael Haneke details the capture and torture a family in his chilling and somewhat surreal remake of his own Austrian feature from 1997. *Trap* (2010) is a micro-budget effort that involves a desperate but doomed young woman seducing one of the men holding her for ransom and is even less of a "feel good" movie than *Hitchhiker*. Equally disturbing is the brutal vigilantism of *Prisoners* (2013), where parents torture a suspect in the abduction of their children. enduring with a much grittier feel.

For the most part, however, neo-noir's abductions are carried out for a more traditional motive: money. On the surface, the title of *Ransom* (1996) says it all. Actually an informal remake of the classic period *Ransom!* (1956), whose wealthy executive is also a multimillionaire, both films consider the emotional toll on the parents and the tangential results of a child's being taken on the police and the press in search of a sensational story. *Breakdown* (1997) also varies the hitchhiking dynamic: a trucker is in cahoots with a gas station attendant who sabotaged their car picks up a stranded couple and holds the woman for money. The husband has to improvise because he has far less money than the criminals believe. The sex scamming couple in *Judas Kiss* (1998) turn to kidnapping for a larger pay day and end up way over their heads. In *The Way of the Gun* (2000) the casual and unrelenting violence of its criminal protagonists has resulted in the movie's cult status; but its noir credentials hinge on the comeuppance of the cocky kidnappers. *Trapped* (2002) adds a few sociopathic twists to another stolen-child story but is mostly uninspired. In David Fincher's *Panic Room* (also 2002) a mother and daughter, the unwitting new occupants of a brownstone, are assailed by three men who are after bonds hidden in the titled location.

While Fincher's film features standard suspense techniques tied to the daughter's need for medication and incorporates extensive "surveillance video" footage, the *The Clearing* (2004) is based on an actual event and alters the dynamic: the wealthy businessman (laconically portrayed by Robert Redford) has two children, but he is the one taken for ransom that, after she discovers that he had not broken off an affair, his wife hesitates over paying. While the docu-context of this movie foredooms its victim, the same year's *Three Way* makes no pretense of realism. Rather it features a combo-plot that moves from infidelity/kidnapping into blackmail, all leading to a glib we-got-away-with-it ending.

The point of the abductions in both *Nick of Time* (1995) and *Don't Say a Word* (2001) are to compel cooperation from an unwitting victim. In the former, the unexpected and deadly riptide lurking in a noir undercurrent just beneath the surface of the normal world is personified by Christopher Walken's performance as conspirator "Mr. Smith." With a manic omnipresence, he dogs the steps of a hapless father (Johnny Depp), whom he seized apparently at random at a Los Angeles train station. As he counters every evasive attempt, Smith's running commentary and wide-eyed gestures—"Tick, tock," while pointing to his watch—are maddening reminders to his victim that his daughter will be killed unless he assassinates the California governor. In the latter an even more convoluted task is imposed on a psychiatrist (Michael Douglas) by the criminals who invade his home and imprison his wife and daughter: extract information from a disturbed young patient of they will die. The more recent *Firewall* (2006) more closely follows the "Desperate Hours" formula with an added fillip: the homeowner is a security expert whose assistance is needed by bank robbers to overcome a client's electronic defenses.

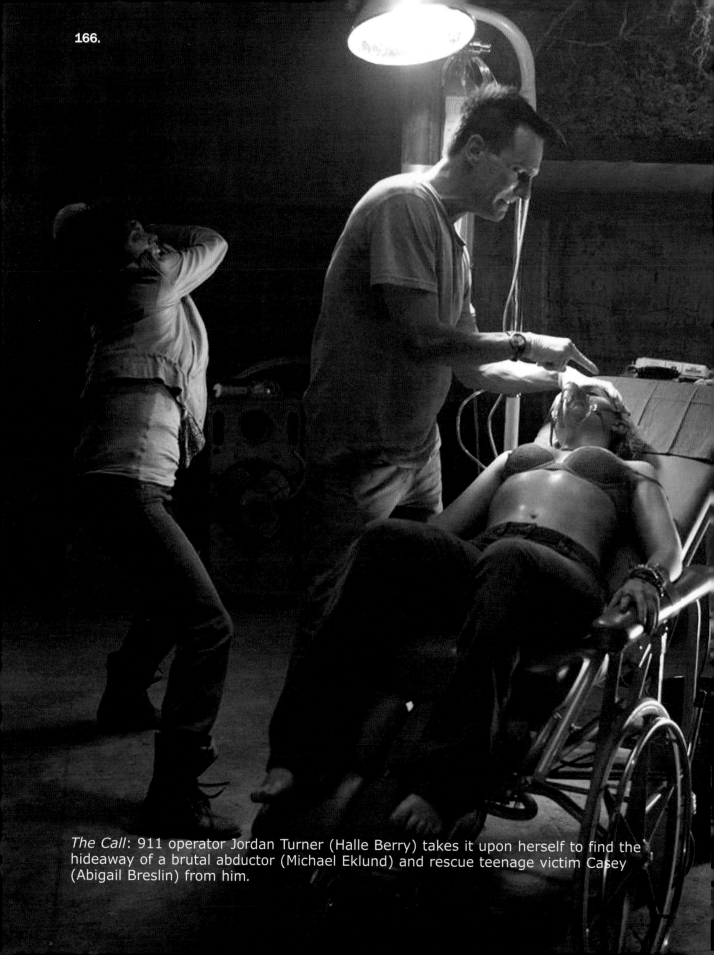

The Call: 911 operator Jordan Turner (Halle Berry) takes it upon herself to find the hideaway of a brutal abductor (Michael Eklund) and rescue teenage victim Casey (Abigail Breslin) from him.

Perhaps the most convoluted of all these narratives is *Hostage* (2005). After elaborate faux graphic-novel credits in the noir style, the movie opens with a bad call by LAPD negotiator Jeff Talley (Bruce Willis) that leaves a family dead. Talley quits the force and moves with his family to an executive job with a rural police department. As luck would have it, another hostage crisis arises—how else could it be in neo-noir—but the twist that strains credulity is when Talley turns the situation over to the local sheriff, only to have mysterious mobsters kidnap his wife and child to force him back to the scene that quickly explodes with the violent action that Bruce Willis fans expect. One could speculate that although there are many hostages over the course of the narrative, the title is singular so that it can refer to Talley as the captive of a dark fate. That is a subtle irony that the concluding shoot-out in a local motel, replete with bullet-riddled bodies spiraling to the floor, belies. *The Box* (2007) inelegantly combines corrupt cop and home invasion stories with the who's-the-perpetrator twist of the previous year's *The Inside Man.*

Another character guilt-ridden over a literal bad call is Jordan Turner (Halle Berry), a 911 operator in *The Call* (2013). She dials back to a kidnapping victim, which reveals her location; and she is killed. Jordan's chance at redemption comes when teenager Casey Welson (Abigail Breslin) is taken by a man with same catchphrase; and she calls 911. Jordan deduces the location of the remote hideout where the kidnapped scalps his victims, goes there, and manages to free Casey. They leave the psychopath trussed in his own lair to die.

Of those falsely accused in the mode of *The Dark Corner* or *The Big Clock*, the early neo-noir detective in *Warning Shot* can bring the skills of his job to bear on his problem. That is also the case for the local police chief in *Out of Time,* who is better able to control an investigation that will implicate him than the journalist in the classic-period original or the naval officer in *No Way Out.* The tech exec in *Disclosure* (1994) reacts with some savvy related to his field, as does the female programmer in the following year's *The Net.* The doctor in *Unforgettable* (1996) takes a mind-expanding drug to find the truth.

While those who are unexpectedly suspected of criminal behavior may have a tangible reason for being paranoid, many neo-noir victims of circumstance start out seeming to be conspiracy theorists. That is clearly the premise of *Conspiracy Theory* (1997), in which taxi driver Jerry Fletcher (Mel Gibson), arguably sketchier than Travis Bickle, finds an unlikely and initially dubious ally in government attorney Alice Stone (Julia Roberts). Ultimately Fletcher is proven right and his death is faked to protect him from an all-too-real and ongoing threat. The previous year' s *Extreme Measures* (1996) detailed discovery by an ER doctor (Hugh Grant) of illegal experiments being performed on New York's homeless population at the behest of a famous neurosurgeon (Gene Hackman), who is ready to crush anyone who imperils his conspiracy. As law student Darby Shaw in the even earlier *The Pelican Brief* (1993), Julia Roberts portrayed a character in deadly peril as the only one who knows the details of an assassination plot. That same year, another John Grisham novel *The Firm*, became a movie about collusion between mobsters and their criminal (pun intended) lawyers, who have their own hit men on staff to sort out new hires who stumble onto their secrets.

From *French Connection*'s loutish cop Popeye Doyle to the P.I.s in *Night Moves* and *The Conversation*, Gene Hackman was already an iconic figure in neo-noir when he took the Charles Laughton role and became the felonious president in *No Way Out*. He was another president/conspirator in *Absolute Power* (1997), a role-reversal story in which a philandering president accidentally kills a sex partner but is brought down by a thief (Clint Eastwood) who witnesses the act. Hackman is also part of a conspiracy in *The Firm*, but a crusading attorney in *Class Action* (1991), a different sort of falsely accused in *Under Suspicion* (2000), and a criminal mastermind in *Heist* (2001).

Hackman's core conspiracy theory performances are in *The Package* (1989) and *Enemy of the State* (1998). In the former movie as Sergeant Johnny Gallagher, Hackman stumbles onto a high-level assassination scheme designed at minimum to reignite the cold war or even start an armed global conflict three. Forced to go on the run with his army lawyer ex-wife, the older fugitive couple does manage to foil the plot.

In the latter movie, Hackman is both sides of the tarnished coin, as Edward Lyle, a former spook for the NSA who now lives off the grid. When his identity is discovered by labor lawyer Robert Dean (Will Smith)—a victim disgraced and discredited by the NSA after he obtains a video of the assassination of a congressman—Lyle must go on the run with Dean and use his tech savvy and insider knowledge to survive.

Opposite, a young Gene Hackman as tough NYPD detective Popeye Doyle in the original *French Connection (*based the actual carreer of Eddie Egan, who is over his right shoulder).   Below, still tough but somewhat dyspeptic as the paranoid ex-spy in *Enemy of the State*.

As in *The Package*, the military investigator in *The General's Daughter* (1999) must unravel a conspiracy, albeit a much smaller scale-one, in order to solve a murder. Released a few months before *Enemy of the State*, *Mercury Rising* (1998) also features a complex scheme at the highest levels by the NSA. In this narrative, a young autistic savant Simon (Miko Hughes) solves a test puzzle and imperils a secret government code. He eludes a government assassin, who does kill his parents, by retreating to his safe place and is discovered by FBI agent Art Jeffries (Bruce Willis), a man demoted from undercover work for striking a superior after a botched standoff and deemed paranoid. The casting of Willis might create expectations of more action, and certainly there is a considerable amount in *Mercury Rising*; and under the direction of Harold Becker, who had made *The Onion Field* and *Sea of Love*, the noir aspects are underscored. Two years earlier Becker had directed *City Hall* (1996), in which another idealist, executive aide Kevin Calhoun (John Cusack) discovers that his boss, New York City mayor John Pappas (Al Pacino), has smeared a dead detective and engaged in an elaborate cover-up to protect himself from the taint of scandal.

Two recent conspiracy tales were adapted from British television series. In *State of Play* (2009), reworked from the six-part 2003 BBC series of the

same name, investigative journalist Cal McAffrey initially gives the benefit of the doubt to his old college roommate Stephen Collins (Ben Affleck) now a congressman, whose mistress has just been found murdered. Goaded to action by Della Frye (Rachel McAdams), a blogger for his paper's on-line department, McAffrey tests her conspiracy theory, which of course proves real and involves yet another ex-military assassin. An actual classified military operation to counter international terrorism, which failed to foretell 9/11, gave its name to *Able Danger* (2008). In this modestly budgeted project shot with a docu-style in New York City, a left-wing bookstore owner and publisher of a 9/11 exposé becomes involved with an Eastern European female fugitive named Kasia (Elina Löwensohn). When he is implicated in the murder an employer, the protagonist probes Kasia's story and discovers she may have undisclosed information about 9/11 itself.

Closing a neo-noir circle, the star of conspiracy theory Mel Gibson portrays Boston detective Thomas Craven in *Edge of Darkness* (2010), whose daughter is murdered in front of him. As transposed and updated from the 1985 British mini-series, the core narrative remains focused on Craven's anguished discovery that, as most of the police department presume, the killer's target was not him but his daughter, who had worked for a company secretly handling nuclear materials.

More D.C. conspiracies: opposite, Congressman Collins (Ben Affleck, left) tries to keep the truth from his reporter friend (Russell Crowe) in *State of Play*.

Below, the docu-style black-and-white *Able Danger*: a wary girl named Friday (Tamara Knausz).

Neo-noir killers are loose. Above, Nicolas Cage as Eddie, the crazed criminal in *Deadfall.*

Below, Christian Bale as the well-groomed sociopath Jim Luther Davis (left, with sidekick Freddy Rodriguez as Mike Alonzo, right), who sports an American flag pin in his lapel.

Opposite, buzz-cut William "D-Fens" Foster (Michael Douglas) places his breakfast order in *Falling Down.*

While one could assert that most of the killers and many of the crooks in neo-noir are like their various classic-period antecedents, socio/psychopaths. some of them are self-aware, like the crazed henchman Eddie in 1993's *Deadfall*. A more notable release from that year was *Falling Down*, in which the impromptu crime spree of the "mad-as-hell, won't take it anymore" William Foster (Michael Douglas) attracts the attention of homicide detective Martin Prendergast (Robert Duvall) who is supposed to be riding a desk on his last day before retirement. The character's self-conscious angst, epitomized by his buzz-cut hair, a pocket protector, and a vanity license plate that reads D-FENS, spreads a patina of social outrage over his behavior, as when he terrorizes the employees and patrons of a fast food outlet that will not serve him breakfast on the cusp of the cut-off time. Ultimately he is closer to Leon "Foggy" Poole, driven to violence out of self-pity in the classic-period *The Killer Is Loose* (1956). For Foster it is more from racist and sexist bias than any authentic moral anger. A more interesting figure is Jim Davis (Christian Bale) the ex-Army Ranger powerfully affected by PTSD in *Harsh Times* (2005). The narrative is as harsh as the title suggests and follows descent of Davis from prospective cop, then aspiring narcotics agent, to drug dealer and finally street-crime casualty.

"I was drugged and left for dead in Mexico and all I got was this stupid shirt": so says the souvenir awarded to a participant in the titular *The Game*, where as early as 1993 David Fincher turned on its head the concepts of a neo-noir underworld rife with paranoia and conspiracy. Although that picture's ending reveals an elaborate hoax remiscent of the awakening at the end of *Woman in the Window*, the director's later *Fight Club* (1999) goes even further into that dark sub-strata. The same fevered atmosphere underlies the story of a demented protagonist who creates a sinister but charming doppelgänger and by whom he is led down a grim trail of physical pain and noir angst toward existential awareness.

That same brand of existential despair envelops the New York executive and whistle blower in *The Caller* (2008): Jimmy Stevens (Frank Langella) hires a private detective named Turlotte (Elliott Gould) to protect him from retaliation without realizing that man has already been tasked to surveille and possibly eliminate him. The circumstances that litter the trails through the neo-noir underworld with a spate of other victims vary widely, as do their attendant ironies. Some are simply the result of a dark past: the photographer and ex-dealer in *Sunset Heat* (1992) sees his friend killed then is tasked to find stolen money the location of which he is entirely unaware. Some are more complex: the nominal protagonist of *Blood and Wine* (1996), a thief whose wine business is on the skids, plans a last score to revive his business. Of course, that goes south and embroils his hapless wife as ancillary victim.

Relationship dysfunction drives many narratives. *The Stepfather* subgenre was born in 1987 from an actual case and a Donald Westlake story and marries (pun intended) the contexts of serial killer and love with the improper stranger. The low-budget original (the success of which generated two sequels) benefits from a performance of Terry O'Quinn as the title psychopath Jerry Blake and a riveting opening that segues from Jerry's transforming his appearance with the same off-handedness as manner of Hitchcock's *Marnie* to a revelation of the bodies of his annihilated step-family. By the time of the larger-budget remake in 2009, the novelty has waned. Harold Becker's studio feature *Domestic Disturbance* (2001) shifts perspective. 12-year-old Matt O'Leary witnesses his stepfather's murder of an associate, but as in the classic-period *Talk About a Stranger*, prior lies makes his parents doubt the story. Ultimately after his parents learn the truth and are imperiled, Matt electrocutes his evil step-parent.

The bloated budget of *Domestic Disturbance* generates predictable suspense through parallel editing and awkward action scenes, with awkward performances by star antagonists John Travolta and Vince Vaughn, as good and evil dads. The "domestic disturbance" in the micro-budget *The Owls* (2010) benefits from a leaner approach: lesbian couples anguished over causing the death of a young woman.

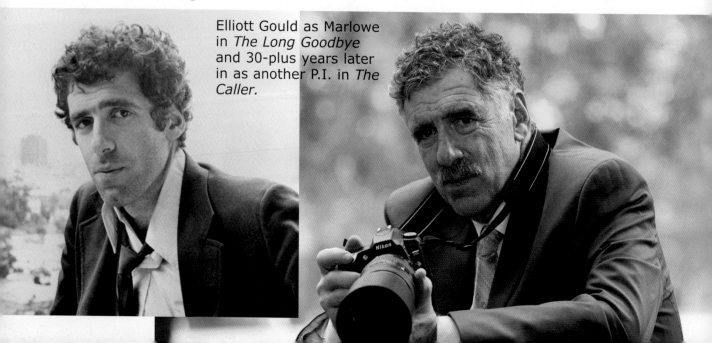

Elliott Gould as Marlowe in *The Long Goodbye* and 30-plus years later in as another P.I. in *The Caller.*

More Love with the Improper Stranger

Few of the encounters in the classic period involve fatal men. While also rare in neo-noir, there are more women who fall prey to a deadly male. As the savvy female lawyer in *Jagged Edge* demonstrated, a woman's common sense can also be overcome by a pretty face. In *The Net* Angela Bennett (Sandra Bullock) meets Jack Devlin (Jeremy Northam) while vacationing in Mexico not realizing until she sees his pistol that the handsome man who rescued her from a mugger actually plans to kill her. Bennett escapes, crashes a boat, and comes to in a hospital. Her body parts are intact, but her identity has been deleted.

In *Fear* (1996) director James Foley follows up on *At Close Range* and *After Dark, My Sweet* with a teen variantion: rebellious high-schooler Nicole Walker (Reese Witherspoon) ignores the misgivings of her parents and gets involved with heartthrob David McCall (Mark Wahlberg). McCall's propensity for violence finals ruptures the relationship; but, of course, he does not take rejection well and bring some friends along to put Nicole and her family through a *Desperate Hours*-style ordeal. In the earlier *Malice* (1993) director Harold Becker had also grappled with a narrative full of pointed misdirection, which veers from bodies in the backyard, to miscarriages, to malpractice awards. That's only the beginning. Husband Andy (Bill Pulman) discovers the con of his scheming wife Tracy (Nicole Kidman), and shortly thereafter she guns down her ex-lover and co-conspirator, handsome Doctor Jed (Alex Baldwin). Irony is stretched to the breaking point, as Tracy is undone by a blind "witness" and a detective in disguise.

Fear: young couple Nicole Walker (Reese Witherspoon) and David McCall (Mark Wahlberg).

As in the classic period, one of the keys to misleading the audience and surprise plot twists in neo noir is casting. Halle Berry and Nicole Kidman are not expected to be killers. Would a prospective viewer (who had not taken a look at the movie's poster) suspect likeable Officer Pete Davis (Ray Liotta) in *Unlawful Entry* (1992) to be something other than a regular joe, the cop who helps yuppie couple Michael and Karen Carr (Kurt Russell and Madeleine Stowe) install a home-security system? Liotta is, of course, a bit edgier than Russell, so is it really a surprise when he comes on to Mrs. Carr in the manner of Joseph Losey's classic-period *The Prowler* (1951) and then frames the inconvenient husband to get close to her?

While it may not be shocking that Officer Davis ends up dead, the same casting dynamic underlies *In the Cut* (2003), where wholesome high-school teacher Frannie Avery (a typecast Meg Ryan) takes a walk on the wild side with Det. Giovanni Malloy (Mark Ruffalo), who is just as anomalous a cop a as his Irish-Italian name might imply. Despite enjoying sexual interludes with Malloy, he has a telltale tattoo that causes Frannie to suspect him of murder. Just when it would seem that common sense will save her from this homme fatal, it turns out the killer's not him.

What Lies Beneath (2000) is perhaps most often cited as an example of casting against type. From his body of work and his insouciant charm, Harrison Ford as Professor Norman Spencer makes an unlikely philanderer, let alone a

Below, *Unlawful Entry*: rogue cop David (Ray Liotta) menaces Michael Carr (Kurt Russell).

Opposite, Michele Pfeiffer and Harrison Ford as Claire and Norman Spencer in *What Lies Beneath*.

killer, especially as the husband of Michelle Pfeiffer. In fairness to this movie, its ad art did not point any fingers, just the blade of a knife held by an unidentified hand. By the turn of the 21st century, neo-noir audiences knew to expect the unexpected. Sure Pfeiffer's character Claire Spencer has memory lapses from a car accident but just like her classic-period antecedents, doesn't she have reason to suspect the bulky bag that a new neighbor Warren (James Remar) dragged to his car contained the body of his wife Mary (Miranda Otto). Hasn't that Remar guy played a villain before? Wasn't that him laughing scornfully at the cop in *48 Hrs.*? Doesn't Ms. Otto look like a victim? A considerable portion of the running time is devoted to this red herring, even including a séance and Claire's imagining messages. Except that just as Claire is pointing the finger at Warren, Mary turns up alive. Oops. But why stop there? Next Claire finds a clipping and after more momentary trances, voila, memory restored: she caught good old Norm boffing his student on the night before her accident. Next thing Claire knows, she has been drugged by Norman and put into a hot bath to drown. Of course, Claire survives, but like Norman *What Lies Beneath* drowns in dark waters.

The recent *No Good Deed* (2014) also seems mired in old formulas. Escaped murderer Colin Evans (Idris Elba) kills his unfaithful ex-fiancée, crashes his car, and charms his way into a suburban home. The subtext, an underappreciated wife, Terri Grainger (Taraji P. Henson), fiercely protects her children

and overcomes her home invader, is a bit facile, particularly when she discovers the man dallying with Evans' former betrothed was her husband and Evans chose her as part of his revenge plan.

The recent *The Boy Next Door* (2015) combines the improper stranger with kid noir and a reverse *Rear Window* (1954) twist in that just-separated high-school English teacher Claire Peterson (Jennifer Lopez) succumbs to the charms of a a young man who just moved in next door, Noah Sandborn (Ryan Guzman). His obsessive response when she comes to her senses, is to rig an accident for her estranged husband and son then blackmail her with a sex tape. Of course, there is an action ending that includes a house aflame.

More Kid Noir

Already mentioned are the many antecedents to *Brick* (2005), where a high-schooler takes it upon himself to investigate a death. The key transposition in *Brick* is writer/director Rian Johnson's decision to populate a plot inspired by Dashiell Hammett and a visualization adapted from *Chinatown* with teenage

Opposite, top, Taraji P. Henson as the victimized in *No Good Deed*.

Bottom, Jennifer Lopez as Claire and Ryan Guzman as Noah, the titled *Boy Next Door*.

Below, Brendan (Joseph Gordon Levitt) and Laura (Nora Zehetner) in *Brick*.

criminals, victims, and investigators. Certainly nothing in *Brick* resembles the retro gangster parody *Bugsy Malone* (1976): the context is realistic (except, perhaps, for the characters' remarkably G-rated language) but the many scenes with hard-boiled dialogue spouting from "the mouths of babes" makes suspension of disbelief difficult if not impossible.

Sleepers (1996) is a revenge film suffused with noir angst and melancholy that relates the story of four boys sent to a reform school run by sadistic guards who abuse them on a regular basis. When the four reach adulthood, they plot revenge against those who twisted their lives. Two of them shoot the chief guard and are brought up on charges. One of them is now a district attorney and asks to be assigned the case so that he can manipulate the trial and free his friends. The key to their defense is their parish priest (played by Robert De Niro), who must lie about the killers' whereabouts in order to destroy the prosecution's case. The film is rife with moral ambiguities like this one: whether revenge and deception is ever justified when the crime committed is so heinous.

Both *Disturbia* (2007) and *Tenderness* (2009) create variations on previously explored noir themes. In the former, Kale (Shia LaBeouf) is a student under house arrest for assaulting a teacher who made remarks about his father is also grounded by his mother. Without TV or games, he turns his attention to his neighbors. Using binoculars to get close views, the young man comes to suspect that the quirky Turner (David Morse), who has been ogling the attrac-

Tenderness: Jon Foster (as Eric) and Sophie Traub (as Lori).

Opposite, Shia LeBoeuf as Kale takes a peek at the guy next door in *Disturbia*.

tive girl next door Ashley (Sarah Roemer), may have committed murder. If that sounds too familiar, the owners of the Woolrich story on which *Rear Window* was based actually sued for infringement. While those plaintiffs did not prevailed, the unmistakable parallels with the classic-period Hitchcock movie failed to elevate *Disturbia* to a similar status in neo-noir.

Much more notable is *Tenderness*: police lieutenant Cristofuoro (Russell Crowe) believes that Eric Komenko (Jon Foster) a soon-to-released juvenile offender who murdered his parents, is also a serial killer. The fixated cop plans to find evidence against Komenko, even sets a trap for him, but is appalled to discover that a 16-year-old named Lori (Sophie Traub), a loner with a groupie fixation of her own on Komenko, has warned him. After he learns that she saw him with an earlier victim, Komenko plans to kill Lori. To prevent that, she drowns herself. In a final, dark twist, although the detective knows the truth, Cristofuoro arrests Komenko and charges him with Lori's murder. Knowing he will be convicted for something he did not do rather than his actual crimes, Komenko is led away.

Harmony Korine's deceptively titled *Spring Breakers* (2012) starts out like an episode of *Girls Gone Wild*. The camera lingers in slow motion on scenes of spring break in St. Petersburg, Florida, the mecca for stressed out college students looking for a Dionysian experience. The film then shifts to a suburban town farther north where a quartet of college students, Faith (Selena Gomez), Brit (Ashley Benson), Candy (Vanessa Hudgens), and Cotty (Rachel Korine) yearn for escape from their stifling bourgeois lives, something they believe the

Above, *Spring Breakers*: Ashley Benson, James Franco and Vanessa Hudgens as Brit, Alien, and Candy respectively, strike a pose in front of his money car.

ideal "Spring Break" offers them. The film cuts between bits and pieces of their everyday lives—smoking dope until they pass out and fetishizing about guns while attending "jacked-up" Christian meetings—as their voice-overs express their disaffection with bourgeois values. Unable to raise the needed cash for their trip, three of the girls—Candy, Cotty, and Brit—steal a car, don ski masks, and rob a "Chicken Shack" with squirt guns, a hammer, and the sheer terrifying force of their performance, all while sporting furry animal backpacks.

Of course, as with any self-respecting neo-noir, darkness enters in the form drug dealer/rapper Alien (James Franco). After the girls are arrested for

Seven: Dets Mills (Brad Pitt) and Somerset (Morgan Freeman, right) at a rain-soaked crime scene.

disorderly behavior, Alien bails them out of jail. With his tattoos of dollar signs and grilled teeth, Alien is seriously disturbed. He owns an arsenal of weapons, has kilos of cocaine, and over his bed a poster of Al Pacino as Scarface (he has the DVD on a loop). Alien is considering a revenge hit on former partner Archie; and, when his nerve begins to weaken, Brit and Candy taunt him into doing it by calling him a "scaredy-pants." Alien goes for it but dies in the initial gunfire, which leaves it to Brit and Candy to finish the job. Dressed in luminescent bikinis and pink ski masks, they eliminate the bodyguards and Archie then kiss the face of the dead Alien, take his sports car, and drive off completing a descent into the dark underside of spring break.

Some Cops Still Bend the Rules

Although long before Miranda warnings and omnipresent video, characters who enforced the law in the classic period mostly conformed to a positive stereotype: dedicated, hard working and willing to bend the rules because they were more concerned with putting criminals away than looking over their shoulders, like Cristofuoro in *Tenderness*.

Seven (or alternately *Se7en*, 1995) is a close-examination of the ebb and flow of existential conflict in criminal investigators, over the course of a career, a case, a day, or a minute. The script by Andrew Kevin Walker has a narrative core that is a simple quest to find a cunning serial killer who keys his murders to the seven deadly sins. The questers are an unlikely partnership: brash, new, and still idealistic detective David Mills (Brad Pitt) and world weary, close–to-retirement Lt. Somerset (Morgan Freeman). As for bending the rules, *Seven* focuses on the causes rather than the consequences. The movie's layered approach makes it a key title in neo-noir; and it has a foundation in the conflicts introduced by Walter Hill in earlier work from *Hickey & Boggs* to *48 Hrs.* In these movies the noir equivalent of a samurai is caught in a *giri/ninjō* conflict, the struggle to adhere to the code when the obligations (*giri*) run counter to the impulse of human emotion (*ninjō*). In terms of both visual style and performance director David Fincher pushes at the margins. The squalor of the first crime scene with its bloated victim that epitomizes gluttony is captured with a dimly-lit and gritty realism that fully immerses the audience in the perspectives of the cops. Both detectives are humanized by their interactions with Mills' wife Tracy (Gwyneth Paltrow). Such normality lulls the viewer into a sense that all may end well. Then as forcefully as any film in the genre, *Seven* demonstrates how all may change in an instant, and the undertow of the noir universe may sweep a character away to destruction. As Somerset grimly notes: ""The world is a fine place, and worth fighting for'—I agree with the second part."

In *In the Line of Fire* (1993), Clint Eastwood is slightly mellower than Dirty Harry Callahan as Frank Horrigan, an old-school Secret Service agent who is not corrupt but marked by guilt over not being able to protect President Kennedy. When a vindictive CIA assassin, portrayed with a creepy angst by John Malkovich, contacts him and promises that the agent will stand over another dead president, Horrigan ignores professional constraints to prevent a new national and personal trauma.

In the long line of corrupt cops in noir and neo-noir, Abel Ferrara's "bad lieutenant" in the 1992 film of the same name is among the worst. He is so "bad" that he is not even given a name. Ferrara has explored the depths of evil from an lapsed Catholic's point of view (much like Martin Scorsese) in many neo-noirs beginning with *Ms. 45*. The lead actor from that film Zoe Tamerlis appears in *Bad Lieutenant* as the cop's druggie girlfriend (and is also one of the script writers). The lieutenant (played by Harvey Keitel) does not inspire the same sympathy as the initially victimized Thana in *Ms. 45*. His descent into drugs and excessive gambling, his willingness to take advantage of his position to obtain sexual favors as well as money, and his general lack of a moral compass make for a protagonist with whom it is difficult for any audience to identify. Even this character does share a moment of epiphany when a nun who has been raped forgives her attackers and refuses to cooperate with him. After seeing a vision of a silent Jesus Christ, the lieutenant decides to try a new path. He finds the boys who had attacked the nun and gives them a second chance. He puts them on the bus with some ill-gotten gains and quietly waits for his own execution, like a Christian martyr, by his bookie's thugs.

Writer-producer Hilary Henkin's *Romeo is Bleeding* (1993) traces the descent of the weak and venal cop named Jack Grimaldi (Gary Oldman) who

narrates the story with typical neo-noir irony from his desert exile in a small Arizona diner where he waits for his "true love," his long-suffering wife Natalie (Annabella Sciorra). Jack freely admits that "the hole"—the way that Jack sees women—in his yard, into which he "fed" his bribes, is the only one he made "happy." Except for occasional outbursts, as when she turns her husband's gun on him, his wife has put up with his behavior. Cocktail waitress Sheri (Juliette Lewis) is a mistress who acts out fantasies for Jack until he murders her by mistake. The only female who defies Jack and maintains erotic power over him—until she, too, is shot by him—is the Russian hit woman Mona Demarkova, played by Lena Olin as part dominatrix/part monster/part sexual predator/part cyborg. Mona acts as an avenger for all the "normal" women whom Jack has betrayed. In a signature scene, she handcuffs Jack to her bed, unstraps her leather harness which holds a prosthetic arm, and furiously assaults him. By dressing Sheri like herself, Mona tricks Jack into shooting her. While handcuffed in the backseat of his car, she chokes him with her powerful legs and then escapes his custody by kicking free through the front windshield. In the end she betrays him and delivers him to the cops.

Jack does make a final attempt at redemption. He sends his wife to safety with the bribe money and asks her to meet him, if he survives, later at the

Opposite, Frankie Thorn (left) and Harvey Keitel as the title figure in *Bad Lieutenant*.

Gary Oldman as Jack Grimaldi has a different sort of epiphany in *Romeo is Bleeding*.

desert diner. While in custody, Jack finally manages to shoot Mona but fails at suicide. Ironically he gets what Mona wanted: a new identity through witness protection. So he waits alone and recounts his twisted tale.

In the early variant *Caroline at Midnight* (1994) that recalls aspects of *Private Hell 36*, the focus is on the wife of corrupt cop—Victoria (Mia Sara) not Caroline—who is also a drug dealer. She dodges her suspicious husband and a female kingpin (Virginia Madsen), while ironically attracted to a reporter who is investigating her husband.

In *Above Suspicion* (1995) a paralyzed cop uses his handicap to put his wife and her lover off their guard. He then plots his revenge through various devious methods. In *City Hall*, corruption is rife, not only among the police but within the political system itself. John Cusack plays the naive deputy mayor to the slick and corrupt mayor, played by Al Pacino. Although co-written by Paul Schrader (*Taxi Driver*, etc.) and Nicholas Pileggi (*Goodfellas*), both no strangers to crime films, and directed by Harold Becker, the noir aspects are undercut by ironies that are more socially conscious than existential. In *Persons Unknown*

Cop Land, another jurisdiction but still corrupt: Harvey Keitel (opposite) as an NYPD cop who lives across the river and tries to control the local sheriff incarnated by Sylvester Stallone (below). Despite the bandage on his nose, it's not hard to guess who wins that contest.

(1996) a womanizing ex-cop (Joe Mantegna) picks the wrong woman to have a one-night stand with. He becomes involved with the woman and her sister in their heist of a fortune of from the mob.

In *Night Falls on Manhattan* (1996, directed by Sidney Lumet), Andy Garcia reprises a variant on his role in *Internal Affairs* as Sean Casey, a young prosecutor assigned to a case because his father was one of many cops killed or wounded by a notorious drug dealer, whose defense attorney claims he was targeted for elimination by corrupt police in the pay of a criminal rival. After prevailing at trial, Casey wins an election to replace the now-ailing district attorney but new facts surface. His father's partner is revealed to have been on the take. Then the senior Casey admits that his warrant was invalid. Rather than reveal all this, the formerly incorruptible and idealistic son enlists the aid of an accommodating judge and creates a valid document after the fact.

Cop Land (1997) gives star Sylvester Stallone a chance to play a more subdued character. He is sheriff in a small town in New Jersey, populated by members of the NYPD. The sheriff's ambition was always to become a New York City cop but loss of hearing in one ear prevented him from achieving his dream. Regarded as a friendly "hick" by the slick New York cops, they never consider him a threat when evidence of their corruption comes to his attention. Although at first reluctant, the sheriff pursues the case, to the anger and dismay of the residents of his small town nicknamed "cop land."

Brown's Requiem (1998) is an adaptation of James Ellroy's novel that focuses on an alcoholic ex-LAPD cop who tries to walk the straight and narrow but is drawn back to the dark underbelly of Los Angeles crime. With the sun-drenched capital city of Arizona as its setting, *Phoenix* (1998) features a police department plagued by corruption. Ray Liotta again plays a marginalized detective, in this case a gambling addict who decides to pull off a heist from the mob in order to pay his debts. In *Negotiator* (1998) a skilled police negotiator named Roman, played by Samuel L. Jackson, accused of corruption and murder, takes hostages in a government office to gain the time he needs to find the truth. A second negotiator, played by Kevin Spacey, is sent out to defuse the increasingly desperate Roman.

Philip Noyce's *The Bone Collector* (1999) anticipates with its chiaroscuro style, conflicted investigators, and detailed procedurals, the long-running neo-noir craze TV series *CSI* and its many spin-offs. Much like her role in the later *Taking Lives*, Angelina Jolie's law-enforcement character, Amelia, is cut off from normal life. Although she has a devoted boyfriend, in an early scene, she is unable to make an emotional commitment to him. She is even uncomfortable on the job, where she faces the typical sexism and condescension of her male superiors. The viewer eventually learns that the chagrin and silence that reify her insecurity are rooted in the traumatic suicide of her cop father.

Amelia's life changes when she comes upon a murder scene in a rail yard. Noticing carefully placed clues on the rail tracks, she stops a train at the risk of her life in order to protect the crime scene. This act earns her the disdain of her captain (Michael Rooney) but links her life to that of paraplegic CSI wizard Lincoln Rhyme (Denzel Washington), whose his injury while investigating a crime scene was withnessed by the audience at the beginning of the movie. Rhyme has subsequently detached himself from life and, after convincing his doctor to assist in his "transition," Rhyme waits for the end; but he is drawn back, unwillingly at first, by his concerned cop buddies into the investigation of the serial killer who kidnaps victims and then leaves clues to his identity.

Seeing potential in the crime investigation instincts of Amelia, Rhyme ignores the direction of his vainglorious captain and brings her on the case. Under his mentorship (she keeps in contact with him via phone as she investigates the various crime scenes), Amelia begins to overcome her natural aversion to the danger and gore of the crime scenes the serial killer has set up and even gains a sense of purpose. Transferring her love for her father onto this new suicidal cop, we see her attachment growing as she caresses his scars as he sleeps. This growing connection lifts both characters out of their despair.

The moody noir night scenes in New York City are particularly well staged as the serial killer kidnaps his victims in his cab and then takes them to abandoned areas of the city to be tortured and murdered unless Rhyme and Amelia can figure out his clues before the time he has set for the killing. Toward the climax of the movie, it becomes clear that the serial killer's real object is Rhyme himself and that all the murders have been bait. As Amelia saves the final victim of the serial killer, a little girl who is tied to the pilings of a pier, the killer (Leland Orser) attacks Rhyme and is revealed to be an ex-cop who was convicted based on Rhyme's testimony. He is about to stab the parplegic when Amelia arrives and shoots him.

The coda of the movie is an affirmation of life. Rhyme is now out of his bed and in a wheelchair, accompanied by Amelia who by her demeanor and actions has become his companion. While the couple host the party, the camera pulls back into the New York City nightscape and the Peter Gabriel/Kate Bush song "Don't Give Up" fades up on the soundtrack, reinforcing the theme of the movie.

In *Cement* (2000) Los Angeles vice detectives Bill Holt (Chris Penn) and Nin (Jeffrey Wright) have allied themselves with a drug dealer. As he tries to stop Holt, Nin narrates the events that led Holt to torture the drug dealer's brother. Director Sean Penn's *The Pledge* (2001) is a moody and melancholic film, much like Penn's earlier directorial effort, *The Crossing Guard* (1995). Whereas *The Crossing Guard* tracked a revenge-obsessed father (Jack Nicholson) intent on shooting the man who killed his daughter in a car accident, *The Pledge* presents a retiring old-school cop Black (Nicholson again), who cannot let go of a case and of a promise he made to a mother to find the murderer of her child. In order to fulfill this pledge, he buys a gas station in the mountains near where the crime occurred.

Black begins his investigation while becoming involved with the single mother Lori (Robin Wright) and her daughter. The duo seems to fill a need in this lonely man's life as he grows attached to both. But Black cannot let go of his obsession. Convinced the killer is going to strike again, he uses the woman's daughter (who is the pedophile's type) as bait, even setting up her playground in front of the house near the road so he can observe any possible suspects.

Below, Officer Amelia Donaghy (Angelina Jolie) consults with paralyzed investigator Lincoln Rhyme (Denzel Washington) in *The Bone Collector.*

Black eventually sets a trap for the man he believes to be the killer, using the daughter again as bait. The killer never arrives but Lori does, outraged at Black's callousness and deviousness. As Black tries to explain himself, she deserts him. In the final scene Black is shown back at his gas station, mumbling to himself as the wind blows through the empty station.

Antoine Fuqua's *Training Day* (2001) takes place over twenty-four hours in the life of two very opposite LAPD narcotic detectives. Jake Hoyt (Ethan Hawke) is an idealistic, young cop, while the veteran Alonzo (Denzel Washington) has made compromise after compromise with the "streets." Because he is unwilling to join in their craven behavior, Hoyt is set up by Alonzo but survives by mere chance, because he had helped the younger sister of his would-be killers. In a noir reversal, Hoyt tracks down Alonzo but lets him live to meet death shortly thereafter at the hands of Russian mobsters. In *True Blue* (2001) a paunchy, middle-aged maverick cop named Rembrandt (Tom Berenger), who cannot keep a partner because of his unorthodox ways investigates the murder of a young woman involved with political corruption and Asian mobs.

Christopher Nolan's *Insomnia* (2002) is a remake of a compelling Scandinavian neo-noir of the same name made in 1997 and starring the remarkable Swedish actor Stellan Skarsgård. Both films trace the disintegration of a personality under pressure from guilt, stress, and sleepless nights. Like Graham Greene's protagonist in his novel *A Burnt-Out Case*, In Nolan's version Detective Will Dormer (Al Pacino) has been sent to Alaska during a period of "white nights"—a time during the summer solstice in higher latitudes when darkness is never complete—partly to avoid an internal affairs investigation, partly to assist the local police in finding a murderer. Pacino, like Skarsgård, projects a "weariness to the bones" in his manner and tone. After shooting his partner during a chase in the fog—a partner who was going to testify against him—Dormer's disintegration accelerates. He begins to hallucinate: seeing glimpses of his partner, of the murdered girl; hearing normal sounds amplified. He speaks almost in a whisper. Even after boarding up the windows with furniture in his hotel room, he still can see the burning sun, a symbol of his guilt as well as his rapidly dissolving psyche.

The only person who can understand Dormer is, ironically, the killer Walter Finch (disturbingly underplayed by Robin Williams). Finch knows that Dormer killed his partner and contacts him to propose a mutually beneficial and convoluted scheme. Nolan underlines the doppelgänger quality of these two men, much as he will later in his 2006 film about two rival magicians *The Prestige.* They are both guilty of crimes which were, at least on a conscious level, accidental. They both are unable to sleep. And they are both clever puzzle solvers: Dolmer unravels real-life crimes; Finch writes mystery novels. Nolan further reinforces their duality by match framing them visually. When they shoot each other in the climax of the movie, the scene plays out symbol-

Opposite, Alonzo (Denzel Washington) and his in-apt pupil Jake (Ethan Hawke) in *Training Day.*   Below, *Insomnia*: a local deputy (Hilary Swank) assists Det. Dormer (Al Pacino).

ically as an attempt by each man to rid himself of his demonic double. After this act of exorcism, both men can finally sleep: Finch floating in the lake; Dormer, dead on the wharf.

The Badge (2002) takes on an unusual subject for neo-noir, a homophobic Louisiana cop, Hardwick (Billy Bob Thornton), who is forced to confront his prejudices when he investigates the murder of a transsexual. His inquiry inevitable leads him up the political ladder to the rich and famous. Director Ron Shelton's *Dark Blue* (2002), like *Training Day* before it, presents a maverick LAPD cop, Eldon Perry (Kurt Russell), who believes he has inherited the right to bend the rules in order to catch the guys he deems "bad" ("I was raised up to be a gunfighter by a family of gunfighters."). He meets his nemesis in the person of Assistant Chief Holland (Ving Rhames) who decides to rid the department of Perry and his elite unit.

The setting is Detroit in *Narc* (2002), where a disgraced ex-narcotics detective, Nick (Jason Patric), is brought back onto the force to investigate yet another maverick cop, Oak (played by a beefy Ray Liotta). Nick battles his loyalties to the "blue code" of silence with his sense that Oak has bent the law one too many times.

Nightstalker (2002) is based loosely on the actual hunt in the 1980s for serial killer Richard Ramirez known as the "Night Stalker." The film narrative is divided fairly equally between the woman-hating, crack-smoking, Satan-wor-

Dark Blue: the espression on the face of Eldon Perry (Kurt Russell) reflects his disdain for uniformed superiors such as Chief Holland (Ving Rhames).

Opposite, Bret Roberts as the menacing figure of the title in *Nightstalker.*

shipping Nightstalker (Bret Roberts) and the LAPD rookie cop Gabriella Martinez (Roselyn Sánchez of *The Perfect Sleep* and the noir TV series *Without a Trace*) in her personal struggles with sexism, male violence, and self-doubt. The film deftly intercuts these two lives until they meet in the final minutes of the film.

The film attempts to externalize the thoughts of its psychopathic and unnamed title figure through alterations of sight and sound. When the Nightstalker smokes crack, the visuals speed up and a naked version of the character morphs onto the screen, to the accompaniment of heavy metal music and sexual growls on the soundtrack. Through most of the film the audience cannot make out the features of the Nightstalker. His long hair covers his face and he is shrouded in darkness. He repeatedly and manicly tells his victims not to look him in the face. His sense of self-loathing carries over to his encounters with street prostitutes, at which times he can only masturbate while he stares at their feet and they verbally abuse him.

Gabriella encounters the bloody handiwork of this killer while on patrol with her father-figure partner Luis (Danny Trejo). Her own father has been killed. She is "filled with attitude"—the words of the Latina woman who asks her for help—despite her inexperience. She vomits at the sight of the mutilated bodies and disturbs evidence at the scene of the first crime; but she is inexplicably—at least to her—promoted to detective and asked to be part of the Nightstalker investigation. She realizes that she is only there because she is a Latina woman. As with the killer's "visions," when her immediate superior, Detective Mayberry (Evan Parke), massages Gabriella's shoulders and propositions her in his office, the motion is sped up. More effects make his head seem to shake in rhythm with growls on the soundtrack. Other distortions happen when younger Detective Elliot (Derek Hamilton) screams for Gabriella to shoot the Nightstalker in an alleyway after Elliot himself has mistakenly killed a homeless man there.

Filled with doubt about her career and her mission, Gabriella prays to a makeshift religious shrine when she enters her house, a ritual interaction with the supernatural that links her to the Nightstalker's behavior. She also defies orders and releases a sketch of the killer to the press to allow the community to protect itself. In reality Ramirez was caught after a mug shot of him appeared in the newspapers. When Gabriella finally corners and wounds the killer in the dark alley, he begs her to finish him. Her answer is simply, "I'm not like you." With this climactic statement she separates herself from the world of male violence and creates an ambiguous ending. Will Gabriella continue to be part of the make-dominated LAPD or will she quit to take that teaching job she has been offered?

Director D. J. Caruso (*Salton Sea*, *Disturbia*, etc.) combined forces with neo-noir star Angelina Jolie in 2004 to produce the serial killer thriller *Taking Lives*. Jolie portrays Illeana Scott, an FBI agent called to Canada to help in the identification and capture of a serial killer. The audience first sees her as she lies flat in the open grave of the latest victim. She seems to be psychically connecting with the scene like the "witch" she has been called by her fellow agents. Her imperious facade and dark beauty give more weight to this description, a description she does not deny. For like profiler Will Graham in *Manhunter*, Illeana is both gifted and cursed by this psychic faculty. As with Graham it forces her into a world of psychopathy and violence.

Also as with other profilers, there is a touch of the psychopath in Illeana that allows her to connect to the serial killers she seeks. She describes how a psychopath has no feelings and can eat dinner while contemplating murder. During the film we see Illeana doing exactly that as she calmly eats dinner while examining photos of a decomposed body or when she has sex with witness/suspect James Costa (Ethan Hawke) and stares up at the photos of corpses plastered on the ceiling above her bed. In *The Silence of the Lambs*, Lecter questions Clarice Starling about a traumatic event from her childhood. For Ileanna her emotional connection to the world of violence stems from her own act of murder as a child, when she comes upon a burglar in her house and stabs him. A variant of this scene is staged at the end of the movie with Martin taking the place of the burglar.

This particularly insidious serial killer not only takes the lives of his victims but then assumes their identities. Abused as a child by his mother, Martin Asher must become what Ileanna calls a hermit crab, who inhabits the shells of his victims because he is so uncomfortable in his own skin. When he goes up against Illeana, to whom he feels connected, he becomes what he calls a "faggy" art dealer named Costa, who purportedly witnessed one of Martin's crimes. Hawke's performance as Martin/Costa is heavily nuanced. Both Illeana and the audience suspect that there is something amiss or off; but he stages an attack by a drug dealer and an ensuing chase with such expertise that he convinces Illeana of his innocence. Ultimately Martin cannot help but reveal himself to Illeana. He even tells her that the only reason she had sex with him was because she was attracted to the serial killer not the art dealer. Finally when Martin's mother comes to identify the body she thinks is her son, the real Martin confronts her in a hotel elevator and, while Illeana watches, rips off her head.

Taking Lives: Angelina Jolie as FBI profiler Illeana Scott and Ethan Hawke as James Costa/Martin Asher.

Pregnant and disgraced by her unprofessional relationship with "Costa," Illeana is terminated by the FBI. She hides out in rural Pennsylvania and waits, the viewer assumes, for the baby to be born. A final twist reveals that she has staged it all to lure Martin to her and re-create the trauma/cartharsis of her childhood confrontation with an intruder. Martin does invade her isolated home in the snow. Claiming his love for the twins inside her, he alternates between beating her and professing his ardor; but as he wrestles with Illeana, he stabs her in the belly. She grabs a pair of scissors, plunges them into his Martin's heart, and before Martin dies she reveals the adjustable prosthetic that she used to fake her pregnancy. Psychologically Illeana has returned to her distant, cold self, the shell that protects her from a world of messy emotions and random violence.

The Academy Award-winning *Crash* (2004) includes several cops in its wide range of characters. The most troubled is Officer John Ryan (Matt Dillon) who reeks of racism and rage. One of many, often contrived ironies, is set in motion early in the narrative film when Ryan molests an African-American woman (Thandie Newton) during a traffic-stop pat down and humiliates her husband; but much later in the film saves her from a burning car.

Miami Vice (2006) is Michael Mann's adaptation of the themes and characters of his landmark neo-noir television series of the same name (1984-1990) to the big screen. The non-traditional cops Crockett (Colin Farrell) and Tubbs (Jamie Foxx) take on another drug cartel while Crockett falls for the wife and adviser, Isabella (played by the femme fatale of Chinese cinema, Gong Li) of a drug and arms cartel boss.

Even discounting his remake of *Cape Fear*, there is no question that Martin Scorsese is as conscious as any filmmaker of the legacy of the classic period. Still his narrative focus, and his reputation, more firmly reside with new entries in the gangster genre from his early *Mean Streets* (1973) through *Goodfellas* (1990) and *Casino* (1995) to the period *Gangs of New York* (2002). A thick gangster thread also runs through *The Departed* (2006), his remake of the Hong Kong *Internal Affairs* (2002) with the interaction transposed to the Irish mobsters of Boston. The other narrative line is closer to *Deep Cover*, as a young officer is sent to infiltrate the mob and discover the corrupt police officials who are protecting them. As in many classic period-movies, the parallel worlds of cops and criminals, through which protagonist Billy Costigan (Leonardo DiCaprio) must navigate, are immersed in issues of loyalty and honor, tradition and transgression. Just as he thinks that he has waded through these murky waters to safety, Costigan discovers that the rip tide in the neo-noir underworld can suddenly pull you under.

Street Kings (2008) was co-written by neo-noir novelist James Ellroy. The film centers on the cop culture of corruption as Detective Ludlow (Keanu Reeves) is forced to go against his buddies in order to clear his own name.

The Bad Lieutenant: Port of Call—New Orleans (2009) is German director Werner Herzog's quasi-remake (Herzog claims never to have seen the original). Set in post-Katrina New Orleans, Herzog brings an expressionist style to the story of a cop descending into a personal hell. The injured and subsequently

Opposite, *Crash*: Officer Ryan (Matt Dillon) profiles and humiliates Cameron Thayer (Terence Howard) as his wife Christine (Thandie Newton) and patrol partner Hansen (Ryan Philippe) look on. Below, big-screen versions of undercover detectives Tubbs (Jamie Foxx) and Crockett (Colin Farrell) in *Miami Vice*.

Michael Shannon as retro P.I. Rosow in *The Missing Person*.

addicted-to-pain-pills Terence McDonagh is portrayed by Nicolas Cage with body contortions and facial distortions that almost resemble Klaus Kinski in Herzog's Nosferatu. Although McDonagh forces female suspects to have sex with him, steals drugs, plants evidence, and hallucinates while on duty, he also defends his prostitute girlfriend from thugs, protects a young murder witness to the multiple murder, and acts as a mediator between his alcoholic father and drug-addicted step-mother. The irony of the film is that his heroic act at the beginning of the movie permits his an ultimate redemption. In a quasi-parody of Hollywood endings, Terence apprehends the murderer of the immigrant family and is promoted to captain while supporting his father, stepmother, and girlfriend as they get clean and sober.

The Missing Person (2009) has its roots securely in the tradition of the neo-noir P.I. back to landmark films like *The Long Goodbye* and *Chinatown* and even further classic-period films *Murder, My Sweet* (1944) and *The Dark Corner*. Like the title figures in *Hickey & Boggs*, the protagonist, John Rosow (Michael Shannon), is an anachronistic figure in the modern landscapes of Los Angeles and New York. He is a sardonic, chain-smoking, alcoholic, technophobic "private dick," who mumbles his way through most conversations and has zero skills when romancing women.

The film begins rather conventionally when Rosow is hired by a mysterious figure to track an even more mysterious figure. As he wends his way through a maze of miscues and lies, the film is an entertaining evocation of classic period noir. Then, suddenly, mid-way through the quest, the film changes gears and becomes a far more psychological examination of two survivors of the 9/11 attack on the World Trade Center. The first survivor, Harold, is the mysterious man Rosow has been hired to bring back to New York. He is a "missing person," who escaped the towers as they collapsed. In an attempt to change his identity as well as jettison his empty stockbroker life, Harold becomes involved in saving children from sex slavery rings.

The audience eventually learns that the second victim is Rosow himself, as he is also suffering from PTSD in the wake of 9/11, when he lost his wife. She is seen with Rosow in dream sequences, where the ashes from the destruction of the towers rain down on them in slow motion. While on the verge of delivering Harold to his wife, Rosow decides to do the "right thing" and lets him return to his new life. In a climax that is again shot in slow motion, Harold runs around a New York City corner, free of his former identity once more, while a chastened Rosow returns his fee of $500,000 to his client, the missing man's perplexed wife.

Director John Curran's *Stone* (2010) is as much about spiritual epiphanies as it is about a burned-out parole office, Jack (Robert De Niro), who becomes involved with a New Age femme fatale, Lucetta (Milla Jovovich), in her attempts to free her imprisoned husband, the eponymous Stone (Edward Norton). In that way it runs counter to the stream of determinism that courses through so much of neo-noir.

Jack has lived his life hiding his rage and alienation (in the opening scene we see a young Jack threatening to throw his young daughter out the window if his oppressed wife leaves him) beneath the facade of a hard-working parole

Milla Jovovich as Lucetta and Robert De Niro as parole officer Jack Mabry in *Stone*.

officer. Jack lives his life shutting everyone out, including his alcoholic wife and estranged daughter. He listens to fundamentalist talk radio and yet does not believe in anything spiritual. He helps prisoners obtain parole but believes everything they say is "bullshit."

Into this empty man's life comes the direct and streetwise Stone, who has been incarcerated for acting as an accessory in the burglary and murder of his own grandparents. With his braided hair and street argot, Stone unsettles Jack, asking him questions rather than sitting obediently while Jack judges and evaluates him. When Stone enlists his sexually alluring wife to seduce Jack and in the process ensure Stone's parole, Jack's ordered, suffocating life begins to unravel. Beyond these neo-noir plot machinations is the theme of transcendence and spiritual growth, symbolized by buzz of an insect in several scenes (possibly alluding to Emily Dickinson's famous poem "I heard a fly buzz when I died") or of a single note that begins to haunt Stone as he struggles with the meaning of his life. Stone's epiphany comes at the moment he witnesses a man's being stabbed to death in prison. As he stares into the dying man's eyes, all sound drops out from the chaotic prison and he hears that single note.

Jack's transformation is much slower and less certain. He does release Stone to "the bricks." But his fear of Stone increases. And when his house burns to the ground, he suspects Stone, who had burned his grandparents' house after their murder. But the culprit is actually his wife, who has finally decided to break free from her emotionally unavailable husband. The despairing Jack stalks the now transcendentally calm Stone and threatens him with a gun. He cannot pull the trigger. In the final scene, Stone, like some pilgrim, straps his pack to his back and takes off on his journey, both physical and spiritual, while

Agnes White (Ashley Judd) and Peter Evans (Michael Shannon) in *Bug*.

Jack sits alone in his empty office. Suddenly he hears a fly buzz near a window. He turns to listen and the film ends. But has Jack learned his lesson, the lesson that suffering is not the purpose of existence but just a lesson to be learned on the road to transformation?

In 2006 William Friedkin directed a modestly budgeted and somewhat noirish adaptation of *Bug*, adapted by Tracy Letts from his own play, in which a paranoid drifter shares nightmares with a waitress expecting trouble from her abusive ex who has just been released prison. There is a new blending of neo-noir subgenres to much greater effect in the more recent collaboration *Killer Joe* (2011). The titled character, a smooth-talking southern lawman who moonlights as a hit man, is not living the noir nightmare, he embodies it. When the hapless white trash family that engages his services cannot collect the life insurance proceeds to pay his fee, Joe takes it out in trade. It's mix of craven behavior and cornpone calamity stretched the limits of the genre, as *Killer Joe* careens freely between peril and parody.

Michael Winterbottom's controversial adaptation of Jim Thompson's grim, naturalistic novel *The Killer inside Me* (2010) featured Casey Afleck as the sociopathic deputy sheriff Lou Ford. Afleck's lanky and laconic aspect were certainly appropriate to what is arguably Thompson's most famous character, whose ability to separate physical and emotional attachments from his casual

Killer Joe: Chris Evans (Emile Hirsh) and killer cop Joe Cooper (Matthew McConnaghey) confer.

brutality, his insanity, was key for Thompson. Winterbottom's intellectual approach to the film's most brutal sequences reached back like the Coens did in *No Country for Old Men* to the gruesome and exhausting murder in Hitchcock's *Torn Curtain* to suggest what a dismal, sweaty, and emotionally bereft experience a murder actually is.

Some P.I.s Are Still Old School

Given the scant number of neo-noir private eyes in recent year, the 1972 lament of Frank Hickey about the meaningless of the profession seems to have taken root. 25 years after *Hickey & Boggs,* that premise itself is at the core of the micro-budget and relatively actionless *Big Empty* (1997), in which grocery clerk Lloyd Meadows decides to hang up a shingle and comport himself with the affectations of an old-school P.I. The fact that, except for his relative impecuniousness, he is obviously not a reincarnated Frank Hickey, let alone a Philip Marlowe injects elements of both nostalgia and parody.

The studio budget of *Twilight* (1998 and certainly not be confused with the more recent series of vampire films) permitted it to engage the services of older name actors, among them such former portrayers of P.I.s as Gene Hackman and James Garner. The actual senior citizen private detective Harry Ross is portrayed, 30 years after *Harper*, by Paul Newman whose character is also a retired cop. Two years after tracking down the runaway daughter of his old friends Jack and Catherine Ames (Hackman and Susan Sarandon), Ross is

Below, Casey Affleck as Deputy Lou Ford in *The Killer Inside Me.*

Opposite, Jack Ames (Gene Hackman) and P.I. Harry Ross (Paul Newman) in *Twilight.*

living in their guest house and mostly playing cards with the terminally ill Jack. The narrative, which unfolds with a gait appropriate to its aging protagonists, ultimately reveals a decades-old murder that was covered up by a former colleague (Garner) and compels Ross to find some new digs.

In the following year's convoluted, mixed-subgenre movie *Eye of the Beholder* (1999), female serial killer Joanna Eris (Ashley Judd) acquires an unlikely "guardian angel," when the undercover operative Stephen Wilson (Ewan McGregor), tasked to surveille one of her victims, becomes infatuated with this literal femme fatale. Wilson becomes so addicted to tracking her that he derails her attempt to settle into a normal life. From that point the movie's verisimilitude goes slightly off the rails, as Eris heads to Alaska, starts slinging hash for a living and seeing a shrink. While not uncommon for private dicks to brood over deadly dames in the classic period, *Eye of the Beholder* is far removed from Spade's mere reluctance to send over Brigid O'Shaughnessy, although if asked Eris might echo Brigid's memorably understated self-assessment: "I haven't lived a good life. I've been bad, worse than you could know." In *Gone, Baby, Gone* (2007), Casey Aflleck portrays disaffected private eye Patrick Kenzie in a narrative (directed by his brother Ben) that conflates a kidnapped child, a disinterested and greedy mother, and a corrupt local cop.

A more recent micro-budget feature (with a micro-running time) is *My Kingdom for a Kiss* (2008), in which another low-rent P.I. romanticizes the job while trailing a woman whose parents were, in more subgenre mixing, victims of a serial killer. From its very title, *Give 'Em Hell, Malone* (2009) is full-on retro. However, the assumption that a few fedoras and large-caliber wheel guns make for compelling neo-noir is a little off-target. After a brief montage of downtown

Thomas Jane as another retro P.I. in *Give 'Em Hell, Malone.*

Los Angeles leads to the rusty neon sign for the Otis Hotel, a body flies out a window and Malone's laconic voice-over begins. As one might expect from a movie inspired by a first-person video shooter game, it is impossible to keep track of the blood spurting from bullet-riddled bodies in what appears to be a 1950s gang fight. Malone walks through it unscathed and invoking his rules "not to die" by: "In my line of work, you have to knife before you're punched, and shoot before you're knifed." Like its titled character's tortured patter, *Give 'Em Hell, Malone* is a mish-mash of stereotypes with visuals inspired less by classic-period noir than the gaudy covers of guns-ablaze dime detective magazines or Mickey Spillane paperbacks. Although pining for a dead wife and son (who, of course, turn out to be alive) Malone strides through a flat, cartoonish pastiche with a constant sneer that recalls Mike Hammer—the only thing badder than his attitude is his movie.

Some Criminals Still Believe in Capers

The title of *A Simple Plan* (1998) says it all. It also describes the mentality of some the rurals/yokels who stumble onto a fortune in ransom money. After their agreement on how to keep it, unravels with deadly consequences: the smartest of them gets off. The only problem: he has to burn the rest of the money to avoid being found out.

Heat (1995, directed by Michael Mann) and *Heist* (2001, directed by David Mamet) are standard capers. As is his wont, Mamet focuses on the long con that underlies the scheme, how the veteran crew led by Joe Moore (Gene Hackman) anticipate betrayals first by their facilitator (Danny De Vito) then by Moore's moll. Whereas Mann shifts points of view in a contest of wills between characters based an actual person LAPD cop (Al Pacino) in charge of the investigation and his criminal counterpart (Robert De Niro), whose violent assault on an armored car sets events in motion. While the twitchy detective cannot manage his messy personal life, the smooth mastermind takes setbacks in stride with a snug sangfroid, which in 1990s neo-noir foreshadows his doom. As troubled capers go, *City of Industry* (1997) more closely channels aspects of *The Asphalt Jungle* and *Point Blank*: a wary ex-thief helps his brother plan a jewelry store robbery but does not expect that his treacherous wheelman will try to kill them and keep all the loot.

Threads from *A Simple Plan* and *City of Industry* intertwine in Sidney Lumet's final feature, *Before the Devil Knows You're Dead* (2007): a desperate attempt by addicted financier Andy Hanson (Philip Seymour Hoffman), who enlists his ne'er-do-well younger brother Hank (Ethan Hawke) to knock over their own parents, who own a small jewelry store in a local mall. Andy expects his parents' clerk to meekly hand over the goods, but a nervous Hank brings along a pal with a gun. In a narrative as full of pathos as irony, the gunsel and

Ethan Hawke and Philip Seymour Hoffman as brothers Hank and Andy Hanson in *Before the Devil Knows You're Dead.*

the mom, filing in for the sick clerk, shoot each other. This precipitates a downward spiral of blackmail, more murder, and a dark conclusion, in which a wounded Andy is suffocated by his own father (Albert Finney), who has discovered his sons are responsible for their mother's death.

The variations on the neo-noir caper are multiform. *Body Count* (1998) is another title that tells all. It has African-American protagonists, as does *Dead Presidents* (1995) and *Juice* (1992), where "the Wrecking Crew" graduates from chronic truancy to "A" felony when a robbery victim is killed. The Coen brothers milk the violent and messy criminal ineptitude in *Fargo* for its dark humor. Like Bart and Annie Laurie in *Gun Crazy*, the murderous jewel thieves Ned (David Caruso) and Jude (Kelly Lynch) in *Cold Around the Heart* (1997) go together like guns and ammunition. The narrative crosses over into fugitive couple mode until they get separated, and then it adds a hitchhiker, albeit an innocent one. *Best Laid Plans* (1999) starts out in the mode of the classic-period *Criss Cross* and *The Asphalt Jungle* and a heavy dose of post-modern, ironic humor. It twists and turns, leaving the audience hanging at various points and like many neo-noirs becomes too complex for its own good. In this film Reese Witherspoon's performance, like most of her early performances in such neo-noirs as *Freeway* and *Fear* (both 1996), is as a sexually liberated nymphet with a sharp tongue. *No Good Deed* (2002) brings a cop and a manipulative femme fatale into a mix that is loosely based on a short story by Dashiell Hammett. In *The Score* (2001) De Niro incarnates another veteran, safe-cracker Nick Wells lured back from a brief retirement by no-less than Marlon Brando as the debt-ridden fence Max.

Left, Samuel L. Jackson as Friar and Milla Jovovich as Erin in *No Good Deed*.

Above, Jackson as Ordell Robbie watches a little TV with Robert De Niro as Louis Gara.

In *Four Dogs Playing Poker* (2000) more amateurs are at work. Threatened with death unless they come up with the $1 million value of a lost artifact, the best plan they can come up with is to purchase an insurance policy on one of them, who will be sacrificed to save the rest, and draw straws to see who loses and who will executioner. The picture mimics the Tarantino style of *Reservoir Dogs* after Tarantino himself had moved on to *Jackie Brown* (1997). Starting with an Elmore Leonard novel and casting blaxploitation queen Pam Grier as the title character, a poorly paid flight attendant struggling to make a living after taking the fall for her drug-dealer husband and supplementing her income by bringing cash from Mexico for Ordell Robbie (Samuel L. Jackson), who is being coerced into betraying Ordell by the authorities. Tired and desperate for a big score, Jackie recruits the assistance of bondsman Max Cherry (Robert Forster) in order to double-cross both cops and the crooks. Set in the drab precincts of Los Angeles' South Bay, Jackie Brown has a docu-look. Much of the criminal planning and activity in takes place at an aging mall, as characters meet in the food court and the shops to exchange contraband currency. As oafish, ex-con Louis Gara, De Niro provides another neo-noir highlight that balances between pathos and parody. Micro-budget *Idleheist* (2004) is a stylized parody that melds Tarantino and *Natural Born Killers*.

Gone in 60 Seconds (2000) and *Confidence* (2003) both feature more hodge-podge gangs of losers and low-lifes. The story line of the former is mostly an excuse for driving exotic cars through L.A. streets at high speed. In *Confidence* the plot turns involved paranoid con men and crooked cops with predictable results.

Former kid noir actor Matt Dillon, who graduated to the racist cop in *Crash*, portrays disaffected driver Mike Cochrane in *Armored* (2009). Inspired by events from the 1960s where armored car personnel gave up their cargo to hijackers to save one of their colleagues and are still suspected of having orchestrated the whole heist, a new generation of guards decides to pull off their own caper. When Mike's promise of no violence fails to stick, his own protégé has a change of heart and locks himself inside one of the trucks hauling $20 million each. In *Takers* (2010) Gordon Cozier (Idris Elba) leads an intergrated crew of hip, young robbers that revels in its notoriety, and, as usual, the karmic consequences of such hubris is a fall. The group is leery about its next job, as it is being pushed by Ghost, who is just released after a prison stretch. At the same time, Det. Welles (Dillon) and his partner are working lead. Ghost does betray his cronies and the caper ends in three-way standoff between cop, criminal, and traitor. Most recently Dillon went back to the other side in *Art of the Steal* (2013), a dark satire told in flashback by a thief (Kurt Russell) entering prison after his brother (Dillon) ratted him out.

As it was for Walter Neff and his filial relationship with the paternal Barton Keyes and the insurance business in *Double Indemnity*, playing the system to get free or just for the hell of it is a frequent underlying motive. Both *Just Cause* (1995) and *Primal Fear* (1996) posit cunning killers, who exploit the hubris of a famous criminal attorney to be exonerated of murder. In *Guilty as Sin* (1993, directed by Sidney Lumet), which lifts some plot dynamics from *Jagged Edge*, the attorney is a woman, Jennifer Haines (Rebecca De Mornay). Although she finds evidence that he handsome and conniving client David

Greenhill (Don Johnson) is guilty, legal ethics prevent her from revealing the truth. None-the-less Greenhill murders her middle-aged investigator (Jack Warden in the Robert Loggia part) then comes for her. She sends them both plummeting of a roof, a fall only she manages to survive.

Opposite, *Heist* mastermind (Matt Dillon) flanked by cronies (Jean Reno, left and Laurence Fishburne) in *Armored*. Above, Paul Walker as John Rahway, one of the smug and stylish crew in *Takers* and Dillon as cop Jack Welles. Below, as an older but not wiser character in *Art of the Steal*.

Above, Det. Brown (Laurence Fishburne) confronts activist lawyer Armstrong (Sean Connery) in *Just Cause.* Opposite, Denzel Washington and Chiwetel Ejiofor as Detectives Frazier and Mitchell in *Inside Man*.

Perfect Murder (1998) is yet another revelatory title and in *Pathology* (2008) a group of medical students actually turn it into a game. *Fracture* (2007) pits an unwary prosecutor Beachum (Ryan Gosling) against wealthy inventor Crawford (Anthony Hopkins), who pretends to be ingenuous and acts as his own attorney when on trial for attempting to murder his wife. Having manipulated a swap of pistols with a detective who was involved with his wife, Beachum is acquitted because of the mismatched ballistics and the revelation of the affair just before his comatose wife dies. Of course, there must be a fatal misstep: protected by double jeopardy a gloating Crawford freely confesses to Beachum. The now-dead wife makes it murder; but when they square off again in court, Crawford has a phalanx of high-priced mouthpieces. Gosling the actor crosses over to the dark side in the recent *Drive* (2011), portraying a new incar- nation of a character known only as the Driv*er*, a wheelman for hire whether it's for a movie stunt or a heist. Unlike Walter Hill's character, this driver gets embroiled with his new neighbors, a boy and young mother, whose husband is doing time. For their sakes he mixes personal and business, leading to a trail of bodies and his undoing.

On the one hand, the bank robbers in Spike Lee's *Inside Man* (2006) are nothing like the amped-up amateurs in *Dog Day Afternoon*. On the other, they both have ulterior motives that are not clarified until the movie's end. Dalton Russell (Clive Owen) sits in what might be a prison cell to address the viewer and initiates a flashback to his "perfect robbery": dressed as painters a crew takes the patrons and employees of a branch bank as hostage. Negotiator Detective Frazier (Denzel Washington) is under suspicion of shady activity that imperils his promotion to first grade. The back-and-forth includes a sidebar between Russell and a woman (Jodie Foster) hired by the bank president Case (Christopher Plummer) to intervene and protect the contents of his personal safe-deposit box, diamonds and documents that reveal he made his fortune by preying on Holocaust victims, inside that branch.

After the captors appear to kill a hostage, SWAT storms in. Since all those inside have been dressed in painter's coveralls, despite hours of interrogations, the cops cannot distinguish the masked perpetrators from the innocent patrons. Russell has, in fact, stayed in the bank hidden behind a false wall. He does not go to prison but simply walks out of the bank a week later, while Frazier happens to be there, then leaks the contents of the box to bring down Case. His full motive is never revealed. He does keep the diamonds, except for one he slips into Frazier's pocket when they pass each other in the lobby.

In his studio project *The Town* (2010), co-screenwriter/director/star Ben Affleck adapts the story of a Boston-based four-man crew of bank robbers. Concerned that a hostage from their last job, teller Claire Keesey (Rebecca Hall), might implicate them, leader Doug MacCray (Affleck) first romances then threatens her to insure silence. Guilty over this, MacCray kills the local mob boss to protect her then reluantly participates in a last big score, a heist of the ticket sales at Fenway Park, which has predictably poor results. MacCray manages an improvised escape while all his cronies are gunned down and realizes that Claire refused to betray him to the FBI. He hides out in Florida still filled with angst over what might have been in his relationship with Claire and his whole sorry life of crime.

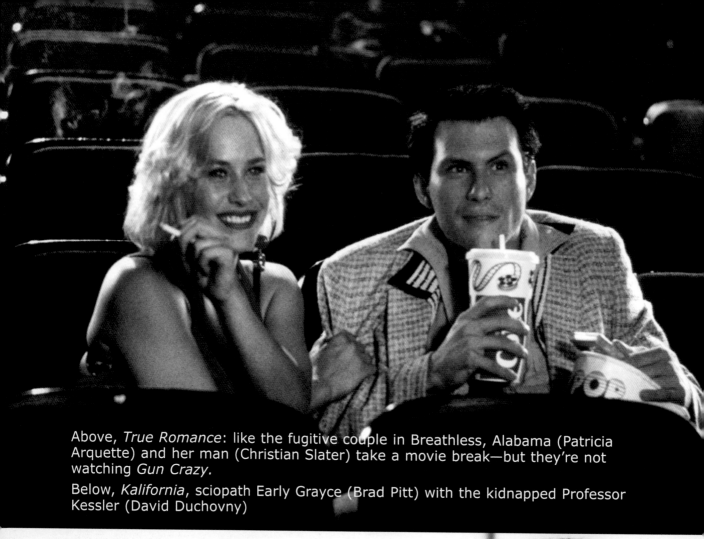

Above, *True Romance*: like the fugitive couple in Breathless, Alabama (Patricia Arquette) and her man (Christian Slater) take a movie break—but they're not watching *Gun Crazy*.

Below, *Kalifornia*, sciopath Early Grayce (Brad Pitt) with the kidnapped Professor Kessler (David Duchovny)

Some Couples Are Still on the Run

In the year before *Natural Born Killers*, two features anticipated its somewhat ageneric fugitive couple that alternates between ultra-violence and sardonic self awareness. *True Romance* (1993), from a script by Tarantino that is replete with variant endings, features a male protagonist named Clarence who has conversations with his inner Elvis and gets hitched to a deadly female named Alabama. Although early drafts of its scripts had more comic elements, the actual *Kalifornia* (1993) is more straightforward in its depiction of psychopathy. Ex-con Early Grayce (Brad Pitt) has a girl, Adele (Juliette Lewis), but his real lust is for blood. Compelled to interview for a job at a local college, Early spots his chance for a cheap getaway: notice of a ride share to the West Coast posted on a bulletin board. The poster Brian Kessler (David Duchovny) is completing a book about serial killers and driving cross-country to visit their hunting grounds assisted by his photographer/girlfriend Carrie (Michelle Forbes). Obvious ironies aside, the movie inserts an element of transference as Early alters Adele's look to resemble Michelle's. As the trail of corpses grows and Early's proclivity is outed, he kidnaps the other couple. When Adele won't hold up her end of the need to eliminate witnesses, she dies instead, Brian is dumped, and the couple is reconfigured. While *True Romance* spared Clarence in one of its endings, there is no version of *Kalifornia* that ends with Early's survival.

The ribald, hard-boiled characters of writer Chester Himes evoke both the ambience of Harlem in the 1950s and '60s and also the noir ethos. In the year before *Deep Cover*, Bill Duke freely adapted Himes' *A Rage in Harlem* (1991), which refocuses on a minor character in the novel, Jackson (Forest Whitaker). Enchanted by the arrival of the possible fatal woman Imabelle (Robin Givens, a newcomer given the role after an extensive casting search for an African-American femme fatale), who has survived a shoot-out and come to Harlem with the loot, the naive Jackson helps her escape. Imabelle's hold on Jackson is a bit like Annie Laurie's on Bart but also like Bess' on Porgy, and Duke turns those characters into a fugitive couple

Mad Love (1995) is marginally noir: the female half of the teen couple is bipolar and capable of violence and their runaway trip to Mexico is hardly a killing spree. Instead of prison, she lands in a hospital. *Desert Saints* (2001) is another example of plot twists without panache, blending hit men with corrupt and obsessive cops into a fictional, fugitive couple. The desert meanderings of hired killer Arthur Banks (Kiefer Sutherland) and Bennie Harper (Melora Walters) involves two impersonations: Banks picks up female traveling companions to mask his movements as a lone killer and Harper is an undercover FBI agent planted by an obsessed superior familiar with the assassin's M.O. Of course, it is not all as it seems to be. In *Firecracker* (2005) young Jimmy from remote Kansas finds love and goes on the road with a carny woman. Elements of Oz are mixed into *Nightmare Alley* (1947) in an oddball, relatively low-budget effort where the same actors portray Jimmy's abusive mother and brother and his love interest and jealous boss. Many of the latest fugitive couples are on the run in micro-budget efforts.

Ironically among the narratives closest to classic-period formulas are in the first chapters of the non-neo-noir "Bourne" series. Many of the key elements in *Bourne Identity* (2002) are shared with the genre: amnesia, assassins, and a couple with separate goals at the start: the man to find his identity, the woman to make a few dollars. When she opts to join him as a fugitive, the plot dynamic shifts. Thrown together by chance, they become a fugitive couple before they become lovers. Their survival together at the end of the first movie is not very noir but also short-lived, ending as *The Bourne Supremacy* (2004) opens. Two new characters in the spin-off *The Bourne Legacy* (2012) do evade assassination by government agents to become an more authentic neo-noir fugitive couple after they flee the Washington D.C. suburbs for Chicago and then the far east. This couple also survives but, as with their predecessors, fate might point a finger towards a different outcome in the next installment.

No Longer Just Hit "Men"

Luc Besson's 1990 French hit *La Femme Nikita* broke the glass ceiling protecting hit men from their female counterparts, while forming the archetype for the neo-noir female assassin: tough, sexy, and emotionally conflicted and consistent with the conflict in traditional cinema between woman as nurturer and woman as destroyer. With *Point of No Return* (1993) mainstream Hollywood remade *Nikita* with its usual compromises. Although the plot, including the action sequence in a restaurant kitchen, are quite close, the casting of the blond and somewhat bland Bridget Fonda in the main part diminished the original character's edginess, a key to that narrative's Gallic irony.

In *The Long Kiss Goodnight* (1996) Geena Davis plays Samantha Caine, a bland woman recovering from amnesia who wakes up to find her middle-class

Opposite, top. *The Bourne Legacy* with Rachel Weisz and Jeremy Renner.

The look (and the weapons) may be similar but Geena Davis, opposite in *The Long Kiss Goodnight*, is much more of a sharp-tongued and ruthless assassin than Bridget Fonde in *Point of No Return*.

life as a teacher and single mom shattered by memories of her other self, a CIA hit woman named Charly Baltimore. As the film develops the viewer comes to understand that the deadly Charly is this woman's "true" persona and that Samantha's amnesia—a staple of film noir—was a coping mechanism to deal with trauma: being shot after discovering her pregnancy. By the end of the film with the aid of low-rent P.I. Mitch Henessey (Samuel L. Jackson), originally hired by Samatha, Charly has fully unraveled her past exacted her revenge on her attackers, while reengaging her warrior woman side. As with his *Lethal Weapon* script, writer Shane Black injects much dark humor into the banter between Charley/Samatha and Mitch and quicky moments such the assassin figure's unexpected encounter with one of Samatha's terrified students.

The title of *The Job* (2003) refers to the last gig before retirement of another blond and glamorous hit woman C.J. March (Daryl Hannah) about which she suddenly gets scruples. In the *Silent Dove* (2007) the ultra-micro-budget filmmakers tried to conform to the sexy female assassin archetype, but the local amateur actor (Chelsee Atkins) might be mistaken for a suburban

Below, *Max Payne*: Mila Kunis as Mona Sax next to Mark Wahlberg as the title figure and opposite in full hit woman regalia, including a pastel bra with décolletage and a butterfly necklace.

Opposite right, Chelsee Atkins as the title killer in *Silent Dove*.

housewife with a Glock. After some botched jobs this hit woman lays low until her father is murdered by the mob then shifts into a reckless and retributive high gear in the manner of *The Outfit*. In *Max Payne* (2008) Mila Kunis plays the single-minded Russian mob assassin Mona Sax who turns against her comrades when they murder her wayward sister (Olga Kurynenko). With the assistance of vengeful cop Payne (Mark Wahlberg) she brings down the organization. In 2010's low-budget *The Resurrection of Serious Rogers*, the eponymous hitwoman (Cooper Harris) wants out of the killing game (much like her older cinematic sister Nikita). In order to accomplish this, she must take out all the criminal roadblocks in her way.

Not to be outdone, the male assassins still outnumber the females. In *Little Odessa* (1994) the filmmakers examine not only the psychology of an emotionally stunted hit man, Joshua (Tim Roth), but also the dynamics of the Russian family he returns to visit while setting up a hit. Estranged from his mother and father (played with understated grace by Vanessa Redgrave and Maximilian Schell respectively), Joshua cannot find his place either within the family or even within the Russian Brighton Beach community so effectively portrayed in the film. By the denouement, Joshua has caused death to visit his own family as well as pushed himself back into his hardened shell.

In *Blown Away* (1994) Tommy Lee Jones, in one of his most out-of-control performances, plays a crazed IRA bomber named Gaerity who targets not

only his ex-comrade, now a cop named Dove (Jeff Bridges)—yes the name is symbolic—but the entire city of Boston. He sets bomb after bomb in this cat-and-mouse game, intent, as he says, on creating chaos and anarchy.

Released the same year was Luc Besson's a very informal sequel to *Nikita*, in which the character of Victor the Cleaner was incarnated by Jean Reno, who has the title role in *Léon: The Professional*. Paranoid and reclusive, Léon discovers his young neighbor Mathilda (Natalie Portman) is the sole survivor of a ruthless family annihilation by corrupt government agents led by Stansfield (Gary Oldman). First he hides her, then Léon becomes her guardian and uses his array of skills and weapons to fend off Stansfield and his cronies.

Director-writer George Armitage, who helmed the odd-ball neo-noir sleeper *Miami Blues*, infuses his *Grosse Pointe Blank* (1997) with the same dark humor. John Cusack stars as Martin Blank, a paid assassin who returns to his suburban hometown of Grosse Pointe while arranging for his next hit in the area. The depressed Blank is convinced by his frightened therapist (Allan Arkin) and his caring assistant (Joan Cusack) to reconnect with his past and hopefully heal himself. At the same time Blank is pursued by fellow hit man Grocer (played hilariously by Dan Ackroyd) who wants to eliminate him and streamline his competition. Blank's attempts at reconciliation with his past do not go well. His ex-girlfriend Debi (Minnie Driver), whom he deserted to join the service, sarcastically upbraids him for his fickleness. His mother has descended into madness and his home has become a convenience store. The film's finale, in which Blank eliminates Grocer by smashing a television on his head is ambiguous, at best, although he does finally convince the stubborn Debi to give him another chance...maybe.

Below, Juvenile hit-girl-in-training Mathilde (Natalie Portman) watches Léon (Jean Reno) with the tools of his trade.

Opposite, *Grosse Point Blank*: local hitman/grocer (Dan Ackroyd) confronts the young interloper Martin Blank (John Cusak).

Anthony La Paglia's Mick in *Killer* (1994) is another hit man who wants out; but his predicament has little of the dark humor of *Grosse Pointe Blank*. Mick is far more existential and nihilistic, as is the film. With another familiar twist, Mick falls for his next target, a psychologically disturbed femme fatale named Fiona (Mimi Rogers), who the audience later learns has commisioned her own death. Mick thinks he has found some hope in life but his hopes are dashed when his partner performs the hit for him and leaves Mick bereft. In *La Cucaracha* (1998) hapless Walter Pool (Eric Roberts) is a broke American writer wannabe living in a Mexican village. How can he refuse an offer from a local gangster of $100,000 to assassinate another villager who is a child killer, especially when he realizes he will be dead if he turns them down. They shoot him anyway, and the subgenre changes from amateur hit man to revenge-seeking cripple. Roberts is again a killer *Hitman's Run* (1999), a low-rent riff on the killer and kid dynamic of *The Professional.*

Forgive Me Father (2001) gives the hit man narrative a religious dimension. Virgil (Ivan Rogers, also the director) is a hit man turned priest who tries to redeem himself with service and good works. But the death of his gangster brother breaks through the thin facade of repentance and Virgil, Bible in hand, returns to his former stomping grounds to eliminate the murderers of his brother. In *No Witness* (2003) the hitman takes on the supernatural. Paid assassin Leiter (Steve Barnes) tries to eliminate a target who boasts supernatural powers. *A Cowboy's Silver Lining* (2004) is a low-budget film shot in Memphis. The cowboy/hit man, like his millennial cohorts, wants to be free of "the life." The story is told in a non-linear fashion which gives the film a not unwelcome complexity. *Killing Mark Twain* (2008) is another ultra low-budget movie in the neo-noir genre. Its main character, who takes the pseudonym "Mark Twain" (Nicholas Calhoun), attempts to start a new life with stolen money. He is pursued by another hit man, Poe (one of many literary references in this movie).

The modestly budgeted (at least in the context of studio work by producer and star Brad Pitt) *Killing Them Softly* (2012) is a variation on *Charley Varrick* and *The Outfit* that features a trio of amateur robbers, who knock off a mob-controlled poker game, and also three hit men. As the featured killer, Jackie Cogan, Pitt moves past the hyper-personas of his psycho and cop performances in *Kalifornia* and *Seven* respectively. His character is smiling, personable...and merciless. Although Cogan knows one of the game bosses was not directly involved, he lobbies for then carries out his murder anyway, just to make a point. This hit man's only soft spot is for fellow assassin Mickey Fallon (James Gandolfini), to whom he farms out work because he knows Fallon needs cash. After Mickey proves no longer capable of anything except substance abuse, Cogan reports him for parole violation, as much to get him into forced rehab as to punish him. Counter-posed against speeches from the 2008 presidential election, in the final scene, as they listen to homilies from candidate Obama, Cogan complains to his employer about being short-charged then denigrates Thomas Jefferson as a hypocritical "rich white snob" before delivering his menacing last words: "I'm living in America, and in America you're on your own. America's not a country. It's just a business. Now fuckin' pay me."

Retro Noir

As with *Chinatown* and *Farewell, My Lovely*, some filmmakers are still reimagining the two decades of the classic-noir period by situating their narratives in the past.

Butterfly (1982) is based on the 1947 novel by James M. Cain, which never could have been adapted earlier as it dealt graphically with the theme of

incest. What ever the movie's incidental history (the young star's older husband produced this showcase movie), the final result on the screen is a pointed example of the Cain strain in noir. The first gimpse is of Pia Zadora as the teenage Kady emerging from the desert like a pedophile's wet dream. Like her literary sister. Lolita, she combines innocence with sensuality, as she runs barefoot across the sand and displays her thighs for a trucker.

Kady is obsessed with control, because, as she tells the man she believes to be her father Jess (Stacy Keach): "Havin' nothin' is being' nothing.'" Initially Jess resists her proposition. He is described by others as a "cold, stony" man who never got over his abandonment by Kady's mother. Knowing she closely resembles her mother, Kady is relentless. She has Jess wash her naked body in the bathtub, so that she can pull his hand down between her legs. When Jess protests that "It ain't right," Kady's reply is, "Feels good to me." Later she taunts him in a bar by flirting with two men and ultimately breaks his resistance. In defiance the social taboo, they become lovers. Eventually society takes notice, and they are arrested for incest. At the trial Jess tries to take all the blame, but Kady will not relinquish control to him. Instead she tells the judge in a shockingly transgressive statement, "What we did was bound to happen. It was good for both of us." The twist in the movie is the revelation that Kady was not really Jess's daughter. Alhough the case is dismissed. Kady decides to leave with the older man who fathered her child because it will be best for both her and the baby. The only consolation she offers Jess is pointedly ironic: no matter what the physical reality, "You're my daddy."

The opening of Howard Franklin's *The Public Eye* (1992), set in the 1940s, features some of Weegee's most famous photos as they appear in the developing tray of "Bernzy" Bernstein (Joe Pesci). When Bernzy rises at 2:00 pm and grimaces at his own reflection in the mirror, he is the daylit equivalent

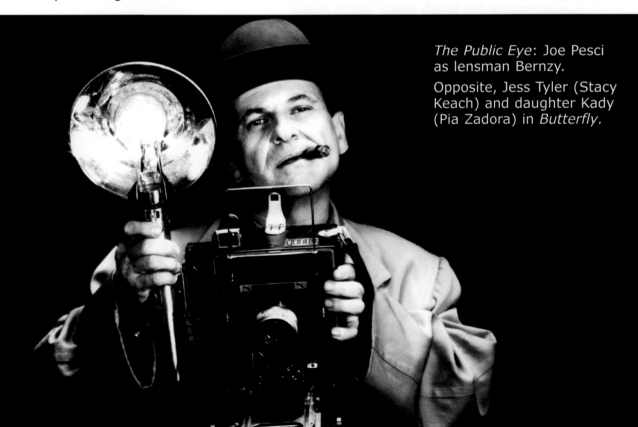

The Public Eye: Joe Pesci as lensman Bernzy.

Opposite, Jess Tyler (Stacy Keach) and daughter Kady (Pia Zadora) in *Butterfly*.

of the images he stalks at night: worn yet resilient, ugly yet beautiful. Like Weegee, this character is at home with cops and crooks as well as New York's hoi polloi. It is this fine line that Joe Pesci as Bernstein walks in *The Public Eye* when he has foreknowledge of a murder that he chooses to photograph rather than to stop. Bernzy's photo-book-in-progress is central to *The Public Eye*'s neo-noir evocation of mainstay emotions from the classic period: alienation and obsession. Rejected by mainstream publishers, Bernzy's work is more than obsession, it is his existential affirmation. Unlike many classic-period femme fatales, Kay (Barbara Hershey) is genuinely drawn to Bernzy because of his talent and by the raw emotion contained in his photographs, especially by his juxtaposition of one photo of her captioned "Beauty" with that of a battered prize-fighter labeled "Beast."

In *The Public Eye*, the quest for recognition as an artist runs parallel to the quest for love. Bernzy points his camera at a sailor kissing a girlfriend good-bye and lurks in the shadows of unfulfilled longing. Artie, a newspaper columnist who has broken through on Broadway, tells him bluntly, "No woman could love a shabby little guy who sleeps in his clothes, eats out of cans, and cozies up to corpses so much that he begins to stink like one." The short, unattractive Bernzy is a classic noir outsider reminiscent of Mickey Rooney's noir portrayals in *Drive a Crooked Road* (1954) and *Quicksand* (1950). Professionally, Bernzy can sustain his pose of self-assurance, even cockiness, even if grilled by cops or slapped by mobsters; but the rush of human feeling can only come to him filtered through the lens of his camera. Fame, recognition, and simple respect are what drive Bernzy to point his camera directly at a loaded gun during the restaurant massacre. When the gunman spots him under the table, Bernzy is

ready to die. He has half-expected that his specially rigged camera on wheels might capture the moment of his own death. But as fate would have it, Bernzy's number isn't up and a stray bullet brings down his would-be killer. As both Artie and his noir antecedents have predicted, Bernzy does not get the girl. Instead he ends up with respect and admission to the Stork Club; but he is alone and obsessed, unable to shut off the police radio that blares nonstop inside his car and inside his fevered brain.

Like many classic noirs *Murder in the First* (1995) combines politics and personal angst in its narrative, based on a true story, of corruption and brutality within the California prison system in the 1930s. Kevin Bacon gives a harrowing performance as the emotionally and physically damaged convict who fights the system with the help of a crusading attorney (Christian Slater). Its attention to detail in production design allows the 1930s to come alive.

Mulholland Falls (1996) deals with the infamous LAPD "hat squad," a group of 1950s detectives who played fast and loose with the rules in order "get their man." Like *Murder in the First*, the filmmakers here lovingly re-create the period, throw in a femme fatale, political secrets, and nuclear secrecy by the nascent military-industrial complex that is much more specific than in *Kiss Me Deadly*. In the end plot twists and mismatched performances—an energetic Chazz Palmentieri sandwiched between the laconic Nick Nolte and Michael Madsen—capsize this vessel before it reaches the falls. *Gangster Squad* (2013) is the latest chronicle of "secret" LAPD operatives set just after World War II,

Opposite, *The Public Eye*: cigar-chomping Bernzy and his femme fatale, Kay (Barbara Hershey).

Below, retro tech-noir: squad member Coolidge (Chazz Palmentieri) threads a 16mm projector while Hoover (Nick Nolte) looks on in *Mulholland Falls*.

specifically in 1949, and focused, as its title suggests, on the West Coast mob-sters of that era. The plot particulars, which include early electronic eaves-dropping, are simpler, so the movie is less focused on neo-noir elements than on violent confrontations and a three-way liaison between cop, gangster, and moll.

Carl Franklin's *Devil in a Blue Dress* (1995) is based on a novel by one of the best-known neo-hard-boiled noir novelists, Walter Mosley. It is one of the few noir films to deal directly with the unmitigated racism in Los Angeles in 1940s and 1950s. The film opens near Central and 24th Streets with a detailed re-creation of the mood and style of the place and time: murals, movie the-aters, bars, jazz riffs emanating from radios, and middle-class African-Americans hanging out. "Easy" Rawlins has been recently laid off from his man-ufacturing job and is desperate to make his mortgage payments. The noirish plot engages as a thug named Albright approaches the desperate Rawlins and offers him work as a "detective," a job Rawlins rejects at first. Eventually his need for funds compels him to accept. The thug then sends him on a quest for Daphne Monet (played with delicate and sultry beauty by Jennifer Beals), the missing fiancée of mayoral candidate Todd Carter.

To find Daphne, Rawlins must venture into all-White areas. On the Westside at the Malibu Pier, White punks from the Midwest harass him. At the prestigious Ambassador Hotel he must enter through the servant's entrance. It is at this swank L.A. landmark that Rawlins finds the mysterious Daphne, dressed in her signature blue. As with Marlowe's Mrs. Grayle or Hammer's "great whatsit" or Spade's "stuff that dreams are made of," many are seeking Daphne. Carter wants her back because he is in love with her. Albright wants her for Carter's political rival, Matthew Terell. And Rawlins wants her to pay his

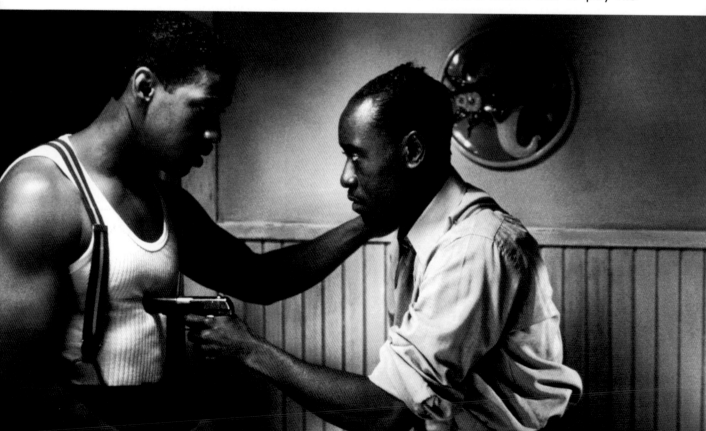

mortgage. In the process Rawlins is beaten by racist LAPD cops and almost murdered by Albright. But the most significant element in the metaphoric nature of Daphne is her revelation to Rawlins that she is half-Black. While not a shocking as the revelation of incest in *Chinatown*, the overt symbolism of someone who is neither one nor the other underscores the artifice of rampant racism, as does her final rejection by Carter, who does not have the courage of his convictions, refusing to risk his political future by marrying her.

In the manner of Robert Towne's scripts to *Chinatown* and its sequel, the *The Two Jakes*, *L.A. Confidential* (1997), based on a novel by James Ellroy and scripted by Brian Helgeland and Curtis Hanson, uses certain events inspired by fact as its narrative core. Also a period film, *L.A. Confidential* is set in 1953, the heart of the classic period of film noir, the year of release for *The Big Heat* and *Vicki*. The ambitious, self-righteous, and obsessed cops of *L.A. Confidential* recall the fictional detectives portrayed by Glenn Ford and Richard Boone in the above movies, and, as in *Mulholland Falls*, are partially inspired by the "hat squad." Despite director Curtis Hanson's assertion that he did not want the picture to be an "homage to a style from the past or neo-noir," *L.A. Confidential* is full of even more overt references to the noir style and the noir era. Lynn Bracken (Kim Basinger), the femme fatale of the piece, is part of a stable of high-class hookers who resemble the glamorous actresses of the era. In one scene, she entertains a local councilman by projecting a 16mm print of *This*

Retro private eyes: opposite, low-rent hood "Mouse" Alexander (Don Cheadle) gets the drop on Easy Rawlins (Denzel Washington) in *Devil in a Blue Dress*.

Below, reprising Jake Gittes, Jack Nicholson, who also directs, finds time to stop and smell the flowers (grown by James Hong as Kahn) in *The Two Jakes*.

Gun for Hire (1942), which stars her look-alike Veronica Lake. When not serving as tipster for a scandal mag, narcotics detective Jack Vincennes (Kevin Spacey) is technical adviser for a fictional TV series modeled on *Dragnet*.

In this context of self-conscious allusions, director Hanson found locations that reflect both the real city and the fictionalized city of the period. Ironically, one of the most striking sequences in terms of topography—Vincennes' arrest of a young actor just down the street from where searchlights accompany a movie premiere at "El Cortez" theater on Hollywood Boulevard—features a location that does not exist. An equally ironic and throwaway moment with Vincennes comes later, as he exits the Frolic Room on Hollywood Boulevard and the marquee on the Pantages Theater behind is for *The Bad and the Beautiful*, Vincente Minnelli's MGM melodrama about filmmakers.

Throughout the narrative, Hanson alternates location types, switching between the monumental and everyday. The steps of City Hall and the neo-baroque fixtures of the Pacific Electric Building, out of which tough cop Bud White (Russell Crowe) dangles a recalcitrant district attorney, contrast vividly with the run-down clapboard of the derelict Craftsman houses of Echo Park and South Central. The power brokers live in the upscale homes, such as Richard Neutra's Lovell House, and exploit women such as Lynn who live in modest but well-kept Spanish moderns in the Larchmont district. Characters die at the Hollywood Center Motel on Sunset Boulevard, a few steps from the one frequented by vice cop Lottie Mason in *Impulse*, or at the "Night Owl" Coffee Shop, on 6th Street, just two blocks from Downtown's skid row and stone's throw from where Sugar Torch is gunned down in *Crimson Kimono* (1959). The office of Sid Hudgens is in Crossroads of the World, a Streamline Moderne "mini-mall" from 1937 that features a central building shaped like a ship with a spinning globe atop a spire. A block east along Sunset is the Hollywood Athletic Club, where Mike Hammer in *Kiss Me Deadly* finds the hot box known as the "great whatsit" in a locker.

This World, Then the Fireworks (1997) brings to the screen another brutal and nihilistic Jim Thompson work. The egomaniacal protagonists of this piece (Thompson's characters, like Lou Ford in *The Killer inside Me*, often feel morally superior to those around them) are an incestuous (another recurrent theme in Thompson's work) brother-sister pair, Carol (Gina Gershon) and Marty (Billy Zane). The trauma that haunts this pair is depicted in the opening sequence and narrated, as is the whole film, by Marty in his sarcastic, flippant tone. The children's father is caught in bed with another woman. The bloody scene that ensues when the woman's cop-husband returns is witnessed by the children and their mother. As the children laugh at what Marty calls the slapstick elements of the action, the mother's face is splattered with blood as fireworks go off in the background.

Opposite, *L.A. Confidential*: top, the hooded Kim Basinger channels Veronica Lake as Lynn Bracken, who enthralls countless clients and two detectives. Center, the crime scene at the Night Owl, with bodies posed in a manner that would have made the real Weegee salivate. Bottom, the aftermath of the all-cop shoot-out at an abandoned motel in the Baldwin Hills, the area where one slept the big sleep in Chandler's novel.

After this event Carol and Marty become inseparable in spirit and body. Eventually, both marry and separate but not for long. Returning to their home, where their Bible-thumping, morphine-addicted mother preaches to them about their "sins," Carol and Marty take up where they left off. Even though Carol plies her sex trade and Marty dates a female cop, Lois (Sheryl Lee), who is drawn sexually to his sadistic ways, it is clear that their first priority is each other. When Carol is tracked by an obese detective, an enraged Marty dispatches him with a letter holder to the eye. When Carol causes a client to go into cardiac arrest, Marty helps dispose of the body. When Carol decides to get rid of their judgmental mother by giving her an overdose of morphine, Marty assents.

The only force that is able to finally separate them is death. When Carol dies from a botched abortion in Mexico, Marty falls into depression. In the end Lois takes her broken lover away (after he has killed her husband, much as his father had killed the cop at the beginning of the story). But a superimposition of Carol over the couple's departing car externalizes Marty's thoughts.

In the gray area between the classic period and neo, a starkly made, independent production, *The Honeymoon Killers* (1969), the only film by musicologist and opera director Leonard Kastle, first dramatized the real-life exploits of Raymond Fernandez and Martha Beck. Kastle's quirky black-and-white movie, full of long takes and underscored with Mahler symphonies, featured a break-out performance by the heavy-set Shirley Stoler as Martha and has moved from succès d'estime to full-blown cult status. *Profundo Carmesi* (1996, aka *Deep Crimson* in the US) was director Arturo Ripstein's unofficial retelling with the deadly couple reimagined as denizens of postwar Mexico.

Lonely Hearts (2006) is a retro noir that again depicts the slightly odd couple who bilked and sometimes murdered war widows and lonely spinsters across the nation in the 1940s. Although somewhat less glamourous than in many other roles, Salma Hayek's portrayal of Martha Beck is certainly different from Stoler's, as the "damaged goods" who answers a lonely hearts ad by con man Ray Fernandez (Jared Leto) and then becomes both the sexual and homicidal engine for the duo. Martha lays her claim to Ray with due speed and even though she goes along with his seductions of wealthy women, her jealousy is

Opposite: *The World, Then the Fireworks*: female cop Lois (Sheryl) competes for the affections of Marty (Billy Zane) with Carol (Gina Gershon, inset).

Above, the fatal couple, Ray Fernandez (Jared Leto) and Martha Beck (Salma Hayek) in *Lonely Hearts*.

what motivates the bloody murders. When Ray is having sex with the first victim in the film, Martha listens in the opposite room. No longer able to stand it, she enters and shoots the woman in the head while she is on top of Ray. She pushes the woman aside and then mounts the bloody and horrified Ray, demanding he continue the sexual act with her.

Whenever Martha feels that the unreliable Ray is beginning to wander, she reinforces her control through the most radical of means. While they are driving, Martha performs oral sex on Ray, causing him to swerve and a policeman to pull them over. When the policeman goes back to check the registration on the stolen car, she follows and performs the same service on the cop while an outraged Ray watches in the rearview mirror. When she returns to the car, she places a gun to his genitals, telling him that she is in charge not him. When the couple is finally apprehended by the obsessed Detective Robinson (John Travolta) and sentenced to the electric chair, Martha tells the officer she committed the murders because "Raymond is mine. He belongs to me." When she enters the execution chamber after Raymond has been "fried," she tells her guards ecstatically, "I can smell him. So sweet."

Josh Hartnett and Scarlett Johansson, neither of whom is *The Black Dahlia*.

Brian De Palma's *The Black Dahlia* (2006) revisits one of the most famous Los Angeles crime stories, the unsolved murder and mutilation of a young starlet. Unfortunately, De Palma's visual excesses and love of pastiche undercuts whatever interest the viewer might have in the subject matter. In the end, this retro kitsch is a some parts Black Dahlia (which De Palma displays in grisly detail on a period autopsy table) and equal parts steamy clinches indulged with a smirking voyeurism, as if Masters and Johnson met Mickey Spillane.

Oliver Parker's *Fade to Black* (2006) melds historical biography with retro-noir stylistics and themes in an attempt to place enigmatic filmmaker Orson Welles (Danny Huston) into a plot resembling many of Welles' own noir oeuvre. Arriving in Italy in 1948 to star in a movie about the mystic and magician Cagliostro, the director becomes embroiled in American machinations on the side of Christian Democrats in their electoral battle against the Communist Party. Drawn into the web by sullen femme fatale Lea (Paz Vega), who resembles his recently divorced ex-wife Rita Hayworth (one reporter calls him repeatedly and derisively "Mr. Hayworth"), Welles attempts to balance the various components of his personality to penetrate the core of this mystery involving assassinations and political corruption. At one level, Welles is a dedicated filmmaker and artist. He jumps out of his car, amateur movie camera in hand, in order to photograph a violent Communist rally. He pursues investors shamelessly, no matter what their shady backgrounds (he wants to make an adaptation of Shakespeare's *Othello*, as did the actual Welles a few years later). In the resolution of the movie, Welles refuses to accept the truth about his femme fatale, even from her own lips, preferring instead, as he did in most of his own movies, to remain in a state of ambiguity.

Parker also conveys Welles' politically leftist sympathies, which exarcebated his disfavor with the studios over his work methods. The actual Welles left the United States before the anti-Communist witch hunts geared up. In the movie he is beaten by Mafia thugs, led by an American attaché, as his punishment for his interference in their plans to assure a Christian Democratic victory. In a particularly effective sequence, Welles uses his magic act and his ability as a filmmaker during a live show, exposing the fascist underpinnings of the Christian Democratic party to the audience. And finally, Welles' infamous character flaws as a person, particularly his basic insecurities about his own worth (mirroring Welles' own portrait of Charles Foster Kane), reappear throughout the movie. After he is beaten by the thugs, his onetime friend the American official delivers the final insult by telling him that all along he was insignificant in this plot, just a footnote. Dejected, Welles lies bleeding in the road, beaten mentally as well as physically, his much vaunted Welles bravado (seen elsewhere in the film) nowhere in evidence.

Clint Eastwood's *Changeling* (2008) is based on a true story of LAPD corruption and female suppression in late 1920s and early 1930s Los Angeles. A single mother's son is kidnapped. The police, with much fanfare, find a boy they believe (or choose for publicity purposes to believe) is the woman's son.

A dowdy (relatively) Angelina Jolie as Christine in *Changeling*.

Angelina Jolie gives a grounded performance as the telephone operator and mother, who tries to convince both the police and the public that this boy is not hers. Only after the police harass and eventually institutionalize her—a common technique for quieting "hysterical" women—is the truth ultimately revealed and the mother vindicated.

Nero Bloom: Private Eye (2009) spends a good deal of its meager budget re-creating the chiaroscuro look of 1940s film noir. The weaknesses in script and acting significantly undermine the effort. *Fairview St.* (2010), also shot in black and white, evidences the same ambitions as *Nero Bloom* but it too stumbles on its performances.

Martin Scorsese's *Shutter Island* (2010) is based on a book by Dennis Lehane, the author behind the neo-noir *Mystic River*. The story is a complex one and related through the perspective of the protagonist, US marshal Edward "Teddy" Daniels, which is intended to mislead. A retro noir set in the 1950s, the movie opens as Daniels (Leonardo DiCaprio) and his partner Chuck Aule (Mark

Below, *Shutter Island* sends its investigator protagonists to an asylum where they occasionally step out of the retro world and into something vaguely surreal, as when Marshals Aule (Mark Ruffalo, right) and Daniels (Leonardo DiCaprio) stumble into an ornate mausoleum.

Ruffalo) arrives at a prison for the criminally insane located on an isolated island near Boston, the gothic iconography of which occasionally gives the visual impression of a horror film. While there to investigate the disappearance of inmate Rachel Solando, from the first scenes Daniels develops migraines and manifests signs of paranoia. Since in the world of noir, there is often a sound basis for paranoia, the viewer is not led toward a particular reading, even when Daniels begins to suspect that the doctors are drugging him, as well as keeping political prisoners. He goes so far as to imagine that Dr. Naehring (Max von Sydow) is an ex-Nazl and flashes back to his own experience liberating a concentration camp. As the events begin to spin out of control, coincident with a powerful storm, Daniels has visions of his dead wife and children, who seem to be calling him from somewhere unworldly.

While the twist at the end is intended to be a complete surprise, a viewer might already suspect from visual cues, or know from reading the novel, that Daniels is not what he seems. As the marshal confronts Dr. Cawley (Ben Kingsley) and his partner in a forbidding lighthouse, he is told that he is actually Andrew Laeddis, husband of Rachel Solando, whom he killed after she murdered their children. In a flashback precipitated by this reveleation, Daniels recalls the truth: he did his kill his wife Dolores after discovering that she had drowned their children. Daniels now has a choice: admit he is Laeddis or accept a lobotomy. In the final scene Daniels/Laeddis refuses to accept this true identity and asks his partner, who is actually his therapist, "Which would be worse: to live as a monster or to die as a good man?" With that question unanswered, Daniels/Laeddis is led away for the procedure.

Sci-fi and Surreal Noir

One cannot overemphasize the importance of Ridley Scott's *Blade Runner* in setting the tone for the universe of sci-fi/fantasy neo-noir in the 21st century. The film helped create a quixotic subgenre of retro-sci-fi, where the film is set in the future with advanced technology but also features old-school architecture, fashion, hair styles and so on.

In *The Crow* (1994) director Alex Proyas creates a dystopic dark city much like the one in his science fiction neo-noir *Dark City,* four years later. Brandon Lee (who was accidentally killed toward the end of shooting the film) brings a balletic performance to his interpretation of Eric Draven, a rock singer who is murdered along with his girlfriend by a group of thugs sent by mobster Top Dollar (Michael Wincott) to punish them for leading a tenant protest. Eric is resurrected from the grave by a crow (along with ravens, a messenger from the underworld in ancient myths), sent from beyond, to aid him in his revenge spree. Lee alternates in his portrayal between overwhelming anguish and white-hot rage. He emerges from the grave, screaming and spasming. He returns to the scene of his girlfriend's rape and murder, again contorting his body before the broken skylight as he remembers the events. And when confronting the gang of murderers, he performs with great agility the martial acrobatics required for the extensive action scenes.

His nemeses in the film are Top Dollar and his half-sister/lover Myca (Bai

Above, Brandon Lee as the title figure in *The Crow*.
Below, a 17-year-old Angelina Jolie as Casella "Cash" Reese, the title character in *Cyborg 2.*

Ling). The viewer is introduced to the couple after they have ravaged a nubile young woman. The gothicly garbed and made-up Myca, obsessed with the symbolism of eyes, dangles her dagger before the cornea of the unconscious woman. When holding court over their motley minions, Myca lies languorously before the men, caressing her lover/brother or holding down with her heel a victim for him to question. The villainous pair epitomizes the decadence that the innocent Eric confronts and eventually conquers. After destroying the brother and sisted, Eric returns to his grave and his dead girlfriend, whose ghost beckons to him, but leaves behind his young ward and the narrator of the film, Shelly (Sofia Shinas), to carry on his crusade against evildoers.

Despite its title *Cyborg 2* (1994) is not actually a sequel to the original *Cyborg* (1989), a Jean-Claude Van Damme vehicle about plague, pirates and a gun-for-hire (Van Damme, not a cyborg) that focuses on action rather than any neo-noir ethos. The writers of *Cyborg 2* took their inspiration instead from both William Gibson, whose noir cyberpunk style was established in his short stories of the 1970s and '80s, and *Blade Runner*, from which they freely mined plot points and character types. Gibson was, in fact, completing his first novel, *Neuromancer*, when he saw *Blade Runner* and was struck by how its visualization of Los Angeles coincided with his own writings about corporate wars in cyberspace and urban underworlds full of dark denizens who are part human and part machine. In Gibson's writing, as in *Blade Runner*, these cyborgs/replicants are conscious of their artificial identities and prone to existential angst.

The competing corporations in *Cyborg 2*, Pinwheel and Kobayashi are unabashedly Gibson-esque in their machinations. The nighttime streets and alleyways of Los Angeles—even its iconic City Hall is used as a background—are the same terrain that many classic-period types criss crossed. The title character is Casella "Cash" Reese (Angelina Jolie), a figure that recalls both the replicant women, Zhora and Pris, in *Blade Runner*, and Gibson's razor-fingered Molly Millions from his story "Johnny Mnemonic" and the Sprawl Trilogy. Although a cyborg designed to infiltrate Pinwheel's competitors and destroy its executives through her pre-programmed immolation, Reese is less angst-ridden than prone to teen infatuation (appropriately, Jolie was just 17 in this first starring role), when she falls hard for her martial arts instructor Colton Ricks (Elias Koteas) and together they become a sci-fi noir fugitive couple assisted by an underground group of hackers and hustlers of the Gibson ilk. There is even a "blade runner" in the form of Danny Bench (Billy Drago), a tracker of fugitive cyborgs, and sundry others recombined from cyberpunk predecessors. The final confrontation in an industrial yard full of surplus ship parts in Long Beach was meant to be visually dynamic but falls far short of such simpler noir archetypes as Cody Jarrett's extinction in *White Heat*. Cobbled together as *Cyborg 2* is, its dramatic impact and noir credentials are predictably uneven.

Kathryn Bigelow's *Strange Days* (1995) is a prime example of the millennial dystopia in neo-noir. Set in Los Angeles as the 20th century draws to a violent close, the protagonist, Nero (Ralph Fiennes), is an ex-cop turned hustler who is peddling "Squids"—a device that records events from one person's brain and then allows another to experience it—on the black market. To the dismay of his former police cohort, Mace (Angela Bassett), Nero is descending further and further into the dark morass Los Angeles has become.

Bigelow creates a vision of a city in flames, controlled by gangs on the streets while the wealthy in the high rises above seek out pleasure and the newest thrill. In addition, Nero's obsession with his volatile former girlfriend, femme fatale glam-punk singer Faith (Juliette Lewis), has turned him into a stalker, hiding in the shadows as she performs onstage and trying to approach her when she rejects him vehemently and cruelly. What finally turns Mace around is the discovery that a local cartel is producing "snuff" Squids for the delectation of the wealthy. When Mace finds one showing Faith being raped and murdered (it is a fake), he becomes frantic. He confronts his buddy Max (Tom Sizemore) whom he now suspects of being behind these "snuff" Squids and in a final struggle kills him.

Terry Gilliam's *Twelve Monkeys* (1995) is based on the seminal short film by Chris Marker, *La Jetée* (1962). Gilliam's film relates the tale of a prisoner—Cole (Bruce Willis)—sent from the ravaged future to the past to stop a virus from being spread throughout the world. Cole is a particularly apt subject for time travel as he is psychically connected to the past via a memory of seeing a man shot at an airport terminal. Cole, with the help of a psychiatrist, eventually tracks down the scientist responsible for the spreading the virus. At the very same airport he had seen in his vision, Cole pursues the man but is shot by security. On the same platform is a young boy who sees the whole event. In a conflation of time dimensions, the young boy is Cole himself as a child.

Johnny Mnemonic (1995) is one of the few actual adaptations (along with the *New Rose Hotel* discussed above) from prose fiction of William Gibson (who also wrote the screenplay for this film). Cyberpunk concentrates on visionary technology and combines it with an edgy, contrarian ethos. Johnny (Keanu Reeves) is an information courier who has given up his childhood memories in order to allow brain space for the information he carries for mega-corporations. Now he wants those memories back but is pursued by rival corporations after his residual tech info. Johnny is aided in his quest by a tattooed cybernetically

Opposite, *Strange Days*: policewoman Mace (Angela Bassett) is concerned about her hallucinating ex-partner Nero (Ralph Fiennes).

Below, the time-warped fugitive couple Cole (Bruce Willis) and Kathryn (Madeleine Stowe) in *Twelve Monkeys.*

Above, *Johnny Mnemonic*: title figure Keanu Reeces is flanked by the rebel J-Bone (Ice T) and bodyguard Jane (Dina Meyer).

Opposite, genetically perfected couple Irene (Uma Thurman) and Vincent (Ethan Hawke) in *Gattaca* in a pastel-tinted scene.

enhanced female bodyguard (Dina Meyer) and the street-wise antiestablishment J-Bone (Ice-T).

In *Fallen* (1997) detective Hobbes (Denzel Washington) tracks down a supernatural killer who is taking the bodies of various individuals in order to commit heinous acts. When Hobbes kills one of those possessed, he is forced to clear his name by proving that the supernatural killer exists.

Gattaca (1997) creates a dystopia which in design owes more to the Bauhaus style than to the German Expressionist lighting of *Blade Runner*. It is an immaculate, orderly universe—sleek, modern, symmetrical, yet somehow still sinister. The scenes at night are tinted eerily red, blue, or green—disorienting the viewer's color expectations. The day scenes are blazingly bright with rockets flying like meteors over the Gattaca headquarters at regular intervals. The Gattaca offices are moderne, minimalist with rows of dark-suited employees marching automaton-like through turnstiles, in a clear homage to *Metropolis.* The central conflict of the film revolves around identity. This "brave new world" will genetically engineer children for the right price, thereby producing a two-tiered society of "valids" and "in-valids." "Valids" occupy the upper echelon positions while "in-valids" perform the menial jobs. As a result society is obsessed with keeping track of each citizen's identity through the use of such methods as electronic scanning and periodic blood/urine testing.

Vincent (Ethan Hawke) is an in-valid, "conceived in love," who narrates the film in traditional noir style. His brother Anton, however, was genetically engineered. Vincent's greatest ambition is to travel in space, even though his father tells him, "The only way you'll see the inside of a spaceship is cleaning it." Although handicapped, he is determined to live out his dream. And so he illegally changes his identity with that of a valid ex-athlete, Jerome (Jude Law). In order to maintain this facade, Vincent/Jerome must painfully scrub away his identity every morning—seen in the first shots of the film in a series of close-ups as Vincent washes away every dead cell and follicle he can find. Although he is scheduled to travel to Titan, he lives in a state of constant fear of being discovered, particularly since a murder has occurred at Gattaca that brings in the police.

Three key scenes in this movie are the swimming contests between Vincent and Anton (Loren Dean) at various ages. These scenes not only crystallize the conflict between the brothers, as well as the class conflict in their society, but they also serve to demonstrate Vincent's perseverance in the face of pain and fear. Although, as he tells the viewer through his narration, he

Jude Law as Jerome, the
who swaps his valid identity
with Vincent in *Gattaca*.

always lost the contests as a boy to his genetically superior brother, as a teen things change and Vincent wins. The spectator sees him outdistance his brother and in fact rescue him from the deep waters. This contest is repeated for a last time, toward the end of the film. It is night and the boys are adults. Vincent finally confirms for his doubting brother the superiority of will over genetics as he beats him and rescues him from the sea once more. As he pulls Anton's spent body back, Vincent stares up at the stars he so longs to visit.

In the final scene of the movie, the filmmakers construct a powerful montage based on the themes of identity and Nietzschean "will to power." The film intercuts between Vincent/Jerome's walking through tunnels and boarding the space ship to Titan while the original Jerome, who has become a second brother to Vincent, prepares to immolate himself in a furnace, thereby giving up completely his identity to Vincent. The rocket rises. Flames spew forth from the boosters as the fire of the furnace devours Jerome, who holds his Olympic medal in a final moment of pride for past accomplishments. The film then cuts to a close-up of Vincent, tears in his eyes, "Every atom in our body was once part of a star...Maybe I'm going home." Noir melancholy and existential doubt color his final victory as it does the entire film.

Like *Blade Runner*, *Dark City* (1998) visually recalls one of the principal stylistic antecedents of classic noir, German Expressionism. Alex Proyas, who also directed the gothically visualized *The Crow*, constructs a world owing much to the German movements in art, theater, and film, typified for many viewers by director Fritz Lang's 1927 *Metropolis*. On a satellite in the sky, a race of dying aliens is conducting a massive lab experiment, seeking there a "cure for mortality," as the human accomplice Dr. Schreber (Kiefer Sutherland) puts it. Each night, from their underground headquarters, the aliens, through an ability called "tuning," destroy and then rebuild parts of the city above, as well as change the identity of any inhabitant in that section of the metropolis. The viewer does not witness this amazing transformation until midway through the film as this city, in which there is never any day, comes to a halt: cars stopping dead on silent city streets, individuals falling asleep in mid-sentence. As they sleep, new buildings arise recalling the bleak future cityscape in the first shots of *Metropolis.* As in Lang's classic, the city is imposing, angular, with edifices that are gothic despite futuristic flourishes. In a departure from this model, and in direct homage to the classic period of film noir, Proyas has given his dark city a 1940s patina through costuming and set dressing. While the city sleeps, the aliens, who resemble Nosferatu with their long black coats, sharp teeth, bent posture, and bald heads, glide through its streets and hallways, accompanied by the Judas-like Dr. Schreber who implants new memories in the brains of the human guinea pigs.

Dark City proposes a supremely existential dilemma. On an allegorical level the inhabitants of this city stand for all humanity caught in the web of a seemingly absurd and meaningless existence over which they have no control. The solution to their cosmic dilemma is the one put forth by writers like Sartre and Camus: consciousness of the absurdity must be followed by action. The protagonist Murdoch (Rufus Sewell) experiences such an epiphany when in close-up he suddenly awakes in his bath to find blood on his forehead from an aborted injection and a dead woman in his apartment.

The remainder of the film tracks Murdoch in his search for his actual

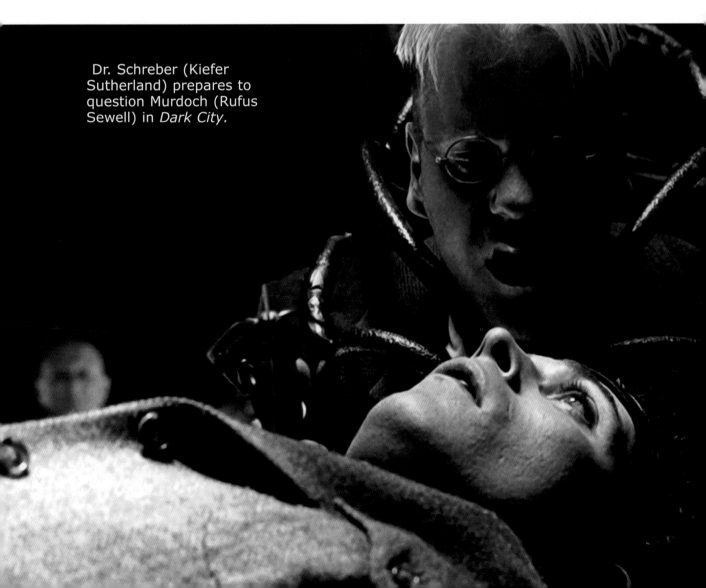

Dr. Schreber (Kiefer Sutherland) prepares to question Murdoch (Rufus Sewell) in *Dark City.*

identity. For the partial injection has erased much of his former memories, and that leaves him unsure of himself or anyone else, including his own "wife" Emma or his "beloved" Uncle Karl, both of whom turn out to be just two more guinea pigs with implanted memories. Even as he is pursued by a melancholy detective (William Hurt), looking much like the classic noir sleuths in trench coat, fedora and suit, who also begins to doubt the reality of his own identity, Murdoch discovers that he has assimilated some of the powers of the aliens, most notably, their ability to transform reality by "tuning." So, the final battle in this Maya-like universe comes down to a contest of wills. Murdoch wins, defeating the aliens at their own game by destroying the underground machinery that operates the city above, again recalling ther destruction wrought by the workers in *Metropolis*. With his victory in hand, Murdoch accepts the unreality of his life and so decides to create a new one. Much like Deckard in *Blade Runner*, Murdoch is haunted by a vision, a dream, possibly even a memory, in this case of a place called Shell Beach where the sun always shines and the colors are vibrant. Utilizing his newly found powers, he decides to construct this beach, flooding the city and then causing the ground to thrust up and create a land's end. In the final scenes he walks down a pier to the waiting Anna (Jennifer Connelly). Together they walk off to Shell Beach, a land of illusion but at least a benign one.

In 1997 Hong Kong director John Woo can to Hollywood to make his most outrageous movie in a career already filled with over-the-top productions. *Face/Off* takes Woo's theme of protagonists/antagonists who are doubles to a literal level by having criminal Troy (Nicolas Cage and obsessed FBI agent Archer (John Travolta) exchange not only personalities but faces in a revolu-

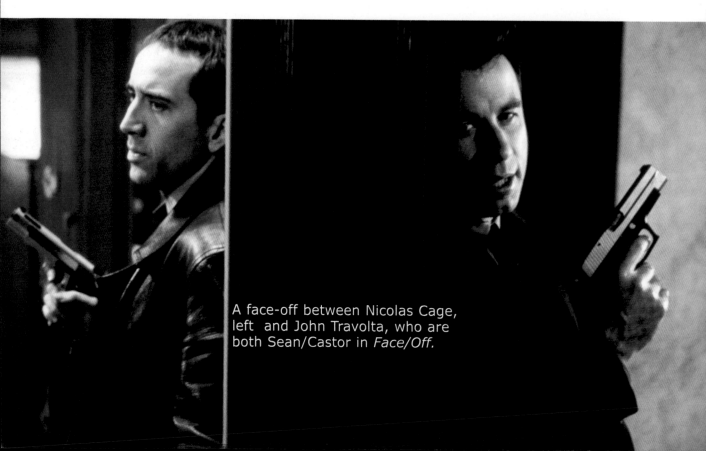

A face-off between Nicolas Cage, left and John Travolta, who are both Sean/Castor in *Face/Off*.

tionary surgical procedure. The purpose of this extraordinary plot device is to allow the Archer to pose as Troy and get the location of a bomb. Not suprisingly the scheme goes wildly awry. Each man finds himself drawn to the people and lives of the other. Troy becomes attached to Archer's suburban life and family while Archer finds Troy's exotic girlfriend (Gina Gershon) and their sybaritic life appealing as well. The ending is more predictable.

The X-Files (1998), brought the successful neo-noir television series of the same name (1993-2002) and its FBI agent protagonists Fox (David Duchovny) and Mulder (Gillian Anderson) to the big screen. As with the original series, Fox is the most tormented of the two agents. His desire to believe in the paranormal and supernatural is fueled by the loss of his sister to, he believes, alien abductors. Mulder, on the other hand, is the more detached and rationalist of the two. She will only believe when confronted with irrefutable facts. And she gets her wish in this movie in the form of a huge alien vessel hidden beneath the ice in Antarctica.

Darren Aronofsky's low-budget, black-and-white *Pi* (1998) is a mystical exploration involving schizophrenic techie Max (Sean Guillette), who is convinced he has stumbled on the key to the universe through his study of numbers. Isolated in his tiny apartment with his computer Euclid, he runs strings of numbers, finally coming upon a 216-digit number. Consulting his Hassidic friend Lenny about his discovery, Lenny references the numerology inherent in Jewish sacred books like the *Kabbalah* while his old mathematics professor warns him away from pursuing numerology.

Max's obsession is aggravated by visions in which he believes he can predict the stock market. With the visions come migraines that debilitate him as

Pi: Sean Guillette as Max.

Cast decidedly against type; Samuel L. Jackson as the very breakable Elijah Price in *Unbreakable*.

well as pulsating tumor (he believes) in his brain. Max is also pursued by Lenny and his Hassidic friends for his knowledge and harassed by a corporation that had funded a new chip for his computer. As visions and reality interface, Max cannot stand the agony in his brain and so lobotomizes himself with a drill. In the final scene of the movie the zombie-like Max sits in the park staring peacefully at nature while a little girl tries to get him to help her with math problems, which ironically Max is no longer able to understand. The price of Max's epiphany was much too great. So instead, he chose ignorance and tranquility.

Unbreakable (2000) foregrounds the meaning of heroism in a modern world. Using comic books as jumping-off point writer-director M. Night Shyamalan sets up a conflict between a tormented modern superhero who refuses to accept his powers of invincibility and a physically and mentally damaged antagonist who will go to any lengths to prove that the comics he loves are relevant in today's world. Price (Samuel L. Jackson) is born with a congenital disease that leaves him with brittle bones. Throughout his childhood he fears the world outside and the pain it can cause with the slightest fall. As he grows up, he walks with a cane but has expanded his ken by opening an art gallery filled with illustrations from comic books. He has also devoted his life to looking for a superhero, an "unbreakable" individual in contrast to his fragility.

Price thinks he has found his man in the person of Dunn (Bruce Willis) who has survived two horrendous accidents without a scratch. Dunn is a reticent man who is estranged from his wife, with whom he still lives, but inextricably bound to his adoring son. After Price approaches Dunn and his son about his conjecture that he might have preternatural powers, Dunn dismisses him but begins to notice qualities in himself that he did not before. With the help of his son, he lifts weights beyond what any person his size should be able to lift.

During his job as a security guard at a stadium, he has visions or "feelings" about people he touches and in that way is able to identify potential criminals. He also remembers that he has never been sick in his life.

But still Dunn is unable, with his melancholy disposition, to accept his findings until in a Philadelphia train station he rubs against a janitor and sees that he has kidnapped a family. Following the man back to the family's house, he struggles with the man. Dunn falls from the second story but is unharmed and eventually strangles the janitor. Returning to Price's gallery, he wishes to thank him for relieving his "sadness" about himself and the meaning of his life; but when he shakes Price's hand, he sees visions of various accidents Price has caused over the years in search for "superman." As Dunn recoils in horror, Price plaintively yells to him, "Now that we know who you are, I know who I am. I'm not a mistake! It all makes sense! In a comic, you know how you can tell who the archvillain's going to be? He's the exact opposite of the hero. And most times they're friends, like you and me! I should've known way back when... You know why, David? Because of the kids. They called me Mr. Glass."

Minority Report (2002) is based on science fiction novelist Philip K. Dick's (the source for *Blade Runner*) short story. The film captures Dick's paranoia about the fate of mankind. In this future world the government can determine who are criminals before they commit crimes. The pitfalls inherent in such an approach are fairly obvious, as are the advantages to a totalitarian entity.

Below, *Minority Report*: Anderton (Tom Cruise) manipulates the pre-crime system

Thomas Janes as the movie rendering of the comic book Punisher (inset).

Daredevil (2003), based on the Marvel comics character, is a superhero at night but during the day he is a blind attorney fighting corruption and seeking to avenge the murder of his boxer father. Complications arise when Murdock/Daredevil (Ben Affleck) meets Elektra (Jennifer Garner), the daughter of an industrialist who has connections to the mob. After a bit of fighting foreplay (she, too, is trained in martial arts), they fall in love. However, the murder of her father changes all that as Elektra comes to believe the murderer is Daredevil.

In a particularly powerful scene, Elektra, dressed in a red leather catsuit, prepares for battle against Daredevil as Amy Lee of the pop group Evanescence wails the lyrics "Wake me up inside." Daredevil fights her reluctantly when attacked and is wounded. But before she can kill him, Bullseye (Colin Farrell), a hitman hired by the mob, murders her. The distressed and broken Daredevil hides out with a priest, agonizing over the loss of Elektra. And when he recovers, he heads out to eliminate Bullseye.

The Punisher (2004) is also based on a Marvel comics character and was first filmed with Dolph Lundgren in 1989. The family of FBI agent Frank Castle (played stoically by Thomas Jane) is destroyed by mob boss Howard Saint (John Travolta) at the behest of Livia (Laura Harring), after Castle killed their son in a shootout. Castle survives and transforms himself into the trench coat-wearing Punisher: "Frank Castle is dead. Call me the Punisher." Since he seeks a more appropriate punishment—rather than simple revenge—Castle's plan begins with an infiltration of Saint's inner circle. Through an intermediary Castle plants "evidence" to convince an insanely jealous Saint that his wife is having an affair with his right-hand man. Consequently and with particular brutality, Saint destroys them both. After that, the Punisher goes postal and kills them all; but he leaves Saint for last and allows time for his nemesis to reflect on the retribution that he has brought down on himself.

Sin City (2005), based on the graphic novels of Frank Miller who co-directs with Robert Rodriguez and Quentin Tarantino, interweaves four stories in a complex visual re-creation of the noir world of the classic period. Using CGI techniques, the film resembles an animated version of Miller's comic books, with chiaroscuro slashes of light and dark interrupted periodically by splashes of color. The four stories themselves ("The Customer Is Always Right"—used only as framing device, "That Yellow Bastard," "The Big, Fat Kill," and "The Hard Goodbye"), which overlap in time and space, recycle for a new generation many of the themes and motifs from the classic period of noir. Obsession, femme fatales, existential "chumps," and corruption abound.

In "The Big, Fat Kill" Dwight is fixated on his ex-lover, the bisexual dom-inatrix Gail, played by Rosario Dawson, who leads the gang of warrior prosti-tutes who have established sovereignty over a part of Basin City called "Old Town." He returns to help them out when a rogue cop and the mob invade their territory but soon learns that these femme fatales are able to defend them-selves. Dressed in fetish outfits and sporting swords, knives, and automatic weapons, these warrior women are "Valkyrie" right out of 1970s warrior women exploitation movies.

Below, self-consciously noir lighting on Gail (Rosario Dawson) and Dwight (Clive Owen in *Sin City.*

In "The Hard Goodbye" (the name, of course, references Chandler's novel), Marv, as played by Mickey Rourke whose own world-weary face requires the minimum amount of prosthetics, is a brute-like "maniac." Not even prostitutes will touch him. After one luminous "goddess" (his word) takes pity on him and spends a night with him in a heart-shaped bed and then is murdered in the morning, he tears apart the town to find her murderer. When he is executed for his "crimes," the camera zooms into his eye to reveal his last thoughts: Goldie's making love to him on that red, heart-shaped bed.

The most classically noir of the pieces is "That Yellow Bastard." Bruce Willis plays an aging cop named Hartigan who has a "bad heart" as well as a strong sense of chivalry. As with the other pieces, he narrates the tale in traditional noir fashion, calling himself "old man" and putting himself through masochistic situation after masochistic situation in order to protect Nancy, the stripper he had saved as a child from a child molester. Their relationship is typical of the perverse couplings in much of noir. Nancy has written him every week while he served time on a trumped-up charge. When he goes to find her she is on stage, dressed as a cowgirl. Deciding to leave, sensing he is being followed, Nancy, who in the person of Jessica Alba is a Lolita stereotype, who jumps from the stage to embrace him. Although Hartigan tries to resist her aggressive advances, he finds himself too drawn to this "granddaughter-lover." In the final scene, Hartigan performs the ultimate act of devotion and chivalry, killing himself in order to save Nancy from the political powers that are bent on his destruction. As he sinks into the snow, he pronounces his own epitaph with an existential fatalism common to noir protagonists, "An old man dies, a young woman lives, fair trade." Alba returns as Nancy to extract revenge for Hartigan's death in the relatively uninspired *Sin City: A Dame To Kill For* (2014).)

As Det. Hartigan Bruce Willis' character again saves a child and reconnects with the adult Nancy (Jessica Alba) after she has become a stripper in a *Sin City* that is black-and-white with splashes of color.

Like Tim Burton's *Batman* and *Batman Returns* in 1989 and 1992 respectively, Christopher Nolan in *Batman Begins* (2005) and *The Dark Knight* (2008) draws heavily on the influence of graphic novelist Frank Miller, the man most responsible for noiring the image of both Batman and Gotham, for his inspiration. *Batman Begins* is a prequel to the Batman myth. It opens at a martial training center in Bhutan, where troubled billionaire Bruce Wayne (Christian Bale) is held by a clandestine group called the League of Shadows. One of their leaders, Ducard (Liam Neeson), who later is revealed as the nefarious Ra's al Ghul, exploits Wayne's guilt and sorrow over the death of his parents.

After years of training, Wayne returns to Gotham to wreak revenge on the man who killed his parents. In the process he becomes a vigilante, fighting the growing mob of criminals running wild in this dark city (the photography is low-key and high contrast in classic noir style). The life-and-death decisions, often morally ambiguous, Wayne is forced to make plus his ambivalence about leading a double life (a major theme in noir) turn the crime-fighter into a stoic, emotionally stunted individual with little trust in others.

Nolan shifts gears in *The Dark Knight* and centers on Batman's chief antagonist, the Joker (played with amazing intensity by Heath Ledger). The Joker is, in many ways, Batman's double and he knows it. He tells the caped

Batman (Christian Bale) and the Joker (Heath Ledger), the freakish doppelgangers posed together in *The Dark Knight*.

crusader that they are both "freaks" and that he (Batman) "completes" him. The Joker is a self-proclaimed agent of chaos or, as Batman's butler tells him, "Some men just want to watch the world burn." His obsession is Batman and forcing him to reveal his identity. In order to accomplish this end, he is willing to turn Gotham into a killing field, which he does in a series of intricately staged action scenes. But the action is not the heart of the movie. It is the Joker himself. Speaking in a hesitant, staccato style, he professes his philosophy of anarchy eloquently while telling several versions of how he received the carved grin on his face. And it really does not matter which version of his story is true. Like Wayne, he is marked by the trauma of living and has chosen, again like Wayne, to live as an outlier in order to assuage his suffering.

The mega-budget *The Island* (2005) revisits the territory of *Blade Runner* as a naive couple escapes from a sanitary and sinister facility. While tracked by a specialized operative, the fugitives discover their true nature, not replicants but clones, raised and reserved at the expense of wealthy individuals who want spare bodies available in case of early death by accident or disease. After a brief moment of existential shock, these clones exploit that fact to survive. While it shares basic credentials with *The Island* as an action movie, the Schwarzenegger vehicle *The 6th Day* (2000) ironically generates deeper angst on the part of its "I didn't realize I was a clone" protagonist. Of course, the emotional source code for the discovery of being a duplicate is Schwarzenegger's much better-known reprisal of the title figure in *Terminator II: Judgment Day* (1990), the reprogrammed killing machine that searches to understand what it means to be human. Like some flesh-and-blood neo-noir hit men, the Terminator sacrifices himself/itself at the end, and prompts the tech noir/pop existential observation: "If a machine, a Terminator, can learn the value of human life, maybe we can, too."

Dark Country (2009) bends the surreal edges of the neo-noir universe imagined by David Lynch even further, all the way into the realm of *The Twilight Zone* visualized in 3-D. There is an explicit irony in the film's opening narration

Below, Ewan MacGregor and Scarlett Johansson as the fugitive clone couple Lincoln Six Echo and Jordan Two Delta in *The Island*.

Richard (Thomas Jane) and Gina (Lauren German) conceal a body that they do not know is a future version of him in *Dark Country*.

and a conscious evocation of classic-period style. The visual treatment of the first scenes is certainly ominous, starting with a pan and 90-degree tilt down and away from a motel sign and into the window of a room. Inside, cut by seemingly endless shadows from Venetian blinds, Richard (*Punisher*'s Thomas Jane, who is also the director) awakens, recaps his situation by talking to himself—newly married to Gina (Lauren German), a woman he has just met in Las Vegas ("You don't even know how to spell her name.")—and suggests a flashback structure that will never be confirmed...or denied. Richard is a man who quit his job, cleaned out his bank account, and hit the road for reasons unknown. He tells his new wife the somewhat incongruous and plaintive story of a girl he saw on a train when he was sixteen but never approached. Now that he is married to a relative stranger, the dialogue as he recalls the girl creates an immediate counter-tone to his earlier questions: "If you knew then what you know now would it make any difference? Do you think you could save her? Do you think you could save yourself?"

The Book of Eli: Denzel Washington as the blmd wamderer with Mila Kunis as Solara.

Does Richard know he is locked in a nightmare? The dichotomy between the narrative set-up, including an odd interaction with a stranger in the diner, creates an appropriate suspense that points toward the elaborate effects shot of the car disappearing into the horizon. Although props and decor—from the drink machine, styrofoam cups, and the price of gasoline—indicate that the film is contemporary, the use of a vintage Dodge Phoenix as the couple's car, inside of which much of the narrative time will be spent, sets a graphic foundation for a sense of amorphous time. The speedometer displays, push-button transmission, old-style AM-FM radio are all vintage high tech, which underscore the aura of time displacement. In the metaphysics of the ending the possibility of a dark past for either Gina or Richard is left unresolved. The various comments by the personnel at the crime scene are appropriately undercut by the focus on Richard trapped in the backseat of the police cruiser. Beginning with the dusty cars at the rest stop, the illogical aspects of the situation are secondary to the protagonist's ever-expanding existential anguish. The payoff comes with the

POV shots from the injured Richard's helpless position in the backseat, where this new perspective reveals to the viewer in its second iteration the true horror of his long, agonizing scream of "No!"

In the Hughes brothers' *The Book of Eli* (2010) Denzel Washington plays a blind swordsman (the audience does not know he is blind until the end) right out of the "Zato Ichi" series in Japan. In a postapocalyptic, "Mad Max" world, Eli protects his Braille version of the Bible as all books are rare, particularly those dealing with ethics. His visions tell him to head west, where he and the book will be safe. On his journey he encounters the embittered Solara (Mila Kunis), a young woman who is sent by the arch-villain Carnegie (Gary Oldman) to seduce him and steal his book. Affected by his kindness and strength, Solara instead joins Eli on his journey. She gains strength and purpose by fighting with him and listening to his words. When Eli reaches his destination, an ashram on Alcatraz island, Solara decides to continue the fight, putting on her sunglasses, like her mentor, to venture out into the world.

In *Inception* (2010) Christopher Nolan returned to the world of the non-linear. This time the protagonist is an information thief named Cobb (Leonardo DiCaprio) who is able to enter the dreams of other individuals, then manipulate them and steal whatever information his client desires from the dreamer. Cobb is a man haunted by his past, in the form of his dead bipolar wife Mal (Marion Cotillard). In planning his newest project with his team (an attempt to plant an idea in the mind of a dreamer), he is sabotaged at each step by the shade of his wife who wants to draw him closer to her. Cobb is torn between his love for Mal, staying with her too long in some dream states, and his determination to succeed in his revolutionary endeavor. In *Source Code* (2011) an army pilot is part of an experiment to implant his consciousness in another's body in another time frame. He finds himself sent back several times to stop a terrorist attack on commuter train. His angst revolves around his ability or inability to change the past and, incidentally, save a woman he has grown to love.

One of the latest dystopian noirs is the modestly-budgeted studio project *The Purge* (2013) that combines a *Desperate Hours* context with a single sci-fi presumption that is a-technological: to purge the violent tendencies of its population, the totalitarian rulers of the United States in 2022 permit one night of deadly mayhem, twelve hours during which murder is permitted if not expressly encouraged when directed at the homeless. James Sandin (Ethan Hawke), the patriarch of the family, has made a fortune peddling security systems; but they come under siege because his young son admits a homeless fugitive. The young killers tracking him are more heavily armed versions of the amped-up droogs from *Clockwork Orange* (1971) hell-bent on "a bit of the old ultraviolence." When the Sandin family confronts its dilemma and refuses to give up the homeless man, the neo-noir nightmare swallows them.

The Purge: the Sandins (Lena Headey and Ethan Hawke) trapped inside their fortified house.

Neo-B: Noir on the Tip of a Shoestring

There are a few quite remarkable ultra-low-budget features, including the neo-B cited in the introduction, *The Death of Michael Smith*, in which the fates of three Detroit men with the same name (detective, killer, and victim) converge. For the most part, however, the ability to create such a feature for a budget of less than $1000 has not yielded many good results. Some interesting narratives failed to secure any meaningful release: In *The Naked Eye* (1995), shot in 35mm despite its meager budget, the seamy aspects of the art world and sex-for-hire are depicted ironically and with a noir style. In *Here Dies Another Day* (1997) a woman is caring for an elder parent whose dementia and attendant paranoia drive him to arm itself. Another regional B, *Dead Dogs* (1999), is a serviceable reimagining of *Blood Simple* shot in Bismarck, South Dakota. Also in black-and-white is *The Poor and the Hungry* (2000), the striking debut feature of native Memphis filmmaker Craig Brewer.

In *Hangman* (2000) a battered wife convinces her shrink to help eliminate her abusive husband. *Ocean Park* (2002) has a relatively large budget (half a million dollars) with which to explore the story of a murdered young woman, whose mate presumes his brother-in-law was responsible. While pointedly neo-noir in its visual style, multiple flashbacks and a *Dark Mirror*-ish twin,

Right, Det. Smith (Chris Moller) in *The Death of Michael Smith*.

Below, *The Poor and the Hungry*: Eli (Eric Tate) and Harper (Lindsay Roberts).

the through line is bit muddied by the manipulations. *The Falls* (2003) is about a missing woman; *The Fall* (2009) a missing girl. *The Parasomniac* (2010) focuses on a missing roommate, who is a somnabulist. *Altered States of Plaine* (2012) mixes somnabulism with narcolepsy to create a micro-budget variant on *Memento*.

It should be clear by now that many neo-Bs have followed the lead of studio pictures and titled their movies in a manner that is best described (with no pun intended) as on the money. *Zen Noir* (2004) concerns a murder in Buddhist temple, an ambitious quasi-Bressonian, quasi-Chaplin-esque exercise that posits a recently widowed private eye who attempts to go all Sherlock Holmes on a Zen puzzle with somewhat comic results.

The title figure of *The Assassin* (2007), a micro-budget effort shot in New York, is a PTSD-ridden and heroin-addicted veteran who tries to make some money as a paid killer. He falls for a neo-femme fatale/chanteuse/moll and botches his first assignment, which leaves him between the rock (police) and the hard place (the gangsters who hired him). In the equally micro *Black Days* (2005), a too-long narrative as dark as its title implies shot in Chicago, a prostitute tempts an ex-con/trick into helping her shed her pimp with the expected consequences. *When Tyrants Kiss* (2005) is a period neo-B that explores the *Chinatown*-like corruption in 1937 Pittsburgh with an even smaller budget. This title is a bit more oblique. *Untitled* (2007) also attempts to re-create the classic period by shooting in black and white and using a first-person narration. Its story also utilizes noir themes like fate and the corruption of the urban jungle.

What to make of a title such as *Sweet Love and Deadly* (2008)? Its sweet but deadly heroine, not a hooker or a singer, just a stripper, already has her hooks in a cop and a sugar daddy, when her own "Moose Malloy" is released from prison and pays her visit. To shed him, she adds a drug dealer to her list of conquests in hopes that he will eliminate "Moose"; but the cops assume she took matters more directly into her own hands. There no strippers in *The Grind* (2009), just a misguided hero, who tries to make money with a hot chick website to pay off a loan shark. The filmmakers may aspire to *Night and the City* or maybe just hothouse Tarantino in suburban Los Angeles (Gardena to be exact); but the results are both predictable and, despite a reasonable budget (over $1,000,000), fairly cheap looking. *Deep River* (also 2009) is hardly a

The Falls: Jennifer (Diedre Kilgore) and David (David Marx).

Altered States of Plaine: Kether Donohue as Violet and George Gallagher as Emanuel Plaine.

mystic one, just a tale of a cut-rate kidnapping gone wrong in the mode of *The Outfit* and *Charley Varrick*, shot in Kansas City. It has many of the elements of *The Death of Michael Smith* and ten times the budget. Admittedly still not much, and KC shot for a fraction of *The Grind* 's million dollars, it holds more visual interest than Gardena; but the movie still misses the mark.

There are more from 2009: *A Good Alibi*, an ultra-low riff on a perfect revenge murder committed by a Jack Mormon with a 7-year plan. Overwhelming guilt, as artificial as that mandated for Criss Cross in *Scarlet Street* by the MPAA-code administraters, undoes him. *Nightbeats* has no day scenes. While that is not a problem on an ultra-low budget, the performances are wildly inconsistent. *Overload* also tries to mask its micro-budget limitations with atmospheric East Coast settings (Boston and Vermont) and also falls short.

Not to be confused with the successful noirish and sci-fi action television series of the same name, *Person of Interest* (2010) is another variation on the Travis Bickle story, and its naked city is Boise, Idaho, where its script and lead performance (by the same person) come off as feeble homages. Soft-core auteur Rolfe Kanefsky dips a low-budget toe into neo-noir with *One in the Gun* (2010) and brings a trio of actors with hard-boiled supporting credentials—Steven Bauer, Robert Davi, and James Russo—along for the swim. Given its profound technical deficiencies, apparently most of its limited means was given over to cast payments. Even before it deviates from its "I'm a femme fatale, so help me kill my husband, handsome homeless guy" premise, this movie is in way over its head and promptly sinks to the bottom.

Unrelated to the 1992 Robert Altman movie, *Player* (2012) is a variant on *The Gambler* movies that adds a conniving fatal woman who shares her sexual favors with the player's son without good effect. *Determinism* (2012) features dual-personality directing on a shoestring by twin co-directors who inexplicably rechristen their shooting location State College, Pennsylvania as Narakaville. The blue and yellow hues add interest to its extensive night photography but cannot redeem the cheap-jack effect of its amateur acting. *Double Tap* (2014, shot 2011, not the Canadian production) follows a pill-taking Latino detective from Los Angeles to Newport Beach. Ostensibly about taking revenge against those who murdered his wife, this stunt-heavy enterprise seems more intent on channeling the martial arts melees in its otherwise unrelated 2000 Hong Kong namesake.

The bizarrely titled *One in the Gun*: Robert Davi as Vincent.

It should be clear from most of these projects that overall the early impact of low-budget neo-noir on the direction of genre in the late 1980s and 1990s has not been sustained in the 21st century. Accordingly, let's wrap it up with *Noirland* (officially 2015 but shot several years ago), also known, although who could imagine why, as *Noirlandia*. Shot in the hinterlands of north Los Angeles country, *Noirland* (2011) features an amnesiac detective in a trench coat who tracks a sometimes catatonic serial killer; but there are no musical numbers. It would be nice to say that despite its very limited means this multilingual pastiche hits the neo-noir bull's eyes; but its titles aside, this movie is hardly noir and entirely unwatchable.

The low-budget world and digital technology permit any number of variations on noir. Among the most self-conscious—certainly more so than *Noirland*—is the recent "vampire noir" *Nightcomer* (2015), which features bitter and pointedly existential voiceovers by an angst-ridden young woman named Rowena (Mackenzie Rosman). By day she panhandles, but by night her compulsion drives her to wander the dark streets of Los Angeles and prey on the criminals that inhabit them.

Mackenzie Rosman as Rowena in *Nightcomer*.

Conclusion

While the neo-noir genre can never be about a simultaneous embrace of a movement or cycle by scores of moviemakers, from features to television to graphic novels to video games, neo-noir continues to reflect the narrative and stylistic influence of its classic-period antecedents. It has been a while since *Dragnet, Naked City, Johnny Staccato, The Fugitive,* and *Run for Your Life* were on American networks, but the troubled and canny investigator continues to be a staple on the small screen that constantly harkens back to the characters of the classic period. As more and more gangster films, science fiction, and even some Westerns—as with the Coens' 2010 remake of *True Grit*—acquire a noir tinge, as more and more adaptations of dark graphic novels such as *Road to Perdition* and *Sin City* appear on the big screen, the outer limits of neo-noir are constantly stretched. Movies-of-the-week and cable originals still frequently explore the noir terrain on a budgets as limited as those in independent features and studios still embrace the genre as with the forthcoming retro noir P.I. tale *The Nice Guys* (2016) written and directed by Shane Black and starring Russell Crowe, Ryan Gosling, and Kim Basinger.

The unremitting resurgence of interest in the themes and styles of film noir since 1990 has benefited filmmakers at all budget levels. If film noir is no longer the American style, certainly no other movement has emerged to replace it. Unless and until filmmakers discover another mirror to hold up to American society, none ever will.

a Robert Evans production of a

Roman Polanski film

Jack Nicholson · Faye Dunaway

"Chinatown"

co-starring
JOHN HILLERMAN PERRY LOPEZ BURT YOUNG and JOHN HUSTON
production designer   associate producer   music scored by
RICHARD SYLBERT   CO ERICKSON   JERRY GOLDSMITH
written by   produced by   directed by
Robert Towne · Robert Evans · Roman Polanski

TECHNICOLOR® PANAVISION®
A PARAMOUNT PRESENTATION

Filmography

There are just over 500 titles in this Filmography. Motion pictures are listed alphabetically and release year is based on the method of the Academy of Motion Picture Arts and Sciences. Given the significant number of titles we include only main technical credits and major cast. Key to abbreviations: "Dir" is Director; "Scr" is Screenplay; "DP" is Director of Photography; "Mu" is Music.

Able Danger (Cinemantics, 2008). Dir: Dave Herman. Scr: Erin Joslyn, Paul Krik. DP: Charles Libin. Mu: Michael Montes. Cast: Elina Lowensohn (Kasia), Adam Nee (Flynn), Tamara Knausz (Friday). 86 min.

Above Suspicion (Rysher, 1995). Dir: Steven Schachter. Scr: Jerry Lazarus, Schachter, William H. Macy. DP: Ross Berryman. Mu: Michael Hoenig. Cast: Christopher Reeve (Dempsey Cain), Joe Mantegna (Alan), Kim Cattrall (Gail Cain). 95 min.

Absolute Power (Castle Rock, 1997). Dir: Clint Eastwood. Scr: William Goldman based on the novel by David Baldacci. DP: Jack Green. Mu: Lennie Niehaus. Cast: Clint Eastwood (Luther), Gene Hackman (President Richmond), Ed Harris (Seth), Laura Linney (Kate). 121 min.

After Dark, My Sweet (Avenue Pictures, 1990). Dir: James Foley. Scr: Robert Redlin, James Foley, based on the novel by Jim Thompson. DP: Mark Plummer. Mu: Maurice Jarre. Cast: Jason Patric (Collie), Rachel Ward (Fay), Rocky Giordani (Bert), Bruce Dern (Uncle Bud). 114 min.

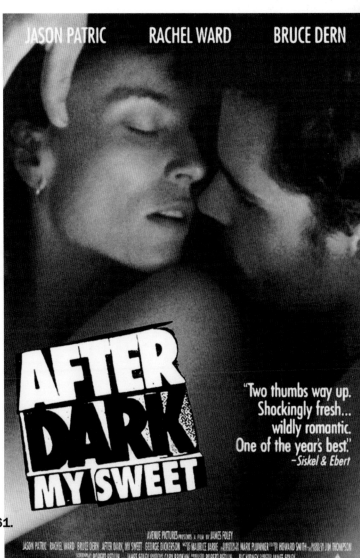

Against All Odds (Columbia, 1984). Dir: Taylor Hackford. Scr: Eric Hughes, based on Daniel Mainwaring's novel *Build My Gallows High*. DP: Donald Thorin. Mu: Michel Colombier, Larry Carlton. Cast: Rachel Ward (Jessie Wyler), Jeff Bridges (Terry Brogan), James Woods (Jake Wise), Alex Karras (Hank Sully). 125 min.

Alien (20th Century Fox, 1979). Dir: Ridley Scott. Scr: Dan O'Bannon based on a story by O'Bannon and Ronald Shusett. DP: Derek Vanlint. Mu: Jerry Goldsmith. Cast: Sigourney Weaver (Ripley), Tom Skerritt (Dallas), Harry Dean Stanton (Brett). 117 min.

Alligator Eyes (Castle Hill, 1990). Dir: John Feldman. Scr: John Feldman. DP: Todd Crockett. Cast: Annabelle Larsen (Pauline), Roger Kabler (Robbie), Mary McLain (Marjorie), Allen McCullogh (Lance). 95 min.

Altered States of Plaine (Over the GW, 2012). Dir: Nick Gaglia. Scr: Justin Swain, Michael Mathis, Kether Donohue, Nick Gaglia, George Gallagher. DP: Jon Fordham. Mu: John Presnell. Cast: George Gallagher (Plaine), Kether Donohue (Violet), Michael Mathis (Doctor). 88 min.

Angel Eyes (Franchise, 2001). Dir: Luis Mandoki. Scr: Gerald Di Pego. DP: Piotr Sobocinski. Mu: Marco Beltrami, Julius Robinson, Michael Sherwood. Cast: Jennifer Lopez (Sharon Pogue), Jim Caviezel (Steven Lambert/Catch), Jeremy Sisto (Larry Pogue), Terrence Howard (Robby). 102 min.

Another Man's Son (Blacklist, 2009). Dir/Scr: Tim Bissell, Craig F. Watkins. Cast: James McGowan. (Mayor Kendrick), Tyler Brent (Ari Hazelle), Doug Millar (Cooper). 72 min.

Armored (Screen Gems, 2009). Dir: Nimród Antal. Scr: James V. Simpson. DP: Andrzej Sekuła. Mu: John Murphy. Cast: Matt Dillon (Mike Cochrane), Jean Reno (Quinn), Laurence Fishburne (Baines), Skeet Ulrich (Dobbs), Columbus Short ("Ty" Hacket). 88 min.

As Good as Dead (First Line, 2010). Dir: Jonathan Mossek. Scr: Eve Pomerance, Erez Mossek. DP: Frank Barrera. Mu: Greg Arnold. Cast: Andie MacDowell (Helen Kalahan), Cary Elwes (Ethan Belfrage), Frank Whaley (Aaron), Matt Dallas (Jake), Brian Cox (Reverend Kalahan). 91 min.

The Assassin (Imperfect, 2007). Dir: Devin Haqq. Scr: Josh Wick, Haqq. DP: Kevin West. Mu: Sean Nowell. Cast: Jerome Bates (Clive), Charles Everett (Detective), Devin Haqq (John Brown). 111 min.

The Assassin Next Door (DPI, 2009). Dir/Scr: Danny Lerner. DP: Ram Shweky. Mu: Nathaniel Méchaly. Cast: Olga Kurylenko (Galia), Ninette Tayeb (Elinor). 103 mins.

At Close Range (Hemdale/Orion, 1986). Dir: James Foley. Scr: Nicholas Kazan, based on a story by Kazan and Lewitt. DP: Juan Ruiz Anchía. Mu: Patrick Leonard. Cast: Sean Penn (Brad Whitewood Jr.), Christopher Walken (Brad Sr.), Christopher Penn (Tommy), Mary Stuart Masterson (Terry). 115 min.

Atlantic City (Paramount, 1981). Dir: Louis Malle. Scr: John Guare. DP: Richard Ciupka. Mu: Michel Legrand. Cast: Burt Lancaster (Lou), Susan Sarandon (Sally), Kate Reid (Grace), Michel Piccoli (Joseph). 104 min.

Bad Boys (EMI/Universal, 1983). Dir: Richard Rosenthal. Scr: Richard Di Lello. DP: Bruce Surtees, Donald Thorin. Mu: Bill Conti. Cast: Sean Penn (Mick), Reni Santoni (Ramon Herrera), Esai Morales (Paco). 123 min.

Bad Influence (Epic, 1990). Dir: Curtis Hanson. Scr: David Koepp. DP: Robert Elswit. Mu: Trevor Jones. Cast: Rob Lowe (Alex), James Spader (Michael Boll), Tony Maggio (Patterson). 110 min.

Bad Lieutenant (Aries, 1992). Dir: Abel Ferrara. Scr: Victor Argo, Paul Calderon, Abel Ferrara, Zoe Tamerlis-Lund. DP: Ken Kelsch. Mu: Joe Delia. Cast: Harvey Keitel (The Lieutenant), Zoe Tamerlis-Lund (Zoe), Anthony Ruggiero (Lite), Victoria Bastel (Bowtay). 96 min.

Bad Lieutenant—Port of Call New Orleans (Millennium, 2009). Dir: Werner Herzog. Scr: William Finkelstein based on the earlier film. DP: Peter Zeitlinger. Mu: Mark Isham. Cast: Nicolas Cage (Terence), Eva Mendes (Frankie), Val Kilmer (Stevie). 122 min.

Badlands (Warner Bros., 1973). Dir: Terrence Malick. Scr: Malick. DP: Tak Fujimoto, Stevan Larner, Brian Probyn. Mu: Erik Satie, Carl Orff. Cast: Martin Sheen (Kit Carruthers), Sissy Spacek (Holly Sargis), Warren Oates (Holly's Father). 95 min.

The Badge (Millennium, 2002). Dir: Robby Henson. Scr: Robby Henson. DP:

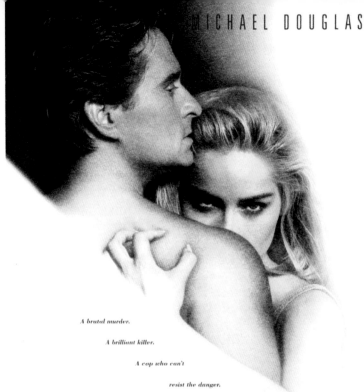

Irek Hartowicz. Mu: Otis Taylor, David Bergeaud. Cast: Billy Bob Thornton (Sheriff Hardwick), Patricia Arquette (Scarlett), William Devane (The Judge). 103 min.

Basic Instinct (Carolco/TriStar, 1992). Dir: Paul Verhoeven. Scr: Joe Eszterhas and Gary Goldman. DP: Jan De Bont. Mu: Jerry Goldsmith. Cast: Michael Douglas (Nick Curran), Sharon Stone (Catherine Tramell), George Dzunda (Gus Moran). 123 min.

The Bedroom Window (De Laurentiis, 1987). Dir: Curtis Hanson. Scr: Curtis Hanson, based on the novel *The Witness* by Anne Holden. DP: Gil Taylor. Mu: Michael Shrieve and Patrick Gleeson. Cast: Steve Guttenberg (Terry Lambert), Elizabeth McGovern (Denise), Isabelle Huppert (Sylvia). 112 min.

Before the Devil Knows You're Dead (Capito, 2007). Dir: Sidney Lumet. Scr: Kelly Masterson. DP: Ron Fortunato. Mu: Carter Burwell. Cast: Phillip Seymour Hoffman (Andy).Ethan Hawke (Hank), Albert Finney (Charles), Marisa Tomei (Gina). 117 min.

Best Laid Plans (Fox 2000, 1999). Dir: Mike Barker. Scr: Ted Griffin. DP: Ben Seresin. Mu: Craig Armstrong. Cast: Alessandro Nivola (Nick), Reese Witherspoon (Lissa), Josh Brolin (Bryce). 92 min.

Best Seller (Hemdale/Orion, 1987). Dir: John Flynn. Scr: Larry Cohen and John Flynn. DP: Fred Murphy. Mu: John Ferguson. Cast: James Woods (Cleve), Brian Dennehy (Dennis Meechum), Victoria Tennant (Roberta). 95 min.

Betrayed (MGM/UA, 1988). Dir: Constantin Costa-Gavras. Scr: Joe Eszterhas. DP: Patrick Blossier. Mu: Bill Conti. Cast: Debra Winger (Katie Philips/Cathy Weaver), Tom Berenger (Gary Simmons), John Heard (Michael Carnes), Betsey Blair (Gladys Simmons). 123 min.

Beyond a Reasonable Doubt (Autonomous, 2009). Dir: Peter Hyams. Scr: Peter Hyams based on the screenplay by Douglas Morrow. DP: Peter Hyams. Mu: David Shire. Cast: Michael Douglas (Mark Hunter), Jesse Metcalfe (C.J.), Amber Tamblyn (Ella). 106 min.

The Big Easy (Kings Road/Universal, 1987). Dir: Jim McBride. Scr: Daniel Petrie Jr. DP: Afonso Beato. Mu: Brad Fiedel. Cast: Dennis Quaid (Remy McSwain), Ellen Barkin (Anne Osborne), Ned Beatty (Jack Kellom), John Goodman (Andre De Soto). 108 min.

The Big Empty (Left of Center, 1997). Dir: Jack Perez. Scr: James McManus. DP: Shawn Maurer. Mu: Jean-Michel Michenaud. Cast: James McManus (Lloyd), Ellen Goldwasser (Jane), Pablo Bryant (Peter). 96 min.

The Big Sleep (United Artists, 1978). Dir: Michael Winner. Scr: Michael Winner based on the novel by Raymond Chandler. DP: Robert Paynter. Mu: Jerry Fielding. Cast: Robert Mitchum (Philip Marlowe), Sarah Miles (Charlotte), Oliver Reed (Eddie Mars), Richard Boone (Canino). 100 min.

The Black Dahlia (Millennium, 2006).Dir: Brian De Palma. Scr: Josh Friedman from the novel The Black Dahlia by James Ellroy. DP: Vilmos Zsigmond. Mu: Mark Isham. Cast: Josh Hartnett (Bleichert), Scarlett Johansson (Kay), Aaron Eckhart (Blanchard), Hilary Swank (Madeleine). 121 min.

Black Days (Premiere, 2005). Dir: Michael Urnikis. Scr: Urnikis. DP: Jeremy Christen. Mu: Michael Sean Colin. Cast: Stephen Cinabro (Trent), Maggie

HARTNETT   JOHANSSON   ECKHART   SWANK

THE
BLACK
DAHLIA

INSPIRED BY THE MOST NOTORIOUS UNSOLVED MURDER IN CALIFORNIA HISTORY.

THE NEW THRILLER FROM THE DIRECTOR OF *THE UNTOUCHABLES* AND *SCARFACE*

McLaughlin (Melanie), Otis Fine (Pope). 123 min.

Black Eye (Warner Bros., 1974). Dir: Jack Arnold. Scr: Mark Haggard and Jim Martin based on the novel *Murder on the Wild Side* by Jeff Jacks. DP: Ralph Woolsey. Mu: Mort Garson. Cast: Fred Williamson (Stone), Rosemary Forsyth (Miss Francis), Teresa Graves (Cynthia). 98 min.

Black Rain (Paramount, 1989). Dir: Ridley Scott. Scr: Craig Bolotin, Warren Lewis. DP: Jan De Bont. Mu: Hans Zimmer. Cast: Michael Douglas (Nick Conklin), Andy Garcia (Charlie Vincent), Ken Takakura (Masahiro), Kate Capshaw (Joyce). 125 min.

Black Widow (20th Century Fox, 1987). Dir: Bob Rafelson. Scr: Ronald Bass. DP: Conrad Hall. Mu: Michael Small. Cast: Debra Winger (Alexandra), Theresa Russell (Catharine), Sami Frey (Paul), Dennis Hopper (Ben). 103 min.

Blade Runner (Warner Bros., 1982). Dir: Ridley Scott. Scr: Hampton Fancher and David Peoples based on the novel *Do Androids Dream of Electric Sheep?* by Philip K. Dick. DP: Jordan Cronenweth. Mu: Vangelis. Cast: Harrison Ford (Deckard), Rutger Hauer (Batty), Sean Young (Rachael), Edward James Olmos (Gaff). 117 min.

Blink (New Line, 1994). Dir: Michael Apted. Scr: Dana Stevens. DP: Dante Spinotti. Cast: Madeleine Stowe (Emma Brody), Aidan Quinn (Detective John Hallstrom), James Remar (Thomas Ridgely). 106 min.

Blood and Wine (Fox Searchlight, 1996). Dir: Bob Rafelson. Scr: Alison Cross, Nick Villiers. DP: Newton Sigel. Mu: Michal Lorenc. Cast: Jack Nicholson (Alex), Jennifer Lopez (Gabriela), Stephen Dorff (Jason). 101 min.

Blood Simple (Circle/Skouras, 1984). Dir: Joel Coen. Scr: Ethan Coen and Joel Coen. DP: Barry Sonnenfeld. Mu: Caster Burwell. Cast: John Getz (Ray), Frances McDormand (Abby), Dan Hedaya (Julian), M. Emmet Walsh (Private Detective), Samm-Art Williams (Meurice). 96 min.

Blown Away (MGM, 1994). Dir: Stephen Hopkins. Scr: John Rice, Joe Batteer, Jay Roach. Cast: Jeff Bridges (Dove/McGivney. Tommy Lee Jones (Gaerity), Suzy Amis (Kate). 121 min.

Blue City (Paramount, 1986). Dir: Michelle Manning. Scr: Lukas Heller, Walter Hill based on the novel by Ross Macdonald. DP: Steven Poster. Mu: Ry Cooder. Cast: Judd Nelson (Billy), Ally Sheedy (Annie), David Caruso (Joey). 83 min.

IT'S THE COOLEST HEAT YOU'LL EVER FEEL.

BLUE CITY

IT'S BELOW MIAMI AND ABOVE THE LAW

Blue Desert (Academy, 1992). Dir: Bradley Battersby. Scr: Arthur Collis and Paul Murphy. DP: Paul Murphy. Mu: Joel Goldsmith. Cast: Craig Sheffer (Randall Atkins), D.B. Sweeney (Steve Smith), Courteney Cox (Lisa Roberts). 93 min.

The Blue Iguana (PolyGram/ Propaganda, 1988). Dir: John Lafia. Scr: John Lafia. DP: Rodolfo Sanchez. Mu: Ethan James. Cast: Dylan McDermott (Vince), Jessica Harper (Cora), James Russo (Reno). 90 min.

Blue Steel (MGM, 1990). Dir: Kathryn Bigelow. Scr: Kathryn Bigelow and Eric Red. DP: Amir Mokri. Mu: Brad Fiedel. Cast: Jamie Lee Curtis (Megan Turner), Ron Silver (Eugene Hunt), Clancy Brown (Nick Mann). 101 min.

For a rookie cop, there's one thing more dangerous than uncovering a killer's fantasy.

Becoming it.

JAMIE LEE CURTIS

BLUE STEEL

22 NYPD

Blue Vengeance (Shapiro-Glickenhaus, 1989). Dir: J. Christian Ingvordsen, Danny Kuchuck. Scr: Ingvordsen, Kuchuck, John Weiner. DP: Steven Kaman. Mu: Christopher Burke. Cast: Joe Ambrose (Chief Cunningham), Tom Billett (Bouncer), Paul Borghese (Heany), Angel Caban (Rivera), Matt Carey (Detective), Deborah Clifford (Peggy). 90 min.

Body Chemistry (Concorde, 1990). Dir: Kristine Peterson. Scr: Jackson Barr. DP: Phedon Papamichael. Mu: Terry Plumeri. Cast: Marc Singer (Tom), Lisa Pescia (Claire), Mary Crosby (Marlee), David Kagen (Freddie). 85 min.

Body Count (Island, 1998). Dir: Robert Patton-Spruill. Scr: Theodore Witcher. DP: Charles Mills. Mu: Curt Sobel. Cast: David Caruso (Hobbs), Forest Whitaker (Crane), Linda Fiorentino (Natalie). 85 min.

Body Heat (Ladd Co./Warner Bros., 1981). Dir: Lawrence Kasdan. Scr: Lawrence Kasdan. DP: Richard H. Kline. Mu: John Barry. Cast: William Hurt (Ned Racine), Kathleen Turner (Matty Walker), Richard Crenna (Edmund Walker), Mickey Rourke (Teddy Lewis). 118 min.

Body of Evidence (De Laurentiis, 1993). Dir: Uli Edel. Scr: Brad Mirman. DP: Doug Milsome. Mu: Graeme Revell. Cast: Madonna (Rebecca), Willem Dafoe (Frank), Joe Mantegna (Robert), Anne Archer (Joanne). 99 min.

The Bodyguard (Warner Bros., 1992). Dir: Mick Jackson. Scr: Kasdan. DP: Andrew Dunn. Cast: Kevin Costner (Farmer), Whitney Houston (Rachel), Gary Kemp (Shelley). 129 min.

The Book of Eli (Alcon, 2010). Dir: The Hughes brothers. Scr: Gary Whitta. DP: Don Burgess. Mu: Atticus Ross, Leopold Ross, Claudia Sarne. Cast: Denzel Washington (Eli), Gary Oldman (Carnegie), Mila Kunis (Solara). 117 min.

LIGHTNING PICTURES IN ASSOCIATION WITH PRECISION FILMS AND MACK TAYLOR PRODUCTIONS PRESENTS
AN EDWARD R. PRESSMAN PRODUCTION A KATHRYN BIGELOW FILM 'BLUE STEEL' STARRING JAMIE LEE CURTIS RON SILVER CLANCY BROWN ELIZABETH PEÑA AND LOUISE FLETCHER
MUSIC BRAD FIEDEL DIRECTOR OF PHOTOGRAPHY AMIR MOKRI EXECUTIVE PRODUCER LAWRENCE KASANOFF PRODUCED BY MICHAEL RAUCH WRITTEN BY KATHRYN BIGELOW AND ERIC RED
PRODUCED BY EDWARD R. PRESSMAN AND OLIVER STONE DIRECTED BY KATHRYN BIGELOW

The Bone Collector (Columbia/Universal, 1999). Dir: Phillip Noyce. Scr: Jeremy Iacone based on the book by Jeffery Deaver. Cast: Denzel Washington (Lincoln Rhyme), Angelina Jolie (Amelia), Queen Latifah (Thelma), Luis Guzman (Eddie), John Benjamin Hickey (Dr. Lehman). 118 min.

The Border (Universal, 1982). Dir: Tony Richardson. Scr: Deric Washburn, Walon Green, and David Freeman. DP: Ric Waite, Vilmos Zsigmond. Mu: Ry Cooder. Cast: Jack Nicholson (Charlie), Harvey Keitel (Cat), Valerie Perrine (Marcy), Warren Oates (Red), Elpidia Carrillo (Maria). 109 min.

Bound (De Laurentiis, 1996). Dir: Wachowskis. Scr: Wachowskis. DP: Bill Pope. Mu: Don Davis. Cast: Jennifer Tilly (Violet), Gina Gershon (Corky), Joe Pantoliano (Caesar), John P. Ryan (Micky Malnato), Christopher Maloni (Johnnie). 108 min.

The Bourne Identity (Universal, 2002). Dir: Doug Liman. Scr: Tony Gilroy, W. Blake Herron based on the novel by Robert Ludlum. DP: Oliver Wood. Mu: John Powell. Cast: Matt Damon (Bourne), Franka Potente (Marie), Chris Cooper (Conklin). 119 min.

The Box (Quorum, 2007). Dir: A. J. Kparr. Scr: Kparr. DP: Sion Michel. Mu: James Sale. Cast: Gabrielle Union (Detective Romano), Yul Vazquez (Finn), A. J. Buckley (Danny). 87 min.

The Boy Next Door (Universal, 2015). Dir: Rob Cohen. Scr: Barbara Curry. Mu: Nathan Barr, Randy Edelman. Cast: Jennifer Lopez (Claire Peterson), Ryan Guzman (Noah), Kristin Chenoweth (Vicky Lansing), John Corbett (Garrett), Ian Nelson (Kevin). 90 min.

Breakdown (De Laurentiis, 1997). Dir: Jonathan Mostow. Scr: Sam Montgomery, Mostow. DP: Douglas Milsome. Mu: Basil Poledouris. Cast: Kurt Russell (Jeff), J. T. Walsh (Red

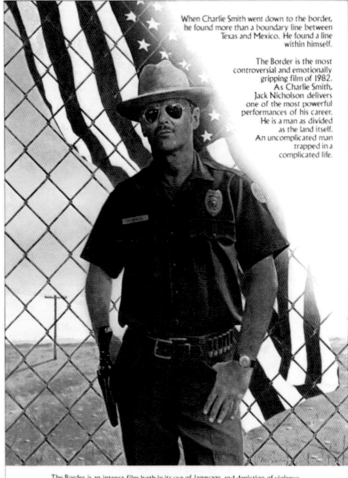

When Charlie Smith went down to the border, he found more than a boundary line between Texas and Mexico. He found a line within himself.

The Border is the most controversial and emotionally gripping film of 1982. As Charlie Smith, Jack Nicholson delivers one of the most powerful performances of his career. He is a man as divided as the land itself. An uncomplicated man trapped in a complicated life.

The Border is an intense film both in its use of language and depiction of violence.

JACK NICHOLSON in THE BORDER

Starring An EFER Production A TONY RICHARDSON Film THE BORDER
HARVEY KEITEL VALERIE PERRINE WARREN OATES
Written by DERIC WASHBURN and WALON GREEN and DAVID FREEMAN Director of Photography RIC WAITE Music by RY COODER
Executive Producer NEIL HARTLEY Produced by EDGAR BRONFMAN, JR. Directed by TONY RICHARDSON A UNIVERSAL PRODUCTION
PANAVISION Original soundtrack on BACKSTREET Records and Tapes

Barr), Kathleen Quinlan (Amy). 93 min.

Breathless (Orion, 1983). Dir/Scr: Jim McBride. DP: Richard H. Kline. Mu: Jack Nitzsche. Cast: Richard Gere (Jesse), Valerie Kaprisky (Monica), Art Metrano (Birnbaum), John P. Ryan (Parmental). 100 min.

Brick (Focus, 2005). Dir/scr: Rian Johnson. DP: Steve Yedlin. Mu: Nathan Johnson. Cast: Joseph Gordon-Levitt (Brendan Frye), Emilie de Ravin (Emily Kostich), Nora Zehetner (Laura Dannon), Lukas Haas (The Pin). 108 min.

Brown's Requiem (J and T, 1998). Dir: Jason Freeland. Scr: Freeland based on the novel by James Ellroy. DP: Seo

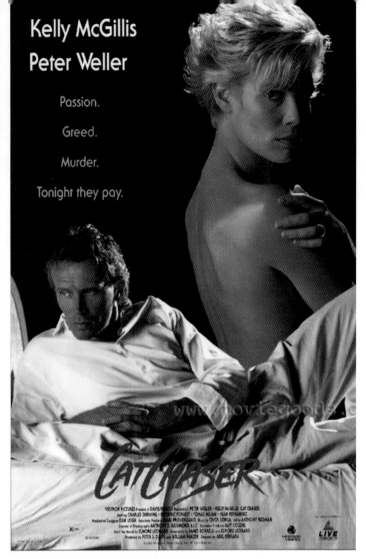

Mutarevic. Mu: Cynthia Millar. Cast: Michael Rooker (Fritz), Jack Wallace (Bud), Will Sasso (Fat Dog). 104 min.

Bug (Lions Gate, 2006). Dir: William Friedkin. Scr: Tracy Letts, based on his play. DP: Michael Grady. Mu: Brian Tyler. Cast: Ashley Judd (Agnes White), Michael Shannon (Peter Evans), Harry Connick Jr. (Jerry Goss), Lynn Collins (R.C.), Brian F. O'Byrne (Dr. Sweet). 102 min.

Butterfly (Analysis, 1982). Dir: Matt Cimber. Scr: Cimber, John F. Goff based on the novel by James M. Cain. DP: Eduard van der Enden. Mu: Ennio Morricone. Cast: Stacy Keach (Jess Tyler), Pia Zadora (Kady Tyler), Orson Welles (Judge Rauch), Lois Nettleton (Belle Morgan). 107 min.

The Call (TriStar, 2013). Dir: Brad Anderson. Scr: Richard D'Ovidio. DP: Tom Yatsko. Mu: John Debney. Cast: Halle Berry (Jordan Turner), Abigail Breslin (Casey Welson), Morris Chestnut (Officer Paul Phillips), Michael Eklund (Michael Foster). 94 min.

Call Me (Vestron, 1988). Dir: Sollace Mitchell. Scr: Karyn Kay. DP: Zoltan David. Mu: David Frank. Cast: Patricia Carbonneau (Anna), Steven McHattie (Jellybean), Boyd Gaines (Bill), Sam Freed (Alex), Patti D'Arbanville (Cori), Steve Buscemi (Switchblade). 93 min.

The Caller (Belladonna, 2008). Dir: Richard Ledes. Scr: Ledes, Alain-Didier Weill. DP: Stephen Kazmierski. Mu: Robert Miller. Cast: Gregory Ellis (Lulu), Frank Langella (Jimmy). 92 min.

Cape Fear (Amblin/Cappa/Tribeca/Universal, 1991). Dir: Martin Scorsese. Scr: Wesley Strick, based on a screenplay by James R. Webb and *The Executioners* by John D. MacDonald. DP: Freddie Francis. Mu: Elmer Bernstein, Bernard Herrmann. Cast: Robert De Niro (Max Cady), Nick Nolte (Sam Bowden), Jessica Lange (Leigh Bowden), Juliette Lewis (Danielle Bowden). 130 min.

Carlito's Way (Universal, 1993). Dir: Brian De Palma. Scr: David Koepp based on the novel by Edwin Torres. Dir: Stephen Burum. Mu: Patrick Doyle. Cast: Al Pacino (Carlito), Sean Penn (Kleinfeld), Penelope Ann Miller (Gail), John Leguizamo (Benny). 144 min.

Caroline at Midnight (New Horizons, 1994). Dir: Scott McGinnis. Scr: Travis Rink. DP: Christian Sebaldt. Mu: Mark Snow. Cast: Judd Nelson (Phil), Mia Sara (Victoria), Tim Day (Ray). 88 min.

Cat Chaser (Vestron, 1989). Dir: Abel Ferrara. Scr: Elmore Leonard, Jim Borrelli, and Alan Sharpe based on Leonard's novel. DP: Anthony Richmond. Cast: Peter Weller (George Moran), Kelly McGillis (Mary de Boya), Charles Durning (Jiggs Scully). 90 min.

Caught (Cinehaus, 1996). Dir: Robert M. Young. Scr: Edward Pomerantz based on his novel. DP: Michael Barrow. Mu: Chris Botti. Cast: Edward James Olmos (Joe), Maria Conchita Alonso (Betty), Arie Verveen (Nick). 110 min.

Cement (Ocelot, 2000). Dir: Adrian Pasdar. Scr: Justin Monjo. DP: Geary McLeod. Mu: Doug Caldwell. Cast: Chris Penn (Holt), Jeffrey Wright (Ninny), Sherylin Fenn (Lyndel). 97 min.

Chandler (MGM, 1971). Dir: Paul Magwood. Scr: John Sacret Young based on a story by Magwood. DP: Alan Stensvold. Mu: George Romanus. Cast: Warren Oates (Chandler), Leslie Caron (Katherine), Alex Dreier (Carmady), Gloria Grahame (Selma). 85 min.

Changeling (Malpaso, 2008). Dir: Clint Eastwood. Scr: J. Michael Straczynski. DP: Tom Stern. Mu: Eastwood. Cast: Angelina Jolie (Christine), Gattlin Griffith (Walter), Michael Kelly (Detective Ybarra). 141 min.

Charlie Varrick (Universal Pictures, 1973). Dir: Don Siegel. Scr: Dean Riesner, Howard Rodman based on the novel *The Looters* by John Reese. DP: Michael Butler. Mu: Lalo Schifrin. Cast: Walter Matthau (Charley Varrick), Joe Don Baker (Molly), Felicia Farr (Sybil Fort). 111 min.

China Moon (MGM, 1994). Dir: John Bailey. Scr: Roy Carlson. DP: Willy Kurant. Mu: George Fenton. Cast: Madeline Stowe (Rachel Munro), Ed Harris (Detective Kyle Bodine), Benicio Del Toro (Lamar Dickey). 100 min.

Chinatown (Paramount, 1974). Dir: Roman Polanski. Scr: Robert Towne. DP: John A. Alonzo. Mu: Jerry Goldsmith. Cast: Jack Nicholson (J.J. Gittes), Faye Dunaway (Evelyn Mulwray), John Huston (Noah Cross). 130 min.

City Hall (Castle Rock, 1996). Dir: Harold Becker. Scr: Ken Lipper, Paul Schrader, Nicholas Pileggi, Bo Goldman. DP: Michael Seresin. Mu: Jerry Goldsmith. Cast: Al Pacino (Mayor), John Cusack (Deputy Mayor), Bridget Fonda (Maybeth). 111 min.

City of Industry (Largo, 1997). Dir: John Irvin. Scr: Ken Solarz. DP: Thomas Burstyn. Mu: Stephen Endelman. Cast: Harvey Keitel (Roy), Stephen Dorff (Skip), Timothy Hutton (Lee). 97 min.

The Clearing (Fox Searchlight, 2004). Dir: Pieter Jan Brugge. Scr: Justin Haythe based on a story by Brugge and Haythe. DP: Denis Lenoir. Mu: Craig Armstrong. Cast: Robert Redford (Hayes), Helen Mirren (Eileen), Willem Dafoe (Mack). 95 min.

Cold Around the Heart (Illusion, 1997). Dir: John Ridley. Scr: Ridley. DP: Malik Sayeed. Mu: Mason Daring. Cast: David Caruso (Ned), Kelly Lynch (Jude), Stacey Dash (Bec). 96 min.

Collateral (Dream Works, 2004). Dir: Michael Mann. Scr: Stuart Beattie. DP: Dion Beebe, Paul Cameron. Mu: James Newton Howard. Cast: Tom Cruise (Vincent), Jamie Foxx (Max Durocher), Jada Pinkett Smith (Annie Farrell), Mark Ruffalo (Det. Fanning). 120 min.

It started like any other night

TOM CRUISE JAMIE FOXX

A MICHAEL MANN FILM

COLLATERAL

Color of Night (Cinergi, 1994). Dir: Richard Rush. Scr: Billy Ray, Matthew Chapman. DP: Dietrich Lohmann. Mu: Dominic Frontiere. Cast: Bruce Willis (Capa), Jane March (Rose), Lesley Ann Warren (Sondra), Brad Dourif (Clark). 121 min.

Confidence (Lions Gate, 2003). Dir: James Foley. Scr: Doug Jung. DP: Juan Ruiz Anchía. Mu: Christophe Beck. Cast: Edward Burns (Vig), Rachel Weisz (Lily), Morris Chestnut (Travis). 97 min.

Conspiracy Theory (Warner Bros., 1997). Dir: Richard Donner. Scr: Brian Helgeland. DP: John Schwartzman. Mu:

FUTURE BEWARE: THE SOUL IS IN THE SOFTWARE

CYBORG²

1993 THEATRICAL RELEASE

Carter Burwell. Cast: Mel Gibson (Fletcher), Julia Roberts (Sutton), Patrick Stewart (Dr. Jonas). 135 min.

The Conversation (Paramount, 1974). Dir: Francis Ford Coppola. DP: Bill Butler. Mu: David Shire. Cast: Gene Hackman (Harry Caul), John Cazale (Stan), Allen Garfield (Bernie Moran), Frederick Forrest (Mark). 113 min.

Cop (Atlantic, 1988). Dir/Scr: by James B. Harris. DP: Steven Dubin. Mu: Michel Colombier. Cast: James Woods (Lloyd Hopkins), Lesley Ann Warren (Kathleen McCarthy). 110 min.

Cop Land (Miramax, 1997). Dir: James Mangold. Scr: James Mangold. DP: Eric Alan Edwards. Mu: Howard Shore. Cast: Sylvester Stallone (Freddy), Harvey Keitel (Ray), Ray Liotta (Gary), Robert De Niro (Moe).104 min.

Copycat (Regency, 1995). Dir: Jon Amiel. Scr: Ann Biderman, David Madsen. DP: László Kovács. Mu: Christopher Young. Cast: Sigourney Weaver (Helen Hudson), Holly Hunter (Insp. M.J. Monahan), Dermot Mulroney (Insp. Reuben Goetz). 123 min.

A Cowboy's Silver Lining (Rusted Sun, 2004). Dir/Scr/DP/Mu: Bevan Bell. Cast: Bevan Bell (Bill), Nicole Britt (Mystery Mira). 83 min.

Crash (Lions Gate, 2004). Dir: Paul Haggis. Scr: Paul Haggis, Robert Moresco. DP: James Muro. Mu: Mark Isham. Cast: Matt Dillon (Officer Ryan), Sandra Bullock (Jean), Don Cheadle (Detective Waters), Terrence Howard (Cameron Thayer), Thandie Newton (Christine Thayer), Ryan Philippe (Officer Hansen). 112 min.

Criminal Intent (Promark, 1992). Dir: Woth Ketter. Scr: Michael Potts. DP: Doyle Smith. Mu: Michael Linn. Cast: Robert Davi (Walker), Joan Severance (Melissa), Jakc Scalia (Yarnell), James Russo (Tanner). 103 min.

Criminal Law (Hemdale/TriStar, 1989). Dir: Martin Campbell. Scr: Mark Kasdan.

DP: Philip Meheux. Mu: Jerry Goldsmith. Cast: Gary Oldman (Ben Chase), Kevin Bacon (Martin Thiel), Karen Young (Ellen Faulkner), Joe Don Baker (Detective Mesel). 117 min.

The Crossing Guard (Miramax, 1995). Dir/Scr: Sean Penn. DP: Vilmos Zsigmond. Mu: Jack Nitzsche. Cast: Jack Nicholson (Freddy Gale), David Morse (John Booth), Anjelica Huston (Mary), Robin Wright (Jojo). 111 min.

The Crush (Morgan Creek, 1993). Dir: Alan Shapiro. Scr: Alan Shapiro. DP: Bruce Surtees. Mu: Graeme Revell. Cast: Cary Elwes (Nick), Alicia Silverstone (Darian), Jennifer Rubin (Amy). 89 min.

La Cucaracha (7.23, 1998). Dir: Jack Perez. Scr: James McManus. DP: Shawn Maurer. Mu: Martin Davich. Cast: Eric Roberts (Walter), Joaquim de Almeida (Guerra), Victor Rivers (Herberto). 95 min.

Cyborg 2: Glass Shadow (Trimark, 1993). Dir: Michael Schroeder. Scr: Schroeder, Mark Geldman, Ron Yanover. DP: Jamie Thompson. Mu: Peter Allen. Cast: Elias Koteas (Colton Ricks), Angelina Jolie (Casella "Cash" Reese), Jack Palance (Mercy). 99 mins.

Dangerously Close (Cannon, 1986). Dir: Albert Pyun. Scr: Scott Fields, John Stockwell, and Marty Ross. DP: Walt Lloyd. Mu: Michael McCarty. Cast: John Stockwell (Randy), J. Eddie Peck (Donny), Carey Lowell (Julie). 92 min.

Daredevil (Regency, 2003). Dir: Mark Steven Johnson. Scr: Johnson based on characters by Stan Lee, Bill Everett and *Daredevil* by Frank Miller. DP: Ericson Core. Mu: Graeme Revell. Cast: Ben Affleck (Murdock/Daredevil), Jennifer Garner (Elektra), Colin Farrell (Bullseye). 103 min.

Dark Blue (Alphaville, 2002). Dir: Ron Shelton. Scr: David Ayer based on a story by James Ellroy. DP: Barry Peterson. Mu: Terence Blanchard. Cast:

Kurt Russell (Eldon), Scott Speedman (Bobby), Michael Michele (Beth). 118 min.

Dark City (New Line, 1998).Dir: Alex Proyas. Scr: Alex Proyas, Lem Dobbs, David S. Goyer. DP: Dariusz Wolski. Mu: Trevor Jones. Cast: Rufus Sewell (John Murdoch), William Hurt (Inspector Frank Bumstead), Jennifer Connelly (Emma/Anna), Kiefer Sutherland (Dr. Daniel Schreber). 100 min.

YOU WON'T KNOW WHO TO TRUST...
WHAT TO BELIEVE...OR WHERE TO TURN.

MICHAEL BIEHN
SARAH TRIGGER
WITH NICOLAS CAGE
AND JAMES COBURN

DEADFALL

...THE ULTIMATE CON.

Dark Country (Sony, 2009). Dir: Thomas Jane. Scr: Tab Murphy. DP: Geoff Boyle. Mu: Eric Lewis. Cast: Thomas Jane (Richard), Lauren German (Gina), Ron Perlman (Deputy). 105 minutes.

The Dark Knight (Warner Bros., 2008). Dir: Christopher Nolan. Scr: Jonathan Nolan, Christopher Nolan, David Goyer. DP: Wally Pfister. Mu: James Newton Howard, Hans Zimmer. Cast: Christian Bale (Bruce Wayne), Heath Ledger (Joker), Gary Oldman (Gordon), Michael Caine (Alfred). 152 min.

The Dark Side (Shapiro-Glickenhaus, 1987). Dir: Constantino Magnatta. Scr: Matt Black, Allan Magee. Mu: Greg Diakun. DP: Gilles Corbeil. Cast: Tony Galati (Russo), Cynthia Preston (Laura), Peter Read (Roscoe), John Tench (Sully), Charles Loriot (Lou). 95 min.

Dark Streets (Capture, 2008). Dir: Rachel Samuels. Scr: Wallace King. DP:

Sharone Meir. Mu: George Acogny. Cast: Gabriel Mann (Chaz), Bijou Phillips (Crystal), Izabella Miko (Madelaine), Elias Koteas (Lieutenant). 83 min.

The Dark Wind (New Line, 1992). Dir: Errol Morris. Scr: Eric Bergren, Neal Jiminez, and Mark Horowitz, based novels by Tony Hillerman. DP: Stefan Czapsky. Mu: Michel Colombier. Cast: Lou Diamond Philips (Officer Jim Chee), Fred Ward (Lt. Joe Leaphorn), Gary Farmer (Albert "Cowboy" Dashee). 109 min.

Dead Again (Paramount/Mirage, 1991). Dir: Kenneth Branagh. Scr: Scott Frank. DP: Matthew Leonetti. Mu: Patrick Doyle. Cast: Kenneth Branagh (Mike Church/Roman Strauss), Emma Thompson (Grace/Margaret Strauss), Andy Garcia (Gary Baker). 111 min.

Dead Bang (Lorimar/Warner Bros., 1989). Dir: John Frankenheimer. Scr: Robert Foster. DP: Gerry Fisher. Mu: Gary Chang. Cast: Don Johnson (Jerry Beck), Penelope Ann Miller (Linda), William Forsythe (Kressler). 105 min.

Dead Dogs (One Eight Five, 1999). Dir: Clay Eide. Scr: Todd Bulman. DP: Don Devine. Mu: Alan Koshiyama. Cast: Joe Reynolds (Tom), Margot Demeter (Carment), Jay Underwood (Derek). 90 min.

Dead Presidents (Hollywood, 1995). Dir/Scr: Hughes brothers. DP: Lisa Rinzler. Mu: Danny Elfman. Cast: Larenz Tate (Anthony), Keith David (Kirby), Chris Tucker (Skip). 119 min.

Deadfall (Trimark, 1993). Dir: Christopher Coppola. Scr: Coppola, Nick Vallelonga. DP: Maryse Alberti. Mu: Jim Fox. Cast: Michael Biehn (Joe), Sarah Trigger (Diane), Nicolas Cage (Eddie). 98 min.

The Death of Michael Smith (Cannon Fodder, 2006). Dir: Daniel Casey. Scr: Casey. DP: Thomas Horvath, Daniel Casey. Mu: Omar Ajluni. Cast: Chris

Moller (Smith), Thomas Galasso (Smith), Michael Mili (Smith). 89 min.

Death Wish (De Laurentiis/Paramount, 1974). Dir: Michael Winner. Scr: Wendell Mayes, based on the novel by Brian Garfield. DP: Arthur J. Ornitz. Mu: Herbie Hancock. Cast: Charles Bronson (Paul Kersey), Hope Lange (Joanna Kersey). 93 min.

Deceived (Touchstone/Silver Screen Partners IV, 1991). Dir: Damian Harris. Scr: Donoghue and Derek Saunders. DP: Jack N. Green. Mu: Thomas Newman. Cast: Goldie Hawn (Adrienne), John Heard (Jack), Robin Bartlett (Charlotte). 103 min.

Deceiver (MGM, 1997). Dir: Jonas Pate, Josh Pate. Scr: Jonas Pate, Josh Pate. DP: Bill Butler. Mu: Harry Gregson-Williams. Cast: Chris Penn (Det. Phillip Maxton), Ellen Burstyn (Mook), Tim Roth (James Walter Wayland), Renée Zellweger, (Elizabeth). 101 min.

Deception (20th Century Fox, 2008).Dir: Marcel Lagennegger. Scr: Mark Bomback. DP: Dante Spinotti. Mu: Ramin Djawadi. Cast: Ewan McGregor (Jonathan McQuarry), Hugh Jackman (Wyatt Bose), Michelle Williams (S), Natasha Henstridge (Simone Wilkinson). 107 min.

Deep Cover (New Line, 1992). Dir: Bill Duke. Scr: Michael Tolkin and Henry Bean. DP: Bojan Bazelli. Mu: Michael Colombier. Cast: Larry Fishburne (John Hull/Russell Stevens), Jeff Goldblum (David Jason), Victoria Dillard (Betty). 112 min.

The Deep End (20th Century Fox, 2001).Dir: Scott McGehee, David Siegel. Scr: Scott McGehee, David Siegel based on the story by Elisabeth Sanxay Holding. DP: Giles Nuttgens. Mu: Peter Nashel. Cast: Tilda Swinton (Margaret Hall), Goran Visnjic (Al Spera), Jonathan Tucker (Beau Hall), Peter Donat (Jack Hall). 101 min.

Deep River (Insert Creative Name Here, 2009). Dir: Scott Kessler. Scr: Kessler. DP: Joey Salomone. Mu: Deriva. Cast: Vincent Mollica (Saul), Steve Williams (Rob), Ari Bavel (Freddie). 95 min.

Deepwater (Halcyon, 2005). Dir: David S. Marfield. Scr: David Marfield based on the novel by Matthew F. Jones. DP: Scott Kevan. Mu: Charlie Clouser. Cast: Lucas Black (Nat), Peter Coyote (Herman), Mia Maestro (Iris), Lesley Ann Warren (Pam). 93 min.

Delusion (Cineville, 1991). Dir: Carl Colpaert. Scr: Carl Colpaert and Kurt Voss. DP: Geza Sinkovics. Mu: Barry Adamson. Cast: Jim Metzler (George O'Brien), Jennifer Rubin (Patti), Kyle Secor (Chevy), Jerry Orbach (Larry). 100 min.

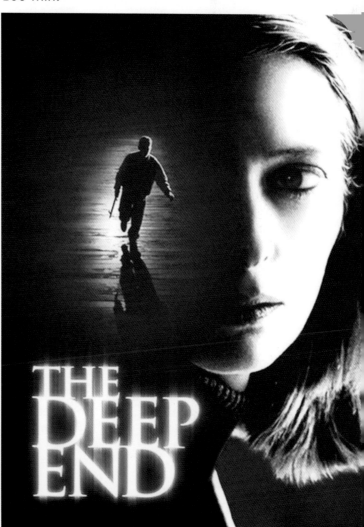

L ISPETTORE CALLAGHAN, NON RISOLVE I CASI DI OMICIDIO. LI ANNIENTA!

CLINT EASTWOOD ... ISPETTORE CALLAGHAN : IL CASO "SCORPIO" É TUO!!

The Departed (Warner Bros., 2006). Dir: Martin Scorsese. Scr: William Monahan based on *Internal Affairs*. DP: Ranju Majumdar. DP: Michael Balhaud. Mu: Howard Shore. Cast: Leonardo DiCaprio (Costigan), Matt Damon (Sullivan), Jack Nicholson (Costello), Mark Wahlberg (Dignam). 151 min.

Derailed (Weinstein, 2005). Dir: Mikael Håfström. Scr: Stuart Beattie based on a novel by James Siegel. DP: Peter Biziou. Mu: Ed Shearmur. Cast: Clive Owen (Schine), Jennifer Aniston (Lucinda),

Vincent Cassel (La Roche), Melissa George (Deanna), Giancarlo Esposito (Det. Franklin). 108 min.

Desert Saints (City Heat, 2002). Dir: Richard Greenberg. Scr: Greenberg, Wally Nichols. DP: John Newby. Mu: Richard Marvin. Cast: Kiefer Sutherland (Banks), Rachel Ticotin (Dora), Jamey Sheridan (Agent Scanlon). 88 min.

Desperate Hours (DeLaurentiis/MGM, 1990). Dir: Michael Cimino. Scr: Lawrence Konner, Mark Rosenthal, Joseph Hayes, based on the novel by Joseph Hayes. DP: Doug Milsome. Mu: David Mansfield. Cast: Mickey Rourke (Michael Bosworth), Anthony Hopkins (Tim Cornell), Lindsay Crouse (Chandler), Kelly Lynch (Nancy Brewers). 105 min.

The Detective (20th Century Fox, 1968). Dir: Gordon Douglas. Scr: Abby Mann based on the novel by Roderick Thorp. DP: Joe Biroc. Mu: Jerry Goldsmith. Cast: Frank Sinatra (Joe Leland), Lee Remick (Karen Leland), Ralph Meeker (Lt. Curran). 114 min.

Determinism (Shami, 2012). Dir: Ranju Majumdar, Sanjit Majumdar. Scr: Majumdars. DP: Ranju Majumdar. Mu: Ranju Majumdar. Cast: Amaobi Anyaogu (Josiah), Lyne Geneste (India), Mike Ghelardi (Dan). 80 min.

Detour (Williams, 1992). Dir: Wade Williams. Scr: Wade Williams, Roger C. Hull based on the novel Martin Goldsmith. DP: Jeff Richardson. Mu: Bill Crain. Cast: Tom Neal Jr. (Roberts), Lea Lavish (Vera), Susanna Foster (Evie). 91 min.

Devil in a Blue Dress (TriStar, 1995).Dir: Carl Franklin. Scr: Carl Franklin based on the novel by Walter Mosley. DP: Tak Fujimoto. Mu: Elmer Bernstein. Cast: Denzel Washington ("Easy" Rawlins), Jennifer Beals (Daphne Monet), Tom Sizemore (Albright), Don Cheadle ("Mouse" Alexander). 102 min.

Diabolique (ABC, 1996). Dir: Jeremiah Chechik. Scr: Don Roos based on a screenplay by Henri-Georges Clouzot. DP: Peter James. Mu: Randy Edelman. Cast: Sharon Stone (Nicole), Isabelle Adjani (Mia), Chazz Palminteri (Guy), Kathy Bates (Cop). 107 min.

Diary of a Hitman (Vision, 1992). Dir: Roy London. Scr: Kenneth Pressman, based on his play, *Insider's Price*. DP: Yuri Sokol. Mu: Michel Colombier. Cast: Forest Whitaker (Dekker), Sherilyn Feen (Jain), Seymour Cassel (Koenig). 91 min.

Dick Tracy (Touchstone, 1990). Dir: Warren Beatty. Scr: Jim Cash, Jack Epps based on the characters of Chester Gould. DP: Vittorio Storaro. Mu: Danny Elfman. Cast: Warren Beatty (Dick Tracy), Glenne Headly (Tess), Madonna (Breathless). 105 min.

Dirty Harry (Warner Bros., 1970). Dir: Don Siegel. Scr: Harry Fink, Rita Fink, Dean Riesner, John Milius based on a story by Jo Heims. DP: Bruce Surtees. Mu: Lalo Schifrin. Cast: Clint Eastwood (Harry), Harry Guardino (Bressler), Reni Santoni (Chico), Andrew Robinson (Killer). 102 min.

Disclosure (Warner Bros., 1994). Dir: Barry Levinson. Scr: Paul Attanasio based on the novel by Michael Crichton. DP: Tony Pierce-Roberts. Mu: Ennio Morricone. Cast: Demi Moore (Meredith), Michael Douglas (Sanders), Donald Sutherland (Garvin). 128 min.

Disturbia (DreamWorks, 2007). Dir: D. J. Caruso. Scr: Christoper Landon, Carl Ellsworth. DP: Rogier Stoffers. Mu: Geoff Zanelli. Cast: Shia LeBeouf (Kale), Sarah Roemer (Ashley), Carrie-Anne Moss (Julie). 105 min.

D.O.A. (Touchstone, 1988). Dir: Rocky Morton and Annabel Jankel. Scr: Charles Edward Pogue. DP: Yuri Neyman. Mu: Chaz Jankel. Cast: Dennis Quaid (Dexter Cornell), Meg Ryan (Sydney Fuller),

Charlotte Rampling (Mrs. Fitzwaring). 96 min.

Dog Day Afternoon (Warner Bros., 1975). Dir: Sidney Lumet. Scr: Frank Pierson, based on the article by P. F. Kluge and Thomas Moore. DP: Victor J. Kemper. Cast: Al Pacino (Sonny), John Cazala (Sal), Charles Durning (Moretti), Chris Sarandon (Leon). 130 min.

Domestic Disturbance (Paramount, 2001). Dir: Harold Becker. Scr: Lewis Colick based on a story by Gary Drucker, William Comanor, Colick. DP: Michael Seresin. Mu: Mark Mancina. Cast: John Travolta (Morrison), James Lashly (Jason), Rebecca Tilney (Laurie). 89 min.

Don't Say a Word (Regency, 2001). Dir: Gary Fleder. Scr: Patrick Smith Kelly, Anthony Peckham based on the novel by Andrew Klavan. DP: Amir Mokri. Mu: Mark Isham. Cast: Michael Douglas (Dr. Conrad), Brittany Murphy (Elisabeth), Sean Bean (Patrick). 113 min.

Double Indemnity (Universal, 1973). Dir: Jack Smight. Scr: Steven Bochco. DP: Jack Smight. Mu: Billy Goldenberg. Cast: Richard Crenna (Walter Neff), Lee J. Cobb (Barton Keyes), Robert Webber (Edward Norton), Samantha Eggar (Phyllis Dietrichson). 75 min.

Double Tap (Da Bronx, 2014). Dir: Ryan Combs. Scr: Combs, Fabian Carrillo. DP: Jim Orr. Mu: Carlos Nicasio.

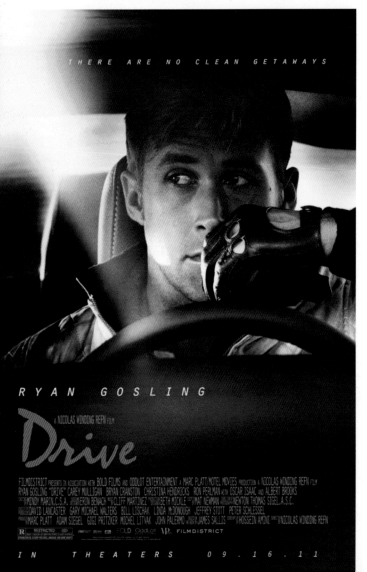

Cast: Fabian Carrillo (Bobby), Richard Tyson (Captain), Elizabeth Di Prinzio (Laura). 100 min.

Dream Lover (PolyGram, 1993). Dir: Nicholas Kazan. Scr: Nicholas Kazan. DP: Jean-Yves Escoffier. Mu: Christopher Young. Cast: James Spader (Ray), Mädchen Amick (Lena), Bess Armstrong (Elaine). 103 min.

Drive (FilmDistrict, 2013). Dir: Nicolas Winding Refn. Scr: Hossein Amini. DP: Newton Thomas Sigel. Mu: Cliff Martinez. Cast: Ryan Gosling (Driver), Carey Mulligan (Irene), Bryan Cranston (Shannon), Albert Brooks (Bernie Rose). 100 min.

The Driver (20th Century Fox, 1978). Dir/Scr: Walter Hill. DP: Philip Lathrop. Mu: Michael Small. Cast: Ryan O'Neal (The Driver), Bruce Dern (The Detective), Isabelle Adjani (The Player), Ronee Blakely (The Connection), Matt Clark (Red Plainclothesman). 91 min.

The Drowning Pool (Warner Bros., 1975). Dir: Stuart Rosenberg. Scr: Tracy Keenan Wynn and Lorenzo Semple Jr., Walter Hill based on the novel by John D. MacDonald. DP: Gordon Willis. Mu: Michael Small. Cast: Paul Newman (Harper), Joanne Woodward (Iris Devereaux), Tony Franciosa (Det. Broussard), Murray Hamilton (Kilbourne). 108 min.

Drugstore Cowboy (Avenue, 1989). Dir: Gus Van Sant Jr. Scr: Daniel Yost and Gus Van Sant, based on the novel by James Fogle. DP: Robert Yeoman. Mu: Elliott Rosenthal. Cast: Matt Dillon (Bob), Kelly Lynch (Dianne), James Le Gros (Rick). 100 min.

Eden (2012). Dir: Megan Griffiths. Scr: Megan Griffiths, Richard Phillips based on the story by Chong Kim. DP: Sean Porter. Mu: Matthew Emerson Brown, Jeramy Koepping, Joshua Morrison. Cast: Jamie Chung (Eden), Beau Bridges (Bob Gault), Matt O'Leary (Vaughan). 98 min.

Edge of Darkness (Warner Bros., 2010). Dir: Martin Campbell. Scr: William Monahan, Andrew Bovell based on television series written by Troy Kennedy-Martin. DP: Phil Meheux. Mu: Howard Shore. Cast: Mel Gibson (Craven), Ray Winstone (Jedburgh), Danny Huston (Bennett). 117 min.

8 Million Ways to Die (TriStar, 1986). Dir: Hal Ashby and Charles Mulvehill. Scr: Oliver Stone and David Lee Henry, based on the novels *A Stab in the Dark* and *Eight Million Ways to Die* by Lawrence Block. DP: Stephen H. Burum. Mu: James Newton Howard. Cast: Jeff Bridges ((Scudder), Rosanna Arquette (Sarah), Alexandra Paul (Sunny). 115 min.

El Cortez (Three-Four, 2006). Dir: Stephen Purvis. Scr: Chris Haddock. DP: Robert F. Smith. Mu: George and Jo Doering. Cast: Lou Diamond Phillips (Manny), Bruce Weitz (Popcorn), Glenn Plummer (Jack). 94 min.

Enemy of the State (Touchstone, 1998). Dir: Tony Scott. Scr: David Marconi. DP: Daniel Mindel. Mu: Trevor Rabin. Cast: Will Smith (Dean), Gene Hackman (Lyle), Jon Voight (Reynolds), Lisa Bonet (Rachel).132 min.

Enough (Columbia, 2002). Dir: Michael Apted. Scr: Nicholas Kazan. DP: Rogier Stoffers. Mu: David Arnold. Cast: Jennifer Lopez (Slim Hiller), Billy Campbell (Mitch Hiller), Tessa Allen (Gracie Hiller), Juliette Lewis (Ginny). 115 min.

Extreme Measures (Castle Rock, 1996). Dir: Michael Apted. Scr: Tony Gilroy based on book by Michael Palmer. DP: John Bailey. Mu: Danny Elfman. Cast: Hugh Grant (Dr. Luthan), Gene Hackman (Dr. Myrick), Sarah Jessica Parker (Jodie). 118 min.

Eye of the Beholder (Ambridge, 1999). Dir: Stephan Elliott. Scr: Elliott based on the novel Marc Behm. DP: Guy Dufaux.

Mu: Marius De Vries. Cast: Ewan McGregor (Stephen), Ashley Judd (Joanna), Patrick Bergin (Alexander). 109 min.

Eyewitness (20th Century Fox, 1981). Dir: Peter Yates. Scr: Steve Tesich. DP: Matthew F. Leonetti. Mu: Stanley Silverman. Cast: William Hurt (Darryl Deever), Sigourney Weaver (Tony Sokolow), Christopher Plummer (Joseph), James Woods (Aldo). 108 min.

Face/Off (Touchstone, 1997). Dir: John Woo. Scr: Mike Werb, Michael Colleary. DP: Oliver Wood. Mu: John Powell. Cast: John Travolta (Sean/Castor), Nicolas

"I need another drink... I need a lot of life insurance... I need a vacation... and all I've got is a coat, a hat, and a gun!"

ELLIOTT KASTNER PRESENTS
A DICK RICHARDS FILM
...BERT MITCHUM · CHARLOTTE RAMPLING · JOHN IRELAND · SYLVIA MILES IN "FAREWELL, MY LOVELY"
ALSO STARRING ANTHONY ZERBE · HARRY DEAN STANTON DIRECTED BY DICK RICHARDS
EXECUTIVE PRODUCERS ELLIOTT KASTNER · JERRY BICK PRODUCED BY GEORGE PAPPAS AND JERRY BRUCKHEIMER
SCREENPLAY BY DAVID ZELAG GOODMAN · FROM THE NOVEL BY RAYMOND CHANDLER   R   RESTRICTED
MUSIC DAVID SHIRE · AN AVCO EMBASSY RELEASE · AN EK ITC PRODUCTION · TECHNICOLOR®

Cage (Castor/Sean), Gina Gershon (Sasha), Joan Allen (Archer). 138 min.

Fade to Black (American, 1980). Dir/Scr: Vernon Zimmerman. DP: Álex Phillips Jr. Mu: Craig Safan. Cast: Dennis Christopher (Eric Binford), Tim Thomerson (Dr. Jerry Moriarty), Gwynne Gilford (Anne), Mickey Rourke (Richie). 102 min.

Fairview St. (New House, 2010). Dir: Michael McCallum. Scr: Michael McCallum. DP: Anthony Griffin. Cast: Michael McCallum (James), Elizabeth Moore (Natalie), Shane Hagedorn (Detective Ferguson). 110 min.

The Fall (Gold Dragon, 2009). Dir/Scr/DP: Jonathan Whittle-Utter. Mu: Simon Gray, Ben Morss. Cast: Gregory Marcel (Bobby Wilkinson), Amanda Cobb (Althea Eshman), Justin Cegnar (Erik Vangaard), Colleen Kerwick (Antoinette O'Sullivan). 95 min.

Fallen (Turner, 1998). Dir: Gregory Hoblit. Scr: Nicholas Kazan. DP: Newton Thomas Sigel. Mu: Dun Tan. Cast: Denzel Washington (Hobbes), John Goodman (Jonesy), Donald Sutherland (Lt. Stanton), James Gandolfini (Lou). 124 min.

Falling Down (Alcor, 1993). Dir: Joel Schumacher. Scr: Ebbe Roe Smith. DP: Bartkowiak. Mu: James Newton Howard. Cast: Michael Douglas (Foster), Robert Duvall (Detective), Barbara Hershey (Beth). 113 min.

The Falls (Locked Horns, 2003). Dir/Scr: Paul DeNigris. DP: Chris Santucci. Mu: Neslon Starr. Cast: David Tully (David), Diedre Kilgore (Jennifer), Johanna Watts (Robin). 85 min.

Farewell My Lovely (Avco Embassy, 1975). Dir: Dick Richards. Scr: David Zelag Goodman based on the novel by Raymond Chandler. DP: John A. Alonzo. Mu: David Shire. Cast: Robert Mitchum (Philip Marlowe), Charlotte Rampling (Mrs. Grayle), John Ireland (Nulty), Sylvia Miles (Mrs. Florian). 97 min.

Fargo (PolyGram, 1996). Dir/Scr: Joel and Ethan Coen. DP: Roger Deakins. Mu: Carter Burwell. Cast: William H. Macy (Jerry), Steve Buscemi (Carl), Harve Presnell (Wade). 98 min.

Fatal Attraction (Paramount, 1987). Dir: Adrian Lyne. Scr: James Dearden. DP: Howard Atherton. Mu: Maurice Jarre. Cast: Michael Douglas (Dan Gallagher), Glenn Close (Alex Forrest), Anne Archer (Beth). 119 min.

Fear (Universal, 1996). Dir: James Foley. Scr: Christopher Crowe. DP: Thomas Kloss. Mu: Carter Burwell. Cast: Mark Wahlberg (David McCall), Reese Witherspoon (Nicole Walker), William Petersen (Steve Walker), Amy Brenneman (Laura Walker), Alyssa Milano (Margo Masse). 97 min.

Fear City (Zupnik/Curtis, 1984). Dir: Abel Ferrara. Scr: Nicholas St. John. DP: James Lemmo. Mu: Dick Halligan. Cast: Tom Berenger (Matt Rossi), Billy Dee Williams (Al Wheeler), Jack Scalia (Nicky Piacenza), Melanie Griffith (Loretta), Rossano Brazzi (Carmine). 96 min.

Femme Fatale (Republic/Gibraltar, 1991). Dir: Andre Guttfreund. Scr: Michael Ferris and John D. Brancato. DP: Joey Forsyte. Mu: Parmer Fuller. Cast: Colin Firth (Joe Prince), Lisa Zane (Elizabeth/Cynthia/Maura), Billy Zane (Elijah). 96 min.

Femme Fatale (Warner Bros., 2002). Dir: Brian De Palma. Scr: Brian De Palma. DP: Thierry Arbogast. Mu: Ryuichi Sakamoto. Cast: Rebecca Romjin-Stamos (Laure/Lily), Antonio Banderas (Nicolas Bardo), Peter Coyote (Watts). 114 min.

52 Pick-Up (Cannon, 1986). Dir: John Frankenheimer. Scr: Elmore Leonard and John Steppling, based on the novel by Leonard. DP: Jost Vacano. Mu: Gary Chang. Cast: Roy Scheider (Harry Mitchell), Ann-Marget (Barbara Mitchell), Vanity (Doreen), John Glover (Raimy). 114 min.

Fight Club (20th Century Fox, 1999). Dir: David Fincher. Scr: Jim Uhls based on the novel *Fight Club* by Chuck Palahniuk. DP: Jeff Cronenweth. Mu: The Dust Brothers, Michael Simpson, John King. Cast: Brad Pitt (Tyler Durden), Edward Norton (Narrator), Helena Bonham Carter (Marla Singer), Meat Loaf (Bob Paulson). 139 min.

Final Analysis (Warner Bros., 1992). Dir: Phil Joanou. Scr: Wesley Strick,

based on a story by Strick and Robert Berger. DP: Jordan Cronenweth. Mu: George Fenton. Cast: Richard Gere (Isaac Barr), Kim Basinger (Heather Evans), Uma Thurman (Diana Baylor). 124 min.

Firecracker (Dikenga, 2005). Dir: Steve Balderson. Scr: Steve and Clark Balderson. DP: Jonah Torreano. Mu: The Enigma. Cast: Karen Black (Sandra/Eleanor), Mike Patton (Frank/David), Susan Traylor (Ed). 112 min.

Firewall (Warner Bros. 2006). Dir: Richard Loncraine. Scr: Joe Forte. DP: Marco Pontecorvo. Mu: Alexandre Desplat. Cast: Harrison Ford (Stanfield), Virginia Madsen (Beth), Carly Schroeder (Sarah). 105 min.

The Firm (Paramount, 1993). Dir: Sydney Pollack. Scr: David Rabe, Robert Towne, David Rayfiel based on the novel by John Grisham. DP: John Seale. Mu: Dave Grusin. Cast: Tom Cruise (Mitch McDeere), Jeanne Tripplehorn (Abby McDeere), Gene Hackman (Avery Tolar), Holly Hunter (Tammy Hemphill). 154 min.

The First Deadly Sin (Filmways, 1980). Dir: Brian G. Hutton. Scr: Mann Rubin based the novel by Lawrence Sanders. DP: Jack Priestley. Cast: Frank Sinatra (Edward Delaney), Faye Dunaway

Doyle is bad news—but a good cop.

The time is just right for an out and out thriller like this.

THE FRENCH CONNECTION

20TH CENTURY-FOX PRESENTS "THE FRENCH CONNECTION" A PHILIP D'ANTONI PRODUCTION STARRING GENE HACKMAN FERNANDO REY ROY SCHEIDER TONY LO BIANCO MARCEL BOZZUFFI DIRECTED BY WILLIAM FRIEDKIN PRODUCED BY PHILIP D'ANTONI ASSOCIATE PRODUCER KENNETH UTT EXECUTIVE PRODUCER G. DAVID SCHINE SCREENPLAY BY ERNEST TIDYMAN MUSIC COMPOSED AND CONDUCTED BY DON ELLIS COLOR BY DE LUXE®

(Barbara Delaney), David Dukes (Daniel Blank). 112 min.

Forgive Me Father (Myriad, 2001). Dir: Ivan Rogers. Scr: Blair Latta, Marisa Caldero. DP: Michael Off. Mu: Gary Koftinoff. Cast: Ivan Rogers (Father Garrett), Charles Napier (Frank). 138 min.

Four Dogs Playing Poker (Half Moon, 2000). Dir: Paul Rachman. Scr: William Quist and Shawn David Thompson. DP: Claudio Rocha. Mu: Bryan Tyler. Cast: Olivia Williams (Audrey), Balthazar Getty (Julian), Arly Jover (Maria). 97 min.

48 Hrs. (Paramount, 1982). Dir: Walter Hill. Scr: Roger Spottiswoode, Walter Hill, Larry Gross and Steven E. de Souza. DP: Ric Waite. Mu: James Horner. Cast: Nick Nolte (Jack Cates), Eddie Murphy (Reggie Hammond), Annette O'Toole (Elaine). 96 min.

Fracture (New Line, 2007). Dir: Gregory Hoblit. Scr: Daniel Pyne and Glenn Gers. DP: Kramer Morgenthau. Mu: Jeff Danna. Cast: Anthony Hopkins (Ted), Ryan Gosling (Willy), Rosamund Pike (Nikki). 113 min.

Frantic (Warner Bros., 1988). Dir: Roman Polanski. Scr: Polanski and Gerard Brach. DP: Witold Sobocinski. Mu: Ennio Morricone. Cast: Harrison Ford (Richard Walker), Emmanuelle Seigner (Michelle), Betty Buckley (Sondra Walker). 120 min.

Freeway (Anchor Bay, 1988). Dir: Francis Delia. Scr: Delia based on the novel by Deanne Barkley. DP: Frank Byers. Mu: Joe Delia. Cast: Darlanne Fluegel (Sarah), James Russo (Quinn). 91 min.

The French Connection (20th Century Fox, 1971). Dir: William Friedkin. Scr: Ernest Tidyman based on the novel by Robin Moore. DP: Owen Roizman. Mu: Don Ellis. Cast: Gene Hackman (Doyle), Fernando Rey (Charnier), Roy Scheider (Russo), Tony Lo Bianco (Boca). 104 min.

Friends of Eddie Coyle (20th Century Fox, 1973). Dir: Peter Yates. Scr: Paul Monash based on the novel by George V. Higgins. DP: Victor J. Kemper. Mu: Dave Grusin. Cast: Robert Mitchum (Eddie Coyle), Peter Boyle (Dillon), Richard Jordan (Dave Foley), Steven Keats (Jackie), Alex Rocco (Scalise). 102 min.

Funny Games (Tartan, 2007). Dir/Scr: Michael Haneke. DP: Darius Khondji. Cast: Naomi Watts (Ann), Tim Roth (George), Michael Pitt (Paul). 111 min.

The Gambler (Paramount, 1974). Dir: Karel Reisz. Scr: James Toback. DP: Victor J. Kemper. Mu: Jerry Fielding. Cast: James Caan (Axel Freed), Paul Sorvino (Hips), Lauren Hutton (Billie), Morris Carnovsky (A. R. Lowenthal), Jacqueline Brookes (Naomi Freed), Burt Young (Carmine). 111 min.

The Gambler (Paramount, 2014). Dir: Rupert Wyatt. Scr: William Monahan. DP: Greig Fraser. Mu: Jon Brion, Theo Green. Cast: Mark Wahlberg (Jim Bennett), Griffin Cleveland (Young Jim), Jessica Lange (Roberta), Omar Levva (Valet). 111 min.

The Game (Polygram, 1997). Dir: David Fincher. Scr: John Brancato, Michael Ferris. DP: Harris Savides. Mu: Howard Shore. Cast: Michael Douglas (Nicholas Van Orton), Sean Penn (Conrad Van Orton), Deborah Kara Unger (Christine). 128 min.

Gangster Squad (Warner Bros., 2013). Dir: Ruben Fleischer. Scr: Will Beall. DP: Dion Beebe. Mu: Steve Jablonsky. Cast: Josh Brolin (John O'Mara), Ryan Gosling (Jerry Wooters), Sean Penn (Mickey Cohen). Nick Nolte (Chief Bill Parker), Emma Stone (Grace Faraday). 113 min.

Gattaca (Columbia, 1997). Dir: Andrew Niccol. Scr: Andrew Niccol. DP: Slawomir Idziak. Mu: Michael Nyman. Cast: Ethan Hawke (Vincent Freeman), Uma Thurman (Irene Cassini), Gore Vidal (Dir: Josef), Xander Berkeley (Dr.

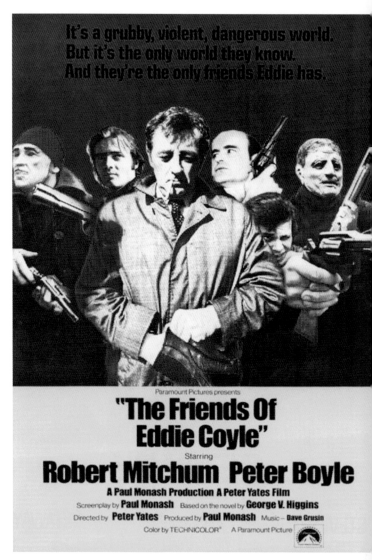

Lamar), Elias Koteas (Antonio Freeman). 101 min.

The General's Daughter (Paramount, 1999). Dir: Simon West. Scr: William Goldman, Christopher Bertolini based on the novel by Nelson DeMille. DP: Peter Menzies Jr. Mu: Carter Burwell. Cast: John Travolta (Officer Brenner), Madeleine Stowe (Officer Sunhill), James Cromwell (Lt. Gen. Campbell). 116 min.

Genuine Risk (IRS, 1990). Dir: Kurt Voss. DP: Dean Lent. Mu: Deborah Holland. Cast: Terence Stamp (Hellwart), Peter Berg (Henry), Michelle Johnson (Girl). 89 min.

STEVE McQUEEN · ALI MacGRAW

GETAWAY
Ihre Chance war gleich Null

The Getaway (Warner Bros., 1972). Dir: Sam Peckinpah. Scr: Walter Hill based on the novel by Jim Thompson. DP: Lucien Ballard. Mu: Quincy Jones. Cast: Steve McQueen (Carter "Doc" McCoy), Ali MacGraw (Carol McCoy), Ben Johnson (Jack Beynon), Sally Struthers (Fran Clinton). 122 min.

The Getaway (Universal, 1994). Dir: Roger Donaldson. Scr: Walter Hill and Amy Jones based on the novel by Jim Thompson. DP: Peter Menzies Jr. Mu:

Mark Isham. Cast: Alec Baldwin (Carter "Doc" McCoy), Kim Basinger (Carol McCoy), Michael Madsen (Rudy Travis), James Woods (Jack Benyon). 115 min.

The Gingerbread Man (Island, 1998). Dir: Robert Altman. Scr: Clyde Hayes based on a story by John Grisham. DP: Changwei Gu. Mu: Mark Isham. Cast: Kenneth Branagh (Magruder), Embeth Davidtz (Mallory), Robert Downey Jr. (Clyde). 114 min.

Give 'Em Hell Malone (Hannibal, 2009). Dir: Russell Mulcahy. Scr: Mark Hosack. DP: Jonathan Hall. Mu: David Williams. Cast: Thomas Jane (Malone), Ving Rhames (Boulder), Elsa Pataky (Evelyn). 96 min.

Ghost Dog: The Way of the Samurai (Artisan, 1999). Dir/Scr: Jim Jarmusch. DP: Robby Müller. Mu: RZA. Cast: Forest Whitaker (Ghost Dog), John Tormey (Louie), Henry Silva (Ray Vargo), Cliff Gorman (Sonny Valerio), Isaach De Bankolé (Raymond), Camille Winbush (Pearline). 116 min.

Gleaming the Cube (20th Century Fox, 1989). Dir: Graeme Clifford. Scr: Michael Tolkin. DP: Reed Smoot. Mu: Jay Ferguson. Cast: Christian Slater Cast: (Brian Kelly), Steven Bauer (Lucero), Richard Herd (Ed), Le Tuan (Col. Trac). 104 min.

Golden Gate (American Playhouse, 1994). Dir: John Madden. Scr: David Henry Hwang. DP: Bobby Bukowski. Mu: Elliot Goldenthal. Cast: Matt Dillon (Walker), Joan Chen (Marilyn Song), Bruno Kirby (Pirelli). 91 min.

Gone (Summit/Lakeshore, 2012). Dir: Heitor Dhalia. Scr: Allison Burnett. DP: Michael Grady. Mu: David Buckley. Cast: Amanda Seyfried (Jill), Daniel Sunjata (Det. Powers), Jennifer Carpenter (Sharon), Wes Bentley (Hood). 94 min.

Gone, Baby, Gone (Miramax, 2007). Dir: Ben Affleck. Scr: Affleck, Aaron Stockard based on the novel by Dennis

Lehane. DP: John Toll. Mu: Harry Gregson Williams. Cast: Casey Affleck (Kenzie), Michelle Monaghan (Angie), Morgan Freeman (Doyle). 114 min.

Gone Girl (20th Century Fox, 2014). Dir: David Fincher. Scr: Gillian Flynn based on her novel. DP: Jeff Cronenweth. Mu: Trent Reznor, Atticus Ross. Cast: Ben Affleck (Nick Dunne), Rosamund Pike (Amy Dunne), Tyler Perry (Tanner Bolt), Carrie Coon (Margo Dunne), Kim Dickens (Detective Boney). 149 min.

A Good Alibi (Confuse a Cat, 2009). Dir: Geoffrey Stephenson. Scr: Stephenson. Mu: Jonathan Fessenden. Cast: Geoffrey Stephenson (Jerry), Lubi Boutdy (Meagan), Sandra Inezz (Detective). 97 min.

Gone in Sixty Seconds (Touchstone, 2000). Dir: Dominic Sena. Scr: H.B. Halicki, Scott Rosenberg. DP: Paul Cameron. Mu: Trevor Rabin. Cast: Nicolas Cage (Randall "Memphis" Raines), Angelina Jolie (Sara "Sway" Wayland), Giovanni Ribisi ("Kip" Raines), Robert Duvall (Otto Halliwell). 118 min.

The Grifters (Miramax, 1990). Dir: Stephen Frears. Scr: Donald E. Westlake, based on the novel *The Grifters* by Jim Thompson. DP: Oliver Stapleton. Mu: Elmer Bernstein. Cast: Angelica Huston (Lilly Dillon), John Cusack (Roy Dillon), Annette Bening (Myra Langtree). 119 min.

The Grind (Flashback, 2009). Dir/Scr: John Millea. DP: Brain Crane. Mu: Kevin Saunders Hayes. Cast: C. Thomas Howell (Luke), Michael Welch (Josh), Tanya Allen (Courtney), Sarah Scott (Alex). 88 min.

Grosse Pointe Blank (Hollywood Pictures, 1997). Dir: George Armitage. Scr: John Cusack, Steve Pink, D.V. DeVincentis, Tom Jankiewicz. DP: Jamie Anderson. Cast: John Cusack (Martin Blank), Minnie Driver (Debi), Allan Arkin (Dr. Oatman). 107 min.

Guilty as Sin (Hollywood Pictures, 1993). Dir: Sidney Lumet. Scr: Larry Cohen. DP: Andrzej Bartkowiak. Mu: Howard Shore. Cast: Don Johnson (Greenhill), Rebecca De Mornay (Jennifer), Jack Warden (Moe). 107 min.

Guncrazy (Zeta/Overseas, 1992). Dir: Tamra Davis. Scr: Matthew Bright. DP: Lisa Rinzler. Mu: Ed Tomney. Cast: Drew Barrymore (Anita), James Legros (Howard), Billy Drago (Hank), Rodney Harvey (Hank), Ione Skye (Joy). 96 min.

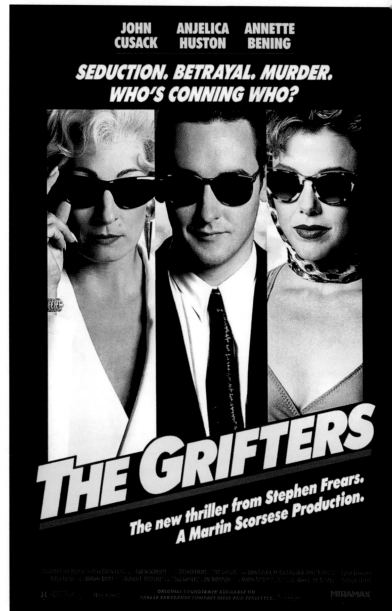

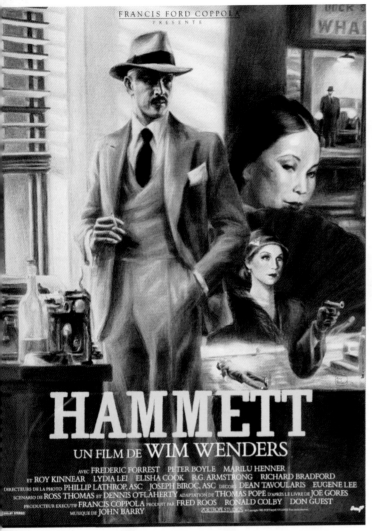

Hammett (Orion/Warner Bros./ Zoetrope, 1983). Dir: Wim Wenders. Scr: Ross Thomas, Dennis O'Flaherty, and Thomas Pope. DP: Philip Lathrop, Joe Biroc. Mu: John Barry. Cast: Frederic Forrest (Hammett), Peter Boyle (Jimmy Ryan), Marilu Henner (Kit Conger). 97 min.

The Hand That Rocks the Cradle (Buena Vista/Interscope, 1992). Dir: Curtis Hanson. Scr: Amanda Silver. DP: Robert Wlswit. Mu: Graeme Revell. Cast: Annabella Sciorra (Claire Bartel), Rebecca De Mornay (Peyton Flanders), Matt McCoy (Michael Bartel). 110 min.

Hangman (Mainline, 2000). Dir: Ken Girotti. Scr: Vladimir Nemirovsky. DP: Gerald Packer. Mu: Steven M. Stern. Cast: Lou Diamond Phillips (Detective Nick Roos), Mädchen Amick (Grace Mitchell), Mark Wilson (Det. Sam Baluzy). 96 min.

Hard Eight (Rysher, 1996). DirScr: Paul Thomas Anderson. DP: Robert Elswit. Mu: Jon Brion, Michael Penn. Cast: Philip Baker Hall (Sydney Brown), John C. Reilly (John Finnegan), Gwyneth Paltrow (Clementine), Samuel L. Jackson (Jimmy). 102 min.

Hardcore (Columbia, 1979). Dir/Scr: Paul Schrader. DP: Michael Chapman. Mu: Jack Nitzsche. Cast: George C. Scott (Jake Van Dorn), Peter Boyle (Andy Mast), Season Hubley (Niki), Dick Sargent (Wes De Jong), Leonard Gaines (Ramada). 105 min.

Harper (Warner Bros., 1966). Dir: Jack Smight. Scr: William Goldman, based on the novel *The Moving Target* by Ross MacDonald. DP: Conrad Hall. Mu: Johnny Mandel. Cast: Paul Newman (Harper), Lauren Bacall (Mrs. Sampson), Julie Harris (Betty Fraley), Arthur Hill (Albert Graves), Janet Leigh (Susan). 121 min.

Harsh Times (Sperling, 2005). Dir: David Ayer. Scr: David Ayer. DP: Steve Mason. Mu: Graeme Revell. Cast: Christian Bale (Jim Davis), Freddy Rodriguez (Mike), Eva Longoria (Sylvia). 116 min.

The Harvest (Curb Musifilm, 1992). Dir: David Marconi. Scr: Marconi. DP: Emmanuel Lubezki. Mu: Rick Boston. Cast: Miguel Ferrer (Pope), Leilani Sarelle (Natalie), Henry Silva (Topo). 97 min.

Heat (Warner Bros., 1995). Dir: Michael Mann. Scr: Michael Mann. DP: Dante Spinotti. Mu: Elliot Goldenthal. Cast: Al Pacino (Lt. Vincent Hanna), Robert DeNiro (Neil McCauley), Val Kilmer (Chris Shiherlis), Jon Voight (Nate), Tom Sizemore (Michael Cheritto). 171 min.

Heist (Warner Bros., 2001). Dir: David Mamet. Scr: David Mamet. DP: Robert Elswit. Mu: Theodore Shapiro. Cast: Gene Hackman (Joe Moore), Danny DeVito (Mickey Bergman), Rebecca Pidgeon (Fran Moore), Delroy Lindo (Bobby "Bob" Blane). 109 min.

Hell Up in Harlem (AIP, 1973). Dir: Larry Cohen. Scr: Larry Cohen. DP: Fenton Hamilton. Mu: Fonce Mizell. Cast: Fred Williamson (Tommy Gibbs), Julius Harris (Papa Gibbs), Gloria Hendry (Helen). 98 min.

Here Dies Another Day (Queen, 1997). Dir: Caryn West. Scr: Martha Moorehead, Caryn West. DP: Samuel Ameen. Mu: Susan Hurley. Cast: Alexa Borden (Girl #4), Natalie Brown (Girl #2), Michael Camacho (Mikey). 88 min.

Hickey & Boggs (UA, 1972). Dir: Robert Culp. Scr: Walter Hill. DP: Wilmer Butler. Mu: Ted Ashford. Cast: Bill Cosby (Al Hickey), Robert Culp (Frank Boggs), Rosalind Cash (Nyona), Sheila Sullivan (Edith Boggs). 111 min.

Hit and Run (MGM, 2009). Dir: Enda McCallion. Scr: Diane Doniol-Valcroze, Arthur Flam. DP: Olivier Cocaul. Mu: Mateo Messina. Cast: Laura Breckenridge (Mary Murdock), Kevin Corrigan (Timonthy Emser), Christopher Shand (Rick). 84 min.

Hit List (New Line, 1989). Dir: William Lustig. Scr: John Goff and Peter Brosnan. DP: James Lemmo. Mu: Garry Schyman. Cast: Jan-Michael Vincent (Jack Collins), Leo Rossi (Frank De Salvo), Lance Henriksen (Chris Calek). 90 min.

Hit Me (Slough, 1996). Dir: Steven Shainberg. Scr: Denis Johnson based on a novel by Jim Thompson. DP: Mark Gordon. Mu: Peter M. Robinson. Cast: Elias Koteas (Sonny), Laure Marsac (Monique), Jay Leggett (Jay). 125 min.

The Hitcher (TriStar, 1986). Dir: Robert Harmon. Scr: by Eric Red. Cast: Rutger

Hauer (John Ryder), C. Thomas Howell (Jim Halsey), Jennifer Jason Leigh (Nash). DP: John Seale. Mu: Mark Isham. 97 min.

The Hitcher (Intrepid, 2007). Dir: Dave Meyers. Scr: Eric Red, Jake Wade Wall, Eric Bernt. DP: James Hawkinson. Mu: Steve Jablonsky. Cast: Sean Bean (John Ryder), Sophia Bush (Grace Andrews), Zachary Knighton (Jim Halsey). 86 min.

The Hitcher II: I've Been Waiting (Universal, 2003). Dir: Louis Morneau. Scr: Molly Meeker, Charles R. Meeker, Leslie Scharf. DP: George Mooradian.

SAFE IS NEVER SEX. IT'S DANGEROUS.

A DENNIS HOPPER FILM

THE HOT SPOT

FILM NOIR LIKE YOU'VE NEVER SEEN.

DON JOHNSON - "THE HOT SPOT" - VIRGINIA MADSEN - JENNIFER CONNELLY
CHARLES MARTIN SMITH · VALERIE TYSON · DEBORAH CAPOGROSSO
BILL GAVIN - DEREK POWER - STEPHEN UJLAKI · UELI STEIGER
WENDE PHIFER-MATE · JACK NITZSCHE · CHARLES WILLIAMS
NONA TYSON & CHARLES WILLIAMS · PAUL LEWIS · DENNIS HOPPER
R   ORION

Mu: Joe Kraemer. Cast: C. Thomas Howell (Jim Halsey), Kari Wührer (Maggie), Jake Busey (Jack, the Hitcher). 93 min.

The Hitchhiker (Asylum, 2007). Dir: Leigh Scott. Scr: Scott, Jeshua De Horta. DP: Steven Parker. Mu: Chris Ridenhour. Cast: Jeff Denton (Jack Carter), Sarah Lieving (Melinda Mann), Shaley Scott (Denise), Sarah Hall (Patty). 86 min.

Hitman's Run (DWP, 1999). Dir: Mark Lester. Scr: Eric Barker. DP: Zoltán David. Mu: Roger Bellon. Cast: Eric Roberts (Tony Lazorka/John Dugan), Esteban Powell (Brian Penny), C. Thomas Howell (Tom Holly). 93 min.

Homicide (Triumph/Cinehaus, 1991). Dir/Scr: David Mamet. DP: Roger Deakins. Mu: Aaeric Jans. Cast: Joe Mantegna (Bobby Gold), William H. Macy (Tim Sullivan), Natalija Nogulich (Chava). 102 min.

The Honeymoon Killers (Cinerama, 1969). Dir/Scr: Leonard Kastle. DP: Oliver Wood. Mu: Gustav Mahler. Cast: Shirley Stoler (Martha), Tony Lo Bianco (Ray). 108 min.

The Horseplayer (Relentless/J&N, 1991). Dir: Kurt Voss. Scr: Voss and Larry Rattner. DP: Dean Lent. Mu: Gary Shuyman. Cast: Brad Dourif (Bud), Sammi Davis (Randi), M.K. Harris (Matthew). 92 min.

Hostage (Miramax, 2005). Dir: Florent-Emillio. Scr: Doug Richardson. DP: Giovanni Fiore Coltellacci. Mu: Alexandre Deplat. Cast: Bruce Willis (Jeff Talley), Kevin Pollak (Walter Smith), Jimmy Bennett (Tommy Smith), Michelle Horn (Jennifer Smith). 113 min.

The Hot Spot (Film Now/Orion, 1990). Dir: Dennis Hopper. Scr: Nona Tyson and Charles Williams, based on the novel *Hell Hath No Fury* by Charles Williams. DP: Ueli Steiger. Mu: Jack Nitzsche. Cast: Don Johnson (Harry Madox), Virginia Madsen (Dolly Harshaw), Jennifer Connelly (Gloria Harper). 128 min.

House of Games (Filmhaus/Orion, 1987). Dir/Scr: David Mamet. DP: Juan Ruiz Anchía. Mu: Alaric Jans. Cast: Lindsay Crouse (Margaret Ford), Joe Mantegna (Mike), Mike Nussbaum (Joey), Lilia Skala (Dr. Littauer). 101 min.

Hustle (Paramount, 1975). Dir: Robert Aldrich. Scr: Steve Shagan. DP: Joseph Biroc. Mu: Frank DeVol. Cast: Burt

Reynolds (Lt. Phil Gaines), Catherine Deneuve (Nicole Britton), Eddie Albert (Leo Sellers), Ben Johnson (Marty Hollinger), Paul Winfield (Sgt. Louis Belgrave). 120 min.

I, the Jury (20th Century Fox, 1982). Dir: Richard T. Heffron. Scr: Larry Cohen, based on the novel by Mickey Spillane. DP: Andrew Laszlo. Mu: Bill Conti. Cast: Armand Assante (Mike Hammer), Barbera Carrera (Dr. Charlotte Bennett), Alan King (Charles Kalecki). 109 min.

Idleheist (Jerseyboy, 2004) Dir/Scr: Joshua M. Dragotta. DP: Carlos E. Moreno. Mu: Jay Verkamp. Cast: Guy Castonguay (Jake), Dan Davis (Ranger), Chris Kemler (Sal). 63 min.

Impulse (Warner Bros., 1990). Dir: Sondra Locke. Scr: John De Marco and Leigh Chapman. DP: Dean Semler. Mu: Michel Colombier. Cast: Theresa Russell (Lottie), Jeff Fahey (Stan), George Dzundza (Lt. Joe Morgan). 109 min.

In the Cut (Screen Gems, 2003). Dir: Jane Campion. Scr: Jane Campion, Susanna Moore, Stavros Kazantzidis based on the novel by Moore. DP: Dion Beebe. Mu: Hilmar Orn Hilmarsson. Cast: Meg Ryan (Frannie), Mark Ruffalo (Det. Malloy), Jennifer Jason Leigh (Pauline), Nick Damici (Det. Rodriguez), Kevin Bacon (John Graham). 119 min.

In the Line of Fire (Columbia, 1993). Dir: Wolfgang Petersen. Scr: Jeff Maguire. DP: John Bailey. Mu: Ennio Morricone. Cast: Clint Eastwood (Horrigan), John Malkovich (Leary), Rene Russo (Lily). 128 min.

Inception (Legendary, 2010). Dir/Scr: Christopher Nolan. DP: Wally Pfister. Mu: Hans Zimmer. Cast: Leonardo DiCaprio (Cobb), Ken Watanabe (Saito), Joseph Gordon-Levitt (Arthur), Marion Cotillard (Mai), Ellen Page (Ariadne). 148 min.

An Innocent Man (Touchstone, 1989). Dir: Peter Yates. Scr: Larry Brothers.

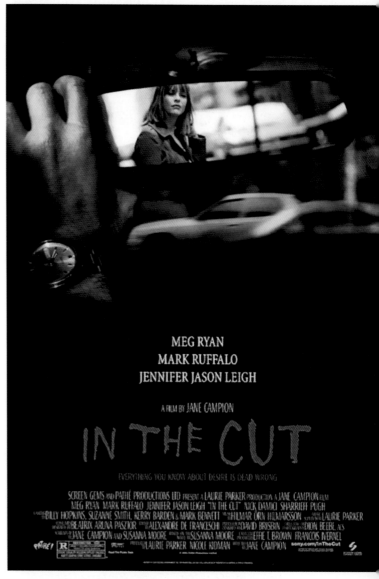

MEG RYAN
MARK RUFFALO
JENNIFER JASON LEIGH

A FILM BY JANE CAMPION

IN THE CUT

EVERYTHING YOU KNOW ABOUT DESIRE IS DEAD WRONG

DP: William Fraker. Mu: Howard Shore. Cast: Tom Selleck (Jimmie), F. Murray Abraham (Cane), Laila Robins (Kate). 113 min.

Inside Man (Universal, 2006). Dir: Spike Lee. Scr: Russell Gewirtz. DP: Matthew Libatique. Cast: Denzel Washington (Det. Frazier), Clive Owen (Dalton Russell), Chiwetel Ejiofor (Det. Mitchell), Jodie Foster (Madeleine White), Christopher Plummer (Arthur Case). 129 min.

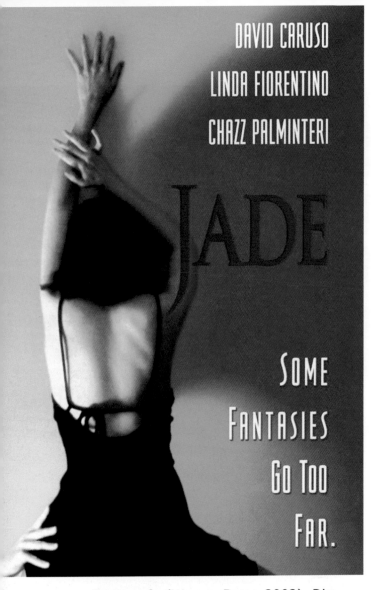

DAVID CARUSO

LINDA FIORENTINO

CHAZZ PALMINTERI

JADE

SOME
FANTASIES
GO TOO
FAR.

Insomnia (Warner Bros., 2002). Dir: Christopher Nolan. Scr: Hillary Seitz based on the screenplay by Nikolaj Frobenius and Erik Skjoldbjaerg. DP: Wally Pfister. Mu: David Julyan. Cast: Al Pacino (Detective Will Dormer), Martin Donovan (Detective Hap Eckhart), Robin Williams (Walter Finch), Hilary Swank (Detective Ellie Burr). 118 min.

Internal Affairs (Paramount, 1990). Dir: Mike Figgis. Scr: Henry Bean. DP: John A. Alonzo. Mu: Mike Figgis, Anthony Marinelli, Brian Banks. Cast: Richard Gere (Dennis Peck), Andy Garcia (Raymond Avilla), Nancy Travis (Kathleen Avilla). 115 min.

Intimate Stranger (SouthGate, 1991). Dir: Allan Holzman. Scr: Rob Fresco. DP: Ilan Rosenberg. Mu: Jonathan Sheffer. Cast: Deborah Harry (Cory Wheeler), James Russo (Nick Ciccini), Tim Thomerson (Malcolm Henthoff). 94 min.

The Island (DreamWorks, 2005). Dir: Michael Bay. Scr: Caspian Tredwell-Owen, Alex Kurtzman, Roberto Orci. DP: Mauro Fiore. Mu: Steve Jablonsky. Cast: Ewan McGregor (Lincoln Six Echo/ Tom Lincoln), Scarlett Johansson (Jordan Two Delta/Sarah Jordan), Djimon Hounsou (Albert Laurent), Sean Bean (Dr. Bernard Merrick), Steve Buscemi (James McCord). 136 min.

Jackie Brown (Miramax, 1997). Dir: Quentin Tarantino. Scr: Quentin Tarantino based on the novel *Rum Punch* by Elmore Leonard. DP: Guillermo Navarro. Cast: Pam Grier (Jackie Brown), Samuel L. Jackson (Ordell), Robert Forster (Max Cherry), Robert De Niro (Louis Gara), Michael Keaton (Ray Nicolette). 154 min.

Jade (Paramount, 1995). Dir: William Friedkin. Scr: Joe Eszterhas. DP: Andrzej Bartkowiak. Mu: James Horner. Cast: David Caruso (David), Linda Fiorentino (Trina), Chazz Palminteri (Matt). 95 min.

Jagged Edge (Columbia/EMI, 1985). Dir: Richard Marquand. Scr: Joe Eszterhas. DP: Matthew F. Leonetti. Mu: John Barry. Cast: Glenn Close (Teddy Barnes), Jeff Bridges (Jack Forrester), Peter Coyote (Krasny), Robert Loggia (Sam Ransom). 108 min.

Jezebel's Kiss (Shapiro- Glickenhaus, 1990). Dir/Scr: Harvey Keith. DP:,Brian Reynolds. Mu: Mitchel Forman. Cast: Katherine Barrese (Jezebel), Malcolm McDowell (Ben Faberson). 97 min.

The Job (Lions Gate, 2003). Dir/Scr: Kenny Golde. DP: Scott Kevan. Mu: Benjamin Newhouse. Cast: Daryl Hannah (Carol Jean "C.J." March), Brad Renfro (Troy Riverside), Dominique

Swain (Emily Robin), Eric Mabius (Rick). 83 min.

Johnny Handsome (Carolco/TriStar, 1989). Dir: Walter Hill. Scr: Ken Friedman, based on the novel by John Godey. DP: Matthew F. Leonetti. Mu: Ry Cooder. Cast: Mickey Rourke (John Sedley), Ellen Barkin (Sunny Boyd), Elizabeth McGovern (Donna McCarty). 94 min.

Johnny Mnemonic (TriStar, 1995). Dir: Robert Longo. Scr: William Gibson. DP: Francois Protat. Mu: Brad Fiedel. Cast: Keanu Reeves (Johnny), Dina Meyer (Jane), Ice-T (J-Bone). 96 min.

Judas Kiss (Bandeira, 1998). Dir: Sebastian Guttierez. Scr: Sebastian Guttierez based on a story by Deanna Fuller. DP: James Chressanthis. Mu: Christopher Young. Cast: Carla Gugino (Coco), Simon Baker (Junior), Alan Rickman (Detective). 98 min.

Juice (Island, 1992). Dir: Ernest R. Dickerson. Scr: Dickerson, Gerard Brown. DP: Larry Banks. Mu: Hank Schocklee. Cast: Omar Epps (Q), Tupac Shakur (Bishop), Cindy Herron (Yolanda). 95 min.

Just Cause (Warner Bros., 1995). Dir: Arne Glimcher. Scr: Jeb Stuart, Peter Stone based on a novel by John Katzenbach. DP: Lajos Koltai. Mu: James Newton Howard. Cast: Sean Connery (Armstrong), Laurence Fishburne (Sheriff Brown), Kate Capshaw (Laurie), Blair Underwood (Bobby). 102 min.

Kalifornia (MGM, 1993). Dir: Dominic Sena. Scr: Tim Metcalfe based on a story by Metcalf and Stephen Levy. DP: Bojan Bazelli. Mu: Carter Burwell. Cast: Brad Pitt (Grayce), Juliette Lewis (Adele), David Duchovny (Brian), Michelle Forbes (Carrie). 117 min.

Kill by Inches (Cineblast, 1999). Dir: Diane Doniol-Valcroze, Arthur Flam. Scr: Doniol-Valcroze, Flam. DP: Richard Rutkowski. Mu: Geir Jenssen. Cast:

Emmanuel Salinger (Thomas), Myriam Cyr (Vera), Marcus Powell (The Father). 80 min.

Kill Me Again (MGM/Progaganda, 1990). Dir: John Dahl. Scr: John Dahl and David Warfield. DP: Jacques Steyn. Mu: William Olvis. Cast: Val Kilmer (Jack Andrews), Joanne Whalley-Kilmer (Fay Forrester), Michael Madsen (Vince Miller). 94 min.

Killer (Republic, 1995). Dir: Mark Malone. Scr: Gordon Melbourne, story by Mark Malone. DP: Tobias A. Schliessler. Mu: Graeme Coleman. Cast:

Anthony LaPaglia (Mick), Mimi Rogers (Fiona), Matt Craven (Archie), Peter Boyle (George). 95 min.

The Killer Inside Me (Devi/Warner Bros., 1976). Dir: Burt Kennedy. Scr: Edward Mann and Robert Chamblee, based on the novel by Jim Thompson. DP: William A. Fraker. Mu: Tim McIntire, John Rubinstein. Cast: Stacy Keach (Lou Ford), Susan Tyrell (Joyce Lakeland), Tisha Sterling (Amy Stanton). 99 min.

The Killer Inside Me (Hero/Muse, 2010). Dir: Michael Winterbottom. Scr: John Curran based on the novel by Jim Thompson. DP: Marcel Zyskind. Mu: Joel Cadbury. Cast: Casey Affleck (Lou Ford), Jessica Alba (Joyce), Kate Hudson (Amy). 109 min.

Killer Joe (Voltage, 2011). Dir: William Friedkin. Scr: Tracy Letts. DP: Caleb Deschanel. Mu: Tyler Bates. Cast: Matthew McConaughey ("Killer" Joe Cooper), Emile Hirsch (Chris Smith), Juno Temple (Dottie Smith). 102 min.

The Killers (Universal, 1964). Dir: Don Siegel. Scr: Gene L. Coon, based on the Ernest Hemingway short story "The Killers." DP: Richard L. Rawlings. Mu: Stanley Wilson, Johnny Williams, Don Raye, Henry Mancini. Cast: Lee Marvin (Charlie Strom), Angie Dickinson (Sheila Farr), John Cassavetes (Jerry Nichols/Johnny North), Ronald Reagan (Browning). 95 min.

Killing Mark Twain (LPD, 2008). Dir/Scr: Lenny Rivera. DP: Gary Powell. Mu: William Niven. Cast: Nicholas E. Calhoun (Ben Maguire /"Mark Twain"), Daniel Gray (Asimov), Ravi M. Iyer (Farouk). 61 min.

The Killing of a Chinese Bookie (Faces, 1976). Dir/Scr: John Cassavetes. DP: Mike Ferris. Mu: Bo Harwood. Cast: Ben Gazzara (Cosmo Vitelli), Timothy Carey (Flo), Azizi Johari (Rachel), Meade Roberts (Mr. Sophistication). 135 min.

Killing Them Softly (Plan B, 2012). Dir: Andrew Dominik. Scr: Andrew Dominik based in the novel Cogan's Trade by George V. Higgins. DP: Greig Fraser. Mu: Jonathan Elia & David Wittman. Cast: Brad Pitt (Cogan), Richard Jenkins (Driver), James Gandolfini (Mickey), Ray Liotta (Trattman), Sam Shepard (Dillon). 97 min.

The Killing Time (New World, 1987). Dir: Rick King. Scr: Don Bohlinger, James Nathan Bruce, and Franklin Singer. DP: Paul H. Goldsmith. Mu: Paul Chihara. Cast: Beau Bridges (Sam Wayburn), Kiefer Sutherland (Brian), Joe Don Baker (Sheriff). 96 min.

The Kill-Off (Filmworld International/Cabriolet, 1990). Dir/Scr: Maggie

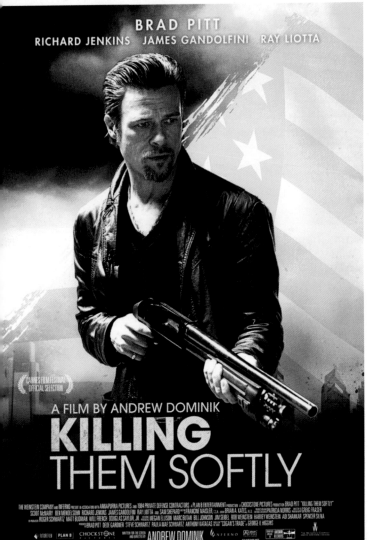

Greenwald based on the novel by Jim Thompson. DP: Declan Quinn. Mu: Evan Lurie. Cast: Loretta Gross (Luane), Jackson Sims (Pete), Steve Monroe (Ralph), Cathy Haase (Danny Lee), Andrew Lee Barrett (Bobbie), Jorjan Fox (Myra). 91 min.

King of New York (Seven Arts/New Line, 1990). Dir: Abel Ferrara. Scr: Nicholas St. John. DP: Bojan Bazelli. Mu: Joe Delia. Cast: Christopher Walken (Frank White), David Caruso (Dennis Caruso), Larry Fishburne (Jimmy Jump). 103 min.

A Kiss Before Dying (Universal/Initial, 1991). Dir: James Dearden. Scr: Dearden, based on the novel by Ira Levin. DP: Mike Southon. Mu: Howard Shore. Cast: Matt Dillon (Jonathan Corliss), Sean Young (Ellen/Dory Carlsson), Max Von Sydow (Thor Carlsson). 95 min.

Kiss Me a Killer (Califilm, 1991). Dir: Marcus DeLeon. Scr: Christopher Wooden and Marcus DeLeon. DP: Nancy Schreiber. Mu: Nigel Holton. Cast: Julie Carmen (Teresa), Robert Beltran (Tony), Guy Boyd (Jake), Ramon Franco (Ramon). 92 min.

Kiss of Death (20th Century Fox, 1995). Dir: Barbet Schroeder. Scr: Richard Price from a Scr: by Ben Hecht and Charles Lederer. DP: Luciano Tovoli. Mu: Trevor Jones. Cast: David Caruso (Jimmy Kilmartin), Samuel L. Jackson (Calvin Hart), Nicolas Cage (Little Junior Brown), 101 min.

Kiss the Girls (Paramount, 1997). Dir: Gary Fleder. Scr: David Klass. DP: Aaron Schneider. Mu: Mark Isham. Cast: Morgan Freeman (Dr. Alex Cross), Ashley Judd (Dr. Kate McTiernan), Cary Elwes (Det. Nick Ruskin). 115 min.

Klute (Warner Bros, 1971). Dir: Alan Pakula. Scr: Andy and Dave Lewis. DP: Gordon Willis. Mu: Michael Small. Cast: Jane Fonda (Bree Daniel), Donald

Sutherland (John Klute), Charles Cioffi (Peter Cable). 114 min.

L.A. Confidential (Warner Bros., 1997). Dir: Curtis Hanson. Scr: Brian Helgeland, Curtis Hanson, based on the novel by James Ellroy. DP: Dante Spinotti. Mu: Jerry Goldsmith. Cast: Kevin Spacey (Jack Vincennes), Russell Crowe (Wendell "Bud" White), Guy Pearce (Edmund "Ed" Exley), Kim Basinger (Lynn Bracken), James Cromwell (Dudley Smith). 138 min.

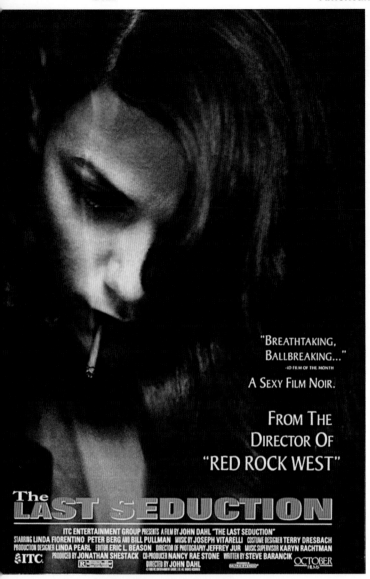

"BREATHTAKING,
BALLBREAKING..."
-ID FILM OF THE MONTH

A SEXY FILM NOIR.

FROM THE
DIRECTOR OF
"RED ROCK WEST"

Lady Beware (Scotti Bros./International Video, 1987). Dir: Karen Arthur. Scr: Susan Miller and Charles Zev Cohen. DP: Tom Neuwirth. Mu: Craig Safan. Cast: Diane Lane (Katya Yarno), Michael Woods (Jack Price). 108 min.

Lady in Cement (20th Century Fox, 1968). Dir: Gordon Douglas. Scr: Marvin H. Albert and Jack Guss, based on the novel by Guss. DP: Joe Biroc. Mu: Hugo Montenegro. Cast: Frank Sinatra (Tony Rome), Raquel Welch (Kit Forrest), Richard Conte (Lt. Santini), Martin Gabel (Al Mungar). 93 min.

The Last Boy Scout (Geffen/Silver, 1991). Dir: Tony Scott. Scr: Shane Black, based on a story by Black and Greg Hicks. DP: Ward Russell. Mu: Michael Kamen. Cast: Bruce Willis (Joe Hallenbeck), Damon Wayans (Jimmy Dix), Chelsea Field (Sarah Hallenbeck). 101 min.

The Last Embrace (United Artists, 1979). Dir: Jonathan Demme. Scr: David Shaber, based on the novel *Thirteenth Man* by Murray Teigh Bloom. DP: Tak Fujimoto. Mu: Miklos Rozsa. Cast: Roy Sheider (Harry Hannan), Janet Margolin (Ellie Fabian), John Glover (Richard Peabody). 103 min.

Last of the Finest (Orion, 1990). Dir: John Mackenzie. Scr: Jere Cunningham, Thomas Lee Wright, George Armitage. DP: Juan Ruiz Anchía. Mu: Jack Nitzsche. Cast: Brian Dennehy (Frank Daly), Joe Pantoliano (Wayne Gross), Jeff Fahey (Ricky Rodriguez), Bill Paxton (Howard Jones), Michael C. Gwynne (Anthony Reece). 106 min.

The Last Seduction (ITC, 1994).Dir: John Dahl. Scr: Steve Barancik. DP: Jeff Jur. Mu: Joseph Vitarelli. Cast: Linda Fiorentino (Bridget/Wendy), Peter Berg (Mike Swale), Bill Pullman (Clay Gregory), Brien Varady (Chris). 110 min.

Last Time Forever (Showcase, 2006). Dir: Adam Bonfanti. Scr: Adam Bonfanti. DP: Ivan Jordana. Mu: Randy Miller. Cast: Daniel Travis (MacDonald), Justine Eyre (Gloria), Tim Ware (Ned). 90 min.

Léon: The Professional (Buena Vista, 1994). Dir/Scr: Luc Besson. DP: Thierry Arbogast. Mu: Éric Serra. Cast: Jean Reno ("Léon" Montana), Gary Oldman (Norman Stansfield), Natalie Portman (Mathilda), Danny Aiello (Tony). 110 min.

Lethal Weapon (Warner Bros., 1987). Dir: Richard Donner. Scr: Shane Black. DP: Stephen Goldblatt. Mu: Milt Kamen and Eric Clapton. Cast: Mel Gibson

(Riggs), Danny Glover (Murtaugh), Gary Busey (Joshua), Mitchell Ryan (General). 110 min.

Lethal Weapon II (Warner Bros., 1989). Dir: Richard Donner. Scr: Jeffrey Boam, based on a story by Shane Black and Warren Murphy. DP: Stephen Goldblatt. Mu: Michael Kamen, Eric Clapton, David Sanborn. Cast: Mel Gibson (Riggs), Danny Glover (Murtaugh), Joe Pesci (Leo). 114 min.

Lethal Weapon III (Warner Bros., 1992). Dir: Richard Donner. Scr: Jeffrey Boam, story Boam and Robert Mark Kamen. DP: Jan De Bont. Mu: Michael Kamen, Eric Clapton, and David Sanborn. Cast: Mel Gibson (Riggs), Danny Glover (Murtaugh), Renne Russo (Lane), Joe Pesci (Leo Getz). 115 min.

Liebestraum (Pathe/MGM/Initial, 1991). Dir/Scr: Mike Figgis. DP: Juan Ruiz Anchía. Mu: Mike Figgis. Cast: Kevin Anderson (Nick Kaminsky), Pamela Gidley (Jane Kessler), Bill Pullman (Paul Kessler), Kim Novak (Lillian). 102 min.

The Limey (Artisan, 1999). Dir: Steven Soderbergh. Scr: Lem Dobbs. DP: Edward Lachman. Mu: Cliff Martinez. Cast: Terence Stamp (Wilson), Lesley Ann Warren (Elaine), Luis Guzman (Eduardo Roel). 89 min.

Little Odessa (Fine Line, 1994). Dir: James Gray. Scr: James Gray. DP: Tom Richmond. Mu: Dana Sano. Cast: Tim Roth (Joshua), Edward Furlong (Reuben), Moira Kelly (Alla). 98 min.

Lonely Hearts (Millennium, 2006). Dir: Todd Robinson. Scr: Todd Robinson. DP: Peter Levy. Mu: Mychael Danna. Cast: Salma Hayek (Martha), Jared Leto (Ray), John Travolta (Detective Robinson). 108 min.

The Long Goodbye (UA, 1973). Dir: Robert Altman. Scr: Leigh Brackett from the novel by Raymond Chandler. DP: Vilmos Zsigmond. Mu: John Williams. Cast: Elliott Gould (Philip Marlowe), Nina van Pallandt (Eileen Wade), Sterling Hayden (Roger Wade), Mark Rydell (Marty Augustine). 113 min.

"Nothing says goodbye like a bullet"... —Philip Marlowe*

ELLIOTT KASTNER presents
A ROBERT ALTMAN Film
ELLIOTT GOULD
in
*PHILIP MARLOWE— THE GREATEST OF ALL 'PRIVATE EYE' CHARACTERS— CREATED BY RAYMOND CHANDLER

"**THE LONG GOODBYE**"

with NINA VAN PALLANDT
STERLING HAYDEN

Executive Producer ELLIOTT KASTNER · Produced by JERRY BICK
Directed by ROBERT ALTMAN · Screenplay by LEIGH BRACKETT
Based on the novel by RAYMOND CHANDLER
Music Composed and Conducted by JOHN T. WILLIAMS · COLOR
United Artists

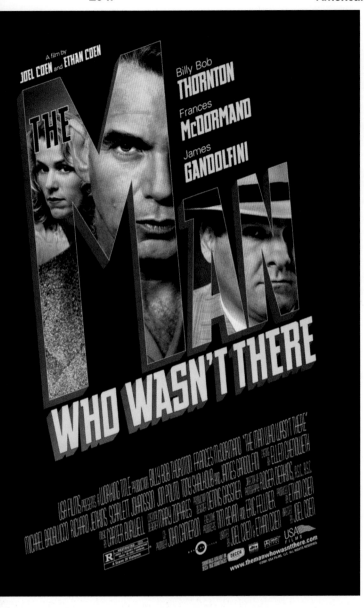

(Renee/Alice), Balthazar Getty (Peter Dayton), Robert Blake (Mystery Man). 135 min.

Love, Cheat & Steal (MPCA, 1993). Dir/Scr: William Curran. DP: Kent L. Wakeford. Mu: Dan Wool. Cast: John Lithgow (Paul Harrington), Eric Roberts (Reno Adams), Mädchen Amick.(Lauren Harrington. 96 min.

Love Crimes (Millimeter/Sovereign, 1992). Dir: Lizzie Borden. Scr: Allan Moyle and Laurie Frank, based on a story by Moyle. DP: Jack N. Green. Mu: Graeme Revell. Cast: Sean Young (Dana Greenway), Patrick Bergin ("David Hanover"). 85 min.

Mad Love (Touchstone, 1995). Dir: Antonia Bird. Scr: Paula Milne. DP: Fred Tammes. Mu: Andy Roberts. Cast: Chris O'Donnell (Matt), Drew Barrymore (Casey), Matthew Lillard (Eric). 93 min.

Madigan (Universal, 1968). Dir: Don Siegel. Scr: Henri Simoun and Abraham Polonsky from the novel *The Commissioner* by Richard Dougherty. DP: Russell Metty. Mu: Don Costa. Cast: Richard Widmark (Daniel Madigan), Henry Fonda (Commissioner Russell), Inger Stevens (Julia Madigan). 101 min.

Malice (Castle Rock, 1993). Dir: Harold Becker. Scr: Aaron Sorkin and Scott Frank. DP: Gordon Willis. Mu: Jerry Goldsmith. Cast: Alec Baldwin (Jack), Nicole Kidman (Tracy), Bill Pullman (Andy). 107 min.

Malone (Orion, 1987). Dir: Harley Cokliss. Scr: Christopher Frank. DP: Gerald Hirschfeld. Mu: David Newman. Cast: Burt Reynolds (Malone), Cliff Robertson (Delaney), Kenneth McMillan (Hawkins). 92 min.

The Man Who Wasn't There (Gramercy, 2001). Dir/Scr: Joel Coen/Ethan Coen. DP: Roger Deakins. Mu: Carter Burwell. Cast: Billy Bob Thornton (Ed Crane), Frances McDormand (Doris Crane), Scarlett Johansson (Birdy Abundas). 116 min.

Long Kiss Goodnight (New Line, 1996). Dir: Renny Harlin. Scr: Shane Black. DP: Guillermo Navarro. Mu: Alan Silvestri. Cast: Geena Davis (Samantha/Charly), Samuel L. Jackson (Mitch), Yvonne Zima (Caitlin). 121 min.

Lost Highway (October, 1997). Dir: David Lynch. Scr: David Lynch, Barry Gifford. DP: Peter Deming. Mu: Angelo Badalamenti. Cast: Bill Pullman (Fred Madison), Patricia Arquette

Manhunter (De Laurentiis, 1986). Dir/Scr: Michael Mann, based on the novel, *Red Dragon*, by Thomas Harris. DP: Dante Spinotti. Mu: The Reds and Michel Rubini. Cast: William L. Petersen (Will Graham), Kim Griest (Molly), Joan Allen (Reba). 118 min.

Marlowe (Cherokee, 1969). Dir: Paul Bogart. Scr: Stirling Silliphant based on the novel by Raymond Chandler. DP: William Daniels. Mu: Peter Matz. Cast: James Garner (Marlowe), Gayle Hunnicutt (Mayvis), Carroll O'Connor (Lt. French). Rita Moreno (Dolores). 96 min.

Masquerade (MGM/UA, 1988). Dir: Bob Swaim. Scr: Dick Wolf. DP: David Watkin. Mu: John Barry. Cast: Rob Lowe (Tim Whelan), Meg Tilly (Olivia Lawrence), Doug Savant (Mike McGill). 91 min.

Max Payne (Abandon/Collision, 2008). Dir: John Moore. Scr: Beau Thorne based on a video game. DP: Jonathan Sela. Mu: Marco Beltrami, Buck Sanders. Cast: Mark Wahlberg (Max), Mila Kunis (Mona), Beau Bridges (BB), Olga Kurylenko (Natasha). 100 min.

Memento (Newmarket, 2000). Dir: Christopher Nolan. Scr: Christopher Nolan based on the story "Memento Mori" by Jonathan Nolan. DP: Wally Pfister. Mu: David Julyan. Cast: Guy Pearce (Leonard), Carrie-Anne Moss (Natalie), Joe Pantoliano (Teddy Gammell), Mark Boone Junior (Burt). 113 min.

Mercury Rising (Universal, 1998). Dir: Harold Becker. Scr: Lawrence Konner, Mark Rosenthal based on the novel by Ryne Douglas Pearson. DP: Michael Seresin. Mu: John Barry. Cast: Bruce Willis (Art Jeffries), Alec Baldwin (Nick), Miko Hughes (Simon). 111 min.

Miami Blues (Orion/Tristes Tropiques, 1990). Dir/Scr: George Armitage, based on the novel by Charles Willeford. DP: Tak Fujimoto. Mu: Gary Chang. Cast:

Alec Baldwin (Frederick J. Frenger), Fred Ward (Sgt. Hoke Moseley), Jennifer Jason Leigh (Susie Waggoner). 97 min.

Miami Vice (Universal, 2006). Dir: Michael Mann. Scr: Michael Mann based on the television series *Miami Vice* by Anthony Yerkovich. DP: Dion Beebe. Mu: John Murphy. Cast: Colin Farrell (Det. J"Sonny" Crockett), Jamie Foxx (Det. Ricardo Tubbs), Gong Li (Isabella), Naomie Harris (Trudy Joplin). 139 min.

It will never happen again!

Ms.45

ROCHELLE FILMS, INC. PRESENTS **Ms.45** A NAVARON FILM PRODUCTION
STARRING ZOË TAMERLIS WITH STEVE SINGER · JACK THIBEAU · PETER YELLEN MUSIC BY JOE DELIA DIRECTOR OF PHOTOGRAPHY JAMES MOMEL
EDITED BY CHRISTOPHER ANDREWS, DA PRODUCTIONS WRITTEN BY NICHOLAS ST. JOHN PRODUCED BY ROCHELLE WEISBERG
PRODUCED BY NAVARON FILMS · DIRECTED BY ABEL FERRARA · RELEASED THRU ROCHELLE FILMS, INC. **R** RESTRICTED

Midnight Heat (New Line, 1992). Dir: John Nicolella. Scr: Max Strom and John Allen Nelson. DP: Charles Rosher Jr. Cast: Michael Pare (Eric), Adam Ant (Danny).Dennis Hopper (Carl), Daphne Ashbrook (Julie). 100 min.

Mike's Murder (Ladd Co./Warner Bros., 1984). Dir/Scr: James Bridges. DP: Rey Villalobos. Mu: John Barry. Cast: Debra Winger (Betty), Mark Keyloun (Mike), Paul Winfield (Phillip), Darrell Larson (Pete). 109 min.

Miller's Crossing (20th Century Fox, 1990). Dir: Joel Coen. Scr: Joel and Ethan Coen. DP: Barry Sonnenfeld. Mu: Carter Burwell. Cast: Gabriel Byrne (Tom Reagan), Marcia Gay Harden (Verna), John Turturro (Birnbaum). 114 min.

Minority Report (20th Century Fox, 2002). Dir: Steven Spielberg. Scr: Scott Frank, Jon Cohen based on a story by Philip K. Dick. DP: Janusz Kaminski. Mu: John Williams. Cast: Tom Cruise (Chief Anderton), Max Von Sydow (Dir: Burgess), Steve Harris (Jad). 145 min.

The Missing Person (Strand, 2008). Dir/Scr: Noah Buschei. DP: Ryan Samul. Michael Shannon (John Rosow), Frank Wood (Harold Fullmer), Amy Ryan (Miss Charley). 95 min.

The Morning After (20th Century Fox/Lorimar, 1986). Dir: Sidney Lumet. Scr: James Hicks and Jay Presson Allen. DP: Andrzej Bartkowiak. Mu: Paul Chihara. Cast: Jane Fonda (Alex Sternbergen), Jeff Bridges (Turner Kendall), Raul Julia (Joaquin Manero). 103 min.

Mortal Passions (Gibraltar Releasing, 1990). Dir: Andrew Lane. Scr: Alan Moskowitz. DP: Christian Sebaldt. Mu: Parmer Fuller. Cast: Zach Galligan (Todd), Michael Bowen (Burke), Krista Errickson (Emily), Sheila Kelley (Adele). 98 min.

Mortal Thoughts (Columbia/New Visions/Polar, 1991). Dir: Alan Rudolph. Scr: William Reilly and Claude Kerven. DP: Elliot Davis. Mu: Mark Isham. Cast: Demi Moore (Cynthia Kellogg), Glenne Headly (Joyce Urbanski), Bruce Willis (James Urbanski). 104 min.

Ms. 45 (Navaron/Rochelle, 1981). Scr: Nicholas St. John. DP: James Momel. Mu: Joe Delia. Cast: Zoe Tamerlis (Thana), Steve Singer (Photographer), Jack Thibeau (Man in Bar), Peter Yellen (Second Rapist), Darlene Stuto (Laurie), Editta Sherman (Landlady). 84 min.

My Kingdom for a Kiss (2008). Dir/Scr/DP: M. Claxton Crawford. Mu: Nicholas Pavkovic. Cast: Sam Brittan (Gordon Fincher), Julie Sufana (Bella Nolan), Michael Massei (Sloan), David Alan Graf (The Emperor), Tom Druilhet

(Malick). 64 min.

Mystic River (Warner Bros., 2003). Dir: Clint Eastwood. Scr: Brian Helgeland based on the novel by Dennis Lehane. DP: Tom Stern. Mu: Clint Eastwood. Cast: Sean Penn (Jimmy), Tim Robbins (Dave), Kevin Bacon (Sean). Laura Linney (Annabeth). 138 min.

Mulholland Drive (Asymmetrical/Canal+, 2001). Dir: David Lynch. Scr: David Lynch. DP: Peter Deming. Mu: Angelo Badalamenti. Cast: Naomi Watts (Diane Selwyn/Betty Elms), Laura Harring (Camilla/Rita), Ann Miller (Coco), Dan Hedaya (Vincenzo Castigliane). 145 min.

Mulholland Falls (MGM, 1996). Dir: Lee Tamahori. Scr: Peter Dexter based on a story by Peter Dexter, Floyd Mutrux. DP: Haskell Wexler. Mu: Dave Grusin. Cast: Nick Nolte (Max Hoover), Melanie Griffith (Katherine Hoover), Chazz Palminteri (Elleroy Coolidge), Michael Madsen (Eddie Hall). 107 min.

Murder in the First (Warner Bros., 1995). Dir: Marc Rocco. Scr: Dan Gordon. DP: Fred Murphy. Mu: Christopher Young. Cast: Christian Slater (James Stamphill), Kevin Bacon (Henri Young), Gary Oldman (Associate Warden Milton Glenn), Embeth Davidtz (Mary McCasslin). 122 min.

Murphy's Law (Cannon, 1986). Dir: J. Lee Thompson. Scr: Gail Morgan Hickman. DP: Alex Phillips. Mu: Marc Donahue, Valentine McCallum. Cast: Charles Bronson (Jack Murphy), Kathleen Wilhoite (Arabella McGee), Carrie Snodgress (Joan Freeman). 100 min.

Nails (Viacom, 1992). Dir: John Flynn. Scr: Larry Ferguson and Roderick Taylor, from a story by Ferguson and Marvin Schwartz. DP: Mac Ahlberg. Mu: Bill Conti. Cast: Dennis Hopper (Harry), Anne Archer (Mary), Tomas Milian (Herrera). 97 min.

The Naked Eye (Bettencourt, 1995). Dir: James Dean Schulte. Scr: Christo Garcia, James Dean Schulte. DP: Michael D. Corbett. Cast: Hellena Taylor (Rachel Weldon), Christo Garcia (Michael Florence), Paul Massie (Davis Parks). 88 min.

Narc (Paramount, 2002). Dir: Joe Carnahan. Scr: Joe Carnahan. DP: Alex Nepomniaschy. Mu: Cliff Martinez. Cast: Ray Liotta (Henry Oak), Jason Patric (Nick), Lloyd Adams (Walter). 105 min.

Narrow Margin (Carolco/TriStar, 1990). Dir/Scr: Peter Hyams, based on the screenplay by Earl Felton. DP: Peter Hyams. Mu: Bruce Broughton. Cast: Gene Hackman (Caulfield), Anne Archer (Hunnicut), James B. Sikking (Nelson). 97 min.

Natural Born Killers (Warner Bros., 1994). Dir: Oliver Stone. Scr: David Veloz, Oliver Stone, Richard Rutowski based on a story by Quentin Tarantino. DP: Robert Richarson. Mu: Brent Lewis. Cast: Juliette Lewis (Mallory), Woody Harrelson (Mickey), Robert Downey Jr. (Wayne). 118 min.

The Negotiator (Regency, 1998). Dir: F. Gary Gray. Scr: James DeMonaco, Kevin Fox. Mu: Graeme Revell. DP: Russell Carpenter. Cast: Samuel L. Jackson (Danny Roman), Kevin Spacey (Chris Sabian), David Morse (Adam Beck), Ron Rifkin (Grant Frost), John Spencer (Chief Al Travis), J.T. Walsh (Terence Niebaum). 140 min.

The Net (Columbia, 1995). Dir: Irwin Winkler. Scr: John Brancato, Michael

Ferris. DP: Jack Green. Scr: Mark Isham. Cast: Sandra Bullock (Angela), Jeremy Northam (Jack), Dennis Miller (Dr. Champion). 114 min.

Nero Bloom (Coldwater, 2009). Dir: Jason Eberly. Scr: Nathan Hartman, Rich Douglas. DP: Jason Eberly. Cast: Philip David Black (Nero Bloom), Bethany Edlund (Veronica St. Claire). 60 min.

Never Talk to Strangers (TriStar, 1995). Dir: Peter Hall. Scr: Lewis Green, Jordan Rush. DP: Elemer Ragalyi. Mu: Pino Donaggio. Cast: Rebecca De Mornay (Dr. Sarah Taylor), Antonio Banderas (Tony), Dennis Miller (Cliff). 86 min.

New Jack City (Warner Bros., 1991). Dir: Mario Van Peebles. Scr: Thomas Lee Wright and Barry Michael Cooper. DP: Francis Kenny. Cast: Mario Van Peebles (Det. Stone), Judd Nelson (Det. Peretti), Ice-T (Scotty Appleton), Russell Wong (Det. Park), Wesley Snipes (Nino Brown). 97 min.

New Rose Hotel (Pressman Film, 1998). Dir: Abel Ferrara. Scr: Abel Ferrara, Christ Zois based on a story by William Gibson. DP: Ken Kelsch. Mu: Schooly-D. Cast: Christopher Walken (Fox), Willem Dafoe (X), Asia Argento (Sandii). 93 min.

Nick of Time (Paramount, 1995). Dir: John Badham. Scr: Patrick S. Duncan. DP: Roy H. Wagner. Mu: Arthur B. Rubinstein. Cast: Johnny Depp (Gene), Courtney Chase (Lynn), Christopher Walken (Mr. Smith). 90 min.

The Nickel Ride (20th Century Fox, 1975). Dir: Robert Mulligan. Scr: Eric Roth. DP: Jordan Cronenweth. Mu: Dave Grusin. Cast: Jason Miller (Cooper), Linda Haynes (Sarah), Victor French (Paddie), John Hillerman (Carl). 114 min.

Night and the City (20th Century Fox/Penta, 1992). Dir: Irwin Winkler.

Scr: Richard Price, based on the novel by Gerald Kersh. DP: Tak Fujimoto. Mu: James Newton Howard. Cast: Robert De Niro (Harry Fabian), Jessica Lange (Helen Nasseros), Cliff Gorman (Phil Nasseros). 105 min.

Night Falls on Manhattan (Paramount, 1996). Dir: Sidney Lumet. Scr: Lumet based on the novel by Robert Daley. DP: David Watkin. Mu: Mark Isham. Cast: Andy Garcia (Sean), Ian Holm (Liam), Lena Olin (Peggy). 113 min.

Night Moves (Warner Bros., 1975). Dir: Arthur Penn. Scr: Alan Sharp. DP: Bruce Surtees . Mu: Michael Small. Cast: Gene Hackman (Harry Moseby), Susan Clark (Ellen), Edward Binns (Ziegler). 99 min.

Night Train (A-Mark, 2009). Dir: Brian King. Scr: Brian King. DP: Christopher Popp. Mu: Henning Lohner. Cast: Danny Glover (Miles), Leelee Sobieski (Chloe), Steve Zahn (Pete). 83 min.

Night Visitor (MGM/UA, 1989). Dir: Rupert Hitzig. Scr: Randal Viscovich. DP: Peter Jensen. Mu: Parmer Fuller. Cast: Elliott Gould (Devereaux), Allen Garfield (Willard), Michael J. Pollard (Stanley), Shannon Tweed (Lisa Grace), Richard Roundtree (Cap. Apollo Crane). 93 min.

Nightbeats (2009). Dir/Scr/DP: Mike Carroll. Cast: Julianne Gabert (Ginger), Missy Bell (Girl), Bonnie Bennett (Edie), Antohny D'Juan (Dubois). 89 min.

Nightcomer (Pendragon, 2015). Dir/Scr: Alain Silver. DP: Danny Belinkie. Mu: Ernest Troost. Cast: Mackenzie Rosman (Rowena Hambleton), Eric Gorlow (Travis), Timothy Busfield (Marty). 91 min.

Nightstalker (Silver Nitrate, 2002). Dir: Chris Fisher. Scr: Chris Fisher. DP: Eliot Rockett. Mu: Ryan Beveridge. Cast: Bret Roberts (Nightstalker), Roselyn Sanchez (Gabriella), Danny Trejo (Frank). 95 min.

No Country for Old Men (Paramount/Vantage, 2007). Dir: Ethan and Joel Coen. Scr: Coens based on the novel by Cormac McCarthy. DP: Roger Deakins. Mu: Carter Burwell. Cast: Josh Brolin (Llewelyn Moss), Tommy Lee Jones (Ed Tom Bell), Javier Bardem (Anton Chigurh), Woody Harrelson (Carson Wells). 122 min.

No Good Deed (Apollo, 2002). Dir: Bob Rafelson. Scr: Steve Barancik, Chris Canaan based on a story by Dashiell Hammett. DP: Juan Ruiz Anchia. Mu: Jeff Beal. Cast: Samuel L. Jackson (Friar), Milla Jovovich (Erin), Stellan Skarsgard (Tyrone). 103 min.

No Good Deed (Screen Gems, 2014). Dir: Sam Miller. Scr: Aimee Lagos. DP: Michael Barrett. Mu: Paul Haslinger. Cast: Idris Elba (Colin), Taraji P. Henson (Terry), Leslie Bibb (Meg), Kate del Castillo (Alexis). 84 min.

No Mercy (TriStar, 1986). Dir: Richard Pearce. Scr: Jim Carabatsos. DP: Michel Brault. Mu: Alan Silvestri. Cast: Richard Gere (Eddie Jillete), Kim Basinger (Michel Duval), Jeroen Krabbe (Losado), George Dzundza (Stemkowski). 105 min.

No Way Out (Orion, 1987). Dir: Roger Donaldson. Scr: Robert Garland, based on the novel *The Big Clock* by Kenneth Fearing. DP: John Alcott. Mu: Maurice Jarre. Cast: Kevin Costner (Tom Farrell), Gene Hackman (David Brice), Sean Young (Susan), Will Patton (Scott). 116 min.

No Witness (Barnesology, 2004). Dir: Michael Valverde. Scr: Michael Valverde, Stephen Antczak. DP: Keith Holland. Mu: James Fairey. Cast: Steve Barnes (Paul), Jeff Fahey (Senator), Corey Feldman (Mark). 95 min.

Noirland (Bloodshot, 2015). Dir/Scr: Ramzi Abed. DP: Ramzi Abed, Jean Luc Meisel. Cast: James Duval (Tiberius Malloy), Wendy McColm (Victoria Finn), Lloyd Kaufman (The Doctor), Twink Caplan (Dr. Zelda). 88 min.

Obsession (Columbia, 1976). Dir: Brian De Palma. Scr: Paul Schrader. DP: Vilmos Zsigmond. Mu: Bernard Herrmann. Cast: Cliff Robertson (Courtland), Genevieve Bujold (Elizabeth/Sandra), John Lithgow (Lasalle). 98 min.

Ocean Park (Surf Digital, 2002). Dir: David W. Warfield. Scr: Warfield. DP: Reinhart Peschke. Mu: Bob Schneider. Cast: Kenneth Hughes (Wilson), James Haven (Youngblood), Julie Ariola (Darlene). 100 min.

Oldboy (Forty Acres and a Mule, 2013). Dir: Spike Lee. Scr: Mark Protosevich based on the manga by Tsuchiya and Minegishi. DP: Sean Bobbitt. Mu: Roque Banos. Cast: Josh Brolin (Joe), Elizabeth Olsen (Marie), Adrian (Sharlto Copley), Samuel L. Jackson (Chaney). 104 min.

One False Move (IRS, 1992). Dir: Carl Franklin. Scr: Billy Bob Thornton and Tom Epperson. DP: James L. Carter. Mu: Peter Haycock and Derek Holt. Cast: Bill Paxton (Dale "Hurricane" Carter), Cynda Williams (Fantasia/Lila Walker), Billy Bob Thornton (Ray Malcolm), Michael Beach (Pluto). 106 min.

One in the Gun (Manmade, 2010). Dir: Rolfe Kanefsky. Scr: Kanefsky.

GOLDEN GLOBE® AWARD WINNER
IDRIS ELBA

FIRST HE GETS INTO YOUR HOUSE.

THEN HE GETS INTO YOUR HEAD.

FROM THE PRODUCER OF **OBSESSED**

NO GOOD DEED

IN THEATERS **SEPTEMBER**

ACADEMY AWARD® NOMINEE
TARAJI P. HENSON

DP: Gigi Malavesi. Mu: Christopher Farrell. Cast: Steven Man (Mickey), Katherine Randolph (Katrina), Steven Bauer (Arthur), Robert Davi (Vincent). 90 min.

The Onion Field (Avco, 1979). Dir: Harold Becker. Scr: Joseph Wambaugh based on his novel. DP: Charles Rosher. Mu: Deodato. Cast: John Savage (Detective Hettinger), James Woods (Powell), Ted Danson (Detective Campbell). 122 min.

Original Sin (MGM, 2001). Dir: Michael Cristofer. Scr: Michael Cristofer based on *Waltz into Darkness* by Cornell Woolrich. DP: Rodrigo Prieto. Mu: Terence Blanchard. Cast: Angelina Jolie (Julia/Bonnie), Antonio Banderas (Luis Vargas), Thomas Jane (Walter/Billy). 118 min.

Out of Bounds (Columbia, 1986). Dir: Richard Tuggle. Scr: Tony Kayden. DP: Bruce Surtees. Mu: Stewart Copeland. Cast: Anthony Michael Hall (Daryl Cage), Jenny Wright (Dizz), Jeff Kober (Roy Gaddis), Glynn Turman (Lt. Delgado). 92 min.

Out of the Dark (New Line/Cinetel, 1989). Dir: Michael Schroeder. Scr: J. Greg DeFelice and Zane Levitt. DP: Julio Macat. Mu: Paul F. Antonelli. Cast: Tracey Walter (Detective), Cameron Dye (Kevin), Karen Black (Ruth), Bud Cort (Stringer). 90 min.

Out of the Rain (Acme Company/Live, 1990). Dir: Gary Winick. Scr: Shem Bitterman, based on his play. DP: Makoto Watanabe. Mu: Cengiz Yaltkaya. Cast: Bridget Fonda (Jolene), Michael O'Keefe (Frank), John E. O'Keefe (Neff), John Seitz (Nat Reade), Georgine Hall (Tilly). 88 min.

Out of Time (MGM, 2003). Dir: Carl Franklin. Scr: Dave Collard. DP: Theo Van De Sande. Mu: Graeme Revell. Cast: Denzel Washington (Matt Lee Whitlock), Eva Mendes (Alex Diaz

Whitlock), Sanaa Lathan (Ann Merai Harrison). 105 min.

The Outfit (MGM, 1973). Dir:/Scr: John Flynn from the novel by Richard Stark [Donald E. Westlake]. DP: Bruce Surtees. Mu: Jerry Fielding. Cast: Robert Duvall (Earl Macklin), Karen Black (Bett Jarrow), Joe Don Baker (Cody), Robert Ryan (Mailer), Timothy Carey (Jake Menner). 103 min.

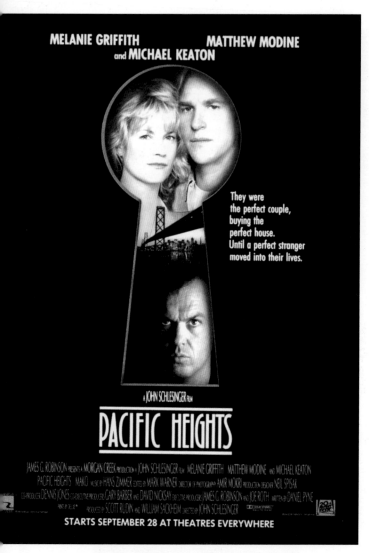

The Outsiders (Zoetrope, 1983). Dir: Francis Ford Coppola. Scr: Kathleen Rowell based on the novel by S. E. Hinton. DP: Stephen H. Burum. Mu: Carmine Coppola. Cast: C. Thomas Howell (Ponyboy Curtis), Ralph Macchio (Johnny Cade), Matt Dillon ("Dal" Winston), Rob Lowe as Sodapop "Soda" Curtis), Patrick Swayze ("Darry" Curtis), Emilio Estevez (Keith "Two-Bit" Matthews), Tom Cruise (Steve Randle). 115 min.

Overload (P-Squared, 2009). Dir/Scr: Robert Fritz. DP: Robert Jordan. Mu: Fritz. Cast: F. Reed Brown (Detective), Verna Brunelle (Granny), Eve Fritz (Brenda). 107 min.

P2 (Summit, 2007). Dir: Franck Kahlfoun. Scr: Khalfoun, Alexandre Aja, Gregory Levasseur. DP: Maxime Alexandre. Mu: tomandandy. Cast: West Bentley (Thomas), Rachel Nichols (Angela). 98 min.

Pacific Heights (Morgan Creek/20th Century Fox, 1990). Dir: John Schlesinger. Scr: Daniel Pyne. DP: Amir Mokri. Mu: Hans Zimmer. Cast: Melanie Griffith (Patty Palmer), Matthew Modine (Drake Goodman), Michael Keaton (Carter Hayes). 103 min.

The Package (Orion, 1989). Dir: Andrew Davis. Scr: John Bishop. DP: Frank Tidy. Mu: James Newton Howard. Cast: Gene Hackman (Sgt. Johnny Gallagher), Joanna Cassidy (Eileen Gallagher), Tommy Lee Jones (Thomas Boyette), John Heard (Col. Glen). 108 min.

Paint It Black (Vestron, 1989). Dir: Tim Hunter. Scr: A.H. Zacharias, Tim Harris, Hershel Weingrod and Michael Drexler. DP: Mark Irwin. Mu: Jurgen Knieper. Cast: Rick Rossovich (Jonathan Dunbar), Sally Kirkland (Marion Easton), Julie Carmen (Gina). 101 min.

Palmetto (Castle Rock, 1998). Dir: Volker Schlondorff. Scr: E. Max Frye based on the novel by James Hadley Chase. DP: Thomas Kloss. Mu: Klaus Doldinger. Cast: Woody Harrelson (Harry), Elisabeth Shue (Mrs. Donnelly/Rhea), Gina Gershon (Nina). 114 min.

Panic Room (Columbia, 2002). Dir: David Fincher. Scr: David Koepp. DP: Conrad Hall. Mu: Howard Shore. Cast: Jodie Foster (Meg), Kristen Stewart (Sarah), Forest Whitaker (Burnham). 112 min.

The Parasomniac (Limitless, 2010).

Dir: George Lin. Scr: Lin. DP: Lin. Mu: Alexander Busi. Cast: Gregory Doyle (Murphy), Chris DeStefano (Hollander), Mariel Rosen (Kelsey). 78 min.

Past Midnight (New Line, 1992). Dir: Jan Eliasberg. Scr: Frank Norwood and Quentin Tarantino. DP: Robert Yoeman. Cast: Natasha Richardson (Laura Matthews), Rutger Hauer (Ben Jordan), Clancy Brown (Steve). 100 min.

Pathology (MGM, 2008). Dir: Marc Scholermann. Scr: Brian Taylor, Mark Neveldine. DP: Ekkehart Pollack. Mu: Robert Williamson. Cast: Alyssa Milano (Gwen), Milo Ventimiglia (Ted), Michael Weston (Jake). 95 min.

Payback (Paramount, 1999). Dir: Brian Helgeland. Scr: Helgeland, Terry Hayes, based on the novel *The Hunter* by Richard Stark [Donald E. Westlake]. DP: Ericson Core. Mu: Chris Boardman. Cast: Mel Gibson (Porter), Gregg Henry (Val Resnick), Maria Bello (Rosie), David Paymer (Arthur Stegman), Bill Duke (Det. Hicks). 100 min.

Pelican Brief (Warner Bros., 1993). Dir/Scr: Alan J. Pakula. DP: Stephen Goldblatt. Mu: James Horner. Cast: Julia Roberts (Darby Shaw), Denzel Washington (Gray Grantham), Sam Shepard (Thomas Callahan), John Heard (Gavin Vereek), Tony Goldwyn (Fletcher Coal). 141 min.

A Perfect Murder (Warner Bros., 1998). Dir: Andrew Davis. Scr: Patrick Smith Kelly based on the play by Frederick Knott. DP: Dariusz Wolski. Mu: James Newton Howard. Cast: Michael Douglas (Taylor), Gwyneth Paltrow (Emily), Viggo Mortensen (David). 107 min.

Perfect Stranger (Revolution, 2007). Dir: James Foley. Scr: Todd Kormarnicki based on the story by Jon Bokenkamp. DP: Anastas Michos. Mu: Antonio Pinto. Cast: Halle Berry (Rowena), Bruce Willis (Harrison), Giovanni Ribisi (Miles). 109 min.

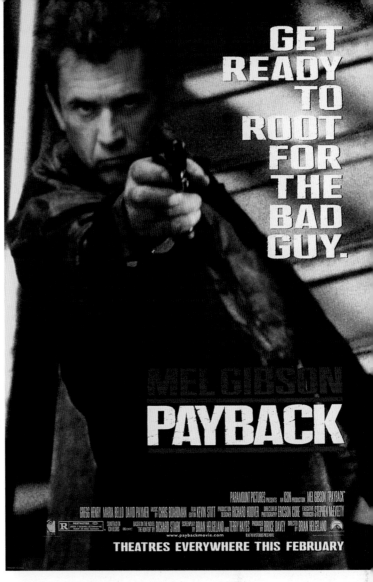

Person of Interest (Lovely Machine, 2010). Dir/DP: Gregory Bayne. Scr: J. Reuben Appelman. Mu: Chris Sorensen. Cast: J. Reuben Appelman (Dyer), Nova Tydings (Nola), Stitch Marker (Stuts). 90 min.

304.

Persons Unknown (Promark, 1996). Dir: George Hickenlooper. Scr: Craig Smith. DP: Richard Crudo. Mu: Ed Tomney. Cast: Joe Mantegna (Jim Holland), Kelly Lynch (Amanda), Naomi Watts (Molly). 99 min.

Phoenix (Trimark, 1998). Dir: Danny Cannon. Scr: Eddie Richey. DP: James Carter. Mu: Graeme Revell. Cast: Ray Liotta (Harry), Anthony LaPaglia (Henshaw), Daniel Baldwin (Nutter). 107 min.

P.I. Private Investigations (Polygram/MGM-UA, 1987). Dir: Nigel Dick. Scr: John Dahl and David Warfield. DP: David Bridges. Mu: Murray Munro. Cast: Clayton Rohner (Joey), Ray Sharkey (Ryan), Paul Le Mat (Lieutenant), Talia Balsam (Jenny). 91 min.

Pi (Harvest, 1998). Dir: Darren Aronofsky. Scr: Darren Aronofsky based on a story by Aronofsky, Sean Gullette, Eric Watson. DP: Matthew Libatique. Mu: Clint Mansell. Cast: Sean Gullette (Maximillian), Mark Margolis (Sol), Ben Shenkman (Lenny). 84 min.

Pilgrim (aka *Inferno*, Barzo, 2000). Dir: Harley Cokeliss. Scr: Peter Milligan, Cokeliss. DP: Stephen McNutt. Mu: Fred Mollin. Cast: Ray Liotta (Jack), Gloria Reuben (Vicky), Armin Mueller-Stahl (Mac). 94 min.

Play Misty for Me (Universal, 1971). Dir: Clint Eastwood. Scr: Jo Heims and Dean Riesner. DP: Bruce Surtees. Mu:

Dee Barton. Cast: Clint Eastwood (Dave Garland), Jessica Walter (Evelyn Draper), Donna Mills (Tobie Williams). 102 min.

Player (B&S, 2012). Dir: Alina Szpak. Scr: Robert Fleet. DP: David C. Smith. Mu: Chris Cano. Cast: Robert Fleet (Sam), Natalie Avital (Princess), Nick McCallum (Jack), Elizabeth Carlson (Marie), Enci (Insa). 100 min.

Playing God (Touchstone, 1997). Dir: Andy Wilson. Scr: Mark Haskell Smith. DP: Anthony B. Richmond. Mu: Richard Hartley. Cast: David Duchovny (Dr. Sands), Angelina Jolie (Claire), Timothy Hutton (Blossom). 94 min.

The Pledge (Franchise, 2001). Dir: Sean Penn. Scr: Jerzy Kromolowski, Mary Olson-Kromolowski based on the novel by Friedrich Dürrenmatt. DP: Chris Menges. Mu: Klaus Badelt, Hans Zimmer. Cast: Jack Nicholson (Jerry Black), Patricia Clarkson (Margaret Larsen), Benicio del Toro (Toby Jay Wadenah), Aaron Eckhart (Stan Krolak). 123 min.

Point Blank (MGM, 1967). Dir: John Boorman. Scr: Alexander Jacobs, David Newhouse, and Rafe Newhouse from the novel *The Hunter* by Richard Stark [Donald E. Westlake]. DP: Philip H. Lathrop. Mu: Johnny Mandel. Cast: Lee Marvin (Walker), Angie Dickinson (Chris), Keenan Wynn (Yost), Carroll O'Connor (Brewster). 92 min.

Point Break (20th Century Fox/Largo, 1991). Dir: Kathryn Bigelow. Scr: W. Peter Iliff, based on a story by King and Iliff. DP: Donald Peterman. Mu: Mark Isham. Cast: Patrick Swayze (Bodhi), Keanu Reeves (Johnny Utah), Gary

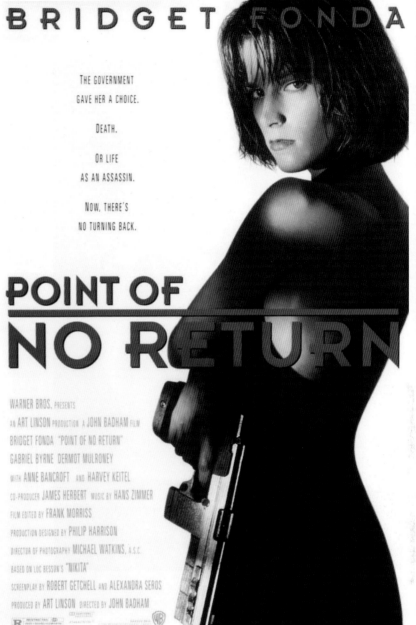

THE GOVERNMENT GAVE HER A CHOICE.

DEATH.

OR LIFE AS AN ASSASSIN.

NOW, THERE'S NO TURNING BACK.

POINT OF NO RETURN

WARNER BROS. PRESENTS AN ART LINSON PRODUCTION A JOHN BADHAM FILM BRIDGET FONDA "POINT OF NO RETURN" GABRIEL BYRNE DERMOT MULRONEY WITH ANNE BANCROFT AND HARVEY KEITEL CO-PRODUCER JAMES HERBERT MUSIC BY HANS ZIMMER FILM EDITED BY FRANK MORRISS PRODUCTION DESIGNED BY PHILIP HARRISON DIRECTOR OF PHOTOGRAPHY MICHAEL WATKINS, A.S.C. BASED ON LUC BESSON'S "NIKITA" SCREENPLAY BY ROBERT GETCHELL AND ALEXANDRA SEROS PRODUCED BY ART LINSON DIRECTED BY JOHN BADHAM

Busey (Pappas), Lori Petty (Tyler). 122 min.

Point of No Return (Warner Bros., 1993). Dir: John Badham. Scr: Robert Getchell, Alexandra Seros based on the film *Nikita* by Luc Besson. DP: Michael Watkins. Mu: Hans Zimmer. Cast: Bridget Fonda (Maggie Hayward), Gabriel Byrne (Bob), Dermot Mulroney (J.P.), Miguel Ferrer (Kaufman). 108 min.

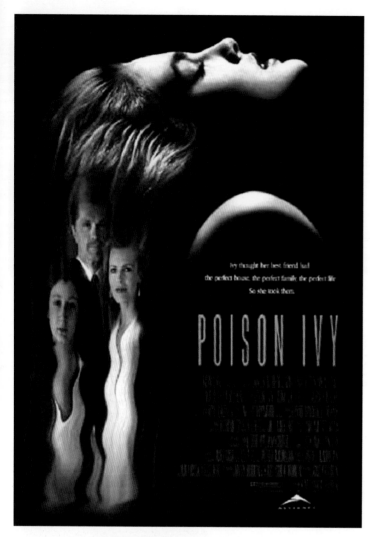

Ivy thought her best friend had
the perfect house, the perfect family, the perfect life.
So she took them.

POISON IVY

Poison Ivy (New Line Cinema, 1992).
Dir: Katt Shea. Scr: Katt Shea, Andy
Rubin. DP: Phedon Papamichael. Mu:
David Michael Frank. Cast: Sara Gilbert
(Sylvie), Drew Barrymore (Ivy), Tom
Skerritt (Darryl), Cheryl Ladd (Georgie).
90 min.

Poison Ivy II (New Line, 1996). Dir:
Anne Goursaud. Scr: Chloe King. DP:
Suki Medencevic. Mu: Joseph Williams.
Cast: Alyssa Milano (Lily Leonetti),
Johnathon Schaech (Gredin), Xander
Berkeley (Donald Falk), Belinda Bauer
(Angela Falk). 108 min.

Poison Ivy: The New Seduction (New
Line, 1997). Dir: Kurt Voss. Scr: Karen
Kelly. DP: Feliks Parnell. Mu: Reg Powell.
Cast: Jaime Pressly (Violet), Megan
Edwards (Joy Greer), Michael Des Barres
(Ivan Greer), Greg Vaughan (Michael).
95 min.

The Poor and the Hungry (BR2,
2000). Dir/Scr/DP: Craig Brewer. Cast:
Eric Tate (Eli Foote), Lindsey Roberts
(Harper), Lake Latimer (Amanda), John
Still (Mr. Coles), Keenon Nikita (Archie).
118 min.

Positive I.D. (Universal, 1987).
Dir/Scr: Andy Anderson. DP: Paul
Barton. Mu: Steven Jay Hoey. Cast:
Stephanie Rascoe (Julie Kenner), John
Davies (Don Kenner), Steve Fromholz
(Lt. Roy Mercer), Laura Lane (Dana). 96
min.

The Postman Always Rings Twice
(Paramount/Lorimar, 1981). Dir: Bob
Rafelson. Scr: David Mamet, based on
the novel by James M. Cain. DP: Sven
Nykvist. Mu: Michael Small. Cast: Jack
Nicholson (Frank Chambers), Jessica
Lang (Cora Papadakis), John Colicos
(Nick Papadakis), Michael Lerner
(Katz).125 min.

Presumed Innocent (Warner Bros.,
1990). Dir: Alan J. Pakula. Scr: Frank
Pierson and Alan J. Pakula. DP: Gordon
Willis. Mu: John Williams. Cast: Harrison
Ford (Rusty Saboch), Brian Dennehy
(Raymond Horgan), Raul Julia (Sandy
Stern), Bonnie Bedelia (Barbara Sabich).
126 min.

Pretty Poison (20th Century Fox,
1968). Dir: Noel Black. Scr: Lorenzo
Semple Jr. based on the novel *She Let
Him Continue* by Stephen Geller. DP:
David Quaid. Mu: Johnny Mandel. Cast:
Anthony Perkins (Dennis Pitt), Tuesday
Weld (Sue Ann Stepanek), Beverly
Garland (Mrs. Stepanek). 89 min.

Primal Fear (Paramount, 1996). Dir:
Gregory Hoblit. Scr: Steve Shagan, Ann
Biderman based on a novel by William
Diehl. DP: Michael Chapman. Mu: James

Newton Howard. Cast: Richard Gere (Vail), Laura Linney (Gail), John Mahoney (Shaugnessy). 129 min.

Prime Suspect (SVS/Sony, 1989). Dir: Mark Rutland. Scr: Alex Josephs. DP: Fernando Arguelles. Mu: Bruce Kimmel. Cast: Susan Strasberg (Dr. Warren), Robert F. Lyons (Hank Fallon), Tom Breznahan (Tod Jennings), Michael Parks (Nevins). 91 min.

Prince of the City (Orion/Warner Bros., 1981). Dir: Sidney Lumet. Scr: Jay Presson Allen and Sidney Lumet. DP: Andrez Bartkowiak. Mu: Michael Chihara. Cast: Treat Williams (Danny Ciello), Jerry Orbach (Gus Levy), Richard Foronjy (Joe Marinaro). 167 min.

Prisoners (Alcon, 2013). Dir: Denis Villeneuve. Scr: Aaron Guzikoski. DP: Roger Deakins. Mu: Jóhann Jóhannsson. Cast: Hugh Jackman (Keller Dover), Jake Gyllenhal (Detective Loki), Viola Davis (Nancy Birch), Maria Bello (Grace Dover), Terrence Howard (Franklin Birch). 153 min.

The Public Eye (Universal, 1992). Dir/Scr: Howard Franklin. DP: Peter Suschitzky. Mu: Mark Isham. Cast: Joe Pesci (Leon Bernstein), Barbara Hershey (Kay), Stanley Tucci (Sal). 99 min.

Pulp Fiction (Miramax, 1995). Dir/Scr: Quentin Tarantino. DP: Andzei Sekula. Cast: John Travolta (Vincent Vega), Samuel L. Jackson (Jules Winnfield), Bruce Willis (Butch), Ving Rhames (Marsellus). Uma Thurman (Mia), Tim Roth (Pumpkin/Ringo), Amanda Plummer (Honey Bunny/Yolanda), Harvey Keitel (the Wolf). 154 min.

The Punisher (New World, 1989). Dir: Mark Goldblatt. Scr: Boaz Yakin. DP: Ian Baker. Mu: Dennis Dreith. Cast: Dolph Lundgren (Castle), Louis Gossett (Jake), Jeroen Krabbe (Franco). 89 min.

The Punisher (Lions Gate, 2004). Dir: Jonathan Hensleigh. Scr: Hensleigh, Michael France. DP: Conrad Hall. Mu: Carlo Siliotto. Cast: Thomas Jane (Castle), Laura Harring (Livia), John Travolta (Saint). 124 min.

The Purge (Universal, 2013). Dir/Scr: James DeMonaco. DP: Jacques Jouffret. Mu: Nathan Whitehead. Cast: Ethan Hawke (James Sandin), Lean Headey (Mary Sandin), Max Burkholder (Charlie Sandin), Adelaide Kane (Zoey Sandin). 85 min.

Q and A (TriStar/Regency/Odyssey, 1990). Dir: Sidney Lumet. Scr: Sidney Lumet, based on the novel by Edwin Torres. DP: Andrzej Bartkowiak. Mu: Ruben Blades. Cast: Nick Nolte (Mike Brennan), Timothy Hutton (Al Reilly), Armand Assante (Texador). 134 min.

Random Acts of Violence (Gutter Bros., 1999). Dir: Drew Bell, Jefferson Langley. Scr: Bell, Langley. DP: Warren Yeagar. Mu: Chergui. Cast: Esteban Powell (Chris), Alex Solowitz (Bryce), Brian Klugman (Johnathan). 77 min.

Ransom (Touchstone, 1996). Dir: Ron Howard. Scr: Richard Price, Alexander Ignon based on a story by Cyril Hume and Richard Maibaum. DP: Piotr Sobocinski. Mu: James Horner. Cast: Mel Gibson (Mullen), Rene Russo (Kate), Brawley Nolte (Sean), Gary Sinise (Detective Shaker). 121 min.

A Rage in Harlem (Miramax, 1991). Dir: Bill Duke. Scr: Bobby Crawford, John Toles-Bey based on the novel by Chester Himes. DP: Toyomichi Kurita.

Mu: Elmer Bernstein, Jeff Vincent. Cast: Forest Whitaker (Jackson), Gregory Hines (Goldy), Robin Givens (Imabelle), Zakes Mokae (Big Kathy). 115 min.

The Rain Killer (Concorde/New Horizons, 1990).Dir: Ken Stein. Scr: Ray Conneff. DP: Janusz Kaminsky. Mu: Terry Plumeri. Cast: Ray Sharkey (Capra), David Beecroft (Dalton), Tania Coleridege (Adele), Michael Chiklis (Reese). 87 min.

Red Dragon (MGM, 2002). Dir: Brett Ratner. Scr: Ted Tally based on the novel by Thomas Harris. DP: Dante Spinotti. Cast: Anthony Hopkins (Lecter), Edward Norton (Graham), Ralph Fiennes (Francis Dolarhyde), Harvey Keitel (Crawford). 124 min.

Red Rock West (Polygram/Propaganda, 1992). Dir: John Dahl. Scr: John and Rick Dahl. DP: Marc Reshovsky. Cast: Nicolas Cage (Michael), Lara Flynn Boyle (Suzanne), Dennis Hopper (Lyle), J.T. Walsh (Wayne). 90 min.

Reindeer Games (Dimension, 2000). Dir: John Frankenheimer. Scr: Ehren Kruger. DP: Alan Caso. Mu: Alan Silvestri. Cast: Ben Affleck (Rudy), James Frain (Nick), Isaac Hayes (Hook). 104 min.

Relentless (New Line, 1989). Dir: William Lustig. Scr: Jack T. Robinson. DP: James Lemmo. Mu: Jack Chattawan. Cast: Judd Nelson (Buck), Robert Loggia (Bill Malloy), Leo Rossi (Sam Dietz). 93 min.

Rent-a-Cop (Kings Road, 1988). Dir: Jerry London. Scr: Dennis Shryack and Michael Blodgett. DP: Giuseppe Rotunno. Mu: Jerry Goldsmith. Cast: Burt Reynolds (Church), Liza Minnelli (Della), James Remar (Dancer), Richard Masur (Roger). 95 min.

Reservoir Dogs (Miramax, 1992). Dir/Scr: by Quentin Tarantino. DP: Andrzej Sekula. Cast: Harvey Keitel (Mr. White), Tim Roth (Mr. Orange/Freddy),

Michael Madsen (Mr. Blonde), Chris Penn (Nice Guy Eddie), Steve Buscemi (Mr. Pink), Lawrence Tierney (Joe Cabot). 99 min.

Resurrection of Serious Rogers (Kiss Hug Five, 2010). Dir/Scr: Angelo Bell. DP: James Rhodimer. Mu: Jon Pierre. Cast: Cooper Harris (Serious), Chip Joslin (Wally), Kasan Butcher (Erby). 80 min.

Revenge (Columbia/Rastar/New World, 1990). Dir: Tony Scott. Scr: Jim Harrison and Jeffrey Fiskin, based on the novella by Harrison. DP: Jeffrey Kimball. Mu: Jack Nitzsche. Cast: Kevin Costner (Cochran), Anthony Quinn (Tibey), Madeleine Stowe (Miryea), Tomas Milan (Cesar). 124 min.

Ricochet (Cinema Plus, 1991). Dir: Russell Mulcahy. Scr: Steven de Souza based on a story by Fred Dekker and Menno Meyjes. DP: Peter Levy. Mu: Alan Silvestri. Cast: Denzel Washington (Styles), John Lithgow (Blake), Ice-T (Odessa). 102 min.

Robocop (Orion, 1987). Dir: Paul Verhoeven. Scr: Michael Miner, Edward Neumeier. DP: Jost Vacano. Mu: Basil Poledouris. Cast: Peter Weller (Robocop), Nancy Allen (Officer Lewis), Dan O'Herlihy (The Old Man), Miguel Ferrer (Morton). 102 min.

Rolling Thunder (AIP, 1977). Dir: John Flynn. Scr: Paul Schrader and Heywood Gould. DP: Jordan Croneweth. Mu: Barry De Vorzon. Cast: William Devane (Major Charles Rane), Tommy Lee Jones (Johnny Voliden), Linda Haynes (Linda Forchet). 99 min.

Romeo Is Bleeding (Polygram, 1994). Dir: Peter Medak. Scr: Hilary Henkin. DP: Dariusz Wolski. Mu: Mark Isham. Cast: Gary Oldman (Jack Grimaldi), Lena Olin (Mona Demarkov), Annabella Sciorra (Natalie Grimaldi). 100 min.

The Rookie (Warner Bros., 1990). Dir: Clint Eastwood. Scr: Boaz Yakin, Scott

Spiegel. DP: Jack Green. Mu: Lennie Niehaus. Cast: Clint Eastwood (Nick), Charlie Sheen (David), Raul Julia (Strom), Sonia Braga (Liesl). 120 min.

The Rosary Murders (New Line, 1987). Dir: Fred Walton. Scr: Elmore Leonard and Fred Walton, based on the novel by William X. Kienzle. DP: David Golia. Mu: Bobby Laurel and Don Sebesky. Cast: Donald Sutherland (Father Koesler), Charles Durning (Father Nabors), Belinda Bauer (Pat Lennon). 105 min.

Rule of Three (Wildlight, 2008). Dir: Eric Shapiro. Scr: Rhoda Jordan based on the story by Shapiro. DP: Eun-ah Lee. Mu: Bilvox. Cast: Rodney Eastman (Russ), Ben Siegler (Jon), Rhoda Jordan (Lo). 85 min.

Rumble Fish (e, 1983). Dir: Francis Ford Coppola. Scr: S. E. Hinton, Francis Coppola based on the novel by Hinton. DP: Stephen Burum. Mu: Stewart

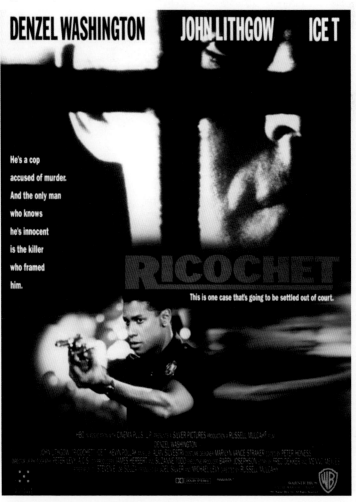

Copeland. Cast: Matt Dillon (Rusty), Mickey Rourke (Motorcycle Boy), Diane Lane (Patty), Dennis Hopper (Father). 94 min.

Run (Buena Vista, 1991). Dir: Geoff Burrowes. Scr: Dennis Shryack and Michael Blodgett. DP: Bruce Surtees. Mu: Phil Marshall. Cast: Patrick Dempsey (Charlie Farrow), Kelly Preston (Karen Landers), Ken Pogue (Halloran). 91 min.

Rush (Zanuck/MGM, 1991). Dir: Lili Fini Zanuck. Scr: Pete Dexter, based on the novel by Kim Wozencraft. DP: Kenneth MacMillan. Mu: Eric Clapton. Cast: Jason Patric (Raynor), Jennifer Jason Leigh (Kristen), Sam Elliott (Dodd). 145 min.

The Salton Sea (Warner Bros., 2002). Dir: D.J. Caruso. Scr: Tony Gayton. DP: Amir M. Mokri. Mu: Thomas Newman. Cast: Val Kilmer (Danny Parker/Tom Van Allen), Vincent D'Onofrio (Pooh-Bear), Adam Goldberg (Kujo). 103 min.

Scissors (DDM, 1991). Dir: Frank De Felitta. Scr: De Felitta, based on a story by Joyce Selznick. DP: Anthony Richmond. Cast: Sharon Stone (Angie), Steve Railsback (Alex/Cole), Ronny Cox (Dr. Carter), Michelle Phillips (Ann). 105 min.

The Score (Paramount, 2001). Dir: Frank Oz. Scr: Kario Salem, Lem Dobbs, Scott Marshall Smith based on a story by Salem and Daniel Taylor. DP: Rob Hahn. Mu: Howard Shore. Cast: Robert De Niro (Nick), Edward Norton (Jack), Marlon Brando (Max), Angela Bassett (Diane). 124 min.

Sea of Love (Universal, 1989). Dir: Harold Becker. Scr: Richard Price. DP: Ronnie Taylor. Mu: Trevor Jones. Cast: Al Pacino (Frank Keller), Ellen Barkin (Helen), John Goodman (Sherman), Michael Rooker (Terry). 113 min.

Serpico (Paramount, 1973). Dir: Sidney Lumet. Scr: Waldo Salt and Norman Wexler, based on the book by Peter Maas. DP: Arthur J. Ornitz. Mu: Mikis Theodorakis. Cast: Al Pacino (Frank Serpico), John Randolph (Chief Green), Jack Kehoe (Tom Keough). 129 min.

Seven (New Line, 1995). Dir: David Fincher. Scr: Andrew Kevin Walker. DP: Darius Khondji. Mu: Howard Shore. Cast: Brad Pitt (Detective David Mills), Morgan Freeman (Detective Lt. William Somerset). 127 min.

Shaft (MGM, 1971). Dir: Gordon Parks. Scr: Ernest Tidyman and John D. F. Black, based on Tidyman's novel. DP: Urs Furrer. Mu: Isaac Hayes. Cast: Richard Roundtree (John Shaft), Moses Gunn (Bumpy Jonas), Victor Arnold (Charlie). 98 min.

Sharky's Machine (Orion/Warner Bros., 1981). Dir: Burt Reynolds. Scr: Gerald Di Pego, based on the novel by William Diehl. DP: William Fraker. Cast: Burt Reynolds (Sharky), Rachel Ward (Dominoe), Vittorio Gassman (Victor), Brian Keith (Papa), Charles Durning (Friscoe). 119 min.

Shattered (MGM, 1991). Dir: Wolfgang Petersen. Scr: Petersen, based on the novel by Richard Neely. DP: Laszlo Kovacs. Mu: Alan Silvestri. Cast: Tom Berenger (Don Merrick), Bob Hoskins (Gus Klein), Greta Scacchi (Judith Merrick), Joanne Whalley-Kilmer (Jenny Scott). 97 min.

Shoot to Kill (Touchstone, 1988). Dir: Roger Spottiswoode. Scr: Harv Zimmel, Michael Burton, and Daniel Petrie Jr. DP: Michael Chapman. Mu: John Scott. Cast: Sidney Poitier (Warren Stanton), Tom Berenger (Jonathan Knox), Kirstie Alley (Sarah). 110 min.

Shutter Island (Paramount, 2010). Dir: Martin Scorsese. Scr: Laeta Kalogridis based on the novel by Dennis Lehane. DP: Robert Richardson. Cast: Leonardo DiCaprio, Mark Ruffalo (Chuck), Ben Kinglsey (Dr. Cawley), Michelle Williams (Dolores).138 min.

The Silence of the Lambs (Orion/Strong Heart, 1991). Dir: Jonathan Demme. Scr: Ted Tally, based on the novel by Thomas Harris. DP: Tak Fujimoto. Mu: Howard Shore. Cast: Jodie Foster (Clarice Starling), Anthony Hopkins (Dr. Hannibal Lecter), Scott Glenn (Jack Crawford). 118 min.

Silent Dove (Dupree, 2007). Dir/Scr: Paul Dupree. DP: David Dupree. Mu: David Dupree. Cast: Chelsee Atkins (Dove), Robyn Berg (Helen), Gary Brumett (Peter). 103 min.

Silent Voyeur (Substream, 2004). Dir/Scr: Georg Koszulinski. DP: Adam Nikolaidis. Mu: Mike Maines. Cast: Eric Cheek (Randy), Jake Molzan (John Doe). 80 min.

A Simple Plan (Paramount, 1998). Dir: Sam Raimi. Scr: Scott B. Smith, based on his novel. DP: Alar Kivilo. Mu: Danny Elfman. Cast: Bill Paxton (Hank Mitchell), Bridget Fonda (Sarah Mitchell), Billy Bob Thornton (Jacob Mitchell).121 min.

Sin City (Miramax, 2005). Dir: Frank Miller, Robert Rodriguez, Quentin Tarantino. Scr: Frank Miller, based on his graphic novels *Sin City*. DP: Robert Rodriguez. Mu: John Debney, Graeme Revell, Robert Rodriguez. Cast: Jessica Alba (Nancy Callahan), Devon Aoki (Miho), Alexis Bledel (Becky), Powers Boothe (Senator Roark), Rosario Dawson (Gail). 147 min.

THERE IS NO JUSTICE WITHOUT SIN

FRANK MILLER'S SIN CITY
A DAME TO KILL FOR

DIRECTED BY ROBERT RODRIGUEZ AND FRANK MILLER
WRITTEN BY FRANK MILLER

IN DIGITAL 3D AND real D 3D

SinCity-2.com

AUGUST 22

Sin City: A Dame to Kill For (Miramax, 2014). Dirs: Frank Miller, Robert Rodriguez. Scr: Frank Miller. DP: Robert Rodriguez. Mu: Carl Thiel. Cast: Jessica Alba (Nancy), Mickey Rourke (Marv), Josh Brolin (Dwight). 102 min.

Slam Dance (Island, 1987). Dir: Wayne Wang. Scr: Don Opper. DP: Amir Mokri. Mu: Mitchell Froom. Cast: Tom Hulce (C.C. Drood), Adam Ant (Jim), Judith Barsi (Bean), Virginia Madsen (Yolanda). 99 min.

Sleepers (PolyGram, 1996). Dir: Barry Levinson. Scr: Barry Levinson based on the book by Lorenzo Carcaterra. DP: Michael Balhaus. Mu: John Williams. Cast: Kevin Bacon (Sean), Robert De Niro (Father Bobby), Brad Pitt (Michael), Jason Patric (Lorenzo). 147 min.

Sleeping with the Enemy (20th Century Fox, 1991). Dir: Joseph Ruben. Scr: Ronald Bass, based on the novel by Nancy Price. DP: John W. Lindley. Mu: Jerry Goldsmith. Cast: Julia Roberts (Sara/Laura), Patrick Bergin (Martin), Kevin Anderson (Ben). 98 min.

Snake Eyes (Paramount, 1998). Dir: Brian De Palma. Scr: David Koepp based on a story by Koepp and De Palma. DP: Stephen Burum. Mu: Ryuichi Sakamoto. Cast: Nicolas Cage (Rick), Gary Sinise (Commander Dunne), Carla Gugino (Julia). 98 min.

Someone to Watch Over Me (Columbia, 1987). Dir: Ridley Scott. Scr: Howard Franklin. DP: Steven Poster. Mu: Michael Kamen. Cast: Tom Berenger (Mike Keegan), Mimi Rogers (Claire Gregory), Lorraine Bracco (Ellie Keegan). 106 min.

The Spanish Prisoner (Jasmine, 1997). Dir/Scr: David Mamet. DP: Gabriel Baristain. Mu: Carter Burwell. Cast: Campbell Scott (Joe Ross), Steve Martin (Jimmy Dell), Rebecca Pidgeon (Susan). 110 min.

Special Delivery (BCP, 1976). Dir: Paul Wendkos. Scr: Don Gazzaniga and Gilbert Ralston, based on a story by Gazzaniga. DP: Harry Stradling Jr. Mu: Lalo Schifrin. Cast: Bo Svenson (Jack Murdock), Cybill Shepherd (Mary Jane), Michael C. Gwynne. 99 min.

The Split (MGM, 1968). Dir: Gordon Flemyng. Scr: Robert Sabaroff from the novel *The Seventh* by Richard Stark [Donald Westlake]. DP: Burnett Guffey. Mu: Quincy Jones. Cast: Jim Brown (McClain), Diahann Carroll (Ellie), Julie Harris (Gladys), Ernest Borgnine (Bert Clinger). 91 min.

Spring Breakers (Muse, 2012). Dir: Harmony Korine. Scr: Harmony Korine. DP: Benoit Debie. Mu: Skrillex, Cliff Martinez. Cast: James Franco (Alien), Selena Gomez (Faith), Vanessa Hudgens (Candy), Ashley Benson (Brit). 94 min.

Stakeout (Buena Vista, 1987). Dir: John Badham. Scr: Jim Kouf. DP: John Seale. Mu: Arthur B. Rubinstein. Cast: Richard Dreyfuss (Chris Lecce), Emilio Estevez (Bill Reimers), Madeleine Stowe (Maria). 115 min.

State of Grace (Orion/Cinehaus, 1990). Dir: Phil Joanou. Scr: Dennis McIntyre. DP: Jordan Cronenweth. Mu: Ennio Morricone. Cast: Sean Penn (Terry), Ed Harris (Frankie), Gary Oldman (Jackie), Robin Wright (Kathleen), John Turturro (Nick). 134 min.

State of Play (Universal, 2009). Dir: Kevin Macdonald. Scr: Billy Ray, Matthew Michael Carnahan, Tony Gilroy based on television series written by Paul Abbott. DP: Rodrigo Prieto. Mu: Alex Heffes. Cast: Russell Crowe (McAffrey), Ben Affleck (Collins), Rachel McAdams (Della). 127 min.

The Stepfather (ITC, 1987). Dir: Joseph Ruben. Scr: Donald E. Westlake. DP: John Lindley. Mu: Patrick Moraz. Cast: Terry O'Quinn (Jerry Blake), Jill Schoelen (Stephanine), Shelley Hack (Susan). 89 min.

The Stepfather (Screen Gems, 2009). Dir: Nelson McCormick. Scr: J.S. Cardone, Donald Westlake based on a story by Westlake, Carolyn Lefcourt, Brian Garfield. DP: Patrick Cady. Mu: Charlie Clouser. Cast: Dylan Walsh (David), Sela Ward (Susan), Amber Heard (Kelly). 101 min.

Still of the Night (MGM/UA, 1982). Dir/Scr: Robert Benton, based on a story by David Newman and Benton. DP: Nestor Almendros. Mu: John Kandler. Cast: Roy Scheider (Sam Rice), Meryl Streep (Brooke Reynolds), Jessica Tandy (Grace Rice). 91 min.

Stone (Relativity, 2010). Dir: John Curran. Scr: Angus McLachlan. DP: Maryse Alberti. Cast: Robert De Niro (Jack Mabry), Edward Norton (Gerald "Stone" Creeson), Milla Jovovich as Lucetta. 105 min.

Straight Time (First Artists, 1978). Dir: Ulu Grosbard. Scr: Alvin Sargent, Edward Bunker, Jeffrey Boam; Michael Mann, Nancy Dowd [uncredited] based on a novel by Bunker. DP: Owen Roizman. Mu: David Shire. Cast: Dustin Hoffman (Max), Theresa Russell (Jenny), Gary Busey (Willy). 114 min.

He's six feet six inches of dynamite. She's crazy. Absolutely crazy!
BO SVENSON and **CYBILL SHEPHERD**
...together they deliver the goods in
"SPECIAL DELIVERY" IN COLOR

America's hottest new stars pitted against each other in more ways than one!
BCP presents "SPECIAL DELIVERY" starring BO SVENSON and CYBILL SHEPHERD
written by DON GAZZANIGA • produced by RICHARD BERG • directed by PAUL WENDKOS • music by LALO SCHIFRIN
executive producer CHARLES A. PRATT • an AMERICAN INTERNATIONAL release
distributed in Canada by AMBASSADOR FILM DISTRIBUTORS, LTD. • foreign distribution by AVCO EMBASSY PICTURES OVERSEAS CORP.

A Maniac is Killing Strippers.
Detective Cody
Has One Weapon To Stop Him.
Her Body.

KAY LENZ · GREG EVIGAN · NORMAN FELL in "STRIPPED TO KILL"
With TRACY CROWDER · DEBBIE NASSAR · PIA KAMAKAHI
Written by ANDY RUBEN & KATT SHEA RUBEN · Executive Producer ROGER CORMAN
Produced by MARK BYERS · ANDY RUBEN and MATT LEIPZIG · Directed by KATT SHEA RUBEN
© 1987 Concorde Pictures

Strange Days (Lightstorm, 1995). Dir: Kathryn Bigelow. Scr: James Cameron, Jay Cocks. DP: Matthew Leonetti. Mu: Graeme Revell. Cast: Ralph Fiennes (Nero), Angela Bassett (Mason), Juliette Lewis (Faith). 145 min.

Street Kings (Fox Searchlight, 2008). Dir: David Ayer. Scr: Kurt Wimmer, James Elroy, Jamie Moss. DP: Gabriel Beristain. Mu: Graeme Revell. Cast: Keanu Reeves (Detective Ludlow), Forest Whitaker (Captain Wander), Hugh Laurie (Captain Biggs). 109 min.

Stripped to Kill (Concorde Pictures, 1987). Dir: Katt Shea Ruben. Scr: Andy and Katt Shea Ruben. DP: John Leblanc. Mu: John O'Kennedy. Cast: Kay Lenz (Cody/Sunny), Greg Evigan (Sgt. Heineman), Norman Fell (Club Owner), Tracy Crowder (Fanny). 84 min.

Sudden Impact (Warner Bros., 1983). Dir: Clint Eastwood. Scr: Joseph C. Stinson, based on a story by Earl E. Smith and Charles Pierce. DP: Bruce Surtees. Mu: Lalo Schifrin. Cast: Clint Eastwood (Harry Callahan), Sondra Locke (Jennifer), Pat Hingle (Chief Jennings). 117 min.

Sunset Heat (Beam, 1992). Dir: John Nicolella. Scr: Max Strom, John Allen Nelson. DP: Charles Rosher Jr. Mu: Jan Hammer. Cast: Dennis Hopper (Carl), Adam Ant (Danny), Michael Pare (Eric). 90 min.

Suspect (TriStar, 1987). Dir: Peter Yates. Scr: Eric Roth. DP: Billy Williams. Mu: Michael Kamen. Cast: Cher (Kathleen Riley), Dennis Quaid (Eddie Sanger), Liam Neeson (Carl Wayne Anderson). 101 min.

Suture (Goldwyn, 1994). Dir: Scott McGehee, David Siegel. Scr: Scott McGehee, David Siegel. DP: Greg Gardiner. Mu: Cary Berger. Cast: Dennis Haysbert (Clay Arlington), Mel Harris (Dr. Renée Descartes), Sab Shimono (Dr. Shinoda). 105 min.

Sweet Love and Deadly (Sweet Love, 2008). Dir/Scr: Paul Clinico. DP: Constantine Kyriakakis. Mu: Russell Steinberg. Cast: Joe Jones (Timothy Jacobs), Peg London (Claire), Elizabeth Mead (Marjorie), Anthony Auriemma (Birdman). 90 min.

Swimfan (aka *Fanatica*, 20th Century Fox , 2002). Dir: John Polson. Scr: Charles Bohl, Phillip Schneider. DP: Giles Nuttgens. Mu: Louis Febre. Cast: Jesse Bradford (Ben Cronin), Erika Christensen (Madison Bell), Shiri Appleby (Amy Miller), Kate Burton (Carla). 85 min.

The Take (Hatchet, 2007). Dir: Brad Furman. Scr: Jonas and Josh Pate. DP: Lukas Ettlin. Mu: Chris Hajian. Cast: John Leguizamo (Felix De La Pena), Tyrese Gibson (Adell Baldwin), Bobby Cannavale (Agent Steve Perelli), Rosie Perez (Marina De La Pena). 96 min.

Takers (Screen Gems, 2007). Dir: John Luessenhop. Scr: Peter Allen, Gabriel Casseus, John Luessenhop, Avery Duff. DP: Michael Barrett. Mu: Paul Haslinger. Cast: Paul Walker (John Rahway), Matt Dillon (Jack Welles), Idris Elba (Gordon), T.I. ("Ghost" Rivers), Jay Hernandez (Eddie Hatcher), Michael Ealy (Jake). 107 min.

Taking Lives (Warner Bros., 2004). Dir: D.J. Caruso. Scr: Jon Bokenkamp based on the novel by Michael Pye. DP: Amir Mokri. Mu: Philip Glass. Cast: Angelina Jolie (Illeana Scott), Ethan Hawke (James Costa/Martin Asher), Kiefer Sutherland (Hart), Olivier Martinez (Paquette). 103 min.

Taxi Driver (Columbia, 1976). Dir: Martin Scorsese. Scr: Paul Schrader. DP: Michael Chapman. Mu: Bernard Herrmann. Cast: Robert DeNiro (Travis Bickle), Jodie Foster (Iris), Albert Brooks (Tom), Peter Boyle (Wizard), Cybill Shepherd (Betsy). 113 min.

Tenderness (Lionsgate, 2009). Dir: John Polson. Scr: Emil Stern based on the novel by Robert Cormier. DP: Tom Stern. Mu: Jonathan Goldsmith. Cast: Russell Crowe (Lt. Cristofuoro), Jon Foster (Eric Komenko), Sophie Traub (Lori). 101 min.

Tequila Sunrise (Warner Bros., 1988). Dir/Scr: Robert Towne. DP: Conrad Hall. Mu: Dave Grusin. Cast: Mel Gibson (Dale McKussic), Michelle Pfeiffer (Jo Ann Vallenari), Kurt Russell (Frescia). 116 min.

The Terminator (Hemdale, 1984). Dir: James Cameron. Scr: James Cameron, Gale Ann Hurd, William Wisher. DP:

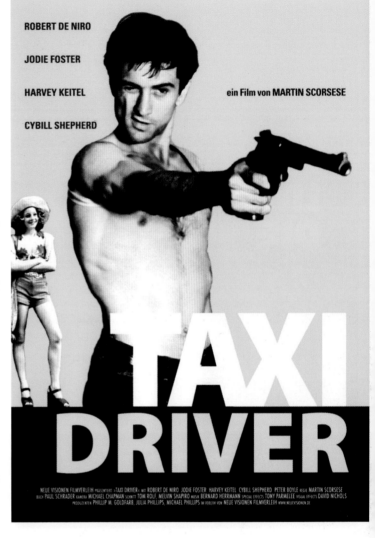

Adam Greenberg. Mu: Brad Fiedel. Cast: Arnold Scharzenegger (Terminator), Linda Hamilton (Sarah Connor), Paul Winfield (Lt. Traxler). 107 min.

Thelma and Louise (Pathe/Percy Main, 1991). Dir: Ridley Scott. Scr: Callie Khouri. DP: Adrian Biddle. Mu: Hans Zimmer. Cast: Susan Sarandon (Louise), Geena Davis (Thelma), Harvey Keitel (Hal), Michael Madsen (Jimmy). 128 min.

Thief (United Artists, 1981). Dir: Michael Mann. Scr: Michael Mann, based on the novel *The Home Invaders* by Frank Hohimer. DP: Donald Thorin. Mu:

Tangerine Dream. Cast: James Caan (Frank), Tuesday Weld (Jessie), Robert Prosty (Leo). 122 min.

Thieves Like Us (United Artists, 1974). Dir: Robert Altman. Scr: Calder Willingham, Joan Tewksbury, and Robert Altman, based on the novel by Edward Anderson. DP: Jean Boffety. Cast: Keith Carradine (Bowie), Shelley Duvall (Keechie), John Schuck (Chicamaw), Bert Remsem (T-Dub). 123 min.

Things to Do in Denver When You're Dead (Miramax, 1995). Dir: Gary Fleder. Scr: Scott Rosenberg. DP: Elliot Davis. Mu: Michael Convertino. Cast: Andy Garcia (Jimmy "The Saint" Tosnia), Christopher Lloyd (Pieces), William Forsythe (Franchise). 115 min.

This World Then the Fireworks (Largo, 1997). Dir: Michael Oblowitz. Scr: Larry Gross based on the story by Jim Thompson. DP: Tom Priestley Jr. Mu: Pete Rugolo. Cast: Billy Zane (Marty), Gina Gershon (Carol), Sheryl Lee (Lois), Rue McClanahan (Mr. Laewood). 100 min.

Three Way (Hyperion, 2004). Dir: Scott Ziehl. Scr: Russell Marleau based on the novel by Gil Brewer. DP: Antonio Calvache. Mu: Christopher Hoag. Cast: Dominic Purcell (Brookbank), Joy Bryant (Rita), Ali Larter (Isobel). 88 min.

Thunderheart (TriStar, 1992). Dir: Michael Apted. Scr: John Fusco. DP: Roger Deakins. Mu: James Horner. Cast: Val Kilmer (Ray), Sam Shepard (Frank), Graham Greene (Walter Crow Horse), Fred Ward (Jack). 119 min.

Tightrope (Warner Bros., 1984). Dir/Scr: Richard Tuggle. DP: Bruce Surtees. Mu: Lennie Niehaus. Cast: Clint Eastwood (Wes Block), Genevieve Bujold (Beryl), Dan Hedaya (Molinari), Alison Eastwood (Amanda). 114 min.

To Die For (Columbia, 1995). Dir: Gus Van Sant. Scr: Buck Henry based on the book by Joyce Maynard. DP: Eric Alan Edwards. Mu: Danny Elfman. Cast: Nicole Kidman (Suzanne), Matt Dillon (Larry), Joaquin Phoenix (Jimmy). 106 min.

To Kill For (aka *Fatal Instinct*, Moviestore, 1992). Dir: John Dirlam. Scr: George D. Putnam. DP: John Dirlam. Mu: Stephen Allen and Bobby Crew. Cast: Michael Madsen (Burden), Laura Johnson (Catherine Merrims). 93 min.

To Live and Die in L.A. (MGM/UA, 1985). Dir: William Friedkin. Scr: Friedkin and Gerald Petrivich, based on his novel. DP: Robby Muller. Mu: Wang

Chung. Cast: William L. Petersen (Chance), Willem Dafoe (Masters), John Pankow (Vukovich). 116 min.

Tony Rome (Arcola, 1967). Dir: Gordon Douglas. Scr: Richard Breen based on the novel by Marvin Alpert. DP: Joseph Biroc. Mu: Billy May. Cast: Frank Sinatra (Tony Rome), Jill St. John (Ann Archer), Richard Conte (Lt. Santini). 110 min.

Tough Guys Don't Dance (Golan-Globus, 1987). Dir: Norman Mailer. Scr: Norman Mailer; Robert Towne [uncredited]. DP: Mike Moyer. Mu: Angelo Badalamenti. Cast: Ryan O'Neal (Tim), Isabella Rossellini (Madeleine), Debra Stipe (Patty). 110 min.

The Town (Warner Bros, 2010). Dir: Ben Affleck. Scr: Affleck, Peter Craig, Aaron Stockard based on a novel by Chuck Hogan. DP: Robert Elswit. Mu: David Buckley. Cast: Ben Affleck (Doug MacRay), Rebecca Hall (Claire Keesey), Jon Hamm as (Agent Frawley), Jeremy Renner (Jem Coughlin). 125 min.

Training Day (Warner Bros., 2001). Dir: Antoine Fuqua. Scr: David Ayer. DP: Mauro Fiore. Mu: Mark Mancina. Cast: Denzel Washington (Detective Harris), Ethan Hawke (Jake), Scott Glenn (Roger). 122 min.

Trap (Zapruter, 2010). Dir/Scr/DP: Jason Horton. Cast: Allen Perada (Walter), Alonzo Jones (Franklin), Ashton Blanchard (Tennessee). 90 min.

Trapped (Columbia, 2002). Dir: Luis Mandoki. Scr: Greg Iles based on his novel. DP: Frederick Elmes. Mu: John Ottman. Cast: Charlize Theron (Karen), Courtney Love (Cheryl), Stuart Townsend (Will). 106 min.

True Believer (Columbia, 1989). Dir: Joseph Ruben. Scr: Wesley Strick. DP: John W. Lindley. Mu: Brad Fiedel. Cast: James Woods (Eddie Dodd), Robert Downey Jr. (Roger Barron), Margaret Colin (Kitty Greer). 104 min.

True Blue (Sandstorm, 2001). Dir: J. S. Cardone. Scr: J.S. Cardone. DP: Darko

Suvac. Mu: Tim Jones. Cast: Tom Berenger (Rembrandt), Lori Heuring (Nikki), Pamela Gidley (Beck). 101 min.

True Confessions (UA, 1981). Dir: Ulu Grosbard. Scr: Joan Didion, John Gregory Dunne, Gary S. Hall from the novel *True Confessions* by John Gregory Dunne. DP: Owen Roizman. Mu: Georges Delerue. Cast: Robert DeNiro (Des Spellacy), Robert Duvall, (Thomas Spellacy), Charles Durning (Jack Amsterdam). 108 min.

True Romance (Warner Bros., 1993). Dir: Tony Scott. Scr: Quentin Tarantino and Roger Avery . DP: Jeffrey L. Kimball. Mu: Hans Zimmer. Cast: Christian Slater (Clarence), Patricia Arquette (Alabama), Michael Rapaport (Dick), Val Kilmer (Elvis). 120 min.

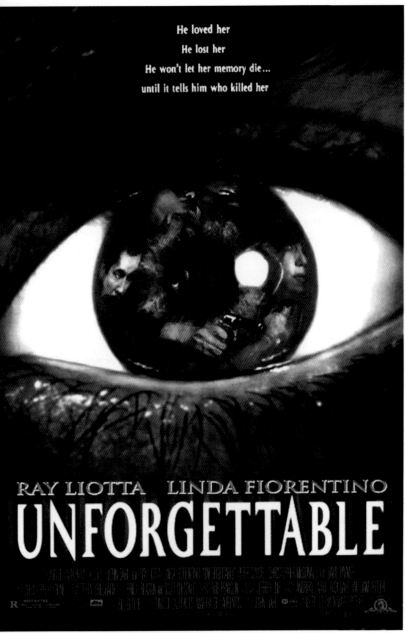

He loved her

He lost her

He won't let her memory die...

until it tells him who killed her

RAY LIOTTA   LINDA FIORENTINO

UNFORGETTABLE

Twelve Monkeys (Universal, 1995). Dir: Terry Gilliam. Scr: David Peoples, Janet Peoples based on the Scr: by Chris Marker. DP: Roger Pratt. Mu: Paul Buckmaster. Cast: Bruce Willis (Cole), Madeleine Stowe (Kathryn), Jon Seda (Jose). 129 min.

Twilight (Paramount, 1998). Dir: Robert Benton. Scr: Robert Benton, Richard Russo. DP: Piotr Sobocinski. Mu: Elmer Bernstein. Cast: Paul Newman (Harry Ross), Susan Sarandon (Catherine Ames), Gene Hackman (Jack Ames), Reese Witherspoon (Mel Ames). 94 min.

The Two Jakes (Paramount, 1990). Dir: Jack Nicholson. Scr: Robert Towne. DP: Vilmos Zsigmond. Mu: Van Dyke Parks. Cast: Jack Nicholson (Jake Gittes), Harvey Keitel (Jake Berman), Meg Tilly (Kitty Berman). 137 min.

U Turn (Phoenix/Illusion, 1997). Dir: Oliver Stone. Scr: John Ridley. DP: Robert Richardson. Mu: Ennio Morricone. Cast: Sean Penn (Bobby), Jennifer Lopez (Grace), Nick Nolte (Jake). 125 min.

Unbreakable (Touchstone, 2000). Dir/Scr: M. Night Shyamalan. DP: Eduardo Serra. Mu: James Newton Howard. Cast: Bruce Willis (David Dunn), Samuel L. Jackson (Elijah Price), Robin Wright (Audrey Dunn). 106 min.

Under Suspicion (Revelations, 2000). Dir: Stephen Hopkins. Scr: Tom Provost, W. Peter Iliff based on the book by John Wainwright. DP: Peter Levy. Mu: BT. Cast: Morgan Freeman (Captain Benezet), Gene Hackman (Henry Hearst), Monica Bellucci (Chantal), Thomas Jane (Detective Owens).110 min.

Undercurrent (Fries, 1998). Dir: Frank Kerr. Scr: Wayne Behar. DP: Carlos Gaviria. Mu: Christopher Lennertz. Cast: Lorenzo Lamas (Mike Aguayo), Brenda Strong (Renee Rivera), Frank Vincent (Eddie Torelli). 94 min.

The Underneath (Gramercy, 1995). Dir: Steven Soderbergh. Scr: Steven Soderbergh as Sam Lowry and Daniel Fuchs based on the novel *Criss Cross* by Don Tracy. DP: Eliot Davis. Mu: Cliff

Martinez. Cast: Peter Gallagher (Michael Chambers), Alison Elliott (Rachel), William Fichtner (Tommy Dundee). 99 min.

Unforgettable (MGM, 1996). Dir: John Dahl. Scr: Bill Geddie. DP: Jeff Jur. Mu: Chris Young. Cast: Ray Liotta (Krane), Linda Fiorentino (Martha), Peter Coyote (Don). 117 min.

Union City (Kinesis, 1980). Dir: Mark Reichert. Scr: Reichert, based on the Cornell Woolrich story "The Corpse Next Door." DP: Edward Lachman. Mu: Chris Stein. Cast: Dennis Lipscomb (Harlan), Deborah Harry (Lillian), Irina Maleeva (Contessa). 87 min.

Unknown (Dark Castle, 2011). Dir: Jaume Collet-Serra. Scr: Oliver Butcher, Stephen Cornwell based on a novel by Didier Van Cauwelaert. DP: Flavio Labiano. Mu: John Ottman, Alexander Rudd. Cast: Liam Neeson (Dr. Martin Harris), Diane Kruger (Gina), January Jones (Elizabeth). 113 min.

Unlawful Entry (Largo, 1992). Dir: Jonathan Kaplan. Scr: Lewis Colick based on a story by Colick, George Putnam, John Katcmer. DP: Jamie Anderson. Mu: James Horner. Cast: Kurt Russell (Michael), Ray Liotta (Officer Davis), Madeleine Stowe (Karen). 117 min.

The Usual Suspects (Gramercy, 1995). Dir: Bryan Singer. Scr: Christopher McQuarrie. DP: Newton Thomas Sigel. Mu: John Ottman. Cast: Stephen Baldwin (Michael McManus), Gabriel Byrne (Dean Keaton), Benicio Del Toro (Fred Fenster), Kevin Pollak (Todd Hockney). 106 min.

The Vanishing (20th Century Fox, 1993). Dir: George Sluizer. Scr: Todd Graff based on the novel by Tim Krabbe. DP: Peter Suschitzky. Cast: Jeff Bridges (Barney), Kiefer Sutherland (Jeff), Nancy Travis (Rita). 109 min.

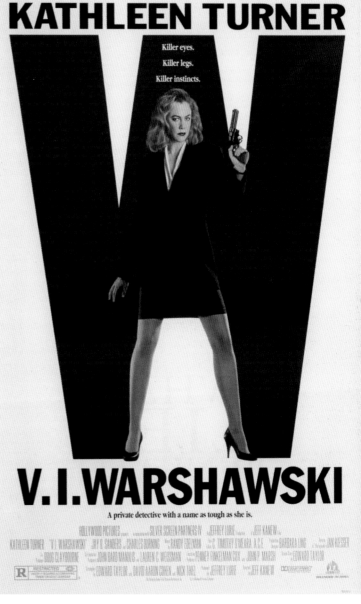

V.I. Warshawski (Buena Vista, 1991). Dir: Jeff Kanew. Scr: Edward Taylor, David Aaron Cohen, and Nick Thiel, based on the novels of Sara Paretsky. DP: Jan Kiesser. Mu: Randy Edelman. Cast: Kathleen Turner (V.I.), Jay O. Sanders (Murray), Charles Durning (Lt. Mallory). 89 min.

HARRISON FORD   MICHELLE PFEIFFER

He was

the perfect husband

until his one mistake

followed them home.

A ROBERT ZEMECKIS FILM

WHAT
LIES
BENEATH

Warning Shot (Paramount, 1967). Dir: Buzz Kulik. Scr: Mann Rubin based on the novel *711–Officer Needs Help* by Whit Masterson. DP: Joseph F. Biroc. Mu: Jerry Goldsmith. Cast: David Janssen (Sgt. Tom Valens), Ed Begley (Capt. Roy Klodin), Keenan Wynn (Sgt. Ed Musso). 100 min.

The Way of the Gun (Artisan, 2000). Dir/Scr: Christopher McQuarrie. DP: Dick Pope. Mu: Joe Kraemer. Cast: Ryan Phillippe (Mr. Parker), Benicio Del Toro (Mr. Longbaugh), Juliette Lewis (Robin). 119 min.

What Lies Beneath (Dream Works, 2000). Dir: Robert Zemeckis. Scr: Clark Gregg; story by Sarah Kernochan, Gregg. DP: Don Burgess. Mu: Alan Silvestri. Cast: Harrison Ford (Norman), Michelle Pfeiffer (Claire), Diana Scarwid (Jody), Miranda Otto (Mary), James Remar (Warren). 130 min.

When Tyrants Kiss (Tyrants, 2005). Dir: Michael Scotto. Scr: Michael Mark Chemers. DP: Laurence O'Neal Suarez. Mu: Alan Shockley. Cast: Alexander Cendese (Harris), Dana Wright (Angel), Melanie Julian (Lucinda). 90 min.

White of the Eye (Paramount, 1988). Dir: Donald Cammell. Scr: Donald and China Cammell, based on the novel *Mrs. White* by Margaret Tracy. DP: Alan Jones. Mu: Nick Mason, Rick Fenn. Cast: David Keith (Paul White), Cathy Moriarty (Joan White), Alan Rosenberg (Mike DeSantos), Art Evans (Mendoza). 113 min.

White Sands (Warner Bros., 1992). Dir: Roger Donaldson. Scr: Daniel Pyne. DP: Peter Menzies Jr. Mu: Patrick O'Hearn.

DREAMWORKS PICTURES AND TWENTIETH CENTURY FOX PRESENT AN IMAGEMOVERS PRODUCTION A ROBERT ZEMECKIS FILM HARRISON FORD · MICHELLE PFEIFFER "WHAT LIES BENEATH" DIANA SCARWID MUSIC COMPOSED ALAN SILVESTRI COSTUME SUSIE DeSANTO FILM EDITOR ARTHUR SCHMIDT PRODUCTION RICK CARTER DIRECTOR OF DON BURGESS, A.S.C.
EXECUTIVE JOAN BRADSHAW · MARK JOHNSON PRODUCED STEVE STARKEY · ROBERT ZEMECKIS · JACK RAPKE STORY SARAH KERNOCHAN AND CLARK GREGG
SCREENPLAY CLARK GREGG DIRECTED ROBERT ZEMECKIS Official What Lies Beneath website at amazon.com DREAMWORKS PICTURES
www.amazon.com/whatliesbeneath

Cast: Willem Dafoe (Ray Dolezal), Mickey Rourke (Gorman Lebbox), Mary Elizabeth Mastrantonio (Lae Bodine), Samuel L. Jackson (Greg Meeker), Mimi Rogers (Mrs. Dolezal), M. Emmet Walsh (Coroner). 101 min.

Who'll Stop the Rain (United Artists, 1978). Dir: Karel Reisz. Scr: Judith Roscoe and Robert Stone, based on his novel *Dog Soldiers*. DP: Richard H. Kline. Mu: Lawrence Rosenthal. Cast: Nick Nolte (Ray), Tuesday Weld (Marge), Michael Moriarity (John), Anthony Zerbe (Antheil), Richard Masur (Danskin). 125 min.

Wicker Park (MGM, 2004). Dir: Paul McGuigan. Scr: Brandon Boyce based on the screenplay by Gilles Mimouni. DP: Peter Sova. Mu: Cliff Martinez. Cast: Josh Hartnett (Matthew), Rose Byrne (Alex), Diane Kruger (Lisa). 114 min.

Wild Things (Mandalay, 1998). Dir: John McNaughton. Scr: Stephen Peters. DP: Jeffrey Kimball. Mu: George Clinton. Cast: Kevin Bacon (Ray), Matt Dillon (Sam), Denise Richards (Kelly), Neve Campbell (Suzie). 108 min.

Wild Side (NuImage, 1995). Dir: Donald Cammell. Scr: Cammell, China Kong. DP: Seo Mutarevic. Mu: Ryûichi Sakamoto. Cast: Christopher Walken (Bruno Buckingham), Joan Chen (Virginia Chow), Steven Bauer (Tony), Anne Heche (Alex Lee / Johanna). 96 min.

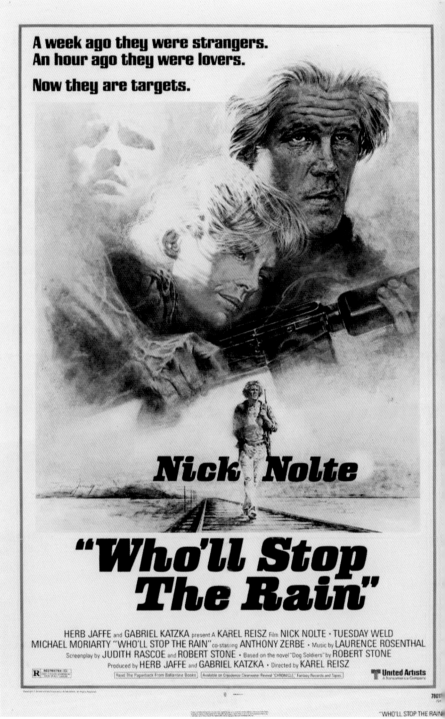

TO FIND THE TRUTH, YOU MUST BELIEVE.

Jarre. Cast: Harrison Ford (John Book), Kelly McGillis (Rachel), Josef Sommer (Schaeffer), Lukas Haas (Samuel), Alexander Godunov (Daniel), Danny Glover (McFee). 112 min.

The X Files (20th Century Fox, 1998). Dir: Rob Bowman. Scr: Chris Carter. DP: Ward Russell. Mu: Mark Snow. Cast: David Duchovny (Mulder), Gillian Armstrong (Scully), William B. Davis (Cigarette Smoking Man). 121 min.

Year of the Dragon (MGM/UA, 1985). Dir: Michael Cimino. Scr: Oliver Stone and Michael Cimino, based on the novel by Robert Daley. DP: Alex Thomson. Mu: David Mansfield. Cast: Mickey Rourke (Stanley White), John Lone (Joey Tal), Ariane (Tracey Tzu), Leonard Termo (Angelo Rizzo). 136 min.

Zen Noir (Dreaming Dog, 2004). Dir/Scr: Marc Rosenbush. DP: Christopher Gosch. Mu: Steven Chesne. Cast: Duane Sharp (The Detective), Kim Chan (The Master), Debra Miller (Jane). 71 min.

Witness (Paramount, 1985). Dir: Peter Weir. Scr: Earl W. Wallace and William Kelley. DP: John Seale. Mu: Maurice

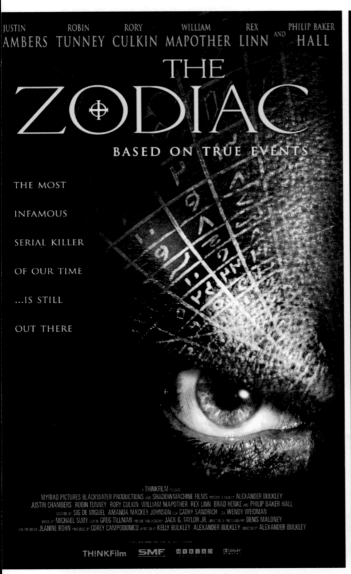

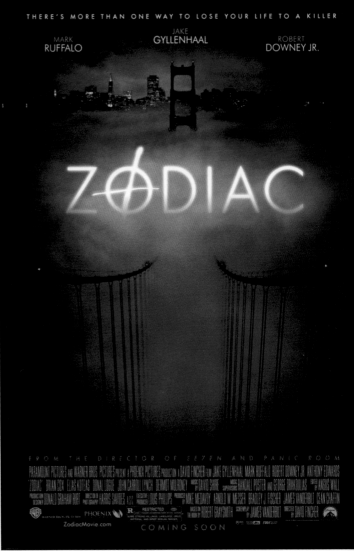

The Zodiac (Think, 2006). Dir: Alexander Bulkley. Scr: Kelly Bulkley and Alexander Bulkley. DP: Denis Maloney. Mu: Michael Suby. Cast: Justin Chambers (Matt Parish), Robin Tunney (Laura Parish), Rory Culkin (Johnny Parish), Philip Baker Hal (Frank Perkins). 92 min.

Zodiac (Warner Bros., 2007). Dir: David Fincher. Scr: James Vanderbilt based on the books *Zodiac* and *Zodiac Unmasked* by Robert Graysmith. DP: Harris Savides. Mu: David Shire. Cast: Mark Ruffalo (Inspector Dave Toschi), Jake Gyllenhaal (Robert Graysmith), Robert Downey Jr. (Paul Avery), Anthony Edwards (Inspector William Armstrong, Chloë Sevigny (Melanie), Brian Cox (Melvin Belli), John Carroll Lynch (Arthur Leigh Allen), Philip Baker Hall (Sherwood Morrill). 158 min.

Metro-Goldwyn-Mayer presents
A Judd Bernard-Irwin Winkler
Production starring

LEE MARVIN
"POINT BLANK"

**There are two kinds of people in his up-tight world:
his victims and his women. And sometimes you can't tell them apart.**

co-starring **ANGIE DICKINSON**
KEENAN WYNN · CARROLL O'CONNOR · LLOYD BOCHNER · MICHAEL STRONG
Screenplay by Alexander Jacobs and David Newhouse & Rafe Newhouse Based on the Novel 'The Hunter' by Richard Stark
Directed by John Boorman Produced by Judd Bernard and Robert Chartoff **In Panavision® and Metrocolor**

Index of Film Titles

As the Filmography is alphabetical, it is not indexed. Alternate titles that do not appear in the text are included below and reference the title used in the Filmography. Page numbers for scenes stills are in *italics*; posters are not indexed. Release years are indicated only when needed to differentiate films with the same title.

Breathless.

The Departed.

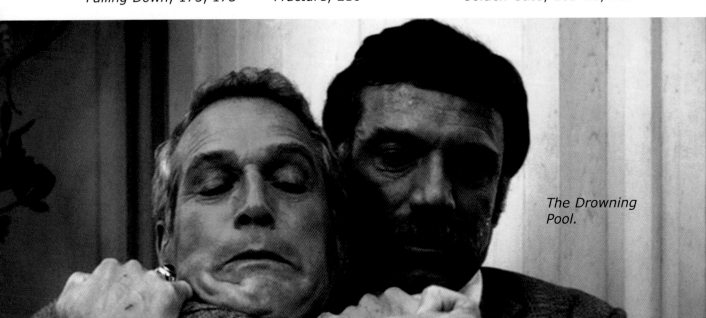

The Drowning Pool.

Hostage.

Liebestraum.

The Narrow Margin.

The Pelican Brief.

A Rage in Harlem.

Sharky's Machine.

Thelma and Louise.

Wild at Heart.